W9-BUM-434

BLOOD ON THE RIVER

Also by Marjoleine Kars

*Breaking Loose Together: The Regulator Rebellion
in Pre-Revolutionary North Carolina*

BLOOD ON THE RIVER

A CHRONICLE OF MUTINY AND FREEDOM ON THE WILD COAST

Marjoleine Kars

NEW YORK
LONDON

Part of the Prolgue was previously published, in slightly different form, as Marjoleine Kars, "Adventures in Research; Chasing the Past in Guyana," *Uncommon Sense* 124 (Fall 2007): 17–20, and used here with permission.

Parts of Chapter 8 are based on Marjoleine Kars, "Policing and Transgressing Borders: Soldiers, Slave Rebels, and the Early Modern Atlantic," *New West Indian Guide/Nieuwe West Indische Gids* 83, 3/4 (December 2009), 187–213, and used here by permission.

Requests for permission to reproduce selections from this book should be made through our website: https://thenewpress.com/contact.

Published in the United States by The New Press, New York, 2020
Distributed by Two Rivers Distribution

LIBRARY OF CONGRESS CATALOGING-IN-PUBLICATION DATA

Names: Kars, Marjoleine, author.
Title: Blood on the river : a chronicle of mutiny and freedom on the Wild Coast / Marjoleine Kars.
Description: New York : The New Press, [2020] | Includes bibliographical references and index. | Summary: "The story of a massive eighteenth-century slave rebellion in the Dutch colony of Berbice (now Guyana) which had been all but forgotten. Historian Marjoleine Kars recovers a riveting tale from the archives, including rare first-person accounts from African-born slaves"—Provided by publisher.
Identifiers: LCCN 2019053892 | ISBN 9781620974599 (hardback) | ISBN 9781620974605 (ebook)
Subjects: LCSH: Slave insurrections--Guyana—Berbice—History—18th century. | Slaves—Guyana—Social conditions—18th century. | Berbice—History—18th century.
Classification: LCC HT1140.B4 K37 2020 | DDC 306.3/6209881—dc23
LC record available at https://lccn.loc.gov/2019053892

The New Press publishes books that promote and enrich public discussion and understanding of the issues vital to our democracy and to a more equitable world. These books are made possible by the enthusiasm of our readers; the support of a committed group of donors, large and small; the collaboration of our many partners in the independent media and the not-for-profit sector; booksellers, who often hand-sell New Press books; librarians; and above all by our authors.

www.thenewpress.com

Composition by dix!
This book was set in Palatino Linotype

Printed in the United States of America

10 9 8 7 6 5 4 3 2 1

For Kate

Contents

BLOOD ON THE RIVER

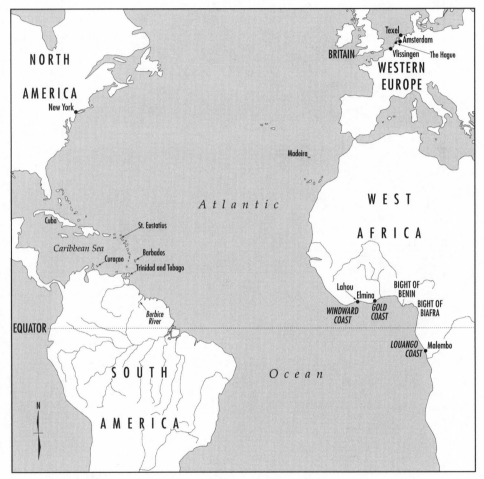

The Atlantic world. (Map designed and produced by the UMBC Cartographic
Services.)

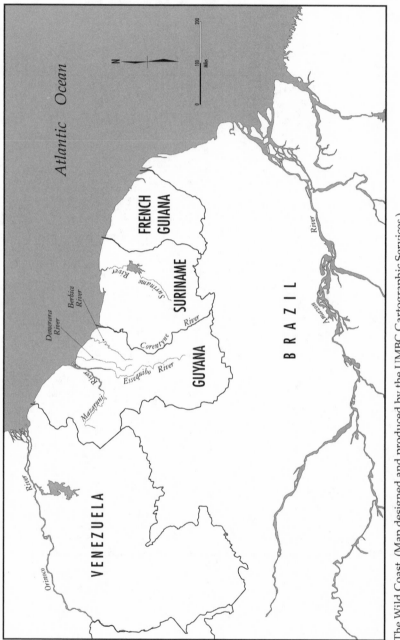

The Wild Coast. (Map designed and produced by the UMBC Cartographic Services.)

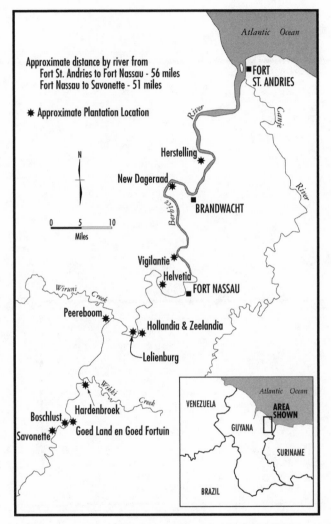

The Berbice River. (Map designed and produced by the UMBC Cartographic Services.)

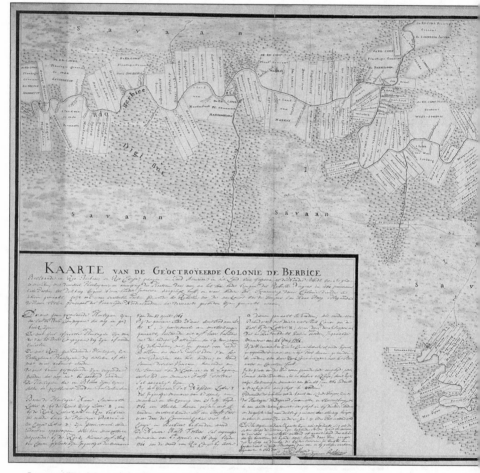

Leupe 1571, Map of the Berbice Colony, 1764. (Nationaal Archief, The Hague.)

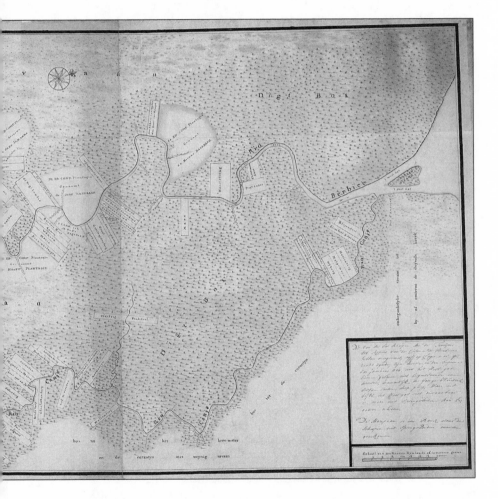

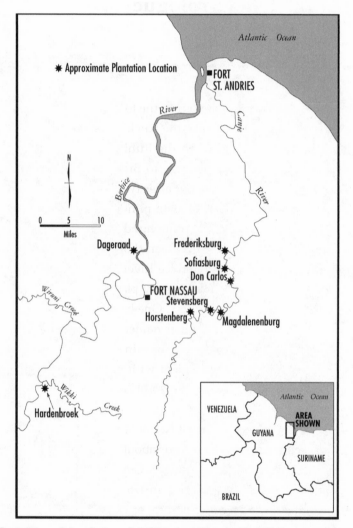

The Canje River. (Map designed and produced by the UMBC Cartographic Services.)

Prologue

Jolting along at sixty miles an hour in the four-by-four, I glanced over at Alex, hoping he wouldn't take the truck into one of the deep gullies pitting the road. We were on the Ituni highway, the main road from Guyana's capital, Georgetown, to Brazil. It was a highway in name only. The pavement gave out after twenty-five miles to become a rutted, sandy path through bauxite mines, savanna, and lowland rain forest. Alex had driven the route hundreds of times. Every year he brings scientists to his seventeen-thousand-acre cattle ranch, Dubulay, ninety miles up the Berbice River, in remote, thinly populated bush country. They come to study plants and animals in Guyana's vast, untrammeled wilderness. One biologist counted forty-one species of bats on the ranch; another named a newly discovered species of lizard after Alex. A large U.S. farming concern runs a research station at Alex's ranch to experiment with hardier species of corn. I was the first historian to visit, the result of an unexpected archival discovery.[1]

A few years before, in the Dutch National Archives in The Hague, I had happened upon a cache of records about a massive slave rebellion. It took place in Dutch Berbice—today's Guyana—on the Wild Coast, the northern edge of South America, in 1763–64. The documents perplexed me. I had never heard of Berbice or of the 1763 slave rebellion. Few have: no one has studied the uprising in depth.[2] Yet the archive was extraordinarily rich. In addition to the daily journal of the colonial governor and reams of European correspondence, it contained five hundred handwritten pages of slave interrogations and—even more tantalizing—letters the rebelling ex-slaves had written to the Dutch authorities. We have few sources for the eighteenth century in which enslaved people actually speak, and here were their voices captured in old Dutch.[3]

As a historian of the Atlantic world, I was well aware that most major slave rebellions were suppressed in a matter of days or even hours, leaving few traces of their organization or how people shaped their freedom. Yet in Berbice, to my astonishment, the insurgents took over the entire colony and held off the Dutch for more than a year. How did they pull this off? What were they after? From prior research on the American Revolution, I knew that during that era, popular myths notwithstanding, colonial Americans did not agree on the meaning of "liberty" or on their future after independence. Not only did colonists divide into patriots and loyalists, but many refused to support either side or oscillated between them.[4] I resolved to find out whether the Berbice uprising had the same complexities.

If the Dubulay ranch is a haven for biologists, it is even richer for historians. Almost four hundred years ago, Dutchman Abraham van Pere started a colony on the Berbice River. He built a house and traded with Indians on the very spot now occupied by Dubulay ranch. Over time, Van Pere's farm, the Peereboom (Pear Tree), evolved into a large sugar plantation. Early in the eighteenth century, a group of Amsterdam investors bought the colony from the Van Pere family, and Peereboom became one of eleven plantations belonging to the Society of Berbice. Early in 1763, slaves in Berbice revolted. The subsequent rebellion lasted more than a year and involved nearly the entire enslaved population of about five thousand people spread over 135 estates. Having researched this rebellion, I knew the Peereboom figured prominently in these events. It was the scene of a massacre where rebels executed, despite promises of free passage, forty-two European men, women, and children who had sought refuge on the Peereboom at the outbreak of the revolt. Later on, a group of Africans accused by fellow rebels of cannibalism built a village in the savanna behind the plantation.

I had arrived in Georgetown after an all-night layover in the Trinidad airport. Bleary-eyed, I had only the vaguest idea of how to proceed. My wish had been to travel up the Berbice River to get to know the terrain. But there is no bus route or train up the Berbice, or even a direct road, and there are no hotels (Guyana's tourist industry is still developing). A month of emailing with a well-known wilderness outfit had resulted in an itinerary and price tag geared more toward a boutique "adventure" tourist than a historian on a modest grant. So on the eve of my departure, I still had no definite plan or reservations, just the assurance of a long-term Guyana resident, a Scottish woman I had contacted at the last minute, that she'd have a driver pick me up at the airport at five a.m. and bring me to her house. Margaret turned out to be an energetic woman in her sixties, experienced in organizing research visits for scientists interested in Guyana's vast biodiversity. She knew all about Dubulay. Alex was an old school friend of her son. As luck would have it, Alex was leaving Georgetown for Dubulay in an hour, just enough time for me to stock up on snacks at the local Shell station. For safekeeping, I left my passport and extra cash with Margaret, my acquaintance of forty-five minutes, and clambered into the cab of Alex's truck. As he wedged his rifle behind the seats my eyebrows went up. Alex explained that highway robbery isn't just a euphemism in Guyana.

Guyana, comparable in size to Idaho or Kansas, faces the Atlantic Ocean in northern South America and shares borders with Suriname, Venezuela, and Brazil. Forty percent of its estimated 773,000 inhabitants are immigrants from India whose ancestors came as indentured servants in the nineteenth century after the abolition of slavery. The descendants of former slaves comprise about 30 percent of the population, and another 20 percent are of mixed descent. Amerindians make up almost 10 percent of the population, and whites and Chinese 0.5 percent.[5] Ninety percent of Guyanese live in the low coastal plain, leaving the rest of the country, vast savannas and rain forests, virtually empty of people. Guyana has only eight thousand kilometers of roadways; fewer than 10 percent are paved. One travels into the interior by jeep or by boat. Locals use dugout canoes on the Berbice, Demerara, and Essequibo Rivers, which run like parallel ribbons from the interior to the coast. In the seventeenth century, the Dutch built settlements on each of these big waterways. Those colonies passed into British hands in the early nineteenth century, making Guyana the only

English-speaking country in South America. In 1966, British Guiana gained its independence.

Many of the country's earliest historical records are housed in the Netherlands. As I surveyed the archive in The Hague, my amazement at the story of the Berbice Rebellion grew. Almost nine hundred people, close to half the surviving enslaved adults, were questioned as suspects and witnesses in the aftermath of the 1763 rebellion. In response to specific, and often leading, questions, the re-enslaved gave careful and strategic answers, mediated by the European clerk, who translated Creole into Dutch, summarized answers, and wrote in the third rather than the first person. Some testimonies were extremely short, while others went on for pages.

The Dutch did not much care about the internal politics of rebellion. They focused their questions on what they were interested in: punishable offenses such as leadership, destruction of property, and, most especially, "Christian murder." Since their own lives and others' lives were on the line, enslaved people had every reason to distort, omit, and lie. And it is hard to know how to read people's words, as written testimony robs us of emotional clues expressed in affect, silences, or hesitations. And yet, as I delved further into these records, I realized that despite such important caveats, this testimony provides a firsthand view of slavery, armed resistance, and the politics of rebellion in intimate, granular detail.

The interrogations told me not only about rebel leaders, but also, more rare in the records of Atlantic slavery, about how the rebellion was experienced by ordinary African-descended people. They chronicle how people fought and evaded the Europeans and their Amerindian allies and how they dealt with the traumas of war as they struggled to survive. Even more intriguingly, the records also expose deep disagreements over what freedom and autonomy meant to people facing slim odds for survival. The Berbice records reveal important intellectual currents usually submerged in the history of Atlantic slavery.[6]

The Berbice Rebellion occurred at the start of the so-called Age of Revolutions, a period of political upheaval stretching from the end of the Seven Years' War in 1763 through the American, French, and Haitian Revolutions to the anti-colonial movements in South America in the 1820s. During this era, not only elites but also peasants, Indians, ordinary whites, and slaves fought for greater autonomy and better lives, though how they defined these values differed greatly. Elites generally sought access to political and economic power, while commoners sought to control their own lives and labor unmolested by elites. The Berbice Rebellion reveals the political perspectives of people ensnared in race-based chattel slavery, an institution central to the Atlantic world, the business of producing wealth, and the revolutions that roiled it. Enslaved Berbicians were among the most oppressed people in the Atlantic world. They rose up, demanding variously liberation and autonomy. One might think that slaves would be united in their vision. But they were not. Popular politics in this rebellion were as complex as any other in this era. Leaders of the rebellion wanted liberty to run a colony of their own with a measure of human bondage in place. Ordinary self-emancipated people wanted autonomy to tend their own gardens. This difference is a common theme in the revolutionary age: elites wanted one thing; commoners wanted another. Both called it "freedom."

I had come to Guyana to get a sense of the place, the landscape, the bewildering "jungle" that frightened Dutch soldiers, and the river that was the lifeblood of the colony. I did not expect to find any trace of the uprising more than three hundred years later, or even of Dutch colonization. Yet to my great surprise, remnants of that past were everywhere: buried in the sediment of the riverbank, hidden in the verdancy of the bush, or poking out of the jungle's soil after a rain. That afternoon Alex cut a path with his machete through the rain forest to show me the grave of a Dutchman, Moses Heyn. Alex didn't know anything about the man except what the stone revealed: born in 1636 and buried in 1715. Above the riverbank, I found shards of pottery and pipe stems emerging from the mud. The next day, Alex's farm manager led me to a rain-washed slope above the river. Within half an hour, I had filled a small bucket with intriguing pieces of china painted with colorful flowers and blue pagodas. On other pottery fragments, I could see the indentations of the fingers that crafted them, their patterns suggesting African or indigenous origin. I even found a few of the tiny glass beads the Dutch at one time traded with the Amerindians.

Today, some two thousand people live along the Berbice River, fewer than on the eve of the 1763 slave rebellion. Their small shuttered houses, built on stilts to capture the winds off the river at night, lack electricity and running water. Locals use the river for drinking, laundry, bathing, fishing, and moving about in small boats and dugouts. The river serves as the spine of the community. All the comings and goings happen up, down, or across the water. When I ventured on the river, my boatsman knew all the people—"but not the small ones"—who lived between Dubulay and the former Fort Nassau, headquarters of the Dutch colonizers, thirty-five meandering miles away. A small, slow ferry travels from New Amsterdam on the coast up the Berbice every few days, but it is too expensive for most river dwellers. People support themselves with a variety of odd jobs. Every few miles someone adds to the family income by running a small bar or a store consisting of a few shelves of canned and boxed goods. As in slavery times, Dubulay is the largest employer for many miles.

Over the next days, I explored this watery world where signs of Dutch colonization remain ubiquitous. Though Dutch plantation buildings are no longer standing, landholdings are still referred to by their former Dutch names. The 1764 Berbice map I carried with me, made for the European soldiers sent to fight the rebels, served just as well as the modern one Margaret gave me. When I put them side by side, half of the 1764 plantations were on the modern map. Berbicians refer to these plantations when they explain where they were born. For instance, the caretaker at Fort Nassau was born at nearby Stadt Danzig, as was my boatman's father-in-law. People pointed out the tall silk cotton trees under which the Dutch allegedly buried their silver at the start of the revolt. The height of the trees made it impossible to forget where the valuables had been hidden. The Dutch bewitched these trees to keep their coins safe from their slaves. Wherever you see such a tree rising above the bush, people say, there would have been a Dutch plantation. Many Afro-Guyanese still consider these trees cursed.

Berbicians actively use the relics history has left behind. Until thirty or forty years ago there were still some Dutch ruins standing, people told me. By now they have been dismantled by neighbors who make use of every spare building material. They opened the graves looking for treasures. They carried off the gravestones to use in foundations or as sharpening stones. They used the old bricks neatly stacked in rows on the former Hardenbroek plantation. Most people own a few colonial bottles, bowls, or pots, dug up from the mud, retrieved from the river, or bought from treasure hunters who sell them in Guyana and abroad.

In spite of the daily presence of the past, or perhaps because of it, the remnants of Berbice's slave history are fast slipping away. The Guyana authorities lack the resources to engage in much historic preservation on the Berbice, and the rain forest reclaims any lost ground quickly. At the site of the former Fort Nassau, newly installed historical markers have already become illegible in the relentless sun. The eighteenth-century gravestones are cracking and the graves filling with water. The foundations of the government building where the colonial governor met with his council, courts tried lawbreakers, and rebel governor Coffij coordinated his attacks on the Dutch are overgrown. The so-called talking tree, an enormous tree some twenty-five feet around at its base, can be reached only by hacking the undergrowth with a machete. Rebels used this tree, so the story goes, to bang out messages to allies on the nearby Canje River. The sound made by hitting the roots of this tree can be heard for miles. If only the archival records rang so clearly.

Back at my desk months later, I found it hard to assess the truthfulness of individual testimonies shaped so deeply by a hostile, murderous judicial system. Still, by comparing them with one another and against other Dutch records, and reading between the lines, I was able to make at least partial judgments about what might actually have occurred. Even if people lied or told half-truths, as they no doubt often did, their stories provide valuable insight into the rebellion at ground level.[7] Take Nero, for instance.

Nero testified that when a band of rebels came to his plantation to recruit fighters, their leader, Adou, recognized him. The two men had been forcibly transported to Berbice on the same slave ship. But the crucible of the Middle Passage had not forged them into kin, as was commonly the case. Rather, an attempt at shipboard rebellion had rendered them rivals. Adou angrily reminded Nero how he "had betrayed him when he had wanted to kill the Christians on the ship." Now in a position to take revenge, Adou threatened to murder him, Nero claimed, but reconsidered and instead had "taken him along . . . as a slave."

We might dismiss this story as the elaborate tale of a desperate man disavowing voluntarily joining the rebels. Clearly, Nero thought being forced to join the rebels was a plausible defense. And that is telling. It suggests that claiming coercion might work, because everyone knew coercion occurred—whether or not it happened in Nero's case. In the American Revolution, too, violence and force were used to turn the hesitant and the doubtful into patriots. Nero's testimony also suggests that people's allegiances during the rebellion were shaped not just by their legal condition as slaves but also by their relationships with one another and so by the dynamics and politics within their own communities. In this they resembled participants in better-known revolutions, who similarly acted on local grievances and alliances as well as on larger revolutionary principles.[8]

As it happens, documents back up, and perhaps confirm, at least part of Nero's story. The provincial archives in Middelburg in the Netherlands contain a long letter written in 1757 by the captain of the Dutch slave ship *Philadelphia*. After chronicling his voyage along the West African coast, his complex negotiations with African merchants, and the number of people he bought at each stop, the captain reported that, "while anchored in Elmina, the male slaves on my ship planned a mutiny but it was betrayed." The captain had 18 enslaved men flogged. He subsequently sold 108 slaves in Berbice, including quite possibly Adou and Nero, though there is no way to be sure.[9]

This book relies on close to nine hundred slave testimonies, the letters exchanged by rebel leaders and the Dutch governor, and the Dutch governor's extensive daily journal, along with officials' copious reports and correspondence. The Dutch sources are also problematic. Like all imperial archives, they were generated by Europeans convinced of their inherent superiority and of their right to use violence to force people to do their bidding. Letters and reports, written for superiors, aim to present European actions in a favorable light. The Dutch were oblivious to much of African-descended people's lives. Yet the documents provide valuable insight into the Dutch experience of rebellion and counterrevolution as well as the fragilities and strengths of their colonial operations. Despite being racist and self-serving, such testimony sheds further light, however distorted, on the experience of the enslaved.[10] And of course we are prisoners of the evidence. Had the rebellion succeeded, participants' stories would have memorialized their victory rather than giving beleaguered testimony under pressure.

Together, the records allow me to chronicle what a slave rebellion and its repression looked like in a remote corner of eighteenth-century America, blow by blow. They highlight the political and military confrontations of rebels with planters and soldiers, but they also reveal the internal dynamics and politics of rebellion. They lay bare the coercion and discipline required to mobilize reluctant people and to organize a new political hierarchy. Berbicians clearly strongly disagreed over strategies and goals, as well as different visions for the future. Large numbers of people did their best to dodge the Dutch and the rebels, to stay uninvolved, eager to remain both masterless and alive.

Despite the eventual failure of the Berbice Rebellion, nowhere else, with the exception of Haiti, did self-liberated people control an entire colony for so long, or come so close to winning.[11] The story of the Berbice rebels attests to the state-supported violence required to make colonialism, slavery, and capitalism work for the Dutch on the Wild Coast and to the determination and resilience of African-descended people as they sought dignity, freedom, and self-governance.

1

Rehearsal, 1762

The young man was forced aboard the newly built Dutch slaving frigate *Magdalena Maria* on the coast of West Africa along with three hundred other captives. We don't know the name his parents gave him, how he fell into Dutch hands, or where along the Guinea coast he embarked. Perhaps he was a prisoner of war, like the majority of West African slaves. Perhaps he was sold to pay a family debt or kidnapped by bandits. Likely he was marched at gunpoint for hundreds of miles before reaching the coast. Stowed in an overcrowded shallow hold belowdecks for the Atlantic crossing, he and his fellow captives continued their journey of forced exile from their families and ancestors, villages and fields—their lives forever divided by the excruciating Middle Passage. Three hundred and three people embarked on that voyage to the Berbice River, a Dutch colony in what is now known as the Republic of Guyana in northern South America. Twenty-four men, women, and children did not reach Berbice alive. Horrific as that figure is, it falls well below the 13 percent overall mortality rate of the Dutch slave trade. Those who survived came to think of one another as kin. The emaciated young African and his fellow captives arrived in Berbice in January 1762.[1]

By that year, well over 5.3 million Africans had been forcibly transported to the Americas since the beginning of the Atlantic slave trade around 1500. Only 4.4 million arrived alive. Most went to Brazil and the Caribbean.[2] Perched on the Atlantic coast of South America, Berbice was part of the greater Caribbean basin. Trade closely tied the region's slave economies to the wider Atlantic world: western Europe, West Africa, and the North American colonies. The Dutch settlement of Berbice was tiny in comparison to British Barbados and Jamaica, French St. Domingue, Spanish Cuba, or South Carolina and Virginia. The riverine outpost held between 4,200 and 5,000 enslaved people, including 300 Indian slaves, and 350 Europeans.

The colony belonged to the Sociëteit van Berbice, the Company of Berbice, which operated under the sovereignty of the Republic of Seven United Provinces, as the Dutch Republic was officially known. The Company directors in Amsterdam appointed a governor who administered the colony to protect their interests and ensure law and order. He was assisted by a council, made up of local planters, that doubled as the colony's court, in charge of civil and criminal justice. Water dominated life in the colony. People moved about in dugouts and "tent boats," light, swift barges with awnings for shade, rowed by six or more enslaved men. Indian trading paths fanned out to neighboring colonies and native towns deep in the interior, where few Europeans dared venture.[3]

Farther north, there were as yet no plantations near the coast since tidal flows would call for expensive flood-control projects. Starting some twenty-five miles inland, plantations snaked south in a long, narrow ribbon along the Berbice River. Berbice lacked a port city, or any city, for that matter. A small hamlet, New Amsterdam, built around the colony's main post, Fort Nassau, some sixty miles upriver from the coast, served as the colony's central administration and defense. Newly appointed governor Wolphert Simon van Hoogenheim and many of his officials lived here. The river widened at the fort into a useful basin to anchor ships before narrowing considerably. The colony extended another fifty-five miles along the winding river to the last plantation in the colony, Savonette. The riverside plantations made for just a tiny sliver of European control. Beyond the fields stretched rain forests and vast savannas, grassy lowlands that became a treacherous morass during the year's two rainy seasons, from mid-December until early February and again from late April to mid-August. This

Dirk Valkenburg, *Plantage Waterlant*, ca. 1608. Detail, tent boat rowed by slaves and canoe paddled by Amerindians. (Amsterdam Museum, Amsterdam.)

larger region was uncharted by Europeans and inhabited, and governed, only by Amerindians.[4]

In Berbice, the young captive from Africa once again faced separation, this time from his new shipboard brothers and sisters. Examined cursorily by a doctor before being sorted for assignment, he was spared the humiliation of the auction block. Planters in Berbice usually signed advance contracts for African captives, as few slave ships could be induced to visit the small colony otherwise. Slaves were designated by lottery. The captive was branded with the initials of his buyer. Laurens Kunkler was a colonial councilman, militia captain, and owner of plantation Goed Land en Goed Fortuin. Kunkler's plantation was located several days' paddling up the twisting river. We do not know at what time of day or night the young man made the trip. The strong tides of the Berbice River rise twice a day. Rowing against the tide was backbreaking work, so boats went up the river only with the tide. Since it moved up by an hour each day, voyagers might be required to travel in the middle of the night. The river would have been calm; there were no rapids until much farther up its 370 miles. Did the captive try to communicate with the men powering the oars, backs glistening, keeping cadence with song?[5]

Night or day, sitting on the floor of the tent boat, the young man would have been able to make out the outline of tropical forest rising up on either side. The winding river's low and muddy banks were lined with impenetrable thickets of red mangroves. Like an upside-down world, sixty-foot-tall palm trees doubled in the still water's reflection. Only the frontage of plantations interrupted the walls of brilliant green and yellow. Abundant and tangled foliage hid the mouths of numerous small creeks and inlets. A cacophony of sounds assaulted his ears: the chattering of howler monkeys high in the trees, the high-pitched shrieks of omnipresent parrots and colorful macaws, the cries of "how-do" birds whose call sounds like a polite inquiry, trilling bird-songs, all over a steady undertone of hissing insects. Depending on where the man was from in West Africa, such sounds were familiar to him, as were some of the plants and grasses. If any riverine predators such as caimans and piranhas caught his eye, they, too, may not have surprised him.[6]

Some thirty-four miles from the coast, the boat passed plantation Dageraad with its green fields of sugar, the first of eleven so-called Company plantations, owned by the Society of Berbice, stretched along the river. During the colony-wide rebellion the next year, Governor van Hoogenheim would set up headquarters on Dageraad. At this point, the riverbank gradually began to rise, throwing up occasional knolls. Around the sixtieth mile, they passed Fort Nassau and the tiny village of New Amsterdam. The seat of government consisted of fewer than thirty wooden houses, sheds, and workshops. Another thirty miles upriver, the boat passed the first of two large creeks, the Wiruni on the west bank and, thirteen miles farther up, the Wikki on the east. These creeks, known by their indigenous names, extended deep into the hinterland. A little beyond, the young man's long journey finally ended at his new place of captivity, a labor camp 115 miles from the Atlantic Ocean and 4,000 miles from home.[7]

At Goed Land en Goed Fortuin, he joined a community of twenty-eight other enslaved Africans and four Amerindian slaves. His new owner called him Coffij, either in reference to the number one crop, coffee, that made Berbice planters wealthy (almost every plantation in Berbice imprisoned at least one boy or man named Coffij) or a Dutch version of the common West African name Kofi. Once incarcerated on Kunkler's plantation, Coffij had to find the resilience and courage to make his life anew. Cut off from family and friends, he had no choice but to reinvent himself, forging new relationships and learning how to survive the brutality of Dutch slavery.[8]

Breakout, July 1762

Coffij arrived in the Dutch colony during a period of starvation and disease. Berbice had been in the grip of a major fever epidemic since the mid-1750s. Illness had struck the Europeans with particular vengeance, but Africans and Amerindians, too, had sickened and died. With less labor power, exports of coffee, sugar, cacao, and cotton had dwindled; so, too, had supplies from food gardens that enslaved people kept outside the plantation grounds. This caused hunger among the enslaved because planters expected slaves to grow part of their own food during their time off. To make matters worse, Dutch supply ships loaded with salted beef, grains, and beans arrived less often as the Seven Years' War (1757–63), a global conflict between Britain and France (Winston Churchill called it the first world war), disrupted Caribbean and transatlantic shipping. As the Wild Coast colonies were not self-sufficient, the shortages that followed were brutal.[9]

The colony's governor, thirty-two-year-old Wolphert Simon van Hoogenheim, had repeatedly requested more food for their slaves from the tightfisted Company directors. He was surprisingly sympathetic, rare for a Dutch official. In frequent letters he described the suffering of the colony's slaves, who often did not get "a bit of meat to strengthen them" for months on end. "It is bitter," he wrote, "to have to labor with a hungry stomach." Hunger made people reluctant to work and obliged plantation managers "to wring labor out of the slaves with violence." Or maybe Van Hoogenheim was simply practical. Planters' violence, he warned, might lead to "bad consequences."[10]

And so Coffij was quartered on Goed Land en Goed Fortuin at a time when there was no good fortune for anyone. Resentful and hungry laborers faced hard-driving planters and overseers keen to meet their production quotas despite diminished numbers of plantation workers resulting from illness and death. Within five months of Coffij's arrival, his fellow plantation slaves decided they had had enough of hunger and enslavement.

On the first Saturday in July 1762, plantation owner Kunkler settled in comfortably in his tent boat as his slaves rowed him downriver to Fort Nassau. Kunkler was headed to a meeting of the governing council made up of the governor and six appointed planters. It functioned as the executive arm of the colony and its criminal court. Once Kunkler, the only European on the plantation, was gone, his slaves seized their opportunity. That Monday, most of them failed to report for work. Instead, they slaughtered and barbecued several cows, raided the plantation house, and loaded three large canoes with clothes, food, and drink. As Kunkler was a captain of the colony's militia, he stored weapons on his plantation. The rebels took control of this cache of thirteen guns and powder. Defiantly flying the militia flag, twenty-six adults and children, including fifteen able-bodied men, pointed their canoes upriver. They called on their gods by singing and beating their drums. They urged the people on the neighboring plantation, Boschlust, to join them, but they declined, just as eight months later they would refuse to join the big rebellion.[11]

The mastermind behind this small-scale rebellion and escape was Adam, Kunkler's driver, or *bomba*. *Bombas* were prominent men on plantations, chosen to direct work crews because of their aptitude, charisma, and good behavior. They received extra rations and other privileges and usually had their masters' complete confidence. Adam had lived at Goed Land en Goed Fortuin for many years and had acquired, adapting African practices, three wives—a sign of his high status and influence. He was Kunkler's surrogate when the planter was absent. After many years of steadfast service, Adam's privileged social arrangement gave way in the face of spreading hunger. Claiming a basic right to subsistence, he declared that people who were not fed should not have to work. He talked persuasively of starting a settlement high up the river. If the place he had in mind proved unproductive or the local native people were hostile, he promised his initially skeptical fellow plantation workers, he would find a better location. Enslaved men knew the terrain of Berbice from running errands for their masters, illicit nighttime visits between estates, working their kitchen gardens in the jungle or savannas behind the plantation, fishing the many creeks in their dugouts, or hunting in the bush.[12]

Adam was a healer. He employed African-derived shamanistic spiritual practices known as obeah, or, in North America, conjure. He assured his followers of his protective powers and vowed to free anyone the Dutch might recapture. He concocted a "fetich" drink, a magic potion of rum, water, and blood, to seal the coconspirators' oath of loyalty. The sacred oath linked those who swore it in bonds of solidarity and ritual protection. Common in West and West Central Africa, obeah was frequently used by Africans planning escape or rebellion in the Americas.[13] Witnesses later testified that only a handful refused to join Adam, among them Kunkler's enslaved mistress, who fought off the man trying to force her into a canoe. As a new arrival, Coffij had little to lose and he threw in his lot with the rebels.

The escape went off without a hitch. As the three canoes approached the last plantation on the river, the Savonette, the manager happened to be at the water's edge. He was about to motion them over when he noticed their guns and thought better of it. When the escapees came upon the Accoway [Akawaio] Post, an Indian trading station on the outer edge of the colony, they attacked. Though vital to trade and diplomacy, such posts were little more than several thatched huts manned by a Dutch officer, known as the postholder, and a few Amerindians. Adam's people wounded the postholder, killed one of his Akawaio assistants, and took more guns and supplies. Well armed, the rebels moved a few miles farther upriver and hid in the mouth of a creek.

The successful breakout proved a stunning embarrassment for the Dutch, who scrambled to respond. The military in Berbice was virtually nonexistent. Europeans in Berbice made up less than 5 percent of the population, holding sway with guns and brutal violence. But unlike Caribbean colonies such as Barbados and Jamaica, which also had huge African majorities, Berbice was tiny, with a poorly developed governmental and military structure. Due to high costs, the Company sent few Dutch soldiers, and most sickened immediately in the tropical climate with its frequent epidemics. Governor van Hoogenheim could spare but fourteen healthy Company soldiers to send after the escapees. Only a handful of planters, led by Kunkler, proved willing to join the expedition; most were reluctant to leave their estates in the hands of their slaves. The plantations dotting the river were small outposts of European dominion. Beyond them, in native country, the Dutch planters had little control. Between European foot-dragging and the difficult tides, it took a week for the governor to get the small force upriver to where the rebels had holed up. Accompanying the Europeans were several Akawaio natives, pressed into service. The posse eventually entered the creek where the escapees camped. Kunkler and the other planters stayed back, leaving the fighting to the military. Adam's men lured the soldiers into the woods and opened fire, killing two and wounding five. Two more soldiers were injured as they tried to retrieve their dead and wounded. The planters made no gesture to help. They fled.

Unwilling to risk their lives, especially in the face of Dutch spinelessness, the Akawaio, crucial as guides, also deserted the expedition. Not even a large reward of axes and cloth could induce them to return to aid the Dutch. A frustrated Governor van Hoogenheim pronounced them cowards, convinced that the unwilling indigenes had it "in their power to mop up such a small number of vagabonds." The governor was forced to supplement the expedition with "Creole" slaves (the blanket term for any enslaved people born in the Americas) as carriers and rowers. Berbice Creoles spoke Dutch and had family and other ties to the plantations where they lived, making them more reluctant to run away. Still, employing slaves was a dangerous proposition, as events in the neighboring Dutch colony of Suriname had shown six years earlier. In 1756, two-thirds of the 345 slaves on a Surinamese expedition against escaped people deserted. A few joined the fugitives; the rest, fed up with abusive soldiers, simply went home. That mission failed.[14]

To bolster his pitifully small commando unit, Governor van Hoogenheim sent a large canoe mounted with six small cannons. The arrival of artillery did little to shore up Dutch courage. The men simply had no stomach for bush fighting. Afraid that the rebels might surprise them, they refused to guard the mouth of the creek, taking post lower on the river. Using their adversaries' timidity to their advantage, Adam's group left the creek and escaped yet farther south. The Dutch made one halfhearted attempt to follow them before beating a hasty retreat when they were met with gunfire. One planter fell into Adam's hands and was killed.

But the Dutch were not the only ones facing obstacles. It was not long before Adam and his band were plagued by the challenges that often doomed slave breakouts. In Suriname, half of all enslaved people who ran off individually did not succeed. We have no statistics for small-group breakouts like the one Adam's band attempted, but the records suggest they were rare and most were not successful. Larger groups struggled with supplies and moving large numbers through the hostile jungle. Escaping one's plantation, alone or with others, was an act of courage and desperation that few attempted, given the overwhelming odds against success.[15]

Eventually, Van Hoogenheim's troops, though small and inept, managed to dislodge Adam and his band, forcing them deeper into the forest. There they confronted environmental obstacles, lack of resources, and interpersonal conflict. The jungle was a treacherous and unknown place. People on the run could never carry much in the way of food if they wanted to move quickly. And leaders disagreed about where to go. Such challenges overwhelmed many slave breakouts, Adam's included.

The escapees found themselves in dense woods flooded by several feet of water in the torrential downpours of the wet season, which made foraging for food impossible. Traveling light in an unfamiliar environment and cut off from the plantation zone, they could not resupply themselves until they could start gardens in the jungle. When the food they brought was gone, extreme hunger quickly set in. Sympathetic Akawaios gave them bread on a few occasions, but Adam's band mostly subsisted on heart of palm, the inner core of the palm tree. Two survivors later claimed that the fugitives resorted to cannibalism. They allegedly ate parts of a woman named Sophia after she was shot to death by Amerindians. Those wounded in the fighting suffered; others fell ill from malnutrition and exposure. Several died. Tempers flared. Unable to provide for his band, Adam reportedly snapped from the pressure and killed three children. He dumped their bodies in the creek. Like hunger, violence and conflict commonly stalked strained people on the run. For some, evil spirits also played a part—the bush was full of unfamiliar forces that even the shaman Adam could not appease.

In early August, after nearly six weeks in the jungle, the remaining fugitives tried to take advantage of a moonless night to escape farther upriver. This time their maneuver failed. The Dutch forces shot their cannon at the canoes, killing or wounding half the group. Despite a hit in the shoulder, Adam got away, along with Anthonij, Pai, Coffij, and a handful of unnamed women and children. Over the next few months, they were hunted by Akawaio Indians, who killed several of them. Reportedly, Anthonij and Pai, perhaps the fathers of the children Adam had killed, beheaded him in his sleep with an ax. Only two fugitives were caught alive: Coffij in mid-August and, a month later, Antoinette, an Amerindian woman who had been one of Kunkler's house slaves. The Akawaio also presented the Dutch with a woman's head and a man's arm, for which they received tools and textiles from India. The Dutch displayed the head on a pike at the execution grounds near Fort Nassau, "as a warning to all." [16]

In the nineteenth century, Joseph Conrad, in *Heart of Darkness*, immortalized the image of heads on pikes as a symbol of Europeans' fall from civilization. Conrad had it wrong. The practice was quintessentially European. In early modern Europe, the spectacle of heads on pikes often served as a reminder to the lower classes about the consequences of challenging the hierarchical status quo. In the colonial world, too, it was a common tactic of revenge and deterrence. English colonists in Plymouth publicly displayed the head of a defeated native leader within three years of their landing, in 1623. [17] During the Stono Rebellion in South Carolina in 1739, pursuing planters killed rebels on the spot and, as one rider claimed, put their severed heads "at every Mile Post they came to." In 1795, twenty-three slaves suspected of being part of a conspiracy in Point Coupee, Louisiana, would be hanged and their heads staked along the Mississippi River. Some twenty years later, again in Louisiana, the heads of defeated slave rebels on the German Coast would be put on public display along a distance of forty miles.[18]

Hauled to Fort Nassau, Coffij and Antoinette were questioned by the court, made up of members of the governor's council. They declared Antoinette innocent. The judges believed her claim, confirmed by Coffij and Kunkler, that Adam had forced her to come along. The court rejected the prosecutor's demand that she be whipped and sold out of the colony. However, the judges took a dim view of Coffij's involvement. Questioned with the aid of several enslaved men as translators,

Jan de Visscher, *Young Archer*, ca. 1650–1701. (Rijksmuseum, Amsterdam.)

he admitted that he had wielded a bow and arrows. Antoinette confirmed that Coffij had "shot many arrows." Since one of the Dutch soldiers fighting the escapees had been killed with a poisonous arrow,
Coffij's fate was sealed. The prosecutor demanded he hang from the
gallows by an iron hook piercing his torso. This gruesome manner of
punishment would later become infamous through a widely published
engraving by the English radical poet and printmaker William Blake.
The court decided against the hook. Instead, Coffij was sentenced to be
tied "to a cross, to be broken alive from his feet up," his body and severed head displayed underneath the gallows "until the birds and air
have consumed it." This was considered a more lenient sentence since
hanging by a hook could take days to bring on death.[19]

The savage execution was performed two days later. The young
Coffij, having spent less than a year in the colony, was brought to the
place of execution near the fort. Before his murder, he received a glass
of *kiltum*, the locally distilled rum. He was asked whether he regretted
his actions. His reply carried an ominous foreboding. What the slaves
had failed to accomplish, he reportedly predicted, "others would soon
carry out."[20]

Becoming Maroons

From the beginning of their forced migration across the Atlantic, enslaved people like Coffij tried to free themselves from their bondage.
Some ran away individually or in pairs, either short-term to visit family or gain some respite, or with the intent to never return. Others escaped as a group. Rather than aiming to overthrow the vast and deeply
entrenched institution of slavery, most runaways aimed for more modest goals: to live independently outside the plantation zone. The great
majority of rebellions were small, like the one on Goed Land en Goed
Fortuin, confined to a plantation or two. Organizing larger uprisings
was extraordinarily difficult. Many escapees died of hunger and disease or were recaptured and punished, sometimes as severely as Coffij.
A few succeeded. They found Amerindians willing to take them in or
they joined existing communities of people who permanently escaped

slavery to live in the hinterlands, known generally as Maroons. Others started their own settlements, as Adam intended; the size of such communities ranged from a dozen people to several hundred or even, more rare, several thousand inhabitants. Yet others found refuge in the colonies of rival European nations eager to undercut one another by promising freedom to deserting slaves and soldiers. The Spanish in Florida populated an entire village outside of St. Augustine with people who had fled slavery in British South Carolina. In the nineteenth century, the Underground Railroad in the United States enabled self-liberating people to find safety in free states, Mexico, and Canada.[21]

The decision to attempt to escape enslavement was not made easily. Except for newcomers, escape meant abandoning one's family and friends, often for good, unless an entire plantation force decided to break out together. Many were reluctant to leave behind ancestral spirits, their intimate knowledge of the local geography, their gardens and poultry, and any hard-won concessions and privileges that might have made their lives under slavery a little bit easier. The most important impediment was family. Difficult decisions had to be made about who should come along: children, old people, pregnant women, the sick? It is not surprising that the overwhelming majority of people decided to stay put. Most runaways were young men recently arrived from Africa, like Coffij, with few ties and loyalties. Women, less mobile due to their responsibilities for children and the elderly, made up a small minority of those who escaped slavery. While some fugitives did not succeed in escaping permanently, others did. To this day, their descendants live in Suriname, Jamaica, and Brazil, as well as elsewhere in the Americas.[22]

For three hundred years, Surinamese Maroons chose to continue to live in remote villages in the hinterlands, visiting the capital, Paramaribo, just a few times a year to buy guns, salt, cloth, and pots. But gold mining and rubber production in the nineteenth century, followed by mining for bauxite, the raw material for aluminum, in the next, chipped away at their seclusion. An enormous dam built on the Suriname River in the early 1960s to provide electricity for the extraction industries displaced thousands of Maroons. In the 1980s, warfare between the Surinamese government and guerrilla opposition groups made the region unsafe. Many Maroons left permanently for neighboring French Guyana or the Netherlands. The majority of the 120,000 remaining Surinamese Maroons now live in Paramaribo.[23]

Present-day Surinamese Maroon historians point to overwork and excessive and cruel punishments to explain why their ancestors made the decision to escape. They use the Dutch verb *afbeulen* (derived from the word *beul*, or torturer) to indicate the kind of impossible labor only a torturer would impose. The *beulswerk* Europeans forced their forebears to carry out angered their gods, who encouraged them to leave their plantations. They also relate stories of punishments that exceeded the bounds of acceptability as reasons that drove people to the bush. Such explanations point to the important role played by West African religious worldviews, which regarded egregious breaches of the social fabric as the result of evil forces that required corrective action. Maroon historians also explain that not all enslaved people felt compelled to escape. Some of their ancestors knew the way to a nearby Maroon village, but they chose to stay on their plantations. "They had no reason to run away as they did not have it so hard," one Maroon explained. "There was no reason to choose life in the bush rather than on the plantation." Enslaved people had to weigh life on the plantation, however onerous and violent, against the dangers of escape.[24]

Escape was treacherous, as the fate of the rebels at Goed Land en Goed Fortuin illustrates. Along the way and in their new locations, Maroons had to contend with Amerindians. Some Indians embraced fugitives as allies against hated colonial occupiers or indigenous enemies. Others rejected them as competitors for natural resources and women. Many turned in fugitives to obtain European commodities like guns and knives. When successful escapees managed to settle down, they had to build houses, plant crops, and organize themselves socially and politically. They basically had to found a colony themselves, but one scantily supplied from the outside.

Maroons deeply challenged the plantation system. They frequently lived on the edges of colonies, raiding plantations for weapons and food, and they even stole women and children, inflicting costly losses on planters and enslaved communities alike. Maroons encouraged slaves to break out, or they welcomed those who arrived in their villages on their own. Their existence reminded the enslaved that a different life was possible. Colonial authorities dealt with these threatening "performances of freedom" in two ways: by trying to wipe out Maroons with military force or by incorporating them into the colonial state as military allies and slave catchers. In Spanish America, Maroons' negotiating for peace started in the sixteenth century. In the British Caribbean, the first treaties involving Maroons were signed in Jamaica in 1739.[25]

Next door to Berbice, in Suriname, the colonial authorities and various bands of Maroons battled one another for much of the eighteenth century. Small Maroon communities had formed in the Suriname hinterland in the 1600s. Within fifty years, they united into several larger societies such as the Okanisi Maroons and the Samaaka, or Saramaka, Maroons. Military expeditions against them were ineffective. European soldiers feared and abhorred the unmapped jungle, with its thirty-foot snakes and vampire bats.[26] During the wet seasons, they easily sickened in the torrential downpours that flooded the rain forest and ruined their weapons and powder. Cannons, Europeans' main tactical advantage, were utterly useless in jungle warfare. They worked only in large open spaces. The isolated Great Dismal Swamp between North Carolina and Virginia provided similar haven for runaway slaves starting in the eighteenth century. In the nineteenth century, American abolitionist and author Harriet Beecher Stowe, famous for *Uncle Tom's Cabin*, wrote her second novel lionizing imaginary Maroons living there.

Realizing that military victory might forever be elusive, one Suriname governor proposed peace with Maroons in 1747, but his council refused to go along. In 1760, after several years of negotiating, Governor Wigbold Crommelin signed a treaty with some Maroon societies. In exchange for their autonomy, the Okanisi Maroons promised to refrain from attacking plantations and, for a price, to return any fugitive slaves. Two years later, the Samaaka assented to a similar agreement.[27]

I have seen no references to Maroon settlements in Berbice before

1763. The colony was narow, leaving little room for Maroon villages. It was surrounded by Amerindians obligated by treaty to kill or return fugitives trying to settle in their territories. Amerindian animosity and collaboration with the colonial authorities also made it difficult for fugitives to reach the Orinoco River, farther west, beyond Dutch territory, where the Spanish offered protection to Dutch escaped slaves and deserting soldiers.

Despite these challenges, small groups of slaves rebelled and fled in Berbice throughout the eighteenth century. In 1734, slaves on a plantation belonging to a powerful Huguenot family from Amsterdam murdered two white servants and escaped into the bush. They were caught by Arawak men. In 1747, enslaved workers injured the estate manager on Petershof, just upriver from Fort Nassau, and took off. But before they could get far, fellow slaves caught them. Five years later, enslaved men on another plantation near Fort Nassau, armed with broadswords and cutlasses, stormed the plantation house and wounded the planter's wife, who was hiding under the dining room table. When her husband came to her aid, they assaulted him too. White, native, and enslaved men from neighboring estates pursued and captured the rebels. In all three instances, those caught were executed. Presumably, these documented breakouts constitute only a few threads in a larger tapestry of resistance.[28]

Balance of Power

The breakout of enslaved people on Goed Land en Goed Fortuin was not unprecedented, but planters were set on edge by their difficulty in suppressing it. They realized they did not have enough men to defend themselves. "Just 15 able-bodied men," a rattled governor wrote to his superiors, "of whom only 13 had guns, have shaken the entire colony, and created such a fright among the inhabitants, that many are still afraid to go to sleep." He implored the Company to hire more soldiers and enforce the decree in the colony's charter that planters settle one white man for every fifteen slaves on their plantations to prevent Europeans from being so hugely outnumbered. "We are completely dependent on the blacks' discretion," the governor emphasized. "If they please," he projected, "they could take over the entire colony and do with us as they wished." The young governor, just two and a half years on the job, knew enough after *bomba* Adam's rebellion to recognize that he was sitting on a powder keg. The colony operated along a finely calibrated scale that balanced enslaved and exploited people against enslavers, many of them absentee, reluctant to risk much to defend the colony. [29]

To the enslaved, the breakout exposed both the possibilities and the dangers of collective action. All along the riverbank, enslaved people likely watched the unimpressive force of soldiers and planters pass by. Carriers and servants came back with stories of Dutch incompetence and cowardice. They told of the Akawaio captain who abandoned the commando unit in disgust after the colonists retreated. Why should he fight, he had asked, if the whites were not willing to risk their lives? They learned that while some Indians made fearful adversaries, others helped fugitives with food. The young Coffij's horrific execution and his heroism spawned new anger and hatred and exposed yet another level of Dutch vulnerability. The colonists' ranks were so thin that they did not even have enough soldiers to circle the execution grounds when Coffij was killed, as military custom dictated. Finally, that an entire plantation broke out together was an inspiration. If the people on Goed Land en Goed Fortuin could organize themselves, others could follow.[30]

Yet, the escapees had not succeeded. News of leader Adam's death devastated those who had hoped for his success or had considered joining him. Tales of murdered children, the men and women dying of injuries and disease, the deprivation, might have strengthened their convictions that hunger on the plantation was preferable to hunger in hiding.

The court, meanwhile, tried to gauge the potential scope of the rebellion. When the councilmen questioned Coffij and Antoinette, the pair denied any collaboration with people on other plantations. But manager Johan Ernst Hoerle of plantation Savonette was convinced that enslaved workers on at least four other estates, including his own, had been in on the plan. Hoerle characterized the Savonette slaves as "corrupted," "impertinent," and "malicious"; they had been upset, he explained to the Company directors, at rarely receiving meat while forced to do heavy labor. The work was hard, he conceded, but he fed them as well as he could.[31]

Hoerle's fears were realized later that fall, when his *bomba*, also named Adam, told him that two male slaves, Pans and Alasso, had plans to take over the Savonette plantation. This news did not surprise Hoerle. On three different nights, he and his two Amerindian house slaves Joris and Philip thought they saw black men armed with cutlasses and knives circle the plantation house. Joris allegedly heard talk that enslaved men on several other estates intended to revolt as well. When questioned, Pans was "very affronted that we would believe such things," Hoerle reported, and "feigned ignorance" of any and all events, despite whippings and threats of torture.[32] Hoerle, unable to get the men to confess, had Pans and Alasso, along with a third man named Accara, rowed downriver to New Amsterdam to be further examined by the court.

Once at New Amsterdam, the prisoners continued to deny everything. Whether their plans went beyond talk is impossible to tell. Pans, who worked as a cooper, had lived in the colony for years. Why would he run away, he asked rhetorically, speaking in Berbice Dutch, given that he was an old man and six of his eleven children were still living? He reminded the judges that the suspects had joined the recent expedition to fight "for their master against Kunkler's Adam." Had they been interested in escape, would they not have run off with Adam at that time? He denied having been upset at the news of Adam's death or proclaiming that "it did not matter, we shall shortly do better." No, Pans now asserted, he was "right glad" Adam was gone. As long as Adam had been on the run, Savonette slaves had not been allowed to tend their kitchen gardens, which were upriver beyond the Akawaio Indian post, increasing everyone's hunger. Moreover, he continued, did the court have examples of Company slaves' intentions to murder their master or take over their plantation? He dismissed the testimony of Joris and Philip. As house slaves they could not know what went on in the *negerij* (slave quarters). And *bomba* Adam? Hoerle had threatened him into making wild accusations.[33]

Alasso, a field hand, was less confident or more evasive. He responded to most questions with a simple "I do not know." Asked whether the Savonette workers had been fed on time, Alasso carefully replied that "when their master had food, he gave it and otherwise they got Saturday off" to grow their own. He concluded his testimony by claiming that he had "a good heart for his master." Accara, who had been a *bomba* but was now a field hand, similarly emphasized his "good heart" for Hoerle. Asked whether the people on Savonette were well fed, he likewise responded, "if their master has something, they get it, though they don't get much." Diplomatically he added, "His master can't help that."[34] The men's careful answers suggest more was going on than they divulged.

In the face of the prisoners' denials, the judges traveled to Savonette to talk to witnesses. They examined Savonette's *bomba* Adam. This Adam was sure that the accused were intent on murdering Hoerle, because the notorious taskmaster punished his slaves too harshly. Yet Adam reassured the commissioners that he did not believe that, beyond the three suspects, any Savonette people were involved in a plot to kill the overseer or wished to live as Maroons.[35] When questioned, two Amerindian house slaves asserted that the breakout on Goed Land en Goed Fortuin that summer set everyone thinking. They believed that the plans had spread to several other plantations where Savonette workers had friends and family.

While the court tried to get to the truth of the alleged conspiracy, manager Hoerle, fearing for his life at the hands of his workers, deserted his post on the Savonette. Claiming he had gotten lost as he took a stroll in the savanna for his health, he somehow ended up in Demerara, several days' walk away. Asserting that he was too ill to make the trip back, he requested his dismissal and his back wages. Outraged, Governor van Hoogenheim ordered Hoerle to return immediately or be considered a deserter, and he appointed a new manager on Savonette. Hoerle's absence put the case of the Savonette conspirators on hold.[36] When the three detainees began to "swell up" in their chains, the court ordered their release during the day to work but that they be locked up again at night.

By now, Governor van Hoogenheim doubted the existence of a widespread conspiracy. He explained to the Company directors that the "sad case" of Goed Land en Goed Fortuin "so captivated the brains of all inhabitants with fear, that we daily hear of nothing but conspiracies that threaten us, and are planned particularly on Company plantations." The interrogations of Savonette workers, he felt, did not indicate a widespread conspiracy, nor indeed any plot at all. Hoerle had pushed his slaves too hard and punished them too severely. Such "poor household governance" had led his workers to hate him, and perhaps some workers had been "wicked" enough to boast that they wanted to kill their manager, the governor concluded. Hunger among the slaves, he wrote to his superiors, was a real problem and might lead to "worse consequences." Again, he "begged and prayed" for the directors to send more food. In the meantime, he had bought barrels of salted meat from a passing ship for the Company slaves, even though he knew his superiors would frown upon such an expense as being lavish.[37]

Only two prisoners remained, as Alasso had died in jail, when late in January 1763 prosecutor Eilardus Harkenroth submitted his findings about the Savonette plot. The heated denials of the prisoners and the wishy-washy witnesses muddled the case. According to Dutch law, the death penalty could be imposed only if a suspect confessed or if there were credible witnesses. But in this case, all the witnesses were slaves (since all the "Christians" involved had not actually seen anything), "and how much credit those should be accorded," the prosecutor reminded the court, "is well-known to you." While the prisoners' denials "opened the way" for the prosecutor to use torture to obtain confessions, he continued, he made clear he had decided against that route. Experience had shown that torture was ineffective, he thought, as it "had little effect on the souls of slaves." Nevertheless, the prisoners' riotous talk and contrary behavior deserved punishment. To that end, he proposed they be whipped and branded.[38] The court agreed.

In the weeks that followed, Berbice planters became increasingly paranoid, as enslaved people appeared emboldened by recent events. The prosecutor had failed to ferret out the conspiracy at Savonette, and colonists worried about another plot. Vastly outnumbered and with few healthy soldiers, they felt understandably horrified by the Goed Land en Goed Fortuin debacle, leaving them anxious and vulnerable.

How on earth, one wonders, had the outnumbered, ill-supplied, and ill-adapted Dutch managed to rule their colony of Berbice for 150 years? How had this tenuous enterprise come about? How had it lasted?

2

Labor Camps in the Making

On January 24, 1629, a biting northeasterly wind strained the sails of two ships leaving the busy port of Vlissingen, or Flushing as the English called it. Vlissingen was located in Zeeland, a coastal province in the southwestern Dutch Republic. A contemporary image of the port shows similar sailing vessels, proudly flying Dutch flags, tacking the river Scheldt to and from the North Sea and the wider world. The panorama depicts a growing merchant town with tall, narrow canal houses, an imposing new town hall, church spires, and a grain mill, along with the entrances to several harbors. On the far right, we can just discern the recently completed fort. In another hundred years, Flushing would become a major slave-trading port. But that was in the future. The two ships, *De Zeeuwse Jager* and *Noordster*, were headed for the "Wild Coast," a region of jungle and waterways between the Amazon and Orinoco Rivers at the top of South America.[1]

The English defeat of the Spanish Armada in 1588 had opened the South Atlantic to northern Europeans. Stirred by Sir Walter Raleigh's discoveries and fanciful tales of gold in Amazonia nearly a decade later, Dutch skippers explored along the many rivers that emptied into the Atlantic. While they found no gold, over the next thirty years, they traded goods off and on with *wilden*, as they called Amerindians, on the Wild Coast. In time, small settlements formed along the major streams to facilitate commerce. The two ships leaving Zeeland that January day were to drop off new colonists on the Amazon River,

View of Vlissingen, 1650. Historisch Topografische Atlas. (Gemeentearchief Vlissingen.)

provision several infant settlements including one on the Berbice River, and make their return with tobacco and annatto.[2]

By then, the Dutch had been involved in the Atlantic trade for several decades. They were looking for new markets as the Spanish Habsburgs, whom they were fighting for their independence, squeezed them out of their traditional trading routes. The Spanish had closed off the Iberian Peninsula to Dutch commerce and occupied Antwerp, the most important port in the region. In response, Antwerp merchants moved north to Zeeland and especially to Amsterdam, injecting money and fresh entrepreneurial zeal. Traders from the Dutch Republic's sea provinces, Holland and Zeeland, expanded their commerce into Russia, the eastern Mediterranean, and the Atlantic Ocean, laying the groundwork for a hundred years of far-flung colonial expansion and spectacular commercial success glossed as "the Golden Age."

By the early seventeenth century, Dutch ship captains were buying gold and ivory in West Africa; salt, tobacco, and hides in the Greater Antilles and the northern tip of South America; and furs on the North American coast. In 1607, the same year the English started a colony in Virginia, the Dutch created the Dutch East India Company, which went on to colonize Batavia (present-day Jakarta in Indonesia), Ceylon (Sri Lanka), and the Cape of Good Hope (South Africa). Fourteen years later, the Dutch West India Company was established to settle colonies like New Amsterdam (New York) and Curaçao. The two companies were tasked with developing overseas trade, colonizing new lands, and damaging the commercial interests of Portugal and Spain. Settlement of the Wild Coast was part of this Dutch offensive.[3]

After fierce winter storms and an encounter with pirates, the ships that left Vlissingen in late January 1629 finally reached the Amazon River in early April. The colonists disembarked and the vessels continued along the Wild Coast. At the mouth of the Berbice River, one of the skippers, Gelein van Stapels, sailed up the river in a small sloop. It is from Van Stapels's account of his brief visit to the river, and his sketch, that we have a first glimpse of the Berbice settlement.[4]

Few historians have studied Berbice, so we have little detailed knowledge about the colony's founding and development. Three visitors to the colony illustrate how a remote Atlantic settlement that started as an Indian trading station grew into a chain of slave labor camps focused on the cultivation of tropical cash crops. Captain Gelein van Stapels arrived at a founding moment in the 1620s. Trader Adriaan van Berkel developed alliances with Indians in the 1670s. Surgeon Rutger Tenhoute ministered to brutalized African slaves in the 1720s. Together, their stories illuminate the centrality of slavery to the development of Berbice. Their experiences showcase how the Dutch, like Europeans elsewhere in the New World, used diplomacy and trade to drive a wedge between Indians and Africans. Amerindians' alliances—sometimes by design, sometimes by accident—helped shape and preserve chattel slavery in the colony. Indian assistance allowed a tiny European minority to keep large numbers of enslaved Africans imprisoned—that is, until 1763.

Van Stapels had visited the Berbice River before his 1629 visit. Just two years earlier, he transported the first colonists there for Abraham van Pere, a rich and influential Zeeland merchant. Van Pere's father had traded with Amerindians on the Wild Coast for thirty years. Van Pere Jr. sought to lay a more definitive claim to the area. In 1627, he sent forty men and forty boys and perhaps six enslaved Africans to the Berbice River under the command of his son Cornelis. The third-generation Van Pere was to develop a private "patroonship," a colonial fief settled under a hereditary lease from the Dutch West India Company.[5] Just as the Dutch government outsourced conquering new lands to companies, so the West India Company itself subcontracted settlement, creating a highly fractured colonial system that mirrored the fragmented government of the Dutch Republic.[6]

In 1629, Berbice was still primarily a native trading post, and in Captain van Stapels's eyes not terribly promising. The colonists were scattered like seeds along a vast stretch of river that took eight days of upstream paddling to traverse. They were isolated and surrounded by impenetrable jungle. Cornelis van Pere built his house far south up the river near the Wiruni Creek. The cabin had a front porch to conduct trade and a storage attic for his merchandise. Captain van Stapels labeled it "Van Pere's house" on his sketch map, the first reference to what would become the Peereboom plantation, today's Dubulay ranch. Archaeological studies suggest that native peoples had foraged and farmed the site for millennia.[7]

The house stood on a bluff overlooking the river. Savanna and rain forest stretched behind it. Van Pere chose the upriver location because of its proximity to Arawak Indians. Native women made the red annatto dye he coveted. They pounded the pea-sized red seeds of the achiote bush, *Bixa orellana L.*, added oil, and shaped the mixture into balls used for body paint, sunscreen, and medicine. Already Van Pere had sent home nine thousand pounds of annatto. Arawak women were planting additional bushes and more indigenes were moving into the area, so Van Stapels expected production to increase. Annatto fetched good prices in Europe, where to this day it colors textiles, butter, and specialty cheese.[8]

While the Van Pere family monopolized the annatto trade, the colonists tried their hand at farming. They lived in small groups near Arawak villages "to plant tobacco," a weed just then taking Europe by storm. The settlers worked on shares—a third of their tobacco went to the patroon, Van Pere; the rest they got to keep. Captain van Stapels judged profit unlikely, noting the poor soil. The European colonists showed even less promise. He believed Van Pere should send most of them home. Old and young were "afflicted by pocks," which commonly struck newcomers, and most could "neither walk nor stand" because of the chiggers, or tiny mites, that burrowed in their feet. A few young men surely would suffice to handle the Indian trade, the captain thought. Once they gained experience, even Cornelis van Pere himself could repatriate. With a smaller workforce, Van Stapels figured, the Van Peres just might make a bit of money. Meanwhile, the captain noted dryly in his logbook, the miserable colonists had better pray that the *wilden* did not live up to their name and "go wild." He left the tiny outpost after three days. The few Dutchmen in Berbice, poorly armed, sickly, and trapped by the jungle, were entirely at the Amerindians' mercy.[9] Such were the meager beginnings of the Berbice colony.

Amerindians on the Wild Coast

A large multiethnic and multilingual indigenous population inhabited the area, dominated by Arawaks (today Lokono), Caribs (Kali'na), Waraos, and Akawaio (Kapon) Indians. They lived in villages that could be as large as several hundred people. Every few years the entire village moved to a new location to avoid exhausting the soil. Men hunted and fished, while women cultivated a variety of crops, especially cassava for bread and achiote for making annatto. The men of each village chose as their chief a charismatic man who had distinguished himself in war. By marrying multiple women, chiefs forged ties of kinship and reciprocity throughout the village, increasing their political authority. Still, their coercive power was limited; they were not authoritarian rulers in the manner of old-world monarchs. This fact would prove a source of frustration to European officials throughout the Americas, who wanted decisive, dependable allies.

As in North America, South American natives were well connected through commerce. Wild Coast villagers traded foodstuffs, handicrafts, information, and captives over hundreds, even thousands, of miles, using rivers and trails that connected them with people living deeper inland, who in turn traded as far away as what is now Colombia.[10]

Native men added regularly to the population of their villages by capturing people through wars, raids, and exchange. The fates of the captives varied. Children were generally adopted. Women were forced to marry into the village to perform domestic and sexual duties, contributing fresh blood and new ideas. Successful combatants increased their prestige by having many concubines. Male prisoners of war were more likely to be killed in elaborate rituals that might include the eating of their flesh. Some captives became servants or slaves or they found themselves repeatedly traded, often across great distances. Prisoners also served as gifts in diplomatic negotiations. As commerce with Europeans deepened, so did the barter in humans. Wars and raids intensified, and, as in North America, captives became increasingly commodified, obtained expressly for the purpose of trade.[11]

The Spanish had arrived in the early 1500s, well before the Dutch. They explored and settled Trinidad and the Orinoco River valley with the help of coastal Arawak Amerindians or "Aruacas." For decades, the natives supported the Spanish with food and indigenous slaves in exchange for iron tools and guns. They received protection from Spanish raiding parties trawling the Wild Coast for slaves for their Caribbean settlements. Spanish goods and protection encouraged the Arawaks' neighbors to join them. Over time, these hybrid peoples developed a more unified and explicit "Arawak" identity, a process anthropologists call ethnogenesis. A similar process set in motion by the arrival of Europeans created the people referred to in early modern sources as "Caribs."[12]

Over time, the Spanish style of ruling poisoned relations with Amerindians. As the Iberians forced indigenous people to work for them, trading alliances between the Spanish and Amerindians unraveled. When Amerindians moved east to escape the Spanish, coastal Guiana became a place of refuge and creative ethnic consolidation. The hostility of many Amerindians toward the Spanish worked to the advantage of Spain's European rivals as they began to explore the area in the late sixteenth century. At that time, the Dutch were struggling to secede from Hapsburg Spain. The United Provinces, as the Dutch Republic was called, fought an eighty-year war for their independence (1568–1648). The Hollanders were especially eager to poach on their enemy's trade. Whenever possible, they engaged in a contraband trade with Spanish colonists, depriving the Spanish Crown of tax revenues, and they harassed and raided Spanish ships. When Dutch traders began exploring the Wild Coast, Amerindians reportedly made clear that "whosoever are enemies, and bear enmity to the Spaniards, are friends with the Indians, and they hope steadily that they shall be delivered from the Spaniards by the Dutch and the English."[13]

With the assistance of Carib and Arawak peoples, Dutch adventurers, sometimes in cooperation with other European traders, established remote trading posts and a few toehold settlements along major rivers in the late sixteenth and early seventeenth centuries. Most did not succeed. The tiny colonies imploded from disease, internal strife, and lack of supplies or were wiped out by the Spanish, Portuguese, or Amerindians. Only two survived—Essequibo (1616) and Berbice (1627), thanks to Amerindian support. Eventually, the Dutch claimed two more colonies on the Wild Coast—Suriname (1667) and, much later yet, Demerara (1746),[14] well known today for its particularly fine, amber-colored sugar. The settlements hugged the riverbanks and extended like slender fingers inland.

Indian Trader Adriaan van Berkel, 1671

After Captain van Stapels's visit to the tiny and sickly colony in 1629, the record is largely silent about the founding of Berbice. Lost are the letters and memoranda to Zeeland describing the Indian trade, the buying of indigenous and some African slaves, the intermarriages of colonists and Africans with Indian women, and the development of farms and the first few sugar plantations.[15]

The Portuguese were the first in the Americas to produce sugar with African enslaved laborers. In the 1500s, they built thriving sugar plantations in Brazil, helped by Dutch merchants who shipped, refined, and marketed their sugar. The Dutch war with Spain interfered with this commerce, especially after the Spanish and Portuguese Crowns united in 1580. By the 1620s, the Dutch schemed to take over Brazil, which they accomplished in 1630, only to see the Portuguese reconquer the colony in 1654. In these same years, western Europeans eagerly pushed against the Spanish in the Americas by developing colonies in the Caribbean. Focused on trade, the Dutch confined themselves to a few small islands, principally St. Eustatius and Curaçao, which would develop into important commercial hubs. The French settled Guadeloupe and Martinique and the western part of Hispaniola, or St. Domingue. But it was the English who would prove the big winners in the seventeenth century. They developed sugar plantations on the islands of Barbados and Jamaica, first with indentured and convict laborers from England and then, when that supply dried up, with enslaved Africans. In time, sugar planters would become fabulously wealthy while enslaved sugar workers died at horrific rates from over-work, poor treatment, and disease.[16]

Like the French and English on their Caribbean islands, the Van Peres grew sugar with enslaved African laborers. But the numbers of plantations, and Africans, remained small. Van Pere Sr., an official in the Dutch West India Company, had encouraged Dutch involvement in the slave trade, likely to obtain Africans for his new colony of Ber-bice. In the early 1630s he had financed a small West India Company fleet, commanded by his son Daniel, to conquer Arguin, an island off the West African coast that served as a Portuguese slaving station. The West India Company followed up with additional successful attacks on slaving stations on the West African coast, conquering Elmina in 1637 and Luanda and Saõ Tomé in 1641. Despite these victories, it is unlikely that Berbice received many African slaves in those early years. Its tiny market simply could not compete with that of the im-portant sugar colony Brazil.[17]

The next account of Berbice and its inhabitants comes more than forty years after Van Stapels's voyage, and more than two decades after the war between the Spanish and the Dutch had ended in 1648. Its author was the young Adriaan van Berkel, a member of a well-to-do Leiden family who was appointed in 1670 as the patroon's clerk and Indian trader.[18] While the Dutch Republic lost its foothold in Brazil in 1654, Dutch merchants steadily expanded their involvement in At-lantic commerce, plantation agriculture, and the African slave trade. Ships from the tiny Dutch Republic carried one in every fifteen cap-tives from Africa to the Americas between 1626 and 1800.[19]

On the Wild Coast, the Dutch increasingly competed with the French and, especially, the English. In 1651, English planters from Barbados, assisted by Caribs, created the colony of Suriname. Well schooled in sugar production, the Barbadians brought their African slaves and quickly developed thriving plantations. During the second Anglo-Dutch War (1665–67) the Dutch conquered Suriname. By then its population—some 2,500 Africans, 800 Europeans, and 500 native slaves—dwarfed that of the other Wild Coast colonies. At the Peace of Breda between the Dutch Republic and England in 1667, the Dutch swapped New York, captured by the English during the war, for Suriname, which promised to be more profitable.[20] Immediately, Suriname became the largest Dutch colony on the Wild Coast.

Indian trader Van Berkel encountered a vastly different settlement on the Berbice River than Captain van Stapels had four decades before. Berbice was stable but small, inhabited by some 50 Europeans and perhaps 150 to 300 Africans and Amerindians.[21] Van Berkel reached Berbice in early 1671 after just five weeks at sea, a surprisingly speedy voyage. The first people he met were Indians, naked except for covering "their private parts." While some of the sailors immediately began to barter, Van Berkel took his first bites of "pepper pot," a native stew consisting of meat, hot peppers, and cassava juice, as hot and spicy as its name implied. On his trip by boat from the coast to Fort Nassau, he quenched his thirst with native *paiwari*, liquor made of "the mastications of women," who chewed charred cassava bread as they went about their work, spitting it into jars to ferment. Everyone in the colony drank it, "for want of better." Van Berkel thought it "tolerably good." After sailing upriver for two days, he reached Fort Nassau, where he was warmly welcomed by the Dutch commander. Van Berkel spent his first night in an Indian hammock, but because he was unaware that the best position was "crossways," he got little sleep.[22]

Van Berkel quickly picked up indigenous ways. During his four years in Berbice, he visited native villages, stayed in Amerindian shelters, slept in native hammocks, attended Indian ceremonies, heartily consumed pepper pot, *paiwari*, and *"berbekot,"* or barbecue, and traded and inventoried native products and people. By that time, the Van Pere family owned five sugar plantations worked by African and indigenous slaves. Van Berkel must have thought their hard lives made for poor reading, because he barely mentions them, erasing their forced labor and hungry existence from his landscape. Instead, the young Dutchman, a proto-anthropologist, was fascinated by Amerindians. He eventually published a book about them, his focus reflecting both his interests as a trader and the strong reliance of Europeans on their native trading partners in Berbice.

Indeed, Van Berkel's account highlights just how dependent the Dutch remained on the Arawak. Annatto, the red dye, continued to fetch good prices in the Netherlands and remained one of the main exports of Berbice.[23] The Dutch also relied on Amerindians for food, hammocks, canoes, timber, gums, household and other services, and native slaves. Native people, for their part, were eager to trade for European iron tools and trading beads made to their exacting specifications. Natives and colonists also cooperated militarily. Amerindians expected guns, powder, and ammunition when they went to war, while the Dutch counted on Amerindian auxiliaries for protection against hostile natives or European competitors.

Van Berkel was fascinated with indigenous people and described them at great length. The men, he reported, were "of ordinary stature." They wore their hair to their shoulders, while chiefs, or "captains," cut it off at the ears. Each man fixed a "small silver plate" to his septum, covering his mouth, requiring him to lift it up to eat or drink. Like natives in eastern North America, they despised body hair and plucked out their beards and eyebrows. They protected their skin from the sun and insects with red paint, giving them a crimson hue. Arawak women adorned themselves with as much as fifteen to eighteen pounds of strung shells around their necks, arms, torsos, knees, and ankles. "A set of between 12 and 16 strings is sufficient to win the finest women," Van Berkel reported. Both sexes covered their "modesty," unless they were in mourning, in which case they went naked. Young women, the lascivious Van Berkel added, "are accustomed to keep their legs close together so that, whatever their position, one can see nothing at all." Young and old bathed daily, and, unlike most Europeans, they were good swimmers.[24]

The young clerk traveled extensively, inspecting the Van Peres' five sugar plantations on the Berbice and negotiating deals in neighboring Essequibo, a week's walk west. When he went by boat, Amerindians paddled him. When he went overland, he needed natives to guide him and carry his belongings. When there was no village to lodge in, the Amerindians built *pleister huisjes*, temporary shelters made of four poles covered with huge palm leaves, which kept him dry in even the

John Gabriel Stedman, *The Manner of Sleeping &c. in the Forest*, 1772–96. Notice the gun and sword suspended below the covering. Enslaved or free African and indigenous guides kindled fires, cooked, and strung up hammocks for European travelers in Guiana. (John Carter Brown Library, Providence.)

most ferocious tropical downpours. A fire smoldering underneath his hammock at night chased away chilly air and mosquitoes. Indians also carried his letters and messages from one colony to another. For all these services, as well as for hunting and fishing, they demanded knives, axes, and kill-devil, the local rum. Yet, as Van Berkel noticed, "they do not stand under the bond of slavery, and will not be forced." Whenever "his" Indians had business to attend to, wanted to fish, rest, or sleep off hangovers, Van Berkel had no choice but to stay home. And when native women did not feel like selling him food, even for double the customary bead strings, he went hungry. Nor could he just take what he wanted, as "the Christians must watch not to make an enemy of them." [25]

Amerindians allowed needy colonists a foothold on the Wild Coast in the first decades of trade. They tolerated their presence as long as it worked in their interests. Dutch slaving practices soon changed that.

Common Cause

In the latter third of the seventeenth century, slavery increasingly shaped the relationship of the Dutch with their Amerindian allies. The trade in indigenous slaves bound them together for decades, but over time mistreatment and indiscriminate enslavement pulled them apart. In 1678, Caribs launched a war against the Suriname colonists, determined to wipe them out. Africans soon swelled Carib ranks. Suriname governor Johannes Heinsius wrote home that a "considerable" number of slaves had joined the Indians and "daily attack us together." By the next year he reported that some eight hundred African slaves had made common cause with the Indians. The Dutch feared, he continued, that the Africans "will cause us more harm than the Indians, as they are braver and more bold than the Indians." Europeans felt increasingly wary of their remaining enslaved workers and worried about trusting "even personal servants and house slaves." [26]

Together, Indians and Africans murdered colonists and burned plantations. It took the Dutch in Suriname eight years to slowly end the uprising by peeling apart the coalition of Indian nations and

Africans with tailor-made treaties. After the last treaty was concluded in 1686, the colonial authorities prohibited Carib and Arawak enslavement; in return, the Amerindians agreed to act as slave catchers and Maroon hunters. They carried out this duty as it suited them over the next hundred years, discouraging any future coalitions between themselves and enslaved Africans. The conflict was not a total loss for African combatants. While many of the Africans who had joined in the long rebellion were killed or fell back into Dutch hands, a considerable number managed to remain free in the hinterlands, where they started the Maroon communities for which Suriname became famous.[27]

After the war in Suriname ended, Berbice experienced a similar uprising, though it was smaller and short-lived. In the fall of 1687, Arawaks and Waraos burned down a number of plantations around Fort Nassau. They, too, made common cause with Africans, together killing several Europeans, including the former commander of the colony and his wife. Contemporaries felt that the Berbice colonists had brought the war on themselves through their "dirty practices, tyranny and unjust trading."[28] Indians in the North American colonies would similarly experience sharp trading practices, indebtedness, and enslavement. They, too, would rise up, as the Tuscarora Indians did in North Carolina in the 1710s.[29]

In response to uprisings that threatened the very existence of Dutch enterprises, Wild Coast officials tried to ensure that all Indian slaves offered for sale in their colonies came from the interior rather than from among "friendly Indians," who might be sold by family members to pay debts or abducted locally for a quick profit.[30] Non-allied inland Indians remained fair game, both because Dutch officials wanted native slaves and because Caribs and other Indians profited by continuing the lucrative human trade. Yet this spatial arrangement regularly broke down. Over and over the authorities had to deal with recalcitrant private traders and planters who, caring little for larger strategic considerations, bartered for local Amerindians, endangering fragile alliances, commerce, and peace.[31]

Colonial officials did what they could to appease their native allies. As in Suriname, Berbice authorities forbade sexual intimacies

Jacob Eduard van Heemskerck van Beest, after Gerard Voorduin, 1860–62, *Arawak Camp*. (Rijksmuseum, Amsterdam.)

and relationships between male colonists and free native women, as this angered the women's "husbands and friends" and caused "great calamities." Such rules were little heeded. Just as futile, they forbade *hoererije*, or fornication, with African women, a crime compounded when European men induced their partners to abort or murder the "fruit" of their "sinful actions." [32]

To manage relations and trade with their Amerindian allies living beyond colonial settlements, the Dutch set up posts on the edges of their territories. The locations of the stations shifted as native politics dictated. At each post, a resident Dutch official, or "postholder," and several assistants managed trade and diplomacy: they urged Amerindians to keep up the supply and production of trade goods; they negotiated their help in returning fugitives; and they defused local disputes that might hamper trade or imperil the colony. Just as English colonies competed with one another for Amerindian alliances in North America, so did Dutch settlements on the Wild Coast. Thus, the postholders were also charged with preventing Amerindians from trading with neighboring colonies or rival Europeans, especially the Spanish on the Orinoco. Some posts were more heavily engaged in slave trading, and others focused more on trade in dyes, balsam, hammocks, or dugout canoes.[33]

By midcentury, the governor of Berbice explained to his superiors that it was of the highest importance to keep natives living near the colony, "as they create a barrier against runaway blacks better than all forts or defensive posts." Arawaks and Waraos living adjacent to the plantations should be treated with the utmost care, for "as long as they live around here," he stressed, "slaves can't conspire to rise up as they will always fall into the hands of the Indians, who if they can't catch them alive, will shoot them dead." Carib and Akawaio peoples living deeper in the continent provided a second line of defense, as "they will never permit slaves to settle in the hinterlands." [34] With native help, a new order was created, one that allowed a tiny European minority to make African chattel slavery a workable enterprise. By 1763, enslaved Africans seeking to escape the torments of slavery faced a gauntlet of Indian slave-catching communities. By providing a loose cordon around the colony, Amerindians helped turn Berbice into one vast prison.

Atlantic Slavery

The new order meant that by the early eighteenth century, Berbice's economy focused less on Indians and the annatto trade and more on export crops grown by enslaved Africans. The colony had transformed from an Indian trading post into a burgeoning slave society, embedded in a larger Caribbean and Atlantic plantation economy. Dutch capital and trade continued to lubricate the Atlantic system, even as the brief moment of Dutch maritime power had passed. France and especially England increasingly dominated the Atlantic world, their navies and armies dwarfing those of the Dutch Republic.

In the 1710s, French state-sanctioned pirates were marauding around the Caribbean, taking over colonies and demanding payoffs. In 1712, they attacked Berbice. Across the Atlantic, the Van Pere family, safe in Zeeland, did not want to pay the ransom because it exceeded the colony's worth. Berbice was sold to a group of Amsterdam investors who raised money by offering stocks in the joint venture, the Society of Berbice. They sold only half the stock, and only half of that was paid for, so funds for the colony were tight. It was an inauspicious beginning for "the Company," as the Society of Berbice became known.[35]

In the early 1730s, the directors opened the colony to new settlers. Many of them were not Dutch but rather German, Swiss, and French. The directors expanded the production of sugar and promoted a new crop, coffee. The Dutch first successfully grew coffee in Java in the 1710s, and seeds for the crop were shared throughout the Dutch Empire, reaching Berbice via Suriname in the early 1720s. In a few decades, coffee would surpass sugar as the main export crop in both colonies.[36] The directors broke ground for additional Company plantations. One of them, called Hooglande, became the home base for the third, and last, Berbice sojourner through whom we can better understand the colony's history and development.

By 1727, surgeon Rutger Tenhoute was desperate to leave the colony.

He had arrived in Berbice three years earlier with an optimistic contract for six years. But his residency as a slave doctor on Company
plantation Hooglande had become a nightmare. Plantation manager
and councilman Anthony van Heesel frustrated the doctor's efforts to
heal slaves and denied him basic comforts. The surgeon's letters to the
authorities chronicle his own distress, but even more, they document
the horrors enslaved people were forced to endure in this colony, horrors that were also more broadly illustrative of slavery in the Caribbean. Though the doctor's claims sound at times unhinged, archival
records confirm his account.

According to the doctor, manager Van Heesel was sadistic toward
his slaves. He was known to bite them on the shoulders when they de-
fied him. His punishments were life-threatening. He brutally whipped
a man for accidentally maiming himself with an ax, and he beat a
woman so badly her legs were permanently injured. A young slave
with a lingering back injury was mercilessly flogged for a minor mistake. When the youth died from the beating, the planter reportedly
joked that this was one way to dispose of ailing slaves. He forbade
bondpeople from visiting the doctor when they were ill, ministering to
them himself with homemade potions. A combination of Van Heesel's
treatments and starvation, the doctor charged, pushed large numbers
into their graves. Van Heesel himself was forced to admit that the
plantation's slaves, despite cultivating additional gardens, could only
"fill their stomachs half full." He lamented that he had suffered "the
great misfortune of losing fifteen slaves within the space of a year."
Estate inventories for 1727 show that proportionately more people died
on Hooglande than on any other Company plantation, even as hunger
was common among enslaved people throughout Berbice.[37]

Like a despotic king, Van Heesel alternated callous brutality with
perverse attention, inflicting scars of a different kind. After thrashing
a teenage boy, the manager tenderly cared for the youth and person-
ally wiped the boy clean when he soiled himself. He took some slaves
to live with him in the main house, where he fed them at his table and
"even," the doctor emphasized to the governor, took some "in the room
where he slept." Evidently, he frequently had sex with the plantation's

enslaved women. Both the doctor's letters and a subsequent inquiry suggest that when the women became pregnant, Van Heesel forced them to drink an abortifacient he had cooked up, causing miscarriages and at least one expectant mother's death. A woman named Abba gave birth to a "Christian child," the phrase used in plantation inventories to indicate a European progenitor. Questioned by officials, Abba named Van Heesel as the father, while he blamed someone else.[38]

Early in 1728, the governor and council reprimanded Van Heesel, less for his atrocious treatment of Hooglande's slaves, at which the officials barely blinked an eye, than for wasting their labor on nonessential tasks. He was sent back to the Netherlands to answer for his poor plantation management.[39] Fed up with Berbice, surgeon Rutger Tenhoute decamped to try his luck in Suriname. A few years later, Hooglande was discontinued and its enslaved population dispersed.[40]

Van Heesel may have been extreme in his cruelty and capriciousness, but chattel slavery exposed enslaved people throughout the Americas to physical abuse and arbitrary management. The records of Berbice are filled with whippings and tortures, including of children. Colonists felt justified keeping Africans enslaved, and they had no moral quandaries about preserving the profitable regime with brutal force. Their fear of slave uprisings, especially given their own small numbers, provided further justification for violence. They relied on terror to keep enslaved people under control. Armed with state support and a firm belief in white supremacy, enslavers wielded tyrannical powers with little check, exacting a deep physical and psychological toll.[41]

When surgeon Tenhoute composed his letters of complaints, 1,100 slaves lived and worked on twelve Company plantations as well as at the fort, the store, the brickwork, the smithy and in the households of Company officials. Almost one in five slaves was Amerindian, a percentage that decreased drastically over the course of the eighteenth century. On the eve of the 1763 uprising thirty-five years later, the Company owned 1,400 enslaved men, women, and children, of whom only 24 were Indians. More than 200 of the Company's slaves were employed at the fort as artisans, cooks, housekeepers, and personal servants.[42] The others grew sugar on a total of eleven Company plantations.

Many more enslaved people were incarcerated on privately owned plantations. In 1732, the Company's charter opened the colony to any Dutch inhabitant. By 1740, a Company map indicated ninety-one "free plantations" on the Berbice and another twenty on the Canje River, though likely not all were actually in production.[43] Private owners could not afford the capital investment associated with sugar production and instead concentrated on cacao, cotton, and, increasingly, coffee. While some owners lived in Berbice on their own estates, others were absentee investors who relied on hired managers. By the time of the 1763 uprising, in addition to 1,400 Company slaves, at least another 3,000 enslaved people lived on 135 so-called private (i.e., non–Company owned) plantations with 96 different owners or combinations of owners.[44] Most private plantations housed fewer than 50 people.[45] Company plantations were larger, but even the largest never exceeded 150 people, making Berbice plantations considerably smaller than those of most Caribbean slave societies. Neither the Dutch West India Company, the monopolistic supplier of Atlantic slaves to the Wild Coast until 1738, nor private traders could deliver the numbers of slaves desired. In the late 1750s, Governor Hendrik Jan van Rijswijk suggested that the colony could easily handle 500 to 600 new slaves a year, double the number it actually received.[46]

Perpetually short on money and more inclined to pay themselves and their shareholders than invest in infrastructure, defense, or officials' salaries, the Company's directors ran the colony on a miserly budget. Incompetent governors and the directors' own blundering administration from afar did little to foster community among planters who hailed from many European nations, felt little loyalty to the Company or the colony, and narrowly focused on short-term profits. One of the few historians to study the Company's records in any detail judged that "no colony was less ably governed than Berbice," at least until the appointment of Governor Wolphert Simon van Hoogenheim in 1760.[47]

By the time Van Hoogenheim arrived, Berbice exemplified empire

Leupe 1586, detail of a survey, ca. 1740. The buildings (including the slave quarters on the left) on Company plantation Johanna. (Nationaal Archief, The Hague.)

on the cheap. It was less a settler colony than a corporate enterprise. A largely transient population of roughly 350 Europeans lived among 4,200 to 5,000 enslaved people on plantations. They were surrounded by thousands of native peoples with varying degrees of allegiance to the Dutch. While the colony had expanded, it remained weak and un-developed in comparison to other Atlantic imperial efforts of the time. Many planters and investors were disappointed in their expectations of profits. Poorly capitalized, reliant on Atlantic trade for supplies and provisions, perpetually short on enslaved workers, plagued by infec-tious diseases, pests, and weather-related crises, and dependent for se-curity on Amerindians, Berbice was a tenuous colonial venture.

Berbice's shaky standing affected the lives of the people incarcerated in the colony. Malnourishment was common, contributing to disease and early death. The small size of plantations meant close contact with Europeans, increasing enslaved people's vulnerability to abuse and lessening their autonomy. A weak colonial government did little to keep brutal planters and overseers in check. The majority of enslaved were African-born; they lacked familial connections and colonial

View of plantation Cornelis Vriendschap in Suriname, 1700–1800. Detail, idealized view of eighteenth-century coffee and cacao labor camp in Suriname. The fields stretched behind the plantation. The rectangular building on the left housed the slaves. Plantations in Berbice would have been equally modest and likely far less orderly. (Rijksmuseum, Amsterdam.)

language skills and they were still processing the trauma of the Middle Passage. On the Wild Coast, as on most Caribbean islands, high death rates and low fertility necessitated constant new slave imports. In Suriname, at midcentury, just a quarter of the enslaved population was Creole—that is, born in the colony. No figures are available for Berbice, but the demographics were likely similar.[48] In eighteenth-century North American settlement colonies, on the other hand, an increase in the enslaved population was fueled in part with new captives but also by natural growth, as sex ratios evened out and Creole women gave birth to more children than first-generation enslaved.

Berbice's frontier conditions also provided enslaved people some reprieve. Outnumbered and unorganized, the Dutch were little inclined to force religious instruction on their slaves. Africans maintained their own religious beliefs and practices, music and dance, and languages. Overall the Dutch share of the 12.5 million captives forcibly shipped to the New World was just over half a million. How many were brought to Berbice up until the start of the uprising is difficult to know because of incomplete records, but the totals far exceeded the number of enslaved people in the colony at that time.[49] In the seventeenth century, the majority of enslaved people were shipped from the Slave Coast (present-day Togo and Benin) and the Loango Coast (from southern Cameroon to the Congo River). The Dutch Creole ("Berbice Dutch") spoken by African-descended people in Berbice until the last speaker died at the end of the twentieth century was deeply influenced by the Ijo of the Bight of Benin, as well as by Arawak and Dutch. In the eighteenth century, the majority of captives came from the Loango Coast, the Gold Coast (present-day Ghana), and, after 1740, increasingly from the Windward Coast (present-day Liberia and Ivory Coast).[50]

Enslaved people in Berbice toiled in the sun ten hours a day, six days a week, with just a few days off at Christmas. During the harvest or while executing time-sensitive tasks, the workday stretched well into the night, and could even, in the case of sugar milling with a tidal mill, include all night. Most people carried out the hot, physically demanding, and often dangerous work of growing export crops. Men, and some women, felled trees, dug trenches to separate fields and discharge rainwater, and built pathways. Both men and women cleared bush and scrubs, prepared fields for planting, and tended to the crops. After the labor-intensive harvest, crops required further processing before they were ready for shipment to Holland. A few people worked as coopers, carpenters, cooks, or servants in the main house. Others grew provisions, principally bananas and cassava, to feed the plantation. Children, teenagers, and old people, too, worked, albeit at lighter tasks.[51] Labor conditions were rough. At any given time, a sixth of adults could not work due to illness, injury, or permanent disabilities.[52]

Wild Coast planters saved themselves the cost of adequately feeding their enslaved workers by providing them with small gardens, a common arrangement in the Caribbean. So in addition to laboring long hours without pay to enrich their enslavers, people worked a second shift to feed themselves. In the evenings and on Sundays, they gardened small patches with bananas and plantains, root crops such as cassava, taro, and sweet potatoes, and okra, pumpkins, peanuts, and sacred and medicinal plants. These small tracts represented for the enslaved more than merely yet more hard labor. Located far from the main house or even deep in the savanna, the plots provided a measure of freedom from scrutiny, yielded a more varied diet, and nourished spiritual lives. Seeds from West Africa, smuggled across the Atlantic on captives' bodies or from slave ship provisions purchased in West Africa, found their way into local plots. Rice, okra, and sesame allowed people to feed themselves in some small measure as they had at home.[53] Gardens enabled enslaved people, many of whom had been farmers in Africa, to sell or barter bananas and peanuts, as well as chickens, ducks, game, fish, and firewood, along with what they pilfered from plantations, to one another and nearby colonists, Amerindians, and soldiers.[54]

And so, despite acute exploitation, brutal violence, and high death rates, enslaved people built lives. Survivors of the Middle Passage coped as best they could with the pain and bewilderment of being ripped from their homelands. They creatively adapted old-world certainties and practices to new-world experiences, forging flexible diasporic cultures. They learned the local Creole, Berbice Dutch. Africans and Creoles built families and communities on their own plantations and across them. Like exploited people everywhere, they accommodated, manipulated, and resisted their *bombas*, overseers, and enslavers. While some small uprisings confined to one or two plantations occurred, most people did not see collective armed resistance as a viable option.

As illness cut short lives, hunger increased, and planter abuse worsened in the late 1750s and early 1760s, some began to reconsider.

3

Overthrow

Governor Wolphert Simon van Hoogenheim felt uncharacteristically optimistic as he picked up his pen early in 1763 to report to the Company. The earnest career soldier had served less than three years as governor of the colony. Fateful years they had been. He had arrived in the middle of a fever epidemic, which claimed his predecessor. Fever and the "bloody flux" (dysentery) felled planters and colonial officials. Others were barely healthy enough to function. Like most newcomers in tropical Berbice, he and his pregnant young wife suffered from fevers, likely malaria. His wife died soon after arrival, after giving birth to the couple's first child, a stillborn baby girl. He buried them both on Christmas Day 1760. He was still frequently sick with headaches and fevers. More than personal misfortune plagued him. The colony was in disarray.[1]

Governing proved hard. The young governor was buried in work. The colony's planters resisted his rule and the Company's financial demands. A faction of prominent planters and officials led by members of the Barkey clan challenged the governor's authority at every turn. He also faced dangerous provocations from below. Overworked and underfed slaves were increasingly unruly. The uprising in the summer of 1762 had starkly exposed Dutch weakness. The governor's repeated requests to Amsterdam for more soldiers had so far gone unanswered. A major global conflict between England and France, known as the Seven Years' War, had impeded shipping in the Caribbean, reducing food imports and causing yet more hunger.[2]

But now, as Van Hoogenheim penned his letter by candlelight, he felt hopeful. After years of epidemics, crop infections, and drought, he informed his employers, the colony showed improvement. The inhabitants were getting healthier, the crops looked promising, and the cotton-devouring caterpillars had finally been beaten off. On the plantations, peace had returned after the revolt the previous year. Planters still jumped at any rumor of conspiracy—the result of overheated imaginations, in Van Hoogenheim's judgment.

Three weeks earlier, the governor had experienced a stroke of good fortune. A slave ship missed the mouth of the Suriname River and landed in Berbice instead. Never had handsomer and healthier slaves been seen than the 350 people on board, the governor enthused. He had purchased for the Company fifty new slaves, "of whom only eleven are wenches." These additional workers would finally finish the new tide-powered sugar mill on the most promising Company plantation, Dageraad. Once these tasks were completed, he predicted confidently, he would be able to ship home six hundred barrels of sugar a year from Dageraad alone.[3]

He was about to close his upbeat letter when he received "calamitous" news. Enslaved people were once again on the rise.

The news was bad indeed. Slaves had deserted two large plantations on the Canje River, a tributary of the Berbice. On Magdalenenburg plantation, they murdered the plantation manager and his assistant and took off. Twenty Creole slaves refused to join the rebels and fled instead to a nearby plantation. On neighboring La Providence estate, plans to kill the director were foiled when his Creole slaves warned him to flee. But the insurgents cut the throat of the *bomba* and the two slaves left in charge. After plundering both estates, eighty men, women, and children left for the Corentyne River on the border with Suriname. Van Hoogenheim had only ten healthy soldiers; he needed them to defend Fort Nassau.[4]

Improvising, the governor armed twelve sailors and sent them up the Canje River. Before the sailors could catch up, the rebels made for a Suriname trading post on the Corentyne River. The station, stocked with trading goods for Indians, was an attractive and poorly guarded target. The residential trader, or postholder, had gone downriver with his wife and child to pick up new shirts the Moravians, a radical Protestant missionary sect, had sewed for him. Warned by an Amerindian of the rebels' approach, several European and native assistants stood guard all night. When they spied thirty well-armed male rebels drawing near in the morning, they lost heart and took off for the woods. The rebels shot the post's baying hounds. They loaded the postholder's large tent boat with clothes, tools, guns, lead for bullets, chickens, turkeys, wine, and several hundred machetes. They also took a thousand Dutch guilders in coin, making for such a heavy load that it took them several trips to ferry the goods to their camp on a nearby island in the Corentyne River.[5] Imagine the pleasure they took from their plunder, as they feasted on a meal of roast chicken and wine, instead of the usual plantains and cassava on the plantation.

At his desk at Fort Nassau, Van Hoogenheim concluded his letter to his superiors on a decidedly less optimistic note. "Who knows what else might be hanging over our heads?" Plenty, as it turned out.

Revolt

Less than a week later, on Sunday, February 27, enslaved people on several estates on the Berbice River revolted. There are no records that connect the insurgencies on the Canje and Berbice Rivers, though they may well have been linked. At the least we can say that both rivers shared the same pervasive culture of resentment and resistance. The breakout at Goed Land en Goed Fortuin eight months earlier may have inspired people on both rivers to think of armed resistance as a viable option.

The latest revolt was located on four plantations in the heart of the colony, some twenty-five miles upriver from Fort Nassau and its hamlet New Amsterdam, where the governor lived. The conspirators timed their insurrection to coincide with the start of the dry season, when savannas and forests became passable again. They chose a Sunday morning because planters would be at church and those fellow slaves who might not support rebellion would be away working their gardens or gone fishing on their day off.

That Sunday morning, *bomba* Cupido of Hollandia, the plantation where the conspirators had been meeting, betrayed the rebels' plans. With tears in his eyes, he appeared before the manager of Rosenburg, a neighboring estate. He reported that slaves on multiple plantations, Hollandia, Zeelandia, Lelienburg, Elisabeth & Alexandria, and Altenklingen, were preparing to revolt. This was the only tip-off the Dutch received. Otherwise, the plan was a well-kept secret. When one of Hollandia's slaves realized Cupido had betrayed them, he rushed to Lelienburg, telling the rebellion's leaders that "it was now high time." At once, the rebel commanders, their faces smeared with clay for spiritual protection and to signify their leadership, gave the signal. On Lelienburg, they overpowered the plantation's *bomba* and secured all guns and ammunition. They pronounced themselves masters of the plantation. On Hollandia, the rebels broke into a warehouse that stored muskets and powder for the militia. Well armed, the insurgents set off to spread their rebellion. The sounding of the drums, heard far and wide, communicated the start of the uprising.[6]

To secure their freedom and to exact revenge on particular masters, the rebels selectively murdered several Europeans that first day. On plantation Juliana, the wife of manager Dell was decapitated, and the rebels, emulating their enslavers, stuck her head on a sharpened pole by the riverbank. Enslaved workers on plantations Essendam and Helvetia killed their managers when they returned from church. On plantation Saintslust, the rebels wounded an Amerindian slave and their manager. The latter managed to escape, making his way to Company plantation Peereboom, where many Europeans cut off from Fort Nassau by the rebellion were gathering. Young Anthony Barkey, the owner of plantation Lelienburg, where the revolt began, survived only because the gun trained on him misfired three times. The rebels narrowly missed their chance to avenge themselves on some of the most hated planters, holed up on a nearby plantation. By the time the rebels caught on to their presence, the men had slipped away.[7]

Governor Van Hoogenheim was awakened before dawn at four thirty on Monday morning by a militia captain bearing the alarming news of the uprising. The governor realized that if "the fury of the rebels was not stopped right away," the conflagration would spread up and down the river. But he had few resources at his disposal. The colony's geography, with estates spread some one hundred miles along the Berbice River, made defense difficult. Just as a year before, he had only a handful of soldiers and officers at the fort. A few remaining soldiers were stationed high up the river. Cut off from the fort by the rebellion, they fled to safety in the neighboring colony of Demerara. Fort Nassau was in poor shape. The governor doubted that its walls could hold up under the recoil of its own artillery. Still, to shore up defenses, he ordered the removal of bushes, and soldiers leveled several small buildings close to the fort to increase visibility for armed marksmen on the ramparts.[8]

The governor's only hope lay in the four ships anchored near Fort Nassau in New Amsterdam. The largest of these was the slave ship *Adriana Petronella*, commanded by Captain Christoffel Kok. Three smaller merchant ships were being loaded with sugar, cacao, coffee, cotton, and other crops for transportation to Holland. The governor had previously ordered the slave captain to ready his ship to go up the Canje River to prevent the rebellion from spreading. Now he commanded Captain Kok to sail his heavily armed ship with thirty-four sailors up the Berbice River to liberate the Dutch trapped on plantations beyond the insurgency "from the hands of these mad Barbarians." He ordered the reluctant captains of the other ships to anchor in front of the fort for its defense. The ships were only lightly armed and many of the sailors were already sick, so the display offered symbolic rather than real protection. Meanwhile, fleeing Amerindians brought news of the uprising's rapid spread.[9]

As the flames of rebellion jumped from one plantation to another, colonists panicked. Instead of rallying to the colony's defense, they acted to save themselves. Rather than protecting their plantations, they hastily prepared to abandon them. They buried their valuables, packed their trunks, and loaded their tent boats. Many deserted their enslaved workers, after arming a few of their male slaves to defend the plantation.[10] Even reservists declined to serve. Goed Land en Goed Fortuin owner and militia captain Kunkler gloomily forecast that "the colony and we ourselves are done for." After hiding his silver and gold and giving his furniture to nearby Amerindians for safekeeping, he abandoned his plantation. In doing so, he deserted the new workers he had just bought from Captain Kok, and the slaves who had refused to join Adam in the July 1762 uprising.[11] Lodewijk Abbensets, a leading member of the governor's council, was one of the few willing to make a stand. He offered to turn his plantation, Solitude, close to the heart of the uprising, into a defensive post. He urgently requested more planters to join him. Few responded.

Not only colonists but even Company officials had little appetite for resistance. Instead of helping the governor, they, too, focused on securing their possessions. Members of the Barkey extended family, hated by the rebels and the governor alike, commandeered the merchant ships riding the current in front of the fort. Over the governor's strenuous objections, one Barkey family member, prosecutor Harkenroth, along with his father-in-law, treasurer and slave auctioneer Abraham Wijs, loaded up their furniture and slaves. Van Hoogenheim entreated them to gather up the Company records for safekeeping on the vessels. They declined. Instead, they moved their families on board and refused to set foot onshore again.

Making matters worse, the captain of the armed slaver failed to sail upriver to liberate the planters cut off from the fort by the spreading rebellion. Barely out of the fort's sight, he anchored in front of plantation Sublieslust, at the request of the council member who owned it. Neither threats nor the promise of generous bounties for every rebel caught dead or alive could induce either the slaver's crew or the militia to aid the colonists upriver.[12]

Peereboom

As the conflagration spread, the settlers trapped upstream huddled on Company plantation Peereboom to defend themselves. The plantation had a large, sturdy house atop a bluff and a commanding view of the river and the adjacent Wiruni Creek. The frightened refugees were a cross section of Berbice's colonial population.[13] Former councilman Ambrosius Zubli arrived in his tent boat with his manager, his plantation surgeon, and a large number of male and female slaves. He brought along his neighbor Jean Zaint with his female cousin, whose plantation had been attacked the previous day. The cousin had saved herself by ducking under the table, while Zaint, shot in the arm, had hidden in the cacao fields.[14] Slaves rowed councilman Johan George, his wife, and their six children down the Berbice from the family's plantation, Beerensteijn. Jan Abraham Charbon, a young man, arrived with his neighbor Christian Mittelholtzer after a sleepless night standing guard at Mittelholtzer's plantation Oosterleek. The next morning they decided there was greater safety in numbers and they rushed to Peereboom.[15] Besides their guns and slaves, they brought two European women. The minister of the Dutch Reformed Church, Jonas van Petersom Ramring, rowed from the church across the creek to Peereboom. He was accompanied by his wife, Elisabeth, and her sister Aletta. The women had taken off their jewelry and buried it before leaving.[16] Three members of a family of mixed ancestry, Philip, Jeremiah, and Hendrik Broer, who owned small plantations upriver from Peereboom, arrived with their wives. Johan Ernst Hoerle had been in charge of Savonette during the 1762 uprising. After he returned from his truancy in Demerara he was reassigned to manage Company plantation Cornelia Jacoba, located downstream of the rebellion. Hoerle got stranded on Peereboom with one of his slaves and a European servant on his way back from business upriver.[17]

All told, close to seventy men, women, and children, or about a fifth of the free colonial population of Berbice, plus an unknown number of their slaves, cowered in the house on the hill.[18]

The Europeans fortified the house on Peereboom as best they could. Slaves were ordered to build a wall around the building and top it with broken glass. To clear the view and deny the rebels cover to sneak up to the house, slaves also razed slave huts and cut down trees. Reconnaissance parties were dispatched to find out how close the insurgents were, and everyone was assigned a place: women and children out of harm's way in the attic, men on the first floor. Some house slaves stayed with their masters; others sought shelter in what remained of the *negerij*, or slave quarters. Councilman George sent an Amerindian messenger with a letter to Governor van Hoogenheim at Fort Nassau, begging assistance in their desperate situation. The man returned the next day with only moral support in the form of a note urging them to "keep up their courage" and expressing hope that "God would provide a favorable outcome." The governor promised that the slave ship was on its way.[19] As the triumphant shouting and drumming of the rebels grew louder and the smoke of torched plantations increasingly darkened the sky, the frightened colonists kept their eyes fixed downriver for the first signs either of welcome rescue . . . or of feared rebellion.

They got the latter. The rebels attacked Thursday morning around nine o'clock, several hundred strong. At first, the Europeans killed several insurgents, and the rebels retreated. But the assailants soon returned. The rest of the day, they wielded their guns from the edge of the forest while the Europeans returned fire from the windows. Hoping to burn out their adversaries, the rebels shot nails covered with cotton at the roof. Gunpowder ignited the cotton as it left the barrel, and the nails pinned the burning cloth to the roof, setting it on fire. The women, sequestered in the attic for their own safety, now frantically doused the flames with valuable drinking water. No one dared dash to the river to refill the water containers. The Europeans were spooked by the rebels taunting them that "they were men, and had another fourteen barrels of powder," and would never give up.[20] Without help, the colonists on Peereboom could not hold out for long.

Short of food and water, the beleaguered colonists were at the breaking point. When the leader of the rebel force surrounding them, Gousarie van Oosterleek, proposed negotiations, they agreed. In the course of the discussions, Gousarie explained that the insurgents mutinied because the Christians were *lomp*, a Dutch term denoting people who are rude and uncivilized. He and his men, he reportedly proclaimed, wanted "no more Christians in their country." The rebels intended "to be the *Heeren* [masters, lords] of Berbice, all the planta-tions would be theirs." The negotiations lasted into the next day.

By Friday morning, the rebels agreed to allow the Europeans to board their tent boats with their weapons and retreat to the fort. Evidently their former enslavers had agreed to pay for their free passage and for Africans to row their boats. But as the frightened Europeans slunk out of the house and filed down the hill to the river's edge, the fragile truce, perhaps a ruse from the start, suddenly fell apart. At the moment that the colonists clambered into their boats, the rebels opened fire. Perhaps they had changed their minds or been unduly provoked. Some people were shot in their boats. Others jumped overboard, only to be fired upon in the water. Many drowned in the river and some killed themselves rather than fall into rebel hands. Of the captured, a good number were taken to rebel headquarters on plantation Hollandia & Zeelandia.[21]

Other captives were selected for immediate punishment. The rebels singled out particular men and their families, including their negotiating partners Johan George and Ambrosius Zubli. George was a member of the governor's council and the criminal court. Six months prior, he had served as interrogator and judge for Coffij after the 1762 Goed Land en Goed Fortuin rebellion. Coffij had been broken on the wheel. Now, George faced retribution. As he and his family were shot at in their boat, his sons jumped overboard and one drowned. Of his three daughters, one drowned and two were captured. George himself was wounded. Over the course of the next day, he and his wife were tortured. Finally, he was killed and his head displayed on a pole. Zubli was shot on his boat and then decapitated. His shooter may have been Gousarie, his opposite in tense negotiations the day before. Zubli's manager killed himself.[22]

The rebels also set their sights on plantation managers and overseers, whose careers depended on whipping as much work out of the enslaved as they could. They may also have earned the wrath of the rebels because of their predatory behavior toward enslaved women. Plantation managers in general were notorious for raping women under their command. Willem Hendrikse, a former sergeant newly appointed as manager on Company plantation Vlissingen, and Johan Muller, who cracked the whip at Peereboom, were both subjected to their own disciplinary measures. Hendrikse was lashed and locked in a *tronk*, a heavy block with iron leg bands used to punish slaves. His wife and children were murdered before his eyes. Muller was whipped to death, then quartered and beheaded.[23] Several other managers were also killed. The managers of two Company plantations, J.H. Schröder and Johan Ernst Hoerle, a notoriously abusive taskmaster, were lucky enough to escape.[24]

The rebels also seem to have targeted the colony's physicians. One got away, but two did not. Mathijs Villiot was whipped to death. Jan Jacob Basch, the Company's former surgeon major, was reportedly skinned alive.[25] The Company's slaves, who were forced to see him when they fell ill, dreaded his ministrations. A year earlier, a Company official had denounced Basch for "unhappy treatments" that caused "great suffering for many, and lowered others into the grave." Even colonists, who had a choice of physicians, avoided him like the pox.[26] Poorly trained and eager to experiment on their charges, surgeons were more likely to kill than to cure.[27] Governor van Hoogenheim agreed in a letter to his superiors that most healers shipped to Berbice were entirely incompetent and given to drink. He would not, he stressed, trust his dog to their care, "let alone a human being." If the directors could not find better people, he would rather do without doctors altogether.[28]

In all, twenty of the seventy European refugees at Peereboom died. There is only one report of the rebels killing a fellow slave. A group of rebels cut down and beheaded Keijta van de Peereboom, perhaps because he, like other Peereboom slaves, had fought alongside the Dutch.[29] A number of enslaved people had huddled in the house with the Europeans, while others had been ordered to hide in the fields. When they were later questioned they claimed they had escaped into the jungle as the Europeans marched to the water.[30]

Planter Jan Broer, of European-Amerindian ancestry, arrived at Fort Nassau on horseback that afternoon to give word to Governor van Hoogenheim of the Peereboom carnage. Jan Broer's brother Philip was among the dead. The news that all Christians had been either "murdered or captured" caused "great dejection" among the colonists holed up at the fort. "From that moment on," the governor noted in his journal, "one could clearly discern that all completely lost heart."[31]

Panic

The Peereboom massacre spelled the end of any pretense of Dutch defense and dispelled any notion of a viable counterattack. As news of the massacre spread, fewer and fewer planters showed any appetite for resistance. They abandoned their plantations not just on the Berbice, but on the Canje River as well. Once again, it was the militia captain who was among the first to abandon his Canje plantation for the coast.

The day after the Peereboom massacre, Saturday, March 5, Dutch Reformed minister Jonas van Petersom Ramring, his wife, Elisabeth, and her eleven-year-old sister, Aletta, arrived at Fort Nassau, their clothes in tatters. They had fled Peereboom by boat but had been captured and taken to rebel headquarters on plantation Hollandia & Zeelandia. The rebel leaders refused to punish Pastor Ramring since he was "a man who spoke to God and prayed for [us]." Instead, they gave Ramring and his female companions something to wear and a secret code to get by the rebel patrols. Exhausted and worse for wear (Aletta had been shot in the buttocks), they brought a verbal message for the Dutch governor. The reason for the revolt, Ramring related, was "the bad and cruel treatment" the enslaved had suffered at the hands of the plantation owners where the rebellion had started. Chief among the men named was Anthony Barkey Jr., the minister's twenty-two-year-old brother-in-law and the owner of Lelienburg. Barkey's management style must have been brutal and stingy. "It is noteworthy," Governor van Hoogenheim wrote to the directors, "that the plantation Lelienburg, belonging to Barkey, has brought forth four rebel leaders," the most prominent of whom were Accara and a new Coffij.[32]

As more Peereboom survivors reached the fort over the weekend and recounted their personal tales of horror, panic escalated. After securing the upper Berbice River, the rebels set their sights downriver.

They were expanding their reach, taking over more and more plantations on their way to the fort. Their example spread in unexpected directions. By Monday, government officials were in open rebellion, announcing they would not take up arms under any circumstances. Secretary and prosecutor Harkenroth publicly declared that he felt no obligation to get shot for his meager wages. The male colonists petitioned the governor, requesting to board the merchant ships riding at anchor. These ships already sheltered several officials. There was no hope of defending the fort, the colonists made clear, given its poor state of repair and the availability of only a few healthy soldiers. They predicted a "general massacre" should the rebels attack. The fires that lit up the sky at night suggested the enemy were advancing rapidly. Despite the fact that his own military officers supported the petition to flee, the governor refused to grant their pleas.[33]

Governor van Hoogenheim was rapidly running out of options. The next morning, the wife of overseer J. H. Schröder arrived at the fort with her child. While her husband had escaped from Peereboom, she and her child had been taken to the rebels' stronghold. The traumatized woman estimated their fighting force at six hundred men with perhaps a thousand "dependents," a rather large estimate. She said the rebels had established a government and exercised strict discipline. She had seen the corpses of seven "Christians." She echoed Pastor Ramring when she explained that the rebels felt "very bitter" about their treatment at the hands of certain planters. The rebels had considered killing her, but leader Coffij chose to release her. He dictated a message for her to deliver to the governor. "The reason for this war," the terse statement explained, "is that many *Heeren* [masters or lords] did not give the slaves what was their due." Coffij named several men in particular, including his enslaver, the young Anthony Barkey. He warned that if the Dutch did not depart Berbice, leaving behind their slaves, "a large number of rebels" would attack the fort.[34]

Coffij's threat elevated the level of panic to hysteria. Later Tuesday afternoon, March 8, the three remaining council members changed their votes in favor of abandoning Fort Nassau, and with it any pretense of governing the colony. Van Hoogenheim was left with no choice. At four p.m., all the colonists went aboard the ships. An hour later, the militia joined them, followed by the governor and his council. A few soldiers remained behind to nail the cannons to the fort walls to make it harder for the rebels to take them, and to set fire to the fort, symbol of Dutch power. An enslaved man named Simon was sent on horseback to go up the Canje River to spread the news of the Dutch retreat. But by this time, most of the colonists there had already fled for the coast. By nine thirty p.m. the fort had burned to the ground. Dutch colonial rule in Berbice had come to an end.[35]

Flight

With the rebels hot on their trail, the ships, crowded with Europeans and an unknown number of slaves, slowly over the course of a week made their way down sixty miles of river to the ocean. Several large canoes laden with enslaved people and goods followed the ships. During high tide, when the current pushed upriver, the flotilla anchored, and when the tide receded they floated downstream once again. Along the way, the Europeans assessed the situation on estates as they passed, occasionally venturing on land. At many plantations, people were busy helping themselves to whatever their enslavers had left behind. When the manager of plantation De Velde left the ship to check on his workers, he found them plundering the house. They chased him back to his rowboat with machetes. Cannon fire from one of the ships kept them from killing him. As the ships drifted by Vigilantie plantation, the rebels shot at them. The ships returned fire. A rebel leader named Prins shouted tauntingly from the riverbank "in good low Dutch" that the rebels "were men" and would meet them at Company plantation Dageraad the next day. Slave auctioneer Abraham Wijs had ordered his twenty-two slaves to follow the Dutch ships in one of the tent boats, but now they used the confusion to turn around, throwing in their luck with the rebels on Vigilantie.[36]

While some plantations were clearly in rebellion, on others the enslaved continued to live in peace. Van Hoogenheim went ashore to inspect Hooftplantage, owned by the Company. He found everyone quietly at work. To keep them from the rebels, he asked the *bomba* to gather the slaves and follow the ships in the plantation's canoes. When they did so, the governor noted in his daily log that he was both "very surprised" and "deeply moved" by their "loyalty." Further downriver, plantation Mara's enslaved workers were continuing their labor, as were slaves on several other estates.[37]

On Friday, March 11, the ships arrived at the last big estate on the Berbice River, Company plantation Dageraad (Daybreak). Most of its enslaved people were still going about their work. The governor and councilmen proposed that the fleeing Dutch take a stand there. Dageraad was well situated. Its extensive kitchen gardens, and those of nearby estates, ensured an ample food supply. And while the rebels had now taken over all of Berbice south of Dageraad, the few plantations situated north of it appeared still unaffected. Van Hoogenheim wanted the Dutch to set up temporary headquarters and wait for provisions and reinforcements from other colonies or the Dutch Republic.

But the governor did not prevail. Amerindians brought news that the rebels were expanding their reach downriver beyond Dageraad, threatening to cut off escape to the coast. Moreover, the ship captains, whose vessels were essential for defense (and, even more important, escape), flatly refused to stay on the river any longer. Their loyalty lay with their merchant employers. To make their case, they cited their orders, sickness among their men, and lack of ammunition. The colonists made known that they would refuse to fight if Dageraad was attacked. They insisted that they had already lost their plantations and most of their possessions; they wished to leave Berbice with at least their lives. Several government officials boldly declared they would no longer recognize the governor or council's authority. The mutiny of Berbice's enslaved workers had spread to its colonists and officials as well. Outnumbered, the governor and councilmen bowed to their wishes. That night they boarded the ships and made for Fort St. Andries near the coast, just below the confluence with the Canje River.[38]

The rebels were closing in. A day after they left Dageraad, the plantation's *bomba*, Piramus, caught up with the governor to tell him that a large group of rebels had arrived on the estate. They had confiscated

View of plantation Cornelis Vriendschap in Suriname. Detail, dugout with bananas. (Rijksmuseum, Amsterdam.)

everything of use. Finding no rum, they had ordered Piramus to make them some, threatening to "break his neck" and those of his laborers "because they had not taken the side of the rebels" and instead had "stayed loyal" to the Dutch. Piramus also reported that several trusted slaves following the ships in a canoe loaded with kitchen supplies and furniture from Fort Nassau had fallen into rebel hands. So had the boat filled with Hooftplantage slaves who had so moved the governor with their loyalty. Van Hoogenheim persuaded a hesitant Piramus to return to Dageraad to guard the plantation and try to prevent his people from joining the rebels.[39]

Meanwhile, Van Hoogenheim's efforts at damage control were being undermined by his own colonists. One ship captain sent armed seamen and soldiers to a northernmost estate, still at peace, to look for provisions. The men broke into the house, took food and wine, and shot dead the plantation's *bomba*. Governor van Hoogenheim was furious but lacked the power to punish them. "All means of executing justice have been taken from me," he noted in his log. "I am entirely dependent on the ship captains, and on dishonorable, disobedient and uncooperative burghers"—truly, he lamented, "a most deplorable and bitter lot for an honest man."[40]

A week after torching their own fort, the Dutch finally arrived at St. Andries, a military outpost near the coast. St. Andries consisted of a low stone building and a few miserable clay huts in the middle of an immense savanna. Utterly exposed, it was armed with only two ancient and defective cannons and surrounded by a parapet, or breast-work, that was not much more than a cattle fence.[41] It lacked gardens and access to fresh water. European refugees from both rivers, many of whom had brought their slaves, were living in hastily thrown-up thatched huts. Each day more desperate and destitute people arrived at the swelling refugee camp. The colonists on board the ships refused to lend a hand. They clamored to be allowed to continue their voyage out of the colony. Officials were now in a complete state of rebellion, no longer recognizing the authority of the governor and his council. "I [find] myself in the most horrible and dire circumstances one can imagine," the governor lamented, "on the very edge of this pitiful col-ony, in a wild savanna, without any expectation of help or deliverance, with few provisions, and many mouths to feed yet few willing to aid in any way."[42]

The governor spent the next two weeks battling not rebels but his own people. He made clear that he intended to remain at St. Andries until help arrived. Any colonist was welcome to stay. Only those who were willing to do military duty and submit to military discipline would be fed. Those who sought to depart, whether on the four ships ultimately headed for Holland or in their own boats to nearby colonies, would be given permission to leave. Few men volunteered to stay; to the governor's astonishment and disgust, even Pastor Jonas Ramring could not be persuaded to remain with his flock. The Lutheran min-ister Salomon Fredrik Müller, born in Berlin and newly appointed in Berbice (he had served less than a year), also departed, reportedly without so much as a goodbye. Next Van Hoogenheim tried repeat-edly to retrieve his own personal belongings, as well as Company goods and provisions stowed aboard the ships. Government officials and captains feigned ignorance of their existence and sailors hid the goods deep in the holds under the cargo. Even a few Company slaves were secreted away. Government officials refused to settle their ac-counts or turn over Company papers, or did so incompletely and with great indifference.

As for the ship captains, they daily asked the governor for clear-ance to leave the colony, eventually threatening to depart without permission. Van Hoogenheim repeatedly impressed upon them and their officers the "dire need of the colony and the dangers to its inhabitants" but could not persuade them to provide any aid. They even refused to move their ships into defensive positions. In fact, on several occasions, those aboard went pleasure sailing on the ocean while a dutiful Governor van Hoogenheim made military preparations to withstand a rebel attack. A few willing colonists and available slaves built additional housing for the refugees, a new battery, and a stronger rampart. They also installed wooden gutters to collect rainwater, while the few soldiers and militia carried out reconnaissance on the Canje River.[43]

Van Hoogenheim spent his nights writing urgent letters to the directors of Berbice, as well as to the Dutch legislature, the States General, begging for speedy assistance. The letters were sent by messenger to Suriname and Demerara, where they were kept until they could be included in the official sealed mailbag when a ship left for Europe. The governor's pleas would not reach the Dutch Republic for months, and any aid from there, he estimated, would take several more months.

Aid from Suriname, some seventy miles east of Berbice, came faster. As soon as he received Van Hoogenheim's desperate request for a hundred fighters, Governor Wigbold Crommelin readied an expedition. Unable to find a Dutch ship willing to transport the troops to Berbice, he hired an "English bark," the *Betsy*, a Rhode Island ship just then in port, commanded by a brother-in-law of future American revolutionary Ben Franklin. In addition to a hundred soldiers, the *Betsy* also carried food supplies for Van Hoogenheim, along with guns, ammunition, and diplomatic gifts to induce Amerindians to stay loyal. Three-quarters of the men were to join Van Hoogenheim. The rest were to patrol the Corentyne River, the border between Berbice and Suriname. Crommelin hoped that the natives and soldiers together could prevent the Berbice Rebellion from spilling into his colony. He assured Van Hoogenheim that his soldiers were experienced slave hunters who had battled Maroons and thus were "well acquainted with the ways of blacks."[44]

The Suriname soldiers reached Fort St. Andries on March 28, 1763, just as the governor had reached the breaking point and was contemplating abandoning the colony. One of the two officers in command was an old army friend of Van Hoogenheim and the other a future governor of Suriname. Both men were veteran Maroon fighters.[45] Buoyed by their arrival, Van Hoogenheim decided to repossess Company plantation Dageraad. Once again, he persuaded the ship captains to postpone their departure for the Dutch Republic and to lend a hand now that help had arrived. The captain of the slaver agreed only after the council authorized a bonus of 300 guilders to "animate" his reluctant sailors. Two of the ships remained near the coast: one at the mouth of the Canje and one at Fort St. Andries, where a small detachment of soldiers also remained. Another twenty-five soldiers and six civilians were sent up the Canje River to determine the situation on that river and eventually to make their way to the Corentyne River. The *Standvastigheid*, the *Betsy*, and the slaver carried the remaining Europeans (including ninety soldiers and civilians capable of fighting), along with an unknown number of enslaved people, upriver. On April 1, at six thirty in the morning, Van Hoogenheim disembarked on Dageraad, the Company's largest and northernmost sugar plantation, where he had wanted to set up temporary headquarters several weeks earlier but had been overruled.[46]

Dutiful and determined, Governor van Hoogenheim had managed to hang on to his colony by his fingernails. Even so, his small contingent still confronted formidable odds. Just under a hundred able-bodied European men, both soldiers and burghers, now faced hundreds, if not thousands, of rebels. The Europeans had access to one plantation and its kitchen gardens, while their opponents controlled the rest of the colony. The relieved governor, deeply disappointed in his fellow colonists but proud to have prevailed against them and, so far, the rebels, had no idea he would be stuck at Dageraad for the next fifteen months.

4

Governing

For at least a year, if not more, rebellion had been in the air. Some enslaved people contemplated starting their own Maroon settlements in the bush. But at some point the conversation turned. Rather than leave themselves, why not force the Dutch to do the leaving? Instead of doing the backbreaking work of starting new farms in the jungle, they could take over the plantations where they lived. The uprising that broke out at the end of February 1763 centered on several adjoining plantations in the heart of the colony. But the speed with which the rebels expanded their uprising suggests not only widely shared discontent, but also the existence of political organization of some sort. Signs indicate elements of self-government, with the leadership likely drawn from men (and some women) who were powerful on their plantations before the rebellion.

The head of the Berbice uprising was Coffij van Lelienburg, who lived on the plantation of the Barkey family. Lelienburg was a mid-sized estate with forty slaves. Coffij identified as Amina, a term the Dutch used for people who had been captured on the Gold Coast of Africa, present-day Ghana. The English used the term Coromantee, or Kromanti. The name Kofi (rendered as Coffij in Dutch) is a common Akan name given to Gold Coast boys born on a Friday. No firsthand testimony survives from Coffij. Many people the Dutch questioned as the rebellion wound down mention Coffij, but unfortunately they provided few personal details. We do not know, for instance, how old he was or whether he was a husband or a father. Did his face bear the scarification tattoos, three parallel lines from ear to eye, typical of the West African Akan, to indicate status, family, and birthplace? The Dutch records rarely remark on physical attributes and never mention filed teeth or facial and body scarification, though many Africans in Berbice carried such "country marks." Perhaps Coffij was stolen from his parents before he received his.[1]

Coffij was a man of broad experience. A contemporary claimed that he was brought to Berbice as a child. Two enslaved women reported crossing the Atlantic with him. He grew up on the plantation of one of the most hated planters in the colony, experiencing firsthand the worst brutality of Dutch rule. He was initially trained as a house servant in the Barkey family, and later became a cooper. His trajectory made him a highly assimilated or creolized African, familiar with the ways of whites. He must have been highly charismatic and spiritually forceful, as Akan people from the Gold Coast prized such qualities in their political leaders. He was chosen as the commander, one insurgent later claimed, because he was a "wise and sensible man." Even a planter admiringly called him a man of "courage and judgement." Coffij was also a man of vision, eager to secure freedom from chattel slavery for himself and his followers with bold ideas about the shape of post-emancipation life. His second-in-command, Accara, also claimed Amina membership and lived on Lelienburg, where he had a wife and at least one grown daughter.[2]

Coffij's and Accara's identities as Amina matter. Enslaved Africans in the Americas created strong ties where they lived and worked. Europeans and slaves alike identified people by the name of their plantation: Coffij van (of) Lelienburg. But people developed ties not just to the estates where they were incarcerated. More so than in North America, many African-descended people in the Caribbean and South America also identified across plantations with members of what Europeans referred to as "nations." Nations were fluid communities of people who came from the same general geographic area and who could communicate because they spoke the same or similar languages. In Dutch colonies, "Amina" or "Elmina" referred to Akan and Ga speakers from the Gold Coast and its hinterland. In Africa they would not have

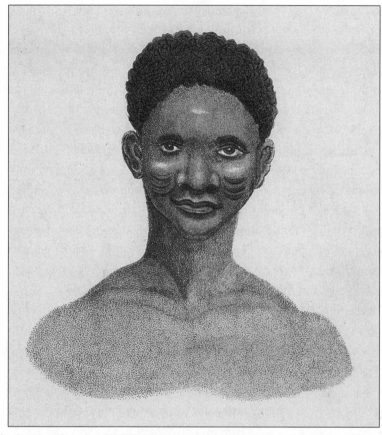

Charles Hamilton Smith; G. B. Whittaker, Akan man with facial marks, 1827. (© National Maritime Museum, Greenwich, London.)

considered themselves one nation, as they would have belonged to different ethnicities and political communities.[3] Nations were American cultural creations for social and religious fellowship. Creoles might or might not claim national membership. Which facet of one's identity took precedence (plantation, nation, or Creole status), and what the affiliation meant at any given time, depended on circumstances. The rebellion, as war tends to do, politicized such difficult choices.[4]

The sources shed little light on the planning of the rebellion. The Dutch did not ask about it in their judicial processes, so people did not speak of it much. One can piece together clues to get a picture of the organization. People strategized first on their individual plantations, and next, across estates through membership in nations. This was especially true of the Amina. The Amina were only one of many nations in Berbice, but they were a sizable and coherent group. The Dutch bought many slaves on the West African Gold Coast, especially after a series of wars there in the 1730s transformed large numbers of people into prisoners of war. Male Amina tended to be well schooled in statecraft and military affairs. They came from hierarchical cultures in which people avidly sought avenues for social advancement, notably through the ownership of slaves. They were behind many rebellions in the Americas—on the Danish island of St. John in 1733 and in British Jamaica in 1760. Time and again, black Berbicians questioned by the Dutch as the rebellion wound down pointed to the Amina as instigators. Africans of many nations as well as some Creoles participated in the uprising, but the Amina formed the senior leadership.[5]

In the first days and weeks of the uprising, the rebels worked to convince, or coerce, as many people as possible to rise up and to do so quickly, before the Europeans had a chance to mobilize. *Bombas* played a crucial role in getting people on board. Depending on whether they behaved like junior managers or shop stewards, *bombas* were resented or respected. Their moral authority could sway people to join, resist, or dodge the insurgents. Moreover, many fleeing planters had left their plantations in the care of their *bombas*, handing over keys and guns. This access made them doubly useful to the rebels.[6]

The judicial interrogations the Dutch conducted in 1764 suggest that when insurgents arrived on a plantation, they moved quickly to gain support and defuse opposition. They searched for weapons and powder and confiscated guns left by Europeans in the hands of trusted slaves. They tied up resisters. They assessed the leanings of the *bomba* or *bombas*, as larger plantations had more than one. Those who refused to join the rebellion were threatened, along with their family members. If that failed, they were whipped, or even killed. The *bomba* at plantation La Providence was flogged by the rebels. *Bomba* Fortuin van Lelienburg and Louis, *bomba* on Hoogstraten, two plantations at the heart of the rebellion, were murdered. Rebelling slaves in

St. Domingue (present-day Haiti), some twenty-five years later, acted similarly toward *commandeurs*, as *bombas* were known in French. The large numbers of *bombas* among the Berbice rebels suggest that many decided to join, or had been in on the planning. They played a similar leading role in St. Domingue's massive uprising in 1791.[7]

Once the rebels took care of opposition, they raided the plantations. They slaughtered fowl and livestock and roasted them on spits. They helped themselves to wine and liquor. They broke into chests and cupboards, shed their rags, and dressed in their enslavers' finest. Some leaders, in significant gestures of social inversion, dined with their families in great style at the tables of the very men and women who had kept them hungry. When the rebels did not want to keep a plantation in production, they torched crops and buildings, making European return difficult. To prevent non-rebellious slaves from staying on their plantation, or to punish them for refusing to join, they burned their huts and gardens as well. Rebels urged or, if necessary, forced women along as wives and men as soldiers. Then they sent tent boats and canoes with plunder, captives, and volunteers to rebel headquarters and moved on to the next estate.[8]

"Getting Their Due"

In the first week of the rebellion, rebel leaders Coffij and Accara sent several messages to the Dutch. Much as the American colonists in 1776 would feel compelled to compose a Declaration of Independence that justified taking up arms and placed responsibility on British officials, so, too, the Berbice rebels decided to explain themselves and assess blame. Their initial brief missives and oral messages pointed to brutal treatment and not getting "what was their due" as the trigger for seeking freedom through armed rebellion. They singled out offending planters by name. Those accused were owners or managers on the estates where the rebellion first started, suggesting that the initial uprising was a local affair. Coffij and Accara did not elaborate, here or in their subsequent letters, on what exactly they meant by not "getting their due." Mistress Schröder, who, as noted earlier, had been captured on Peereboom plantation, taken to rebel headquarters, and released to carry the insurgents' first message to the Dutch governor, filled in some of the details. The rebels, she said, had pointed to particular masters for withholding food and the customary allotment of rum. They had mercilessly flogged the slaves to work beyond their endurance. And, Schröder testified, they had forced themselves on enslaved men's wives.[9]

In pointing to ill treatment and "not getting one's due," the Berbice rebels joined a long revolutionary tradition. In human history, people have repeatedly overturned the status quo because they felt that on some fundamental level they did not get what they deserved. Other revolutions, too, began out of a sense of injustice when the moral understanding between rulers and ruled was violated. To justify their actions, revolutionaries worked to transform concrete violations into abstract principles. Not long after the Berbice Rebellion, American colonists would feel ill-treated when the British imposed taxes, which threatened their livelihoods and violated their sense of what they rightly deserved as British subjects. They transformed this affront into the more abstract political principles of "liberty" and "independence." By 1775, their peaceful efforts at redress rebuffed, many colonists felt justified in resorting to collective violence to create a more just social order.

Historians of slavery have argued that enslaved people held similar understandings. In lives of incessant violence and acute exploitation, enslaved people, like oppressed workers everywhere, nevertheless expected a modicum of fairness and predictability. They labored with an expectation of sufficient food to do the work, time off, some autonomy, reasonable rules with clear consequences, and a chance at building families and communities. The terms of social "contracts" differed from place to place, shaped by local law and custom, the particular plantation economy, and the historical contingencies that shaped the struggles between enslavers and enslaved. Such expectations about conditions do not mean that people accepted their enslavement. Nor do they mean that the enslaved people did not resist their exploitation in daily life. Rather, ruled by terror, and wary of armed rebellion, most begrudgingly accommodated themselves to their enslavement as long as certain minimum standards were observed, in order to survive.[10]

When planters violated such customary understandings, their victims had limited recourse. In some colonies in the Americas, notably those under Spanish rule and in New England, aggrieved slaves had access to the courts. In most English and Dutch colonies in the eighteenth century, people could only informally complain to a master, overseer, neighboring planter, or government official. Once in a while, enslaved people succeeded in reining in a cruel master or getting an offensive overseer fired. More often, such risky challenges were unsuccessful, as law, custom, and an ideology of white supremacy granted planters enormous leeway in treating enslaved people as they saw fit.[11]

In addition to lodging complaints, enslaved people resorted to what social scientist James Scott calls the "weapons of the weak." They protested their enslavers' unacceptable treatment through lewd gestures, disrespectful talk, and subversive behavior. The people on plantation Hooglande, for instance, expressed their contempt for their abusive owner by making "fun of him in all things," the surgeon on the plantation reported; "even the little ones give him all kinds of nicknames." When mocking could not bridle hurt, anger, or fear, people turned to sabotage, theft, or violence. Every once in a while, an overseer or slaveholder was murdered, though such occurrences were surprisingly rare. Some people sought a change of masters, or ran away, either temporarily or permanently. When the infractions were egregious, long-lasting, and widely shared, and other measures had been exhausted, people might organize and break out collectively, as happened on plantation Goed Land en Goed Fortuin in 1762. In resorting to collective armed rebellion reluctantly, and only as a last resort, enslaved people acted like other exploited people in history. When hunger and oppression grew intolerable, armed rebellion became the only way out.[12]

Yet armed revolution brought people in search of freedom and self-mastery face-to-face not only with their colonial oppressors but with one another.[13]

Ruling

As they expanded their grip on the colony, and even before the Dutch fled to the coast, Coffij and his next in command, Accara, formed a government. They expanded on the rudimentary organization they had set up in the first weeks of rebellion, drawing on Akan and new-world political understanding and practices. Coffij set policy and headed up the civil administration. He upgraded his title from captain, as he designated himself in his first message to Governor van Hoogenheim, to governor. Captain Accara was in charge of military affairs. Separation of political and military affairs was common practice, too, among Maroons in Suriname and elsewhere. Coffij picked councilmen, a prosecutor, and an executioner.[14] They, like Governor Coffij, were known by the Dutch terms for their offices. They were given servants, chosen from both the rebellion's opponents and its supporters.

They added ceremony. High-ranking officials and their wives dressed in fancy European clothing and jewelry to symbolize their new authority, power, and status. Their comings and goings were announced with drumming and gunshots. Some were given the tent boats of plantation owners. Berend, the *bomba* of Sublislust, was "ferried about like a *Heer*," or big man, in the boat of councilman Abbensets, rowed by some of Abbensets's former slaves. While at first the insurgents were too busy for elaborate festivities, it is likely, though no accounts exist, that in the weeks that followed, some in positions of power and prestige participated in Akan "ennobling" ceremonies to legitimize their new elite status, which carried with it the right to own slaves.[15]

Rebel leaders selected *heren* (lords), trusted supporters to run the plantations that the rebels decided to keep in production and to ensure that plantation workers stayed at their jobs. Much as *bombas* had been beholden to their European masters, *heren* were obligated to Coffij— and to the rebellion's success, if they wanted to keep their new positions. Others were encouraged or forced to work at their previous occupations, but now to aid the rebellion. One man claimed he was outed as having been a butcher, in a revealing phrase, "under the previous governor." Apprised of this, Governor Coffij, the current governor, likewise set the man to slaughtering.[16] Governor Coffij ordered Jan Kat, a former colony slave trained as a smith, to make arrows with metal points and drill open any cannon the Dutch had spiked. Others worked as carpenters, masons, and cooks.[17]

On the military side, Captain Accara designated captains and lieutenants to train and lead army units. No doubt some were chosen because of their wartime experience in Africa. Pokko van Hollandia, an Amina, for instance, knew how to "command with flags," meaning that he used signals to direct soldiers in battle. Others were promoted because they proved their mettle in the early stages of the rebellion. Fortuin van Helvetia brought Coffij the heads of two European men, which reportedly gained him a commission as a "great Captain." Gousarie van Oosterleek led the uprising on his plantation and was also in charge during the attack on Peereboom plantation in the first week of the rebellion. Entrusting these men and others to lead their own bands tied them to the rebellion.[18]

While the great majority of leaders were male, a few female counselors exerted crucial leadership early on in the rebellion.[19] Their roles reflected old- and new-world practices. Among the Akan, female counselors served as social critics who helped regulate people's behavior. On plantations, senior women played important roles in informal slave tribunals that dealt with community infractions such as theft, sexual transgressions, and accusations of poisoning. No doubt drawing on such customs, Amelia van Hollandia & Zeelandia, Coffij's sister from the Middle Passage, was said to have counseled him about people's loyalty. Other rebels, later charged and questioned by the Dutch, claimed that at the word of this powerful woman heads rolled. She defended herself against such claims by asserting that she had merely served as "[Coffij's] cook." As on the Gold Coast, a wife's duty to cook for her husband was of great importance, second only to bearing his children. Amelia in fact may well have been one of Coffj's wives.[20]

Her fellow slaves did not buy Amelia's defense. One man related that he had even seen her "walking around with a broadsword like a man." Accara's wife Barbara, also from Lelienburg, acted in a similar

African woman with a hand drum, 1675–1725, detail. (Rijksmuseum, Amsterdam.)

capacity. Likewise, leader Atta van Altenklingen, who became governor at a later stage, was said to pay close attention to the advice of
a woman named Pallas from Antonia plantation. The Dutch accused
her of being "an instigator of the rebels through pretend magic." They
were referring to obeah, the channeling of special spiritual powers to
cure ills or correct social wrongs. Obeah provided a path to power for
women in West African societies where female diviners played important roles in criminal justice. According to Veronica van Lelienburg,
Barbara, who functioned as a counselor to her husband, Accara, urged

the death penalty for Veronica's husband, the *bomba* of Lelienburg, who had opposed the rebellion. When Accara acted on her recommendation, Barbara watched the *bomba*'s execution approvingly while she smoked a long pipe. She then made Veronica her servant. Perhaps women like Barbara and Pallas operated as "female reign-mates," or queen mothers, in Dahomey (present-day Benin), helping new rulers establish legitimacy and control.[21] While these women did not have formal titles, they functioned as informal advisers to top male leaders to whom they were closely related. As the rebellion progressed, and war eclipsed governing, the sources no longer identify women in leadership roles. The rebellion provided men with many opportunities for social mobility and prestige as soldiers and leaders—opportunities from which women were largely excluded.

In addition to creating civil and military administrations, Coffij and Accara also stockpiled and distributed supplies. In exchange for a reward, rebels were ordered to bring to rebel headquarters all confiscated goods, especially guns and powder, but also food, clothes, jewelry, money, tobacco, liquor, canoes, tent boats, and livestock. Coffij redistributed supplies to the army and loyal followers or kept them for future use. Rebel leaders also made a careful inventory of what, and who, remained on the various plantations. One rebel later reported that Coffij sent his lieutenant Atta van Altenklingen to Company plantation Savonette, several hours upriver, "to count the people and the cows." Some cattle were left on the plantations to be slaughtered at a later date, but most were picked up right away.[22]

As one might expect in wartime, the bulk of the supplies went to the army. Coffij and Accara handed out the estimated three hundred to four hundred guns they had collected to their most trusted and capable men (no records indicate that women received guns).[23] Some rebels, such as *bomba* Claes van Petite Bretagne, "did not know how to handle a gun." He and men like him were given sharp tools like axes, for hand-to-hand combat. Archers relied on skills they brought from their home countries.[24] Governor Coffij had iron-tipped arrows made for them. But, as in the precolonial Akan kingdom of Asante in West Africa, the powerful carried guns.[25] In fact, some rebels refused to fight without one. One man later explained that he had resisted going on a particular mission since he lacked a firearm. "A soldier, when he goes to war, has to have a gun," he had insisted. Coffij allegedly promised him that he would "get the musket of the first one killed." The man then reluctantly agreed to join, armed with a cutlass. Officers were further distinguished from common soldiers with sashes to wear over their clothes.[26]

Lookouts were set out around plantation Hollandia & Zeelandia, which served as rebel headquarters until Coffij moved into Fort Nassau. An advance post was created on Vigilantie, a plantation downriver, some three hours south of Dageraad. Iron discipline was imposed—soldiers "had to jump," people later testified, when their officers commanded them. A similar strict discipline would be maintained among rebel soldiers in St. Domingue during the slave uprising in the 1790s.[27]

In addition to organizing their army and government, Coffij and Accara had to decide what to do with their hostages. Their men had captured perhaps two dozen Europeans at Peereboom and elsewhere throughout the colony. Rebels punished and killed prisoners or put them to work. Captives' fates depended on how much they were hated, whether they had advocates among the rebels, and their potential usefulness. Widow Jansen was seized at Peereboom and put in the stocks at rebel headquarters. She had owned a small plantation, named Vrijheid, or Liberty, with four slaves. One of them, Favoriet (Favorite), now repeatedly threatened to cut off her ears—retribution for a punishment the widow herself may well have inflicted. Female rebels also regularly flogged her. Slave women were particularly active in punishing European women, whose white gender privilege was based on black women's degradation. Widow Jansen's ordeal ended when she was killed on the rebels' execution grounds across the river from plantation Hollandia & Zeelandia. One of the European female captives, later set free, claimed she saw seven dead colonists; all had been killed at the same time.[28]

Despite a desire for revenge and retribution, the insurgents kept alive a few Europeans, at least for the moment. The widow Hosch and her three daughters were put to work in the kitchen gardens. They were eventually killed. Coffij took Georgina Sara Helena George, a young woman of about twenty, whose father had commanded the Europeans at Peereboom, as one of his "wives." Sara's ten-year-old sister served as her lady-in-waiting. Despite historians' documentation of pervasive European anxieties in the Atlantic world about rebellious slaves wanting to marry white women, Georgina appears to have been the only Dutch woman to have wed one of the rebels. Other hostages were spared so they could be used to communicate with the Dutch. For instance, Coffij had sent Pastor Ramring, "a man who spoke with God," to carry a message to Governor van Hoogenheim the day after the Peereboom massacre. [29]

A few days later Coffij sent Mistress Schröder on a similar mission. She had been captured at Peereboom with her toddler. Rebels had undressed and whipped her before bringing her to their headquarters. Her husband had, until very recently, been the manager of the Company plantation Cornelia Jacoba and she claimed that people who had been enslaved there had stood by her. Using "strong language," she related, they proclaimed "that woman shall live or we will die with her." "They insisted," she added, that "she has always treated us right and done right by us." Figuring Schröder could be of help, and eager to retain the goodwill of the Cornelia Jacoba people, Coffij relented. He gave her new clothes and employed her as a stenographer, dictating a note to Governor van Hoogenheim explaining why the people had risen up. Coffij then dispatched Schröder and her child to take the note to Van Hoogenheim at Fort Nassau. As we have seen, she arrived just before the Dutch abandoned the fort.[30]

Besides dealing with European captives, rebel leaders had to decide what to do with their opponents among the liberated. This was a delicate task because loyalties and social ties overlapped and conflicted. Detractors were more than likely to have family, friends, and neighbors among the insurgents. The rebellion was organized both on the individual plantation level and along lines of nation across plantations. To be successful, the rebels had to forge these various communities into a coherent unit. So no doubt Coffij, Accara, and their councilors,

perhaps acting as a formal tribunal, had much to consider when de-
ciding each person's fate. Like the European captives, some opponents
were punished with beatings or the stocks and then put to work, while
others were killed.[31] *Bombas* who opposed the rebellion were generally
beheaded, so they could not use their influence to encourage resistance
to the new regime. On the other hand, the rebels spared *bomba* Cupido
van Hollandia & Zeelandia, who had betrayed the rebellion, allegedly
out of mercy because he "had many children," some of whom might
already have been of fighting age.[32]

Competing Loyalties

In the first few weeks, enslaved people would have watched the rebellion unfold with mixed emotions. Presumably, many felt exhila-
ration and satisfaction. Hated masters and mistresses were gone and
former slaves were in charge. There was food and drink, drumming
and dancing. People appropriated their owners' clothes and other possessions. A man named Cesar likely spoke for many when he justified emptying his plantation house's closets by reportedly asserting
that "he was old, and had worked for it all, and therefore it was all his
due."[33] People must have heard about the murder of Europeans and
the burning of their masters' houses and fields with grim satisfaction
and even glee. Not surprisingly, no one admitted to such feelings in
their interrogations a year later by the Dutch. But we find clues in the
actions of enslaved people in neighboring Suriname. In no time, they
composed songs celebrating the events in Berbice.[34]

But there must have been other reactions as well. Rebellions are not
just electrifying and promising, but scary and unpredictable. The uprising of the Dutch against the Spanish during the Eighty Years' War
(1568–1648) or the American colonists against their colonial masters
during the American Revolution (1763–83) were slow events that gave
people months if not years to decide their loyalties. And many remained apathetic throughout these conflicts. But slave rebellions happened fast, requiring split-second decisions in chaotic and dangerous
circumstances. No matter how much people hated their enslavement,

survival was foremost. For many, keeping themselves and their families alive and together and protecting their meager but hard-earned possessions, gardens, and privileges trumped the dicey overthrow of a brutal regime. People also worried about the right moment to join in: too late might be as costly as too soon. There were those who had no desire to join but were eager to keep their masters' food, drink, and clothing for themselves, rather than yield them to the rebels. Many later claimed they wanted to stay out of the fray altogether.[35]

Then, too, people may well have been weary of the Amina. They had been behind the uprising on St. John in 1733 as well as the 1760 rebellion in Jamaica. In both cases, their objective was to create a West African state with themselves on top. Rumors of their attempts to enslave the majority of the people may have circulated among black Berbicians. On the Gold Coast, powerful and militaristic Amina elites were known to be deeply involved in slaving and, according to West African informants on St. John, eager to leave work to others. The coercion involved in the first weeks of the uprising likely led many to stay away from the rebels.[36]

And so, not surprisingly, as is common in rebellions and revolutions, people's responses to the insurgency, and their alignments, ran the gamut from strong support to evasion. Their decisions hinged as much on their own personal circumstances and social tensions on plantations as on larger ideological, political, and strategic considerations. A few chose to side with the Dutch. Many more joined the rebels. Most stripped their own plantation houses, taking back what their labor had wrought.[37] Yet whatever their sympathies, in terms of committing themselves to rebellion, it appears that many remained noncommitted where possible, attempting to stay autonomous, or holding off on choosing their allegiance until it became clearer who would prevail. By their own accounts, they hid in the rain forest and savanna behind their plantations as soon as they heard the rebels approach, and they moved back to their plantations when the rebels, or the Dutch, had passed by. Some no doubt claimed disengagement to avoid prosecution. Others likely spoke the truth. The very fact that so many thought such claims believable is suggestive. It makes sense that people would have been wary, and preferred watching events from afar. They would have wished to keep their children and elderly safe, their garden produce from confiscation, and their chickens from the rebels' barbecues. They may have disliked or mistrusted those who supported the insurgency on their plantations, especially *bombas* who may have unfairly disciplined them in the past.[38] They feared Dutch or rebel retaliation if they bet on the wrong side. And as the rebels became more coercive, forcing people to work for them, many must have felt that the choice the Amina offered, at least in the short run, was tantamount to exchanging one set of masters for another.

Hiding from the rebels, in other words, signaled more than a fearful refusal to participate in rebellion. Avoiding the rebels was a political statement about preferring life without masters, a declaration of independence if you will. Like self-governing people throughout history, they sought to evade war, the appropriation of their labor, and outside rule. In dodging all combatants, ex-slaves in fact became fugitives in their own backyards, living independently of both the Dutch *and* the rebels. They camped in their own communities near their gardens and plantation pantries—subsistence agriculture did not require much coercion. This alternative, especially for women, children, and the less able-bodied, would have been preferable to joining a military campaign or being incorporated into the rebellion as workers. One man probably spoke for many when he told Dutch investigators later, "he did not want to be anyone's slave, and so he stayed home."[39] During the American Revolution, many people similarly struggled to remain neutral, less because they were anti-patriot or pro-British than because they wanted a "different kind of revolution" than the one they got.[40]

What happened on plantation Boschlust provides a revealing example. When the uprising started, the inhabitants of Boschlust, high up the Berbice River, charted their own future. Rather than kill their enslavers, as the rebels demanded, they urged them to flee. "They besieged me," Boschlust's owner, councilman Pierre Perrotet later reported, "that I had better leave as soon as possible, if we wanted to avoid getting murdered." But Perrotet's eighteen slaves declined his invitation to accompany him and his family to neighboring Demerara.

"Why would we go with you," they reportedly told him, "we have always had a good life on this plantation, we have good food, gardens we don't want to leave, and if the bad people [rebels] come, we'll kill them." They promised him they would not abandon the plantation and that they'd harvest his cotton, cacao, and coffee as they had done before. Perrotet wrote out a note that his slaves "had not rebelled against me nor had done the least bad deed." He hoped the declaration would stand them, and him, in good stead should the Dutch retake the colony. Four enslaved men agreed to accompany the family on their flight to Demerara, ostensibly to carry the luggage, but perhaps also to ensure the planter's prompt departure. A free Amerindian family living on the plantation came along as well, likely as guides. As soon as the party reached Demerara, the slaves abandoned the family, taking back the luggage, as they may have intended from the start. The Indians took off as well.

With their enslavers in Demerara, Boschlust's workers were now effectively free. They continued to live on the plantation, at least for the moment, occasionally hiding in the bush when they detected rebels or Europeans. Despite earlier promises, it seems unlikely that they continued to work the cash crops cotton, cacao, and coffee. They would certainly have maintained, and expanded, their provision grounds to feed themselves and their families. Their story illustrates how refusing to join the rebellion was not a statement of loyalty to the Dutch, even if plantation owners like Perrotet wanted to interpret their behavior (or their words) that way.[41] Rather, they calculated that armed insurgency likely spelled suicide, whether in battle, on the gallows, or from hunger in the bush.[42] They would have quickly figured out that joining the rebels might mean a new regime of forced labor. Above all, they were keen to work what they considered their land—their plots— as they wished, without any kind of masters. Dodging rebellion, in other words, was a way to live on their own terms as autonomous subsistence farmers.[43]

The risk of being re-enslaved by the rebels was an especial threat for Company slaves. For Coffij and his fellow insurgents it was crucial to keep the Company plantations in production, for they, along with just one private plantation, were the only sugar estates in Berbice. These plantations supplied all Berbicians with their staple drink, a crude intoxicant distilled of molasses (milled from sugarcane), known as *kiltum*, or dram.[44] These estates also produced the cash crop the rebels would need to participate in the larger Atlantic economy in the future. Yet Company slaves were least disposed to join the rebellion—or so the Dutch believed—and available evidence supports this. Company plantations were among the oldest in the colony; several had been in continuous existence for a hundred years. Many of the workers on these estates were Creoles with strong ties to one another and to the land. They were leery of rebellion and more attuned to the risks than newcomers from Africa with fewer familial attachments. Creoles had more children, more kin and older family members to worry about. Moreover, the prospect of continuing to produce sugar, albeit under a new set of masters, could not have been attractive.[45]

We can peek in at Company plantation West Souburg, for instance. Just over a hundred enslaved people lived on West Souburg: thirty-five men, forty-eight women, and twenty-three youths and children. At the start of the rebellion, the plantation manager and his wife took off for Peereboom. "Christian servant" Jacob, who took care of the mill horses, fled into the woods. Captured, he was murdered by a rebel acting on orders.[46] A militia captain took all of West Souburg's guns and ammunition to Fort Nassau, leaving the enslaved defenseless. When the insurgents approached West Souburg, *bomba* Mathebi, a middle-aged man with grown children, warned everyone "that something was going on among the blacks." He no doubt urged women such as Kikomba and her five children, pregnant Jacomijntje and her toddler Roselyn, and seniors Gratie, Maria, and Cecilia to keep out of sight in the sugar fields and forest across the river. He reportedly was determined not to hand over the plantation, declaring he would "stand like a man."[47]

When the rebels arrived at West Souburg, they captured Mathebi. The insurgents set fire to the plantation house and the sugar mill but spared the cane in the fields. They rounded up the Amina people and marched them, along with Mathebi, his wife, Klaartje, and other captives, to Coffij's headquarters on Hollandia & Zeelandia. There, two West Souburg people sympathetic to the rebellion told Coffij about Mathebi's resistance. He was beheaded and his wife Klaartje was allegedly sold to a rebel leader.[48] The two men who denounced Mathebi were promoted to command West Souburg. The majority of West Souburg inhabitants spent the next few months much as they had before the rebellion: forced to work cane.

The story was much the same on other Company plantations. Coffij reportedly told the people on Company plantation Vlissingen that "since they tried to help their manager, they now had to be the slaves of the others and work for them, just like they had done for the Christians."[49] Rebels then tortured the *bomba* on the plantation such that, according to the man's son, he hanged himself.[50] Company plantation Hardenbroek's people later testified that rebel leaders whipped them when they refused to cut cane "and do the work." Little wonder that Indian spies repeatedly told the Dutch that the people on Company plantations, especially those high up the river, at least for the moment, wanted nothing to do with the rebels.[51]

And so black Berbicians quickly learned, if they did not already know it, that freedom and coercion went hand in hand. A successful revolution required control of resources, of territory, and of people. To feed their followers, rebels had to cultivate kitchen gardens in the hinterlands. In order to prevent the Dutch from retaking the colony, and to save themselves from death or re-enslavement, they had to conscript, drill, and supply a sizable army. To maintain that army, they needed cash. To grow cash crops, they had to have workers in the fields. To do all those things, they needed a government to enforce compliance with their rule and to neutralize opponents. Their own political and cultural traditions, including notions of honor, held that officers and officials be attended by servants and slaves, a sure sign one was no longer a slave. And so, perhaps not surprisingly, rebel leaders began in some small measure to resemble the very masters they had just booted out.[52]

Afro-Berbicians also came to realize that not everyone shared the same vision for post-rebellion Berbice. Some, it appears, sought freedom in an African state that employed coerced labor to participate in the Atlantic economy, while others, wary of a centralizing and hierarchical state, desired autonomy—to be left in peace to farm their own plots for subsistence and local barter.

In the months that followed, allegiances shifted as people continued to gauge how best to reach their goals and stay alive.

5

The Long Atlantic Reach

As the Dutch floated down the Berbice from St. Andries to repossess Company plantation Dageraad in the last two days of March 1763, rebel soldiers along the lower Berbice retreated, warned by spies of their enemy's approach, while women and children hid in the forest behind their plantations.

By the time the Dutch arrived at Dageraad on April 1, the rebels had left, joined by several men from the plantation. But the majority of Dageraad's 160 people had stayed behind, loyal to *bomba* Piramus. Some weeks earlier Piramus had visited Van Hoogenheim, who had promised him a reward for protecting the estate and its people, as he had evidently done. The slaves appeared, the Dutch judged, "somewhat apprehensive and afraid," yet "reasonably well disposed" toward them.[1] Their attitude was no doubt influenced by the difficulties they had endured since the start of the rebellion. Rebels had repeatedly raided the plantation's gardens and supply room and had forced them to brew dram. It is, of course, impossible to know how "well disposed" toward the Dutch Dageraad's enslaved people really were. One imagines they felt anxious and ambivalent: while the return of the Europeans provided some protection from rebel raids, it also spelled re-enslavement.

The Dutch also found on Dageraad an enslaved carpenter who had just escaped from the rebel encampment on plantation Hollandia & Zeelandia. He related that the rebels had "killed many Christians and

blacks" and had tossed so many bodies into the Berbice at that locale
that he feared drinking from the river. [2]

As soon as the Dutch disembarked at Dageraad they prepared for an
attack. Van Hoogenheim posted soldiers around the plantation. That
night, a former Dageraad *bomba* turned rebel slipped onto the plantation to see what the Dutch were up to. Warned by his young son that
he had been spotted by *bomba* Piramus, the rebel spy hastily fled the
plantation. As soon as Van Hoogenheim woke up, he questioned the
child, who refused to talk until "a few strokes with a wooden spoon"
led him to divulge that rebels were hiding in the fields all around.[3]

Attack

Within an hour, on Saturday, April 2, at sunrise, a day after the Europeans arrived at Dageraad, the rebels attacked. Directed by war
drums, they yelled and screamed to disorient their opponents, whom
they outnumbered three or four to one. The Europeans scrambled to
get to their assigned posts while Van Hoogenheim established a command center on a nearby slope. The insurgents congregated near the
recently completed sugar mill complex, where newly built slave huts
provided cover. The rebels attacked and retreated three times over the
course of the morning and early afternoon, firing especially heavily at
the European soldiers protecting the sugar mill and at the merchant
ship anchored to protect the plantation. Only constant fire by the Europeans kept the rebels at bay.

Descriptions of the attack, penned by Europeans eager to empha-
size their military prowess, are short and few, providing scant details
about the battle or the rebels' style of fighting. Did they, for instance,
fall eerily silent once the attack was under way? Did spiritual leaders
encourage the men with spells? Did rebel soldiers employ archers, as
armies did in West Africa, to protect their infantry? They were short
on guns, yet the Dutch reported that rebel musketeers targeted Europeans both on the plantation and aboard their ships. It is likely the Africans fought three to a gun in the manner of Suriname Maroons: one
fired the weapon; the second took over if the shooter became injured;

and the third dragged the wounded off the battlefield. West Africans cared deeply about retrieving those who died. Leaving a corpse behind provoked the deceased person's spirit to visit terrible revenge on the survivors.[4]

The fighting lasted until the early afternoon, when, Van Hoogenheim boasted, the rebels "retreated to the woods with bloodied heads." The Dutch governor estimated the rebel force at 300 to 400 men. That estimate crept up to 400 to 500 men in a letter to Suriname a few days later, and to 600 to 700 in a subsequent report to the Company. Since the attackers were not the entire rebel army but only the men stationed at plantation Vigilantie, located some two hours from Dageraad, Van Hoogenheim's first estimate seems closest to the mark. The rebels may have lost as many as twelve men, in addition to their injured. Among the Europeans, only one died, a valuable civilian, the engineer in charge of the costly new water-powered sugar mill, who was shot in the thigh and bled out within the hour.[5]

The rebels failed to defeat their enemies, but they badly rattled the colonists' nerves. In the days following the attack, the Europeans rushed to better secure Dageraad. Van Hoogenheim rearranged his small forces and tore down buildings used as cover by the rebels. He also divided his men into groups, each with specific instructions in case of a future attack. Most important, as it turned out, he ordered the creation of a battery of four cannons to cover Dageraad's waterfront.[6] And he wrote his neighbors for assistance with increased urgency.

Neighbors

Ever since the rebellion broke out, Governor van Hoogenheim had penned pleading letters to the Society of Berbice and the Dutch government, the States General, begging for ships, soldiers, and supplies. But with aid at such a distance, he also turned to his Dutch neighbors on the Wild Coast for faster assistance. His letters to his neighbors took a while to reach their targets, carried by messengers on foot or taken by boat. Yet the news also spread quickly the old-fashioned way, by mouth, as Amerindians and colonists, some with their slaves, fled

Berbice. Word of the uprising deeply alarmed planters in Berbice's neighboring colonies, east and west. They feared its spread to their colonies. Officials rushed to minimize contagion. Hobbled by limited resources—these colonies, too, were run by commercial companies that economized on soldiers and supplies—those in charge did what they could to help Van Hoogenheim hold out until aid from the Dutch Republic could arrive.

News first reached Berbice's closest neighbor, Demerara. European refugees shared alarming tales of torched plantations and murdered "Christians." (No doubt, enslaved Berbician refugees told different tales in the quarters.) In the next days and weeks, more terrified Europeans crossed the fifty miles of jungle and savanna separating the two colonies, while others arrived by sea. They brought frightening and garbled news: Fort Nassau had been abandoned, "Mulat Frederick" was the new governor of Berbice, and the "mutineers" (rebels) planned to invade Demerara on March 28. Incredulous, the authorities sent a "trusted person" to Berbice for confirmation, but the man returned empty-handed, too afraid to venture into the colony. By then, Governor van Hoogenheim's letters had arrived, confirming the worst. An official summed up the dread felt in his vicinity: "To see a colony like Berbice totally ruined and deserted in nine days, more than forty whites (according to report) massacred in the most barbarous manner, the Fort burnt and abandoned by the governor, who retreated to the river mouth whilst the mutineers had the assurance to attack the vessels as they dropped down stream, these occurrences fill everyone with terror and amazement."[7]

To defend himself against Berbice rebels and his own slaves, Demerara's chief official, Laurens van Bercheijck, pooled defenses with his father-in-law, Laurens Storm van 's Gravesande, the governor of Dutch Essequibo, thirty-five miles farther west. The pair acted swiftly to secure Demerara, so close to Berbice. The governors grilled refugees from Berbice for information. They readied their militias and ordered their citizens to keep a sharp eye on their slaves. To prevent the massive flight of Europeans that aided the rebellion's spread in Berbice, they forbade all able-bodied male colonists from departing the colony.

(European women and children were allowed to leave, and many did, rushing to Essequibo on foot or securing a precious berth on a ship just then departing for the Caribbean.) They assembled a small army of thirty "trusted Creoles," enslaved men born in the colony, to quell rumored slave unrest upriver. To protect against a rebel invasion, they ordered an armed ship to anchor where the path from Berbice ended at the Demerara River. After learning that "Cormantine Blacks" were the "first rebels," they even requested that the Dutch West India Company limit their importation "from the [Caribbean] islands."[8]

The two commanders also pleaded for aid from abroad. Van Hoogenheim had been reluctant to ask for the help of foreign powers, especially without the knowledge and approval of the Dutch authorities. What if such forces, he fretted, "came to play master, or tried to stay," or "with rough ways destroyed good and bad negroes at the same time?" But his fellow governors did not share his qualms about asking for British help; they appealed to their trading partners and worked their informal networks in the Caribbean and North America without regard for imperial boundaries. They sent letters about the rebellion to the governor of Barbados, a British island in the westernmost Caribbean some 450 miles to the northeast of Berbice. Without a formal request from the States General, the governor of Barbados was reluctant to send troops. Perhaps his hesitation stemmed in part from recent tensions in Anglo-Dutch relations over the extensive illicit trade by the neutral Dutch in the Caribbean during the Seven Years' War. More successful was their appeal to Gedney Clarke, an Atlantic trader and Barbados official originally from Salem, Massachusetts. Well connected, the merchant planter regularly entertained high-level British officers and colonial officials, including a teenage George Washington, who during his only trip abroad in 1751 was delighted to dine at Clarke's house. Clarke and his son owned eleven plantations in Demerara and Essequibo.[9]

Eager to safeguard the family's extensive investments, Clarke mobilized quickly. Without any official authorization from London, he assembled three armed ships with several hundred mercenaries and British sailors stationed in Barbados, made available informally by a friend in the British navy. These troops reached Demerara in early April, an astonishingly fast deployment. Van 's Gravesande later claimed that "the succour" sent by Clarke was, "after God, the salvation of Demerara." The British sailors were recalled in early May, but Clarke's mercenaries ended up staying for almost a year. It is unclear whether the Dutch West India Company ever paid Clarke's bill of 41,000 guilders (equivalent to more than 900,000 euros in current purchasing power), allegedly just half what he spent.[10]

As we have seen, Governor Crommelin of Suriname sent a hundred soldiers in late March, as soon as he received Van Hoogenheim's urgent pleas. Like the other Wild Coast colonies, Suriname was not administered by the Dutch government but jointly by the West India Company and the city of Amsterdam. Much larger than its neighbors on the Wild Coast, Suriname was in a better position to send fighting men. Yet when Van Hoogenheim requested additional forces after the April 2 attack, Crommelin declined, citing the need for "conservation" of his own colony, and his desire to send additional men to guard the Corentyne River, the border with Berbice.[11]

Like his counterparts in Essequibo and Demerara, Governor Crommelin worried about Berbice rebels tempting his colony's slaves to revolt. Demographics were not in his favor, as his 1,300 colonists were vastly outnumbered by 36,000 people of African descent. Within weeks of the uprising in Berbice, Suriname workers could be heard talking and singing about the event—testimony to enslaved people's well-developed communication networks. Trying to put a stop to dangerous loose talk and song, Surinamese officials urged colonists to be careful about spreading news and to punish their slaves for conversation or songs that demonstrated, as they put it, "their malevolence or rebellious inclinations and pleasure in the adversities of Europeans." Crommelin secretly censored his colonists' letters and urged Van Hoogenheim to do the same.[12]

Suriname authorities knew only too well the dangers posed by slave resistance. They had been at war with Maroons for most of the century. Colonists had lost their lives, estates had gone up in flames, and valuable slaves had escaped or been abducted. Hundreds of soldiers from the Dutch Republic had proved no match for the Maroons or the jungle. Starting in 1760, after lengthy negotiations, Crommelin signed peace treaties with several Maroon bands. Worried that Berbice rebels might try to ally themselves with so-called pacified Maroons living closest to the Berbice border, he ordered an emissary to urge the Samaaka Maroons, "with the greatest delicacy," not to assist the Berbice rebels but "to turn them over to the whites alive, or to exterminate them," as the recent treaty required.[13]

In addition to providing soldiers and discouraging a rebel-Maroon alliance, Crommelin sent Van Hoogenheim weapons and ammunition, Indian trade goods to reward his native allies, and medicine, candles, meat, fish, flour, and rum for colonial consumption. The governor of Essequibo similarly sent fish, plantains, beer, and tobacco, as Van Hoogenheim was dangerously low not only on soldiers and weapons but also on basic supplies.[14] Over the course of the rebellion, Berbice's neighbors would from time to time dispatch ships with aid to the colony, drawing on their commercial contacts in Amsterdam, Philadelphia, Connecticut, Rhode Island, and elsewhere in the Atlantic world to procure provisions and supplies for their sister colony, charging hefty sums to the Society of Berbice.[15] War and commerce—as is well known—go hand in hand.

Further aid came from St. Eustatius, a tiny but thriving Dutch commercial hub and smuggling center in the northeastern Caribbean, eight hundred miles from Berbice. Governor Jan de Windt heard about the uprising at the end of March via sailors freshly arrived from Demerara. Letters followed from Gedney Clarke and Van Hoogenheim, requesting help. During the American Revolution, St. Eustatius, or "Statia," merchants would supply the American anti-British rebels with much-needed weapons; not surprisingly, in 1763, they took the side of the Dutch, the colonial masters. Still, De Windt was reluctant to spend government funds without authorization from his superiors at the West India Company. Instead, he and his colonists privately raised 15,000 guilders to outfit three ships for two months, an effort

St. Eustatius with British warships whose soldiers are rowing to the island during an attack, 1781. (Rijksmuseum, Amsterdam.)

to provide relief to their "countrymen" in Berbice. The 150 Statia men arrived in Berbice in early May, where they would remain for close to a year at a cost of 100,000 guilders, billed to the Company of Berbice.[16]

Barbados merchant Gedney Clarke was highly critical of the way the Dutch States General outsourced colonial responsibilities to commercial societies, convinced that companies could never adequately

develop, or defend, Dutch interests overseas. "I am far from ascrib-
ing any merit to myself," Clarke claimed, "but it is certain had I not
sent the timely aid and in the manner, I did, Demorary and Isequebe
wou'd have been cut off; and Surinam wou'd in time have followed;
and in course the States wou'd have lost that whole Continent."[17]
Clarke exaggerated his own importance—soldiers from Suriname and
St. Eustatius were just as crucial, if not more so. But he was correct
that Van Hoogenheim would have had to abandon his poorly supplied
and underfunded colony without massive international aid. In another
thirty years, the States General would rethink this decentralized colonial structure. For the moment, transnational European solidarity,
based on shared fears of slave rebellion and entangled commercial interests, trumped national borders and enabled the Dutch to remain in
Berbice.

Native Alliances

Even as the might of international finance and transatlantic supply
lines swung to take aim at the small band of Berbice rebels, the response appeared inadequate. In order to hold on, and eventually to reconquer, the Dutch needed more. Just days after the April 2 attack, Van
Hoogenheim and his councilmen urged the authorities in Essequibo to
mobilize the Caribs in their vicinity. They suggested that Van's Gravesande appeal to his indigenous allies' self-interest by impressing on
them that "if the Christians were to be exterminated, it might be their
turn next, to give way to the fury and savagery of the blacks."[18]
Of the four Dutch colonies on the Wild Coast, Essequibo had long
been, and remained, the most deeply involved in Amerindian trade.
Although all Dutch colonies turned from trade to plantation agriculture in the eighteenth century, Essequibo continued to buy indigenous slaves and native-produced goods, especially the much-desired
dye annatto. The Caribs' dominance of this commerce and a shared
interest in containing the Spanish on the Orinoco formed the basis of
a continued strong partnership. Much like the Haudenosaunee, or Iroquois, in North America, Caribs had parlayed Dutch need for allies

Squatting Carib or Arawak man with a knife in his left hand, ca. 1810. Detail of a diorama made by Gerrit Schouten, a Surinamese artist of African and European descent. (Rijksmuseum, Amsterdam.)

into a virtual trading monopoly that gave them ample access to European guns and turned them into a regional power.[19] Van 's Gravesande
did what he could to protect his allies from the Spanish on the Orinoco, whose aggressive conversion policy worried him. He was well
aware that the Spanish used the missions to expand their settlements
and influence, threatening Dutch territorial claims. Spanish priests
also interfered in slave raiding, which undermined Carib power in the
region and hurt Dutch trade.[20] And, though it is not clear that Van 's
Gravesande understood this, the missions introduced deadly epidemics among the native populations with disastrous effect. One modern
estimate suggests that the Carib population on the Orinoco would di-
minish from 120,000 in 1730 to 20,000 by 1780.[21]

Yet Van 's Gravesande well knew the risks, and costs, of calling on
his native partners. Were he to summon the Caribs, he explained in
the midst of an earlier crisis to his superiors, they would come "several
hundred strong," demanding not only "bread and other provisions,"
but also "guns, powder, and shot, and in such quantities that I hesitate
about putting all these weapons into their hands, the Indians being as
a rule not greatly to be trusted." Van 's Gravesande realized that Dutch
manufactures and arms turned Amerindians into allies. They are, he
summed up his understanding, "friendly towards us through fear and
by reasons of the profit they make out of trading with us rather than
from inclination."[22]

Yet when Van 's Gravesande heard about the Berbice rebellion, he set
aside scruples about security and costs. He immediately dispatched
upriver a mixed-race trader, Joseph de Meijer, who had "criss-crossed
the highlands and speaks the Indian languages fluently," to persuade the Caribs to take on the rebels in Berbice. Van 's Gravesande
offered to arm any Carib willing to go to Berbice since they "cannot or
will not fight without guns." The Amerindians received trade goods
for any rebels killed, submitting the right hands of their victims as
proof. In the next century, King Leopold II would deploy this grisly
tradition in the Belgian Congo.[23]

More immediately helpful natives were closer at hand—in Berbice.
Designated "free Indians" or "our Indians," they lived individually

behind plantations in the savanna or in villages under chiefs whose authority the Dutch worked to strengthen. They formed the first line of defense against absconding slaves and soldiers. In addition to catching escapees (or, sometimes, concealing them), Berbice Indians fished and hunted for colonists and the Company, cut firewood in the jungle, roofed buildings with giant leaves, hired out as boatmen, and carried out odd jobs. Archival records list the iron axes, chisels, and cloth native men received for catching escaped slaves—including Coffij and Antoinette, who were part of the 1762 rebellion on Goed Land en Goed Fortuin.[24] Even indigenous men living in the Protestant Moravian mission were not exempt from the expectation of slave catching. The brethren reassured suspicious colonial authorities that their disciples "diligently hunt runaway blacks."[25]

When the rebellion broke out, Van Hoogenheim was eager for these local allies to come to his aid. Several joined the Dutch at besieged Dageraad, carrying out daily reconnaissance missions to spy on the rebels. Ironically, while these "Indian patrols" provided indispensable service, the Dutch did not entirely trust them, aware that native interests did not always align with their own. With some regularity, Van Hoogenheim sent soldiers and "loyal blacks" to spy on his spies, "to see whether they properly reconnoiter and deal with us faithfully."[26]

Most local Indians fled the colony in fear at the first sign of rebellion. Others decamped over time to avoid being pressed into service by either the Dutch or the rebels. Even native peoples living as far away as the border with Suriname packed up their households and hurried east.[27] Moravian missionaries on the Corentyne River reported that the Indians in their vicinity took great fright after hearing rumors that rebels not only killed Amerindians, but cooked and ate native children. (Such stories persisted. An elderly man living in an Arawak village on the Wikki Creek, reportedly well versed in his people's history, told me when I visited in 2006 that fugitive slaves barbecued and consumed Amerindians, especially children.) The brethren also noted indigenous wishes that "the white people were in Holland with their blacks," rather than, presumably, turning Amerindians into refugees by bringing strife into their lands.[28]

Despite strong and long-standing treaties and partnerships, native cooperation was never a foregone conclusion. Individual groups made their own decisions. Guided by indigenous ideas about reciprocity, community, and kin, Amerindians' willingness to fight on behalf of colonists depended on local circumstances, relationships with other native communities, and their connections with individual colonial representatives. Just as the Six Nations Iroquois, in North America, for instance, did not always act as a body but frequently as independent villages or nations, so not all Caribs, Arawaks, or Akawaios supported the Dutch. Powerful natives living inland, such as Caribs and Akawaios, agreed to fight to obtain guns and trading goods, to protect their most-favored trading status, and to prevent the settlement of Maroons who competed for natural resources and indigenous women.[29] Local Amerindians joined the Dutch to revenge themselves on rebels who had attacked their villages or killed family members. Yet all Amerindians cooperated with the colonists on their own terms. They came and went as they pleased, and they refused to fight when they felt mistreated or when they judged the risks too high. Even those local Amerindians who were most dependent on the Dutch retained enough autonomy to refuse assignments they deemed too dangerous. In the months to come, colonial governors, postholders, and intermediaries would do all they could to press native allies into service.

Had colonial neighbors of all stripes not come to colonial Berbice's rescue within weeks of the rebellion's start, the colony would have disappeared, sinking into the jungle like a tropical Atlantis. If it had been reborn as an independent entity, Governor Coffij might have preempted Haiti's leader Toussaint Louverture as the first black liberator to defeat colonial powers. Instead, Coffij and his followers, like the Dutch, struggled with shortages of key resources. They faced the constant need to get their hands on supplies and additional supporters for their cause. Lacking the long Atlantic reach of early modern European capitalists, the rebels had to resort to different measures to sustain themselves.

6

Expanding the Revolution

On the morning of April 3, 1763, the day after the rebel attack on Dageraad, two Amerindians paddled their canoe briskly downriver toward the plantation that had become the precarious stronghold of the Dutch. Within hours they had covered the fifteen miles from the rebel headquarters at Vigilantie to Dageraad. They carried important cargo, a European prisoner of war named Jan Abraham Charbon, who had a message from the rebels.

Charbon had a harrowing tale to tell. When he first got wind of the uprising, he had fled to plantation Peereboom with his neighbor Christian Mittelholtzer. During the massacre there, he was wounded, his back and chest peppered with shot. Despite his injuries, Charbon had saved himself by swimming across the Berbice to the opposite shore, where he stumbled upon Mittelholtzer. The two men wandered the savannas and woods for days, hungry and thirsty but too afraid to seek food and water at a plantation. By week's end, hunger overcame fear. As they crammed their mouths with corn in a plantation garden, rebels found them. The men dove onto their bellies in the field but Mittelholtzer was discovered. Wielding his saber, he severed the hand of one of his assailants, and he briefly chased away the others with his gun. But Mittelholtzer could not save himself for long; from under a bush, Charbon heard his friend's "pitiful screaming."[1]

Now alone, Charbon hid out on two different plantations, where self-emancipated people fed him. After five days, he was captured and taken to rebel headquarters on plantation Hollandia & Zeelandia.

There he joined three other European captives, two men and one woman, in a disciplinary device known as "the stocks," once used on slaves and now turned on their erstwhile masters. The four endured daily whippings, and eventually two were executed. Over the next few weeks, several more Europeans were beheaded, always at the water's edge, perhaps so the bodies could be pushed into the river, saving the labor of digging graves and intimidating any non-rebels downstream. Others were kept alive, among them, as mentioned, Georgina, daughter of council member Johan George. She was installed as Coffij's "wife." Her little sister and another girl were spared to attend her.

Charbon spent his days alternating between fearing death and hoping that he would be reprieved to serve as the rebels' clerk. One day, he was told that Governor Coffij wanted him to take a message to the Dutch. Charbon was given a set of clothes, some gold coin, and a silver pocket watch. Putting little trust in European promises, Coffij made Charbon solemnly swear "in the manner of the negroes" that he would return with the governor's answer. Accompanying the two Indians in their canoe, he reached Governor van Hoogenheim's headquarters on April 3, 1763. "You may easily apprehend," Charbon later wrote to friends with considerable understatement, "how happy I was to be thus delivered of them."[2]

The young man conveyed a note from the rebels, along with an oral message.

Rebellion into Revolution

The note from the rebels, and the additional information proffered by Charbon, had a tone that was at once assertive and conciliatory, and betrayed tactical disagreements among the insurgents. As they had done in their first communications in early March, the rebels justified their actions. They reiterated that they were willing to fight but now added that they would rather negotiate. Van Hoogenheim mentions only one letter in his daily journal, but when he met with the council he showed them two. One was signed by Charbon as clerk. The other one was not signed, and it is not clear who brought it or when.[3]

Copies of the rebel letters, but unfortunately not the originals, are in the National Archive in The Hague in several slightly different versions. They are difficult to understand because neither syntax nor spelling is in standard Dutch. Yet their general meaning seems clear, especially when combined with the governor's insights based on what he learned from the envoys, who had likely been told by Coffij what to say.[4]

As in their previous messages the rebels sought to explain themselves. "Coffij Governor of the *Neegers van de Berbice*" and "Captain Accara," the note brought by Charbon read, assured "your right honorable governor of the colony Berbice" that they had been forced into rebellion by mistreatment and brutality. They singled out, again, the abusive behavior of specific plantation owners and managers who were the "ultimate culprits of all the evil that has happened in Berbice." The attack on Dageraad on April 2 had happened, according to the note and the oral message, without Governor Coffij's knowledge or approval, and it had made him "very angry." The rebels wanted to negotiate, but they emphasized that if the Europeans wanted war, they would fight for their freedom "so long as there is a Christian in Berbice."[5]

They then offered a radical proposal to divide the colony in two. The rebels would take the upper half, returning the lower half to the Dutch. In the first note they suggested the Dutch had to buy part of Berbice. In the second, they offered to "give" the Dutch the lower half. Leaving no doubt about their political aims, they warned in a bold declaration of self-emancipation that the Dutch "should not think that the *neegers* will be slaves." They added to the governor, however, that "the blacks you have on the ships can be your slaves."[6] Did Coffij and Accara mean to suggest that while they intended to be free, they would accept the continued existence of slavery in the Dutch half of Berbice? Or was this a dig at African-descended people who had not joined the rebellion but had chosen to remain with their oppressors? Inverting the usual colonial power relationships in which slaves were the supplicants, they closed by inviting "your honor" to come talk to them in person.[7]

Coffij was not the first self-liberated man to engage in negotiations with his colonial enemies. While there are few letters directly from slave rebels, formal peace negotiations between Maroons (formerly enslaved people living in independent communities) and colonial authorities were not uncommon. Starting in New Spain in 1609, there are examples of peace treaties in Colombia, Brazil, Mexico, Jamaica, Cuba, Suriname, and elsewhere. In exchange for recognition of their freedom, settlement in the hinterlands, and necessary European goods, Maroons agreed to refrain from attacking plantations for supplies and additional recruits. They usually obligated themselves to return fugitives who sought to join them and to hunt down escaped slaves. Some also promised to help fend off foreign attacks. Coffij may have heard, through the transcolonial slave grapevine, about the well-known treaties between the British and Maroons in Jamaica in 1739 and 1740.[8] No doubt he knew about the negotiations in Suriname that resulted in treaties, modeled on those in Jamaica, between the colonial government and the Okanisi or Ndyuka Maroons in 1760 and with the Samaaka as recently as 1762.[9]

But Coffij was proposing an agreement on a much grander scale. He initiated the negotiations, not the colonial authorities, and he approached Van Hoogenheim as one head of state to another. His proposal to divide the colony in half was unprecedented. Coffij did not offer to retreat with his people to villages in the jungle. Rather, he suggested living alongside the Dutch as equals, as one nation next to another. Did he and his men intend to exploit the plantations in order to trade sugar with the Dutch or other Europeans, as Amina rebels had planned on St. John in the 1730s? If so, they would obviously need access through Dutch territory to the sea. Reportedly Coffij told Charbon that he wanted "free trade" with any ships that called on the colony. This suggests that he was not after freedom and subsistence in Maroon fashion, but had in mind capitalist-style production and trade. He also reportedly intended to exchange plantation products from his half of the colony for salted meat and bacon from the Dutch governor. No record remains in which the colonists discuss their reaction to the proposal, but they must have been aghast, as many Europeans and

Americans would be forty years later at the establishment of Haiti, the first black independent republic in the Atlantic world.[10]

The offer to negotiate nevertheless created a welcome opening for the Dutch. They decided to start a correspondence "to buy time and lull the rebels." Much was at stake. The attack on Dageraad had exposed the vulnerability of the colonists, and it was hardly certain they could withstand another rebel assault. Stringing the rebels along through diplomacy bought the Dutch time that proved essential to their survival.[11]

Correspondence

Purposely imitating the insurgents' writing style, the council composed a patronizing letter in Dutch that asked many questions and, the colonial governor noted, "contained nothing essential."[12] Van Hoogenheim sounds like a minister berating his parishioners, or, even more, a father chastising his children. Pointedly addressing the rebel leaders, not as Governor and Captain, but condescendingly as "*Negers* Koffij en Accara," the letter explained that Charbon was ill and could not keep his promise to return. "We don't quite understand your letter," the Dutch asserted. What did the rebels mean by "half the Berbice for you and half for His Lordship the governor?" "Why are you so cruel and angry," they asked, "killing so many good Christians who never hurt you?" Did Coffij and Accara not know there was a God who sees everything and punishes all evil? Surely they knew the Dutch governor was a good man who would discipline all bad Christians, so why had they not come to talk to him the previous day, before they attacked? Why had they come to fight? The rebels should prove their good intentions by writing back to explain whether they "know who God is, and that he punishes all evil in his time," so the governor and councilmen would know that the rebels could be trusted.[13] Coffij and Accara could use the two Amerindian messengers who brought this letter to send a response.

The Amerindians set off immediately, late on April 3, paddling the letter upstream to the rebels within several hours.

The very next day, the Amerindians returned downriver, carrying the surprisingly deferential and conciliatory reply from the rebels. Now calling themselves merely *"Neger* Cofi and acarra,"* as the Dutch had addressed them, the two men repeated their invitation for the governor to come negotiate in person. They assured him that they knew who God was and they pointed out that the nonviolent act of writing letters provided proof of their good intentions. They suggested that Accara had attacked the Dageraad plantation because the rebels had been told by hostages that the Dutch were "expecting them"—in other words, that the Dutch had been spoiling for a fight. Coffij had been upriver "with his people" (probably at Fort Nassau) when he heard of the attack. It had deeply angered him, implying that the offensive had happened against his orders. Neither he nor Accara, Coffij assured the Dutch, harbored any "bad intentions." As a sign of diplomatic goodwill, he sent along a pair of golden shoe buckles as a present for Van Hoogenheim. Such gestures were common, too, in Suriname, where both Maroons and colonial authorities sent along gifts with their proposals for peace. The same practice occurred in West Africa.[14]

The Amerindians relayed an oral message as well. Coffij was deeply sorry, he stressed, turning the blame away from his own people, that the governor had to suffer because a number of evil planters had badly abused their slaves. Black people loved the governor, he assured Van Hoogenheim, and did not wish to harm him. The Dutchman was not convinced, however. He noted in his journal that clearly, no matter how Coffij might feel, the people under him remain "deeply bitter, and persist in their design to attack and exterminate us."[15]

In his next reply to the rebels, on April 5, Van Hoogenheim reiterated that he was confused about what the insurgents wanted, inviting further explanation. He requested that they return a Dutch helmsman held hostage as a gesture of goodwill. This was an odd request, as the Dutch had just the previous day heard that the rebels had executed the man. Was Van Hoogenheim trying to point out that the rebels were still killing Dutchmen? He acknowledged the gift the rebel leaders had sent him. But he went on to explain that he could not accept it until he was convinced that they were "good friends, who would hurt no one, and could be trusted." [16] He received no answer to his missive. For now, the back-and-forth correspondence came to a halt.

The Dageraad attack on April 2 had been carried out by Captain Accara and signaled that the military leader, an African, and his African soldiers were less enthusiastic about negotiating than the highly creolized Coffij. No documents explain why this would be so. It seems likely that Accara trusted more in the military prowess of his men than the goodwill of the Dutch. Africans likely were more mistrustful of Europeans than were Creoles, who had lived among the Europeans much longer. Moreover, Africans may have been suspicious of letters many could not read, in a language they may not have understood. An example from neighboring Suriname may be illustrative. There, a Maroon charged with writing a letter to the authorities in the 1750s was closely watched by his fellow leaders, who crowded around him as he wrote. The man became so nervous that his hand trembled, causing both his penmanship and the letter itself to turn out, he apologized to his correspondents, "badly and confused." [17]

Accara and his men may also have feared that treaties endangered their independence. Some Maroons in Suriname initially rejected peace proposals "because," they explained, they "needed many tools to work their land, and other things, which they obtained by attacking plantations, which they could no longer do once there was peace with the whites." They would then "have to do without, unless the whites gave them what they needed," a dependency they adamantly rejected, at least at first.[18] Or, as likely, Coffij and Accara had decided on a more subversive, two-pronged, strategy: negotiation furthered by military action, as was common among European generals and West Africans such as the Asante.[19]

Canje River

While the rebels engaged in diplomacy with Van Hoogenheim, and even before, they also reached out beyond Berbice to their neighbors. Like the Dutch, they, too, needed shoring up—more food, weapons, and soldiers. But the rebels could not just call on existing allies, as the

Dutch could; they had to create them, either through liberation or by force. Within the first week of their revolt, they may have sent emissaries westward to Demerara, allegedly warning the enslaved there that "those that will not join them they will cut off."[20] If that information is correct, the arrival in that colony of the ships from Barbados may have altered such plans, as there are no reports of Berbice rebels operating in Demerara.[21] The Barbadian soldiers also helped quell any slave unrest in Demerara. A better option for supplies and reinforcements presented itself among the self-liberated people on plantations along the Canje River, a tributary of the Berbice River, that had been abandoned by frightened Europeans.

Sometime in the second half of March, Coffij and Accara had reportedly sent organizers eastward to the Canje River, to encourage people there to "pursue the Christians to the coast." By then, most Europeans and Indians had deserted the Canje River, the militia captain in the lead. Some planters managed to take along a portion of their goods and slaves; others armed their bonded workers and left them behind, effectively leaving the river, and some fifty plantations, in the hands of local black inhabitants. While some of them remained quietly on their plantations, or took shelter in the woods, others organized.[22]

Most likely before the April 2 attack on Dageraad, and certainly thereafter, Coffij and Accara decided to strengthen their hand by incorporating Canje's people and resources into their rebellion, if necessary by force. They put Berbice rebel Fortuin van Helvetia in charge of the Canje River campaign. When the uprising began, the manager of plantation Helvetia had armed several trusted male slaves and fled to a nearby plantation, only to be killed and decapitated.[23] Several men and women on Helvetia, meanwhile, eagerly joined the rebellion, including those entrusted with guns. Among them was Fortuin, a married man who identified himself as "Timmine," suggesting he was a first-generation African, perhaps a Temne from Sierra Leone, or the adjacent "Upper Guinea" coast.[24]

Fortuin had proved his loyalty to the rebellion when he delivered the head of a European planter to Governor Coffij. He was made captain in the rebel forces and given a Creole boy, Marquis van Helvetia, to carry his ammunition. Captain Fortuin scoured his neighborhood, confiscating guns, drumming up support for the rebellion, and urging men to behead their masters. To reward him for his efforts, Coffij put him in charge of plantation Vigilantie, near Dageraad, where he fired on the Dutch ships as they passed by on their flight to the coast in early March. Impressed by his courage and commitment, Coffij promoted him again. Within weeks, Captain Fortuin was sent to Canje with a group of soldiers. He quickly proclaimed himself "governor of the Canje." Dressed distinctively in blue, he placed an eye-catching "red plume and a red cockade" on his hat. With that exquisite feather, Fortuin appropriated political power in the ways that kings and clerics did in Europe and Africa, signifying his new authority and command. Among Gold Coast people, a red feather was reportedly associated with war and leadership, as the color red was elsewhere in West Africa, including Senegambia and Sierra Leone. Fortuin also took three additional wives as a sign of his new status, casting aside his pre-rebellion wife, Lisette—at least for the time being[25]

Fortuin did not run the Canje campaign alone. Post-rebellion, when the Dutch questioned Canje people, they repeatedly brought up the names of two prominent Berbice men: Adou van Schirmeister and Accara van de Brandwacht. Adou had been a *bomba* on two plantations near Helvetia, owned by Christopher Schirmeister, a councilman. Adou led the rebellion on his plantation. There is no firsthand testimony from him; he died before he could be questioned. His funeral was reportedly a grand affair. One of his plantation mates, Fortuin, claimed to have deserted the rebels when he realized that he was expected to accompany Adou in the grave.[26] Killing dead leaders' servants and close associates so they could travel with them into the next world was a common practice in West Africa.

The other powerful figure named by slaves, Accara van de Brandwacht, would play an ominous role in the rebellion. Accara was evidently a *tovenaar*, in Dutch parlance, or *wisiman*, as witches and poisoners were known among Suriname slaves. Unlike obeah men and women, who employed their knowledge of plants and spirits for the greater good, *wisimen*'s aim was "sinister." Accara had initially been an elite "forts neger," employed since at least 1750 by the Company at Fort Nassau. But within a few years he was banned to the isolated, newly built signal station Brandwacht near the coast in response to the many complaints from his fellow fort slaves about his *tovenarij*, or sorcery. A few years later still, he was accused of killing a number of Africans and Indians, including several children, with poisoned bananas. A father of one of the children, "Mulat Frederik," an enslaved smith at the fort, would subsequently support the Dutch in the rebellion, serving as interpreter and guide to commando units of soldiers and Amerindians.[27]

Commanders Fortuin, Adou, and Accara brokered the rebel takeover of the Canje River, where Fortuin turned plantation Stevensburg into his headquarters. Located high up the river, Stevensburg was well situated. At the back, a creek ran to Horstenburg, just a few estates over, where the only route from the Canje to Fort Nassau began. In the dry seasons, it took only three hours to walk to the Berbice River. Fortuin put an advance post on Horstenburg to guard the trail.[28]

From their headquarters on Stevensburg, Fortuin's men made forays up and down the Canje River, proceeding much as they had during the initial rebellion on the Berbice River. They raided plantations for food, supplies, weapons, and recruits. When they came across coffee, cacao, or cotton stored for transportation, they cut open the carefully packed bales and barrels, burning their hated contents, or dumping the valuable products into the river. People who offered opposition, wanting to retain their independence or their former masters' goods and food for themselves, were quickly neutralized by the rebels. Uncooperative *bombas* were killed or tied up and taken away.[29] Some people were forcibly relocated to Canje plantations upriver where the rebels consolidated their forces, or to plantations turned rebel camps on the Berbice, to grow food, haul water, and cut firewood. Those who hid in the bush ran the risk of finding their houses in ashes upon their return, making it hard for them to stay on their plantations.[30]

Take plantation Sophiasburg. Its people claimed after the rebellion that they had fled their homes under duress. Rebels whom they alternately identified as "the Amina," the "bad *neegers*," or "the Berbice *neegers"* had tied them up and moved them to two plantations high on the Berbice River, where they worked in the gardens under a rebel overseer they called "Alla or *heer."* A few detailed their ordeals to the Dutch at the end of the rebellion. Africa-born Simba related how during the fight over her plantation, the "Amina" had killed her baby Jantje as she clutched him in her arms. Her breast, she pointed out, still showed the cutlass mark. La Haije, also pointing to his scar, claimed he had been sold to a rebel captain who slashed his arm when he did not work hard enough. Husband and wife Sam and Adriaantje and their toddler ended up hiding in the woods along with former slaves from a Company plantation, occasionally dodging rebels.[31]

A few people told more ambiguous stories. After rebels took him to Fort Nassau on the Berbice River, Cacauw explained, he "became Coffij's drummer but ran away from him." Flip, a Creole, related that he had been separated from the others and forced to make weirs and catch fish for the rebels. When the examiners pressed him on whether he had not served as a guide to Accara van de Brandwacht on local trails, Flip claimed, plausibly, that he had been forced "on pain of death." When the examiners questioned his possible participation in several military engagements, he vehemently denied having fought, claiming "they never trusted him with a *snaphaan* [gun] because he was a Creole." Flip was not punished, which means either that the Dutch believed him or that no one testified against him. Nor were any other Sophiasburg people convicted of rebellion.[32]

It is possible, of course, that Sophiasburg's workers coordinated their coercion narratives to deny their support of the rebellion. Arguing that "one had no choice" is a well-worn defense. But it seems equally likely, as we also saw on the Berbice River, that many labored against their will. They cooperated when they had no alternative, or perhaps, like Flip or Cacauw, they joined for a spell when it seemed opportune. Men who were fingered by others as bona fide rebels used the same defense, suggesting that precisely because everyone knew choice was limited, coercion made for a plausible story. And we do have the testimony of one Canje slave, Mars van La Providence, who

View of Coffee Plantation Leeverpoel Suriname, ca. 1700–1800. Detail, pontoon boat with barrels of coffee. (Rijksmuseum, Amsterdam.)

liberally denounced many in his examination, yet made no charges against people from Sophiasburg; in fact, he claimed specifically that no one from that plantation was involved.[33]

In contrast, others joined with enthusiasm. Quadia van Stevensburg made his way to the Berbice River as soon as he heard about the uprising. He was eager to join Atta van Altenklingen, whom he called his brother, perhaps suggesting that they had been captives on the same slave ship. Atta promoted Quadia right away. On the whole, however, few men from Canje seem to have occupied leadership positions in the rebellion, suggesting that the original leaders from the Berbice incorporated Canje people largely on a subordinate basis.[34]

Recruits

The Berbice insurgents fortified their ranks with Canje recruits. Some people became workers among the rebels. Others, set to soldiering, were brought to plantation Stevensburg, where they were turned into fighters. Fortuin van Helvetia and Accara van de Brandwacht handed out arms and conducted initiation ceremonies to call on their gods, reduce animosity, and create new social bonds. They swore a blood oath, common among conspirators, which linked the men in an insoluble and sacred political pact. Fortuin and Accara prepared cups of rum or water with, as some recruits later related, "something black in the bottom," probably soil. To this they added drops of blood taken from each of the Berbice rebels and the new Canje recruits and made everyone drink, vowing to stand together "to fight the Christians and kill them." The oath put the men under a sentence of death if they defected to the Dutch or betrayed one another.[35]

The new soldiers had a chance to prove themselves right away. Governor van Hoogenheim had dispatched twenty-five Suriname soldiers and five European burghers to take command of strategically placed plantation Stevensburg, high up the Canje River (unaware it had become Fortuin's training camp). The men never made it that far into enemy territory, choosing instead to post themselves on Frederiksburg, one of two remaining Dutch strongholds on the Canje.[36] Eager to rid the Canje River of Europeans, Fortuin and his associates launched a surprise attack on Frederiksburg in the early afternoon of April 6, just days after Coffij had sent prisoner of war Charbon to Dageraad with an offer of negotiation. Perhaps Fortuin acted without authorization, or, more likely, Coffij was strengthening his hand on the Canje at the very same time that he was negotiating for a possible peace on the Berbice. As they had done in the Dageraad assault, the rebels attacked Frederiksburg overland from three different angles. Three times the insurgents retreated, regrouped, and came back in greater numbers, or so it seemed to the outnumbered Dutch.

After almost four hours of heavy firing on both sides, everyone's guns began to fail from overuse. But by then, with nightfall nearing, Frederiksburg was "in full flame" and the rebels forced the Dutch to abandon the outpost. The Europeans retreated to Fort St. Andries at the confluence of the Canje and Berbice Rivers, leaving behind the corpses of three of their soldiers. Several weeks later an Indian patrol sent out by the Dutch found one of the dead men's heads on a stake at the water's edge—an imitation of Dutch practice and a bold marker of rebel authority.[37] The Dutch also suffered seven wounded, several of whom subsequently died of their injuries.

The Dutch commander at Frederiksburg concluded that rebels on the Canje and Berbice had united; he estimated that his attackers had added up to "circa 400 blacks, all well armed." Even if we allow for exaggeration on the part of a man badly beaten, this was a large force, though it seems unlikely that all rebels had arms. Many carried fake

A Rebel Negro armed & on his guard.

Rebel armed with musket, bandolier for ammunition, and hatchet, 1794, engraving after John Gabriel Stedman. (John Carter Brown Library, Providence.)

guns, made of table legs, with leather straps over their shoulders. Dutch soldiers identified the rebel commander as a "mulatto, tall and corpulent, dressed in blue with a red plume and red cockade on his hat." There is no way to know how many casualties the rebels sustained. The Dutch commander reported that he believed, again no doubt exaggerating, that the rebels had suffered twenty-five to thirty dead, though he admitted he could not be certain "because it is their habit to drag off their dead right away." Fortuin himself, it was later established, sustained a wound: he lost a thumb to a malfunctioning gun.[38]

By the end of April, the rebels had full control of the Canje River, cutting off Dutch communication overland between Berbice and Suriname. As on the Berbice River, the revolutionaries concentrated their forces upriver, where most plantations were located, abandoning the lower river. While they destroyed many estates, they left others intact. Van Hoogenheim was reduced to stationing a few men on a plantation near the coast, to protect access to drinking water for the soldiers posted at Fort St. Andries, where there was none. Also, they could sound the alarm, should any rebels show themselves downriver. If Governor van Hoogenheim had obtained reinforcements and new supplies through his long Atlantic reach and the ready-made alliances among European colonists, Governor Coffij had done so by virtue of his wits. The issue now became whether the rebel leader could turn this advantage into victory.[39]

7

Stalemate

After the Dageraad attack in early April 1763, the Europeans struggled to get their bearings. With the Canje River in rebel hands, most Indians gone, and the Europeans barely able to defend themselves, the Suriname officers gloomily predicted "little glory" for their mission in Berbice. The Dutch could do little more than send enslaved men and native scouts to spy on the nearby rebel camp Vigilantie. Tracks around Dageraad suggested that the insurgents similarly kept a sharp eye on their adversaries. Two of the ships, including the slaver that had transported the Dutch to Dageraad, set sail for Holland. As the ships' cannons had provided protection, their leaving increased the plantation's vulnerability.[1]

Disease worsened the situation. By mid-April, as the seasonal rains began, European soldiers and sailors sickened. Most suffered from unspecified wasting fevers. These likely included yellow fever and malaria, initially brought to the Americas by slave ships, and spread by female *Aedes aegypti* mosquitoes, plentiful then as now in tropical areas around the equator. Newcomers from Europe had no immunity to such diseases, while people who had survived yellow fever as children, either in West Africa or on the Wild Coast, were immune. By the end of the month the soldiers were dying. As one Scottish officer wrote home, "This is a most terrible Climate, few moments are there betwixt the most perfect health, & non-Existence of which we have had but too many proofs."[2]

The torrential rains hatched large numbers of mosquito eggs, releasing swarms of loudly buzzing insects aptly nicknamed "Devils Trumpeters" in neighboring Suriname. One Scottish officer in Suriname explained the pesty insects were "so very thick . . . that by Clapping my two hands against each other I have kill'd in one Stroke to the number of 38 upon my honour." Other servicemen suffered from *rode loop* ("bloody flux"), or dysentery, a highly contagious disease characterized by uncontrollable diarrhea mixed with blood. It spread through contaminated feces when latrines were located too close to provisioning gardens or near the river's edge where people drew their drinking water.[3]

European newcomers' crippling vulnerability to tropical fevers was not the only challenge. Dutch officials increased Van Hoogenheim's burdens by quarreling, complaining, and boozing. Food supplies ran low. Several important enslaved men deserted, including one named Otto. As the personal valet of Suriname commander Bernard Texier, Otto had accumulated valuable intelligence. The Dutch feared he joined the rebels, no doubt sharing all he knew.[4]

Worst of all, another attack seemed imminent—one the Dutch were not likely to withstand. Given this precarious situation, the Dutch governor saw only one option.

Negotiations

Hoping to stave off an attack, Van Hoogenheim reopened negotiations. He sent two "faithful" Company slaves, carpenter Christiaan and bricklayer Pieter, upriver in a canoe in early May with a message "for the chieftains of the rebels." The note asked why they had not responded to Van Hoogenheim's last letter. Perhaps the two Amerindians had failed to deliver it? Van Hoogenheim reiterated that he bore "the blacks" no ill will, proven by the fact that he had not mounted an expedition with his Suriname reinforcements. Still probing to understand the rebels' presumption of equality and power, he asked again what they meant about dividing the colony in half.[5]

Pieter returned the next night with an enslaved indigenous man, but without Christiaan, who was held hostage. Pieter brought an oral message. The rebels were very pleased with Van Hoogenheim's letter. Indeed, the Amerindians had never delivered his last letter in early April. Assuming from the lack of a response at that time that the Dutch wanted war, not negotiation, the rebels planned to attack Dageraad. Now they renewed their invitation for unarmed talks on plantation Vigilantie.[6]

As instructed, Pieter had made careful observations while among the rebels, and he had much to report. He and Christiaan had been locked in the "trunk," outside at Fort Nassau, before Coffij decided to send him back while keeping Christiaan hostage. The majority of rebels were stationed near the fort, now their headquarters, and they appeared well armed. Coffij lodged in the former *secretarij* (clerk's office) of the town hall, one of the few stone buildings in New Amsterdam, which he had fortified with two cannons in the grand entranceway. His office was well guarded. The rest of the town's twenty or so houses, Pieter related, were "overflowing" with people.[7] Sentinels kept a close watch, and daily patrols spied on the Dutch.

Plantation Vigilantie had been downgraded to an advance post with two hundred fighters and a battery of four cannons at the river's edge. A rebel leader named Prins was on his way to neighboring Demerara with two hundred men, to capture weapons and supplies and spread the revolution. Like Captain Fortuin of the Canje campaign, Prins hailed from plantation Helvetia, where he had been a *bomba*. Prins was evidently literate, as it was he, Pieter divulged, who had so far penned most of the letters to the Dutch. The rebels spoke of Van Hoogenheim with "love and respect," Pieter assured the governor, but they continued to express hatred toward certain planters and officials whom they intended to murder if they had the chance. Based on what he had overheard, Pieter was sure the insurgents planned another attack. It would come soon and the rebels seemed confident of their success. Several had inquired where the governor slept. Pieter urged Van Hoogenheim to bunk on the ships from now on, as he was sure the rebels meant to capture him as leverage in the negotiations. Pieter confirmed that Otto, Captain Texier's servant, was at the fort, as feared.[8]

Pieter's alarming information about the rebels came at a time of mixed news for the Dutch. At the end of April, a Surinamese bark with supplies and weapons for the Corentyne Post, a military station on the border between Berbice and Suriname, shipwrecked, drowning ten of the fourteen men aboard. But the Dutch had also learned that in late April a coalition of Carib, Arawak, and Warao Indians had attacked the camp of the Magdalenenburg Canje rebels high on the Corentyne River. This skirmish had considerably weakened the group of eighty-three men, women, and children. The rebel survivors had escaped in the dense jungle carrying along their wounded but leaving behind twenty dead. To pay themselves for their services, the Indians plundered the rebel camp, carrying off the loot that rebels had taken from plantation Magdalenenburg and the Corentyne trading post. The Suriname postholder demanded that the Indians return this booty, but Governor Crommelin hastily ordered him to let them have it for their encouragement.[9]

Most welcome was word in early May that two armed vessels with a total of 146 soldiers from the Dutch Caribbean island of St. Eustatius had arrived at Fort Andries. Indeed, as soon as they heard about their arrival, Van Hoogenheim and his councilors considered an offensive expedition against the rebels with the fresh troops. But Suriname commanders Van Rijssel and Texier, veterans of anti-Maroon missions in their own colony, discouraged them. While an expedition might drive off the rebels, they explained, the insurgents would retreat upriver, moving from plantation to plantation along the way, reducing everything to ashes. Moreover, the retreating rebels would no doubt take with them by force all blacks "who might otherwise be willing to return" to the Dutch, as it was understood that "many of them must stay with the rebels under duress." The enemy would then settle high upriver in the jungle, where they would attract new fugitives and could not be defeated. Better to wait until Indians, hopefully soon, cut off all escape routes. With native allies securing the colony's borders, the Dutch could then strike at Fort Nassau, the heart of the uprising.[10]

After discussion, the governor and council decided to follow the Suriname commanders' advice to abstain from any offensive action in the short term. Instead, Van Hoogenheim prepared to secure Dageraad. He persuaded the council to agree to establish "premiums," or bounties, to motivate the sailors and soldiers: 50 guilders for every "rebellious black" caught alive and 20 for a dead rebel's severed right hand. Adults found quietly living on plantations "or otherwise in hiding and who don't resist capture or show hostility" would be worth 10 guilders, and each child 2½. Top money was reserved for the two rebel leaders. The Dutch offered 500 guilders for catching the "*Neger* Coffij, who has elevated himself to governor," and 400 guilders for Accara. Any treasure recovered from the rebels, whether gold, silver, jewelry, apparel, household goods, or weapons, would have to be turned in to pay for the premiums. The Dutch in Berbice were not the only Europeans at this time to pay bounties to soldiers. During the Seven Years' War, provincial legislators in North America, along with a few British commanders, offered prize money to their soldiers for indigenous captives or scalps.[11]

As he prepared for a likely attack, Van Hoogenheim continued the correspondence with his opponents. He sent the Amerindian messenger back to the rebels with a misleading letter intended to string along his opponents once more. He chided them for keeping his messenger Christiaan, asking how he could trust them "because if you treat thus the blacks whom the Honorable Governor sends you, perhaps you will treat the Honorable Governor worse?" He invited Coffij and Accara to Dageraad, "because you know that the Honorable Governor is a kind man, who has done the blacks no harm." At the very least, they should clearly spell out in a letter what they wanted, he urged. He still could not understand in practical terms what they meant by "half the Berbice for them and half for the governor." His letter was proof, he asserted, that the Dutch did not seek war, so if the rebels similarly wanted to avoid fighting, they should send Christiaan back with a letter of their own or send representatives to talk to the governor in person. Van Hoogenheim also requested the return of his favorite horse, now in rebel hands, as well as Suriname *neeger* Otto. No harm would come to those who would deliver them. The Dutch requested an immediate response. None came for five days.[12]

Gearing Up

On May 9, a letter from Coffij and Accara finally arrived. It was short, likely reflecting growing exasperation and increasing skepticism about Dutch sincerity. Perhaps it also represented a last-ditch effort to avert violence on Coffij's part, even as Accara was preparing for military action. The two leaders again issued what Van Hoogenheim in his journal described as a "friendly invitation" to visit them at camp Vigilantie, where they would meet him unarmed. They ignored most of the questions and requests in the governor's letter, rightly perceiving them as diversions. With regard to Christiaan, they explained that they had kept him as a substitute for Charbon, who had promised to return but had failed to do so. They pointedly asked why, if the Dutch did not want war, they had "invited the English and the Carib" to join them. Their question indicated that they knew of efforts to mobilize Amerindians in Demerara and of the arrival there of British troops from Barbados. This intelligence had been gained either through their own spies or, more likely, through Otto. Coffij and Accara reiterated their proud and defiant emancipation proclamation, made in previous letters: "if the governor wants part of Berbice, you'll get it if you come to Vigilantie, but you'll have to get new slaves, because we are free."[13]

The two natives who delivered the note brought other news. Prins van Helvetia was said to have abandoned his mission to Demerara "because of bad roads." That made sense given that it was the rainy season. Perhaps, too, the rebel leader had been scared off by word of Demerara's defensive measures and the recent arrival of troops from Barbados. Regardless, Prins's lack of success meant that the rebels, at least for now, were unable to obtain new supplies or recruits from Demerara. More important, the two messengers confirmed prior accounts of discord among the insurgents, reporting that "Coffij and Accara had repeatedly been at loggerheads" and that Coffij was "good" (i.e., well intentioned) "but Accara very angry."[14] Such intelligence suggested that disagreements over strategy—whether to seek a political solution, as Coffij appeared to favor, or a military one, as Accara advocated—continued to divide the rebels.

The latest information heightened Dutch fears, so they stepped up their defensive preparations, all the while continuing their dialogue with the rebels in a bid to buy time. Charbon was ill, they explained in their response, and had wished to leave for Holland. He was a free man so the governor could not prevent him from departing. The Dutch would not trust the rebels as long as they held messengers hostage, so the rebels should return Christiaan. If they did, perhaps Van Hoogenheim would visit Vigilantie with the Suriname commander Texier, who was a decent man and would not hurt them as long as their intentions proved good. Van Hoogenheim had not sent for the English and the Caribs because he was angry, but because he thought the rebels were, and wanted to kill him. But if the rebels did not seek war, the governor would in turn not hurt "good blacks."[15] This letter received no response.

War

For the rebels, the moment for diplomacy had passed. Few sources help us understand how or why Coffij and Accara decided to abandon negotiations and trust once more to force, although letters like the last one they received likely convinced them of Dutch duplicity. And perhaps Accara, seeing Coffij fail at diplomacy, could no longer restrain the men under his command, who, like himself, placed more confidence in their own weapons than in Dutch words. Then, too, the rebels knew about the arrival of the armed ships from St. Eustatius, now anchored in front of Dageraad. No doubt Coffij and Accara hoped to defeat the Dutch before they received yet more reinforcements. There is some indication that they aimed to take over one of the ships, to gain the military advantage of shipboard artillery.[16]

Still, the leaders faced a major decision. After all, launching an attack no doubt would cost the rebels dearly in men and ammunition. They did have reason for guarded optimism: they had gained new recruits from the Canje River, and as the Dutch on the Berbice were as yet unaware, Berbician rebels (likely Fortuin's men) had reached the upper Corentyne River, on the border with Suriname. They had reportedly scared off Caribs and other Indians, disrupting plans for those allies to come to aid the Dutch. Ammunition stockpiles remained a sticking point. Prins's aborted mission to Demerara had represented a major setback in that regard.[17] Nevertheless, on balance, Coffij and Accara must have surmised that the time had come for one gigantic push to defeat the Dutch once and for all before their opponent gained further strength. "Scrap[ing] all their ammunition together," they assembled their men on Vigilantie. From there, advance forces cut a path to Dageraad, two hours' paddling away.[18]

On Friday, May 13, a little more than a month after beginning negotiations, the rebels were ready for war. They advanced on Dageraad early in the morning. Some came on foot along the freshly cut path; others paddled in canoes and tent boats, which they pulled ashore about an hour away from Dageraad, drumming and cheering loudly as they advanced on foot.

At the start of the battle, the rebels held the advantage. Three large groups, estimated by the frightened Dutch at five hundred to six hundred strong, took position in the woods surrounding Dageraad. Over the course of several hours, the fighters advanced to the plantation's buildings, despite steady fire from the besieged Europeans. The attackers burned to the ground the expensive new water mill, so recently finished. Surrounded and outnumbered, the Dutch found themselves in dire straits. But they still had one crucial advantage: cannons. As the rebels left the cover of the trees and approached the buildings, they became targets for the artillery, set up to protect the perimeter of the plantation. Meanwhile, the three ships anchored in front of Dageraad kept up a steady barrage of shelling, unmolested. Time and again, the rebels surged forward, met with cannon fire, and were forced back to the forest.[19]

By early afternoon, the rebels had sustained serious losses and were probably running out of ammunition. Realizing they were no match for cannons, they retreated. Around two thirty p.m., a Dutch force of some eighty men, most of them from St. Eustatius, took off in pursuit. Van Hoogenheim figured the rebels would flee by water and ordered the ship *Zeven Provintien* to sail upriver to destroy their boats. When they saw the ship set sail, rebel warriors, fearing they would be cut off, raced back to their canoes. Not all of them managed to paddle away safely. Slack wind and an outgoing tide foiled the perfect execution of Van Hoogenheim's plan, but the ship got close enough for its sailors to bombard several canoes and larger boats "overflowing with goods and blacks," as the Dutch put it, forcing their occupants to save themselves by swimming in the river's piranha-infested waters.[20]

It is unclear how many casualties the insurgents sustained. As always, they carried off their dead and wounded. They left just eight men behind, whom the Dutch decapitated, staking the heads at the water's edge and burning the bodies. But later that day, the Europeans may have found another fifty dead rebels in the woods; Van Hoogenheim estimated more than a hundred total casualties. The Dutch lost eight men, and another ten were wounded, some of whom died later. The Dutch governor had a close call when a lead ball passed through his coat.[21]

Discontent

Van Hoogenheim was exceedingly grateful for the reinforcements from St. Eustatius who had landed just ten days before the attack. "The arrival of the two barques [boats] from St. Eustatius has likely preserved us," Van Hoogenheim penned in his daily journal after the attack, "for which we praise and thank God." In fact, everyone agreed that had the St. Eustatius forces not shown up when they did, the Europeans would have had to flee to the coast once more. The Statia mercenaries had fought, the governor enthused, "with great courage if great irregularity."[22]

But Dutch elation at repulsing the rebels did not last long. The battle was barely over before the Statia men approached the governor and, pressing up closely around him, wanted to know "what premiums they would earn in case they brought in *neegers*, dead or alive." Until they knew, they boldly proclaimed, they "would neither come ashore nor pick up a gun again." They relented when they were told about the newly established bounties. They also requested, and received, assurance of *soulagement*, or relief payments, for any "mutilations" they might suffer in battle, ranging from 1,500 guilders for the loss of two eyes or both arms to 200 guilders for the loss of a foot. The council declined the men's requests to be paid for retaking plantations.[23]

If Dutch officials hoped that by offering bounties they had solved their labor problems they were mistaken. The sailors and soldiers sent from St. Eustatius and Suriname to help fight the rebels quickly grew dissatisfied with the conditions under which they labored.

By the end of May, fully two-thirds of the Statia mercenaries were sick. On one ship, seventy-four of the eighty men were incapacitated; "most," Van Hoogenheim reported, "are unconscious." One of their captains asked for permission to take his ship to the coast, where the fresh sea air might help his men convalesce. Fearing an attack if the largest armed vessel left, Van Hoogenheim denied this request, offering instead a large canoe roofed with leaves to transport the sickest men downriver. Several died along the way, slowing down the evacuation, as comrades stopped to bury their dead onshore. By early June, hasty interments had become a daily event on Dageraad. The remaining healthy sailors, supported by their captain, went on strike and demanded to return home. Only severe threats could get them back to work.[24]

More than illness plagued the men. The rainy season added to their misery. They were harassed by mosquitoes during the day, and vampire bats occasionally sucked their blood at night, creating festering sores. Adding to their woes, they lacked adequate clothing. Moreover, all of them often went hungry because the gardens at Dageraad were meager, forcing the governor to stretch provisions. Van Hoogenheim was largely dependent on supplies from other colonies, especially Essequibo, which arrived by boat irregularly. A shortage of ovens meant the men ate moldy ship's biscuits rather than fresh bread. Since the soldiers and sailors were partially paid through room and board, poor or reduced rations amounted to wage cuts. The men from St. Eustatius and Suriname repeatedly protested their short or inedible allowances. They complained about irregular payments, as their wages more often than not arrived late from their home colonies. Such deprivations often caused unrest and recalcitrance among sailors and soldiers throughout the early modern world. Clearly, enslaved people were not the only disaffected workers in Berbice.[25]

As most in the European camp lost faith that they could prevail against the rebels, morale slipped lower and lower. Few felt much loyalty to the colony or Company. The rebellion of the slaves and the terror that followed had loosened the bonds of community and authority among the Europeans, splintering them into atomized individuals hard-pressed to set aside narrow self-interest. Many, officials included, were critical of the governor and council, voicing their complaints "both in secret and publicly." Officials dragged their feet in carrying out their duties and obligations, or refused to do so altogether. The grumblers were not all men; in their official warning to the colony, the governor and council emphasized the duty of all, "men and women of whatever station . . . to behave as behooves loyal inhabitants of the nation."[26] Encircled and besieged, living close to death, set everybody on edge.

Unfortunately, the council failed to set an example; its members bickered like children at the slightest provocation. Van Hoogenheim wrote home that he could no longer stand the constant petty disputes between his councilmen "at every meeting." Lodewijk Abbensets in particular, the governor reported, applied himself to "criticize and contradict" anything anyone said. "The sad situation of this country and its inhabitants" stopped the governor from reprimanding the man as he deserved. The ships' captains, too, were ornery. As their men wasted away, their boats became increasingly inoperable and the remaining sailors, with little left to lose, harder to govern. The commanders resented having to accommodate entitled burghers, including women and children, billeted on their vessels. Indian patrols deserted Dageraad without warning. A frustrated and increasingly dispirited Van Hoogenheim lamented that it was hard to see "so little honor or sentiment in my fellow beings, over whom I have the misfortune to rule, and whose behavior brings us to the brink." He suffered from fevers and, although just in his early thirties, his eyesight and memory deteriorated under the strain.[27]

Late in May, "all the new slaves" on Dageraad went missing. They had gone fishing in the creek behind Dageraad, "as usual on a Sunday," and failed to return. A patrol sent after them came back empty-handed. It seems likely that these were the fifty captives Van Hoogenheim had bought in January 1763, just before the rebellion broke out. As there is no mention of them again, it is not clear whether they escaped into the jungle or joined the rebels.[28]

The loss was somewhat offset by the news, brought by Amerindians, that enslaved people on the Company plantations upriver had "no communion with the rebels and remain at peace." Van Hoogenheim immediately hired Jan Broer Jr., who was partly of Amerindian ancestry, to travel upriver to persuade the *bombas* of those plantations to remain loyal. If they prevented their people from joining the rebels and kept the plantations from being torched, Van Hoogenheim promised to ask the directors at home for the men's freedom. Disguised as an Amerindian, and accompanied by two Indians, Broer left on his dangerous errand on May 29, "well instructed about how much to divulge to the loyal blacks." Three weeks later Van Hoogenheim learned that the mission had failed. Less than a week into their journey, the three men were spotted by several rebels who, as fate would have it, had belonged to Broer's father. The men were not fooled by Broer's native disguise, and he was, Van Hoogenheim recorded, "badly abused and cruelly murdered." His head was staked at the river's edge at one of the rebel camps. One of his Indian companions escaped; the second went missing. Van Hoogenheim feared, correctly as it turned out, that he would never again find anyone willing to take on this kind of mission.[29] Without non-European go-betweens, Dutch communication with those behind enemy lines became impossible.

Deadlock

The Dutch were not the only ones at an impasse that spring and early summer. The rebels, too, faced crippling internal and external challenges. Coffij had been unable to turn numerical preponderance into a clear victory. It is hard to know how many men participated in the

May 13 attack. Van Hoogenheim believed that his opponents "had gathered their entire force together, to exterminate us all at once." He estimated their number at two thousand, which seems too high, especially if intelligence was correct that most Company people had not participated. Nevertheless, if at the first Dageraad attack there were some five hundred freedom fighters and the second time perhaps as many as twelve hundred, then that would suggest that in the second attack Coffij and Accara had fought together in that last battle, and that rebel support had grown. Yet despite outnumbering the Dutch at least three to one, if not four to one, the rebels were unable to dislodge them from their stronghold at Dageraad.[30]

Like his European counterpart, Governor Coffij faced internal discord and shortages of supplies. If Coffij and Accara disagreed over strategy in April and May, when Coffij insisted on negotiating with the Dutch while Accara wanted to crush them militarily, by June, if not before, similar disagreements divided the rank and file. Amerindian spies reported conflict between Creoles, people born in the Americas, and "soutwaterse neegers," or saltwater slaves, as first-generation Africans were commonly called. In June, a native man who had spent time among the insurgents told Van Hoogenheim that the Creoles had issues with Africans, whom they accused of being the instigators of "all the bad actions in the rebellion." The man alleged that the Creoles had threatened to kill Coffij and Accara but that "at long last they had made up." A subsequent report confirmed discord between the two groups and claimed that among the Creoles "there were still many who meant well by the Christians." By the end of the month, according to native reports, the slaves on Company plantations upriver "had been brought to obedience with force."[31]

How should one interpret these reports? Conflict between Creoles and Africans is not surprising since Creoles were more familiar with colonial culture and spoke the colonial language. They monopolized elite occupations, worked well-established gardens, and owned property such as chickens and ducks. They had families. No matter how much they hated their enslavement, they had a greater stake in the existing colonial order. In fact, Creoles often considered themselves a separate nation. Throughout the Atlantic world, Creoles frequently looked down on Africans. Africans, for their part, were more deeply shaped by their home cultures, including ethnic and regional affinities and antipathies. African-born men likely had military experience, as many had been enslaved after defeat in war.[32]

By late June, Indian scouts were also reporting that while the rebels were "deeply embittered" about the Europeans and eager to force them out of the colony, lack of powder and shot tied their hands. They were also running out of food. But, the scouts surmised, as soon as the dry season started, the rebels would no doubt do whatever they could to obtain new ammunition "to drive out the Christians." In fact, it appears that the insurgents once again planned a trip to Demerara as soon as the woods and savannas became passable after the rains stopped in early August. Local Indians reported that rebels forced natives to work as guides and wanted the Amerindians to guide them to Demerara. Unwilling to perform this service, the Indian families fled to the Dutch.[33]

Why did the insurgents not leave Berbice to set up Maroon camps in the interior after their May attack failed to push out the Dutch? The rebels' opponents were too weak to keep them in the colony and the Indians had as yet not closed off the hinterlands. Governor Coffij may still have hoped to install his people in the upper half of Berbice. But even if he had been willing to settle in the bush, two obstacles prevented insurgents from choosing that course. The first was food. How would they feed themselves? It would have been impossible to nourish several thousand people in the jungle without adequate preparation. Leaders knew they needed to clear and plant provision gardens in the interior before they could leave Berbice. But cultivating gardens big enough to feed large numbers of people would take time. In Suriname, new Maroons often stayed in the plantation zone for months or even several years while they prepared fields farther inland. They gradually moved away once they were able to sustain themselves.[34]

This had been the tactic in a recent slave revolt in the Tempati area of Suriname, as Governor Crommelin told his Berbice counterpart. "The first care of the blacks," he explained, "was to keep us busy and worn out with attacks while a good many went into the bush to create a place for retreat, plant gardens with corn, casave, *napjes* [potatoes], yams, peas, etc." Once that was done, Crommelin continued, "they moved their wives and children and then, at once, all the others left." [35] Likely the Berbice rebels employed a similar strategy, keeping the Dutch off-balance through aggressive posturing to buy time until they could create gardens upriver when weather conditions permitted.

Indeed, weather was the other key factor. The long rainy season spanned from mid-April to August, flooding savannas and forest with as much as two feet of water, making travel and the building of new habitations impossible. It seems likely this caused the rebels, much like the Dutch, to play a waiting game, albeit for different reasons. The Dutch eagerly anticipated reinforcements from home and busied themselves cajoling their Amerindian allies into position to close off the colony. The rebels, for their part, needed the rain to stop so they could send people into the interior to cultivate gardens and prepare settlements. Perhaps, too, they planned one more try to vanquish the Dutch and take over Berbice for good, if they could secure additional guns and ammunition from Demerara. On each side, internal divisions may have complicated strategizing.

By the start of summer, both governors found themselves enmeshed in deadlocks and unable to act decisively. Each struggled to hold on to his leadership position in the face of growing discontent, crippling shortages, and worrisome factionalism. Which one would manage to hold on the longest?

8

Rebellious Soldiers

The midsummer escapade of a ragged regiment of European soldiers would upend the tenuous balance that prevailed between enemy camps along the Berbice River. In May, the governor of neighboring Suriname had sent the men to the Corentyne River, the border with Berbice. He hoped to block the rebels from entering his colony. But his move backfired.

The soldiers arrived at Post Auriarie on the Corentyne River already disgruntled. Several had served "over their time," indicating that their customary four-year contracts had expired but they had not received their "passport," a written discharge from service. Without this document, the men could not repatriate. Attracting new recruits proved difficult given low wages and the high demand for soldiers in Europe, so the colonial authorities basically turned contract work into forced labor. They withheld passports until replacements arrived. Before the long-serving men could leave, officials forced them to pay money owed for the cost of clothes and passage, debts they incurred at the time of enlistment. The policies kept soldiers in a state of bondage or indenture; at any time, almost a quarter of the men in Suriname were serving well beyond their contracted four years. Similar practices contributed to the wave of mutinies that were plaguing British armies in North America in 1763 and 1764.[1]

Under such circumstances, how the men were treated and whether or not they received what they considered their due gained additional importance. In the minds of the soldiers, it was precisely their treatment that set bonded white male laborers like themselves apart from slaves. It is not surprising that even before they left Suriname, there had been talk that if they were not treated well in Berbice, they would try to make off for the Spanish on the Orinoco. Like Coffij's troops, their vision of escape amounted to a renunciation of enslavement.

As it turned out, once on the Corentyne River, the soldiers found plenty to gripe about. They were overworked, subjected to harsh discipline, and treated disrespectfully by their own officers. With the enslaved workers gone, they wore themselves out in the sticky heat, forced to perform the labor of slaves: clearing brush, cutting wood, and building their own huts. Officers drove the men hard, reinforcing harsh words with frequent use of the whip. The soldiers began to complain, "We are not *Negers*; we don't want to work or be treated like them." The assertion suggests the depth of their resentments over the blurring of lines between military bondage and slavery.[2] Their commanders could have pressed local Amerindians into service, but they had orders not to involve indigenous men for fear of alienating valuable military allies.[3] And so the soldiers felt doubly insulted: they deeply resented being treated like slaves, particularly in the presence of indigenes who were exempted from harsh usage.

Anxieties about status and identity were not confined to comparisons with Africans and Amerindians; they played within the European community as well. Many of the soldiers were foreigners. The Frenchmen among the Suriname soldiers resented what they perceived as a pervasive anti-French climate. Everything that went wrong, they complained, was blamed on the French. Some of the officers were quite brazen about their anti-French (and anti-Semitic) sentiments. Particularly galling had been the comment of one of the officers that he "thought the French as bad as the Jews and would rejoice to see both nations hanged."[4]

Affronts to soldiers' dignity and anger about perceived injustices increased in the weeks leading up to the mutiny. In the middle of June, at the height of the rainy season, forty of the soldiers, along with some seventy Native American allies, were sent on a weeklong

Private soldier, n.d., watercolor by Dirk Langendijk (1748–1805). (Rijksmuseum, Amsterdam.)

slave-hunting expedition. They sought the people who had rebelled on the Canje River in February, and who had been attacked by Indians in late April. These self-emancipated people were thought to be hiding in a nearby creek. Crashing thunderstorms soaked the miserable contingent to the bone as they paddled up the Corentyne River. At first, they found only several small deserted rebel camps, the huts washed out by flash floods. But at last an Indian scout located the insurgents.

The troops left their canoes at river's edge and slogged all night in single file, "one holding the other," through the pitch black of the rain forest. At dawn, they forded a swollen creek, those who could by swimming, the others grasped under the arms and pulled through the water by natives. Once across, the commando unit surprised the rebels. In the fighting that ensued over the course of a week, six rebel men and sixteen women and children were killed, most of them reportedly beaten to death by Indians as they tried to escape by swimming across the creek. A young woman was taken captive. Only one European, a Dutchman, lost his life.[5]

Yet despite this victory, a series of ill-advised actions by the commanding officer brought the soldiers to the breaking point. When apprised of the Dutchman's death, Captain Frederik Willem Baron von Canitz, an aristocrat and recent veteran of the Tempati Maroon wars in Suriname, proclaimed that he would rather lose a Dutch soldier than an Indian one. This comment infuriated his men. Von Canitz added insult to injury by confiscating the contraband his men had taken from the rebels. Almost 300 guilders had been recovered, along with trade goods the rebels had seized from the Corentyne Post. The native allies had immediately claimed the merchandise as their payment. The soldiers expected to get the cash. At the start of the expedition, Von Canitz had promised that "whatever they would seize, would be for them."[6]

Instead, Von Canitz now took most of the money, declaring it would have to be shared with the Indians at a later date. In its place, each man got two shillings for drinks. Yet another affront since custom dictated that drinks should be served for free as reward for a dangerous mission. The young female captive, coveted by some of the soldiers, was likewise kept from them. The men "cursed and murmured" among themselves "that they got none of the spoils for which they had risked their lives." No one dared complain openly for fear of reprisal, but when the expedition returned to camp and the time seemed ripe, the soldiers transformed anger into action.[7]

Mutiny

The mutiny started well before sunrise on July 3, just days after their return. Those unaware of the plans recalled being startled awake in their hammocks, hearts pounding, fearing the commotion signaled a rebel attack. Instead, they found their officers, still in their nightshirts, pleading with the mutineers for their lives and promising that if the soldiers returned to their duties, all would be forgotten. Such negotiations were common: angry men threatened mutiny, chastened officers made concessions, and eventually authority was restored. In this case the mutineers were not so easily appeased. The soldiers listed their grievances, emphasizing slave work and physical abuse, prejudice toward the French, and the confiscation of the plunder.[8]

The mutineers, in fact, nursed grievances similar to those of the rebellious ex-slaves they had attacked weeks earlier. The rebels in their notes and messages at the start of their rebellion had singled out particular plantation owners by name as the worst offenders. Likewise, the mutineers now pointed to their commander and Captain von Canitz as the two officers whose conduct was most reprehensible. A few mutineers proposed to kill these men. One even took direct aim, but his gun misfired.[9]

The leaders of the mutineers, among them a Frenchman from Languedoc named Jean Renaud, prevailed against murder, and the officers in question got off with a mere beating. Thereafter the commander fled, still in his nightclothes, to Ephraim, a Moravian missionary settlement. A few soldiers tried to persuade two junior officers to lead them on a march to inform Governor van Hoogenheim in person about their maltreatment. It was quite common for European soldiers to complain to civil authorities. The officers refused and tried to talk the troops out of deserting. When several soldiers began to waver, surgeon Johan Carolus Mangmeister, a thirty-year-old Prussian veteran, broke up the discussion with the reminder that the officers could not be trusted to keep their word and that the soldiers "had much to do."[10]

Having rejected negotiation and compromise, the men reached the point of no return. Much like the rebels who appropriated their masters' possessions, the mutineers helped themselves to the officers' liquor, fancy clothes, and weapons. They then escorted the three remaining officers to the river's edge, where they allowed them to board a canoe with what was left of their belongings. When Von Canitz requested a few Indians to man the paddles, the soldiers responded cheekily that they had learned the skill; surely he could too. Surgeon Mangmeister, cutlass drawn, prevented Von Canitz's servant, a "free Christian mulat" named Steven Andries, from boarding the canoe. "You have been free a long time," Mangmeister allegedly told Steven, "but now you'll be my slave."[11]

With the officers gone, the rebelling soldiers debated their options, none of them good. Some wanted to make their way west to the Orinoco River to hire themselves out as mercenaries to the Spanish in Venezuela. Surgeon Mangmeister gave them erroneous information, claiming mistakenly that the Orinoco, which was several hundred miles away, was only a three-day march once they got to the "breede [broad] water," a large lake between the Corentyne and Canje Rivers. Distance aside, no one knew exactly how to get to the Orinoco, though several people (including the black female prisoner whom Jean Renaud had set free in order to take her along) claimed to know the route. There was talk of making common cause with the rebels but also of attacking them, to demonstrate the mutineers' loyalty to the Dutch. Then, they reasoned, the governor of Berbice would realize they had not actually deserted but had merely left their post to acquaint him with the bad behavior of their officers.[12]

In the end, the men decided to make for the Spanish settlements on the Orinoco River, which meant crossing through or around the colony of Berbice, as well as Demerara and Essequibo. Before they set out

on what would prove to be a long, and for many fatal, odyssey, the mutineers destroyed everything of value they could not carry and tossed
extra guns and powder in the water. They bundled their belongings in
their hammocks, chose Sergeant Adam Niesse as their leader, took an
oath to stick together, and vowed to shoot the first man who changed
his mind. Then they set off, the ringleaders decked out in the officers'
colorful finery, and the "swarte meyd" (black wench) with Jean Renaud
at the head.[13] The soldiers also took along, possibly by force, several Indians knowledgeable about the terrain, one of whom, unlike most of
the mutineers, spoke Dutch well. Twenty-two soldiers stayed behind,
having hidden from their rebelling comrades in the bush when the
mutiny broke out.[14] As with the enslaved community, rebellion was
not for everyone.

The exact events of the following days are sketchy. By their own account, some of the men celebrated their new freedom with the officers'
liquor and a murder spree. They reportedly killed a native boy before
the mutineers broke camp. The men spent their first night in an Indian
village. There, they allegedly killed three more Indians and abducted
nine native women, which, if true, would certainly have turned potential allies into resentful enemies.[15]

The next morning, the mutineers lost some of their members. Eight
men volunteered to return to the post to look for stragglers. When they
got there, the three subaltern officers and five soldiers, perhaps scared
or repentant (or, as the court-martial later alleged, too drunk to keep
walking), decided to abandon their comrades and turned themselves
in. The remaining forty-one mutineers, guided by the slave woman
and the Indians, continued west toward the distant Orinoco River.[16]
They would have been quite a sight. The hungover soldiers, unshaven,
in haphazard officers' dress; the reluctant Indian guides, their bodies
smooth, plucked clean of hair; the traumatized young African woman,
who may or may not have known the way. An odd pilgrimage of people bound by their disaffection for the colonial order.

The Berbice authorities could not pursue the group: local Indians
were not willing and their own soldiers were not capable. Mistrustful
of the soldiers who did not join the mutiny, the Dutch commanded the

Indians living near post Ephraim to keep any intelligence about the whereabouts of either rebels or mutineers secret from them. They also asked the natives to return any soldiers who were found beyond the view of the sentries, and, inverting the usual social order, they authorized them to use force if necessary.[17]

As in all rebellions, the initial act of emancipation was less of a challenge than trying to hold on to freedom. The rainy season made travel difficult. Water and thunder poured from the sky in the late afternoons. The men waded through flooded savanna and boggy forests, pestered by swarms of insects. The mutineers were of several nationalities and spoke different languages. Not surprisingly, they did not trust one another. Some men required coercion to keep going, and guards accompanied anyone who went into the bush to relieve himself. The soldiers had a poor idea of the region's geography to say the least. Before the mutiny the surgeon apparently had claimed to possess a regional map, a rare and valuable treasure, but it turned out he did not even bring part of a map.[18]

Without a map, the men were dependent on the local knowledge of their indigenous guides and that of the African girl. Two of the Indians, perhaps forced to go against their will, did not remain with the soldiers long. One native man ran off after drinking a bottle of wine and hitting a drummer on the head with the empty bottle; another was shot in the head in retaliation.[19] Despite these setbacks, the soldiers finally found a path. Ironically, it may have been a well-worn trail the Indians called "the slave path," as it was used by Carib traders to lead captive natives for sale to the Dutch.[20]

After several days the men reached the "breede water" (perhaps Lake Ikuruwa), where it took them forty-eight hours to build rafts. Some later claimed they tricked a native man into guiding them across under the pretext that they were patrols looking for slave rebels. After another two days traversing the soggy savanna, they crossed the Canje River. Then, a week into their journey, they "lost the path to Spain" and ran out of food. The rebel woman led them to an abandoned plantation but they failed to find the provisions she had promised.[21] At this point, the mutineers, desperate, made a radical decision.

Rebellion Redux

The mutineers resolved to contact the rebels. Much later, some of the men blamed the change of plans on hunger, the unexpected distance to the Orinoco River, and the persuasive words of the slave woman. We know almost nothing about her, yet she was a pivotal figure in the mutiny. She apparently made the bold suggestion that the men negotiate with the slave rebels for permission to travel through the colony of Berbice rather than taking the long way around. Or perhaps the men themselves decided to join the rebels, given their desperate situation and lack of options. Either way, on July 11, a small delegation of soldiers led by Mangmeister, Renaud, and the captive woman made their way to plantation Stevensburg, the main rebel camp on the Canje River, to negotiate. The rebel girl had to do most of the talking, though at some point a rebel was found who spoke some Dutch. Quasie, the commander of Stevensburg, was understandably mistrustful. He inquired about the mutineers' numbers, ordered them to hand over their weapons as a gesture of goodwill, and promised to send a messenger to Governor Coffij, at Fort Nassau, for instructions.[22]

When the rest of the mutineers arrived on Stevensburg plantation, they were disarmed and stripped of their clothes. Quasie, anxious to protect his post, did not wait for Coffij's answer. He had the testimony of the captured woman that these were the same soldiers who had killed so many rebels the previous month. He moved quickly, out of revenge, decisiveness, or fear, to thin their ranks. Based on his estimation of each soldier's usefulness, Quasie selected twenty-eight mutineers, who, still naked, were walked to the cacao fields and shot to death. When the Dutch authorities were informed of these events later on, they smugly characterized it as "a miraculous instance of divine providence" that the mutineers had been executed by "those they had chosen as their deliverers."[23]

The remaining thirteen mutineers, including several of the original leaders, were taken to Governor Coffij's headquarters at Fort Nassau. On their journey from the Canje to the Berbice, the group met up with Fortuin van Helvetia, the leader on the Canje River. According to

Renaud, Fortuin "was very displeased that the other whites had been murdered." Once they got to the fort, the men were clothed and put to work. Like Fortuin, Governor Coffij was angry about the murder of the majority of the mutineers. He sent "Brother Accara" to chew out the Canje rebels and, again according to Renaud, "Accara even murdered one of the Canje blacks." Coffij ordered that all the mutineers' loot, ammunition, and guns be brought to his headquarters at the fort.[24]

Relations between the black and white mutineers were tenuous and shifting. Most of the testimony comes from the courts-martial of the surviving men, who portrayed themselves as having been betrayed and coerced by the rebels. It is not surprising they claimed to have been victims. Their lives were on the line for having mutinied during a war. The men would have wanted to avoid the impression that they had compounded their original offense of mutiny by also committing treason by voluntarily joining the enemy, and a "heathen" enemy at that. This would only have increased their chances of receiving the death penalty.[25] For their part, the rebels had every reason to treat the soldiers, so deeply implicated in the maintenance of colonialism and slavery, as prisoners.

Yet, as time passed, driven by fear, need, and a shared interest in defeating the Dutch, the mutineers and the rebels built bridges across the many divides that separated them. Rebel leaders knew full well that the soldiers' presence among them dealt a powerful psychological blow to the colonial authorities. Indeed, the Europeans were greatly alarmed at reports that, in the priceless phrase of one Dutch officer, the "Christian Rebels and Rebel Negroes" now lived in "close harmony."[26] And so Coffij kept the remaining Europeans alive and set them to work. Over time, some became trusted allies and advisers. Others remained little more than slaves. In other words, the mutineers were absorbed into the rebel hierarchy.

Such incorporation rekindled among the European soldiers many of the resentments that had led them to mutiny in the first place. The rebel leaders gave the mutiny leaders preferential treatment and jobs of greater importance compared to the common soldiers. Sergeant Niesse assisted Governor Coffij by exercising troops, writing letters, and ordering the other mutineers about. He set some to painting Coffij's quarters. For his service, Niesse was rewarded with fancy clothes, good food, and a comfortable hammock. Johan Mangmeister, the surgeon, ministered to the rebels' health and received an African slave boy named Andries to attend to him as a mark of his status.[27] Jean Renaud had saved himself from execution at Stevensburg by claiming to know how to make gunpowder. Now he busily tried to hide his ignorance by mixing sand and water, only to be unmasked when the surgeon provided him with the necessary saltpeter he claimed he lacked. To save Renaud from beheading, rebel leader Fortuin, who had evidently taken a liking to him, took the Frenchman with him to the Canje River.[28]

The rest of the mutineers were set to work as tailors and carpenters, occupations they had no doubt carried out before they mustered. They also cleaned and repaired guns and stood guard, and a few even accompanied the rebels on raids against the Dutch. Most of them were eventually sent away from Fort Nassau to other rebel posts to serve alongside African captives as "footboys" to deserving rebel leaders, once again overturning customary colonial racial hierarchies. Ironically, the men who had resented enslavement now ended up working for ex-slaves.[29]

Desperation

As soon as Van Hoogenheim received the "most regrettable and upsetting tiding" of the mutiny, he and his councilors assumed the mutineers would make common cause with the rebels and "come to fight us."[30] The Dutch were deeply apprehensive that the deserters would replenish the rebels' stock of weapons and ammunition. Even more disconcerting was the idea that the unfaithful soldiers would exponentially increase the effectiveness of the rebel army. Not only would the new arrivals provide training in European warfare; they would also, as experienced slave hunters, pass on knowledge about "the maneuvers of the Suriname [Maroons]," along with "all their wicked tricks and tactics."[31] In mid-July, Indian spies related that they had heard much gunfire at rebel camp Vigilantie. This was puzzling to the Dutch, who had been told that the rebels were running low on powder. Van Hoogenheim surmised, rightly as it turned out, though under circumstances quite different than he imagined, that the mutineers had arrived at the rebel camp and these were "victory salutes." [32] The thought that defected European soldiers had restocked the munitions of their former enemies vastly increased his misgivings. Even more alarming, as a result of the mutiny, the path to the Corentyne River and even the "entire river" was now unprotected. Perhaps the rebels would try to retreat that way, foiling all hope that they would stay on the Berbice and Canje Rivers until soldiers from Europe arrived. [33] The devastating consequences of continuing disease and low morale did not help matters for the forces at Dageraad.

Worst of all, the example of the Corentyne mutineers proved infectious. By the end of July, the officers of the Suriname regiment informed Van Hoogenheim and his council that they little trusted their men, who were "mostly French deserters" serving beyond their contracted time. Astoundingly, the officers feared they could not guarantee their soldiers' loyalty in case of another rebel attack. A surgeon working on Dageraad proclaimed to anyone who would listen that he would "rather join the slave rebels than serve the colony" any longer. He had, Van Hoogenheim noted by way of explanation, served previously "a long time among the French" and in Berbice had allied himself closely with French soldiers, "all libertines without any discipline." While the man deserved harsh punishment, "under the circumstances," redeployment to St. Andries was all Van Hoogenheim dared impose. [34]

To prevent the Suriname soldiers serving in Berbice from following the example of their compatriots, the councilors tried to appease the men with cash. To do so they used money recovered from officers who had died of disease in order to pay the men who had "murmured" about the slow arrival of their wages from Suriname. [35]

In mid-September, two French soldiers stationed on Dageraad deserted to the insurgents just before daybreak. They took with them not only their weapons and shot, but valuable intelligence about the desperate situation of the Dutch. The Indians sent to catch them spotted the two men but refused to attack without reinforcements, allowing the deserters to get away. Van Hoogenheim berated the native "captain" about his men's lack of courage. "This wild man answered," an unnerved governor reported, "that he was surprised I'd reproach him, given that I could not count on my own soldiers." How could Van Hoogenheim admonish him, the man pointed out with biting words, when "before their eyes" the governor's men "turned into enemies, joining the rebels." [36]

Deeply shaken, Van Hoogenheim confided to his journal that "since the desertion of the last two soldiers, we can count on nothing anymore." Even a 100-guilder premium to catch the deserters, dead or alive, yielded no result. Early in October, a major altercation between soldiers and Dageraad slaves, noted in Van Hoogenheim's journal without any further detail, created yet more worries.[37]

In this climate of discontent, along with shifting (and shifty) loyalties, a new issue took on ominous meaning—food. Van Hoogenheim's dwindling supplies, and forces, had been somewhat replenished over the summer with the arrival of two ships. One turned up from Holland in late June, dispatched by the Company directors before they knew about the uprising, carrying replenishments and twelve new soldiers. The other appeared a few weeks later from St. Eustatius with forty additional men. Van Hoogenheim distributed peas, oats, and flour from Holland to the soldiers and sailors to supplement their usual rations, knowing the men had suffered hunger and many were ill. Yet the newly arrived mercenaries from St. Eustatius judged this not enough and had the "intolerable insolence," in Van Hoogenheim's judgment, to also demand salted bacon and fish, along with linen shirts and pants. "They know," the governor noted, "that I am depended on them and they refuse obedience but under certain conditions." The men repeatedly badgered him for more victuals.[38]

Soon after, the Suriname soldiers at Dageraad rejected the ship's biscuits ("made of good rye, of excellent taste, without any sign of spoilage or mold," all officers agreed after close inspection) handed out to them. A delegation approached the governor and his councilmen on the veranda of the main house. The men retorted that the biscuits were fit for beasts, not men, and they demanded bread. Outraged at their "impudence," the usually restrained governor, a former army officer after all, ran to his room to get his gun, "with the intent of shooting at the feet of one of the spokesmen." Thankfully, "God Almighty" cooled his head, which prevented the incident from escalating into outright military rebellion. That evening, the men accepted the biscuits, now supplemented by the desired white bread. "We can no longer doubt," a shaken Van Hoogenheim wrote in his journal, "that evil conspiracies are afoot among them." Along with the men's commanders, he feared that another mutiny was imminent.[39]

Such apprehensions were amplified when in October the mercenaries resorted to collective work stoppages. One day, men from one of the St. Eustatius ships did not receive their promised allotment of bread; the Suriname soldier hired on at Dageraad as baker could not keep up with daily demand for fresh loaves of bread for several hundred men. Against the orders of their captain, the discontented sailors lifted anchor and abandoned their crucial position upriver from Dageraad. The precipitous action prompted Indians stationed in several nearby creeks to leave their posts, fearing for their own safety without the protection of the ship. When Van Hoogenheim threatened to punish the ringleaders among the sailors *and* promised that the men would have their bread, they agreed to sail their ship back to its former position, upon which, as the governor observed, "the entire safety of this plantation depends."[40]

Discontented workers whose tools were weapons represented a serious danger, as the Dutch leaders well understood. The rebellious sailors and soldiers in Berbice were expected to be faithful and compliant instruments of state power. But they were also workers, subject to the power, and exploitation, of the state. They received wages, like free laborers, but the conditions of their contracts kept them in a state of bondage, suggesting to the men uncomfortable comparisons to the slaves they had come to fight. Yet despite their lowly position, the men were not without power. Their martial labor, especially in the midst of a slave rebellion, was crucial to the survival of the colony. Soldiers and sailors used their leverage to protest poor compensation and working conditions, forcing the colonial authorities into making concessions. The mutineers took their insubordination a step further. They not only deserted their post but committed treason as well. They saw their own plight as akin to that of slaves and so made common cause with the rebels, undermining the racial boundaries on which white power, colonial exploitation, and empire building depended.

Van Hoogenheim accurately informed the home authorities that he had more to worry about than merely "Swarte" (blacks). "We have to be as much prepared at all times," he impressed upon the colony directors in Amsterdam, "for bad faith and treason from within, as for attacks from without." Shared new-world enemies at the gate, he understood, did not necessarily mute old-world labor conflict inside the colony.[41]

9

Palace Revolution

On a night in late July, the guards at plantation Dageraad spotted a dugout canoe moving swiftly downriver with the tide. In the light of the full moon, they could make out an Amerindian at the paddle and a European passenger. As the boat approached the shore, they observed that the European was cut and bruised. He turned out to be a Dutch soldier, recently captured by rebels on the Canje River, selected by Governor Coffij to deliver a letter to Governor van Hoogenheim. Cupido, an Amerindian, had been ordered to paddle the soldier downriver. The two men had set out after sunset, traveling through the darkness and arriving after midnight.

Woken by a guard, Van Hoogenheim ordered the soldier brought to his chamber right away. He, too, did not fail to notice that the young man was in bad shape, evidently beaten by his rebel captors. He eagerly studied the unexpected letter from the adversary he referred to as "so-called Governor Coffij." It was the first communication since the rebels had broken off the initial round of correspondence two and a half months earlier, in May. The struggling Dutch inhabited a topsy-turvy world. The former slaves commanded troops and controlled most of the colony, while the former masters held only a handful of plantations and had a tenuous hold on their soldiers. Van Hoogenheim lived in fear not only of the rebels, but of his own fighting men as well. His hopes hinged on help from Holland. "God give," he prayed, "that the wished for deliverance from the homeland may arrive and turn our situation around." Until such assistance arrived, his position was desperate. The rebel letter provided a respite.[1]

Out of the summer darkness, the Dutch were tossed a slim lifeline, but one that would eventually sink Coffij.

Gamble

Coffij's letter projected confidence. "Highly born Lord Lord Governor and General of these lands Berbice &c &c &c," the note started, imitating the elaborate salutations of early modern correspondence. "I hereby notify your Lordship governor van Hoogenheim with a little note, to let him know, whether he has not changed his mind about making an agreement with me, with respect to the land Berbice, or, is he still set on having war." "Governor Coffij" had sent the soldier (a "prisoner," the letter emphasized) to find out whether the Dutch wanted peace. Was Governor van Hoogenheim ready to change his mind about negotiating? Was he willing to divide the colony? Coffij stated once again that he would give the Dutch half of Berbice while "I and my *negers*" would "keep the other half."[2]

With this deceptively simple sentence, Coffij reiterated the revolutionary proposal he had made in the spring—to create a sovereign state alongside that of the Dutch. He added, "I will allow you to negotiate as before." The word *negotieeren* carried a double meaning in Dutch in the eighteenth century (rather as it does in English today), since it could refer to both trading and talking. Earlier in the letter, Coffij used the verb *accodeeren*, "to come to an agreement," several times to refer to previous negotiations. Given that word use, it seems most likely that with the word *negotieeren* he was assuring his counterpart that the former slaves would allow the Dutch to carry on trade as they had before the revolution—another assertion of control and superiority.[3] Or, Governor Coffij continued, the Dutch governor could reject the rebels' offer and "wait for something better," either a backhanded reference to the length of time that had already passed without any troops from Holland or perhaps a threat of an imminent rebel attack.

Coffij used the rest of his letter to trumpet his good fortunes. He confirmed Dutch fears with the news that forty-one mutineers had joined him "as good friends, well supplied with powder and shot," while omitting that his men had executed two-thirds of them. He boasted that he had ample supplies of ammunition. No doubt aware through spies of the high Dutch mortality rates, he emphasized his own good health for which he "thanked God." He reiterated that if the Dutch wanted to negotiate, they should let him know soon or, he warned, "expect something else."

Coffij closed with a final and visceral reminder to the Dutch of the new state of affairs. He offered not only a "friendly greeting" to Van Hoogenheim but also a message from the young Dutch woman he had kept as his hostage and to whom he now referred as "my young wife Schorzina [Georgina] Sara Hebina George." Georgina sent greetings to a friend of her father, councilman "Mr. Schirmeister and also to my two brothers." In a "postscript from the young wife," Georgina, or someone writing for her, warned Van Hoogenheim that "many blacks have joined them of late and you will not be able to prevail but through a good accord." The letter was simply signed "Cooffij [the scribe spelling his name phonetically rather than in Dutch], governor."

Why had Coffij chosen to reopen negotiations at this time after more than two months of silence? Was he operating from a position of strength, as it at first appears, or of weakness?

Coffij's confidence must have grown after recent psychological and military victories over the Dutch, chief among them the defection of the Suriname mutineers, which deeply damaged Dutch morale. The mutineers had replenished the insurgents' gunpowder supply, severely depleted after the May attack on Dageraad. Moreover, Canje rebels had just overpowered a Dutch post on that river, killing eight of the nine defenders. They captured one soldier, the man Coffij used as courier, as well as his commander, a corporal.[4] And the Dutch remained feeble. Coffij no doubt was aware that while the Dutch had recently received a few new soldiers, illness and discord were decimating their forces. The desperately awaited aid from the Dutch Republic was clearly taking a long time to arrive, but the balance of power might shift drastically when fresh troops from Europe reached Berbice. Coffij must have calculated that his opponents' immediate situation appeared so dire that he might induce them to sue for peace.

Coffij's decision to return to diplomacy was also propelled by less advantageous circumstances and events. Like the Dutch, Coffij was short on provisions and weapons. Amerindians and Creoles who had escaped from the rebels reported that insurgents were eating "dogs and cats" and were forced to slaughter valuable horses and mules to provide for their people.[5] Governor Coffij had many more mouths to feed than Governor van Hoogenheim and so faced steeper challenges in staving off shortages. And unlike his adversary, Coffij could not count on resupplies from helpful neighbors. Rather, the insurgents had to travel far and wide in search of provisions or risk their lives poaching food from Dageraad's gardens. Canje insurgents ranged as far as the Corentyne River on the border with Suriname scavenging for food, but they were increasingly harassed by patrolling Dutch-allied Indians. And while the rainy season was coming to an end, the jungle was still under a foot of water. Once those waters receded, the rebels intended to cultivate gardens in the upper Berbice and to travel to Demerara for weapons and ammunition. But those plans had recently been put into doubt.[6]

Coffij had sent a hundred people, many of them women, upriver to start provision gardens near the southernmost plantation, Savonette. But their mission met with disaster when they were attacked one night in late July. Carib and Akawaio fighters recruited in Demerara killed more than half the Africans and abducted two girls before help from surrounding plantations dispersed the Indians. As soon as rebel authorities learned of the raid, Captain Accara led a large force of well-armed men, including several mutineers, upriver to take revenge and drive out the natives. There had been no word about the outcome of this mission.[7] The reality that Indians were closing off the hinterlands and coming to the aid of the Dutch must have greatly troubled Governor Coffij.

Yet reopening negotiations carried major political risks. Many rebels, especially Africans, opposed any kind of dialogue with the Dutch. Coffij's second-in-command, Captain Accara, the insurgency's military leader, was foremost among them. He had attacked Dutch headquarters at Dageraad in April against Coffij's wishes, undermining the first round of talks with the Dutch. Perhaps Coffij chose this moment to contact the Dutch governor again because Accara and his most formidable fighters were away. Despite the risk to his authority, Coffij had a small window to try diplomacy once more to save his people from costly warfare.

When Van Hoogenheim read Coffij's missive, he noticed that it was not written by the same person who had penned the rebel leaders' notes in April and May. In spring, the notes had been written by Prins, an enslaved man from plantation Helvetia whose Dutch was poor. The current letter, Van Hoogenheim judged, showed much more German inflection, and the sentences were longer and more complex. According to the bearer, it was written by one of the mutineers, Sergeant Adam Niesse.[8]

The use of a European scribe raises fascinating questions about how this note and those that followed were produced. Did Coffij dictate them, or did he and his scribe collaborate? Could Coffij read the letters himself, or did the scribe read them back to him when they were finished? Were other rebels around, listening? Can we be sure that the scribe read what he had in fact written? Did he have the power to alter Coffij's meaning or even secretly add sentences to the notes? The scribe's shaky syntax makes the writing not only difficult to understand and ambiguous at times, but impossible to render literally into clear English. One can only paraphrase.

The letter, as well as the reports of the soldier-courier and the Amerindian, provided the Dutch with confirmation that the mutineers had made common cause with the rebels. This was an outcome they had expected and dreaded. Van Hoogenheim closely questioned Cupido. All we know about this man, besides his Dutch name, is that he had been a slave on plantation Herstelling. But whether Cupido was enslaved or free among the rebels is not clear. Nor is it clear how much of what he told the Dutch was what Coffij had ordered him to say. Cupido claimed, for instance, "that not one *neger* remained outside the rebellion," and that in the entire colony, on every plantation, the Dutch would meet only enemies. If true, this would indicate that by this time, Coffij and Accara had either convinced everyone to join or effectively forced all to submit to their regime. The fact that both Cupido and Georgina, in her postscript, emphasized Coffij's overwhelming support could also suggest that Coffij was eager to assert what might not in fact have been the case, as it is doubtful that Georgina could write freely.[9]

Cupido also relayed to the Dutch the news of the Akawaio and Carib attack near the Savonette and Accara's subsequent quest for revenge. Lastly he claimed that the Suriname soldiers had handed over two barrels of powder and large quantities of bullets to the rebels, along with many guns. He did *not* tell the governor, though he must have known, that only thirteen mutineers had joined the rebels, not forty-one. As soon as the sun rose at seven, a worried governor called his council together to compose an answer.[10]

Renewed Negotiations

The situation had deteriorated for the Europeans. The mutiny of the Suriname regiment had dealt a devastating blow, and illness continued to take its toll, in lives, in morale, and in military preparedness. One of the officers reported that during the summer, "over a hundred men have been put in the earth." Several of the ships had lost so many sailors they had to be manned by enslaved Africans, a potential security risk for the Dutch. Few officers remained alive, leaving the sailors largely to rule themselves. By early August, fully one-third of the soldiers and sailors were sick, and another third had died, making funerals a daily occurrence and rendering the situation of the Dutch absolutely desperate. The remaining men, "officers, soldiers, and sailors," Van Hoogenheim reported, "are losing all courage," convinced that if the rebels did attack, "they could not withstand their superior numbers." Now only two Dutch posts remained: the Dageraad and the small fort of St. Andries near the coast. Rebels had just wiped out the third one, on the Canje, and news of this setback had caused the flight of the last Europeans still living on that river.[11]

Despite recent fresh supplies, the Dutch were also running low on food and watched helplessly as their opponents regularly raided the Dageraad's gardens. Normally the annual "Indian fishery" replenished their stores. When the rains abated, native men blocked the creeks on the Canje River to haul in large quantities of fish that fed colonists and slaves for months. But this summer, most of the indigenes were gone. Besides, the Dutch did not have the food and drink required to pay the natives regardless, so the fish catch did not take place. Moreover, the Dutch were so vulnerable that any change in rebel positions caused great panic. "Given our scant force," Van Hoogenheim reported, "every small movement of even a few enemies causes here immediately many difficulties and worries."[12]

On top of it all, the change in season filled the Europeans with dread. When the floodwaters receded in mid-August, the forests and savanna would become passable and the rebels could attack again overland. The Dutch were dangerously low on ammunition, especially on cannon balls, which they could not manufacture themselves. "If the heavens do not provide speedy *secours* [help] from patria, we will be forced to leave Dageraad and retire to the ocean," one officer reasoned, "because once the woods fall dry, it will be impossible to remain here." Van Hoogenheim's war council concurred. "God has lifted up his hand heavily against us," the governor concluded, evoking with Psalm 106:26 the biblical scale of Dutch misfortune: "Therefore he lifted up his hand against them, to overthrow them in the wilderness."[13]

Still, colonial officials were not sure how to respond to Coffij's overtures. The Suriname officers urged abandoning Dageraad and sailing back to the coast to hole up once again in Fort St. Andries. The air at the seashore was healthier, they argued, and it was harder for soldiers to desert to the rebels from there. Barring flight, the officers favored negotiations, given that their men could not be trusted and in case of an attack by the rebels "might not stay loyal." To the governor's chagrin, the council members were divided on the wisdom of writing back, and even on what to say if they did reply. Convinced that as long as he made no concrete promises, correspondence not only could be to Dutch advantage but, given their precarious situation, was "of the utmost necessity," Van Hoogenheim decided to compose an answer himself. He entrusted his letter to Amerindian Cupido to take to Governor Coffij the very next day.[14]

War of Words

Dispensing with any honorifics in a bid to assert dominance he did not possess, Van Hoogenheim addressed his letter merely "Aan den Neeger Coffij." As in spring, he wrote in a style geared for children and referred to himself in the third person. Van Hoogenheim feigned surprise that the insurgents thought he might want war—had not the rebels themselves "started the war with the Christians, and mistreated them terribly"? He reminded Coffij that the rebels had proposed dividing the colony in April. "His Lordship the governor," as he referred to himself, had not been sure then either what Coffij meant by "half" and had asked for clarification, so he could explain the situation to the Company directors in Amsterdam. But instead of providing an answer, Van Hoogenheim charged, "you brought your entire force here to fight," referring to the attack on Dageraad on May 13. So the governor could "not trust the *neegers'* promises or words." If this time they were willing to be more sincere and act without deception, he would entertain their proposal, as long as "*Negers* Coffij and Accara" would explain clearly "what half entails for you."

The soldier-courier had been so badly mistreated by the rebels, Van Hoogenheim charged, that he needed time to recover before he could convey any more messages. Instead, "*bok* Cupido" (*bok* being a derogatory term for Amerindians) would bring the letter to the rebels and could also convey their answer. To prove their sincerity, the rebels should give up their most recent hostage: "return Corporal Sneebel, whom you captured in Canje, because that man's misfortune will do you no good." In closing, Van Hoogenheim conveyed that "*Heer* Schirmeister sends friendly greetings to *Juffrouw* [Miss] George, as do her two brothers." [15]

By noon the next day, on August 2, two Indians arrived with Governor Coffij's answer. Van Hoogenheim kept the two messengers sequestered on one of the ships "to hide from them our weak situation on Dageraad." [16] The letter, likely again written by one of the Suriname mutineers given the German-inflected Dutch, was a remarkable missive. Not only did it detail the specific demands of the rebels; it also presented powerful and provocative political statements on behalf of both the rebels and the mutineers, their fates now inescapably yoked.

The note began by specifying what Coffij had in mind by "half." "I want to keep no more than four plantations," Coffij explained, naming Company plantations Savonette, Markey, Oost Souburg, and Peereboom.[17] "The rest," he added magnanimously, either emphasizing his control of the colony or trying to minimize his request, "is for you." Coffij understood, he wrote, that the Dutch governor himself had nothing to do with the triggers for the rebellion, "as it is the Planters and Directors who are the cause of the war, while they badly mistreated the people, with excessive beatings and lashings, so we could stand it no longer." [18] "Because we know," Coffij continued, asserting God's approbation for his actions, "who God is, and that God rewards good and punishes evil." He said he and his people also understood that Berbice did not belong to the governor and that Van Hoogenheim would need to consult his superiors in Holland. In the meantime, if Van Hoogenheim wanted to make a (preliminary) agreement, he should send the Amerindian messenger back. And if Mr. Schirmeister wanted to see the two George sisters returned, Coffij would hand them over for a ransom.

While it sounds as if Coffij scaled back from his former bold position of demanding half the colony, the area covered by the four plantations he mentioned, from Savonette upriver to the Peereboom on the Wiruni Creek, did in fact entail the entire upper section of Berbice. He was asking for about half the cultivated area of the colony, which included, besides the four valuable Company sugar plantations mentioned, some forty private plantations. It seems from this demand that Governor Coffij intended to keep the sugar plantations in production, likely with forced labor, growing sugar to distill rum and perhaps to sell on the European market just as Dutch colonists did. Coffij, a self-liberated former slave holed up in a remote corner of the imperial

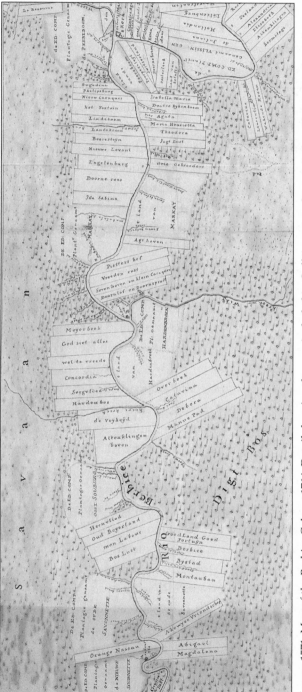

Leupe 1571, Map of the Berbice Colony, 1764. Detail showing the area included in Coffij's proposal to retain four Company plantations. Between Savonette on the far left and Peereboom on the far right, a large part of the cultivated area of the colony was included. (Nationaal Archief, The Hague.)

world, understood that the grinding force of capitalism meant some people toiled against their will while others commanded. Some thirty years later, after their rebellion succeeded, Haitian leaders would insist on the same thing, compelling newly liberated people to grow sugar on plantations as they had as slaves.[19]

The rest of the letter leaves Coffij behind. Amazingly, there is a new voice and a defiant statement on behalf of the mutineers by Sergeant Niesse. Were these sentences written with Coffij's approval or even his knowledge? It is possible that Niesse added them secretly, taking advantage of the opportunity to send word. "With respect to us Christians," the letter switched abruptly, "we know very well that God is the source of all order and we will stay with these people [the rebels] until the end." [20] Niesse proclaimed on behalf of the mutineers that they did not want to get any more letters from the Dutch "because they [their officers] mistreated us badly and we do not desire to return to you." "God rules over all," Niesse, or the mutineers, repeated emphatically in closing, "we commend ourselves to our dear Lord [*den lieben god*] every day." [21] If this astonishing letter was signed, the clerk omitted it from the record.[22]

The mutineers' portion of the letter revealed that the Suriname officers had secretly been in touch with them.[23] Indeed, when Van Hoogenheim inquired, the officers confirmed that they had written the deserters as soon as they learned they had joined the insurgents. Their letter had stressed the officers' shock and abhorrence to hear that Christian soldiers "had united themselves with heathens to wage war and exterminate their fellow brethren in Christ," for which, they had emphasized, God, and man, would judge them harshly. The officers nevertheless beseeched the mutineers to return to the Dutch before the reinforcements from Holland arrived to "exterminate you and your Barbarian friends." The officers pledged to work hard to obtain "a complete pardon" for any mutineer who returned and fought against the rebels.[24] The mutineers' assertion of godliness and Christianity in response to accusations of religious and political infidelity was a strong, even revolutionary, declaration that they, despite joining "heathen" rebels, continued to belong to Christendom.

Van Hoogenheim sharply questioned the two messengers, one at a time, with the aid of a translator. Their separate testimonials matched. The most important news, and, for the Dutch, the best news, was that the mutineers did not number forty-one, but only thirteen. The emissaries did echo what Cupido had claimed about the unity of the ex-slaves, that "all is rebel, that has the name of *neger.*" But they also qualified this blanket assertion. The Indians related that the *bomba* of the Company plantation Hooftplantage had declared that he and his people "had a good heart for the Christians and desired that they'd repossess the country."[25] Such statements continued to suggest that Company people were overall less enthusiastic about the revolt and less involved than those from private plantations.

Van Hoogenheim wrote back immediately. He ignored the mutineers, responding only to Coffij. He now understood what the rebels wanted, but he could not agree to anything until he received instructions from home. He assured Coffij that he had already written to the directors in Holland. An answer might take as long as three to four months, he claimed, two at best. However, since the four requested Company plantations were currently "in your possession," and (again using the third person to refer to himself) the Dutch governor "had not yet come to fight" to repossess them, the rebels should be content to live quietly and show him they were sincere in their desire for peace. Heer Schirmeister would gladly pay ransom for the daughters of the deceased councilman George, as well as for all other European children still held by the rebels. To continue the diplomatic dance, Van Hoogenheim urged his opponents to spell out their requirements for the return of the hostages in a letter. "At least you can be assured," the Dutch governor closed, "that the Heer Gouverneur, de Heer Schirmeister, and the other *Heeren* mean well by the *neegers* and" (in either a dig at or a nod to the mutineers) "all good Christians."[26]

Five days later, Van Hoogenheim received what would turn out to be Coffij's last letter, delivered by the same Amerindians, paddling the river, as before. Governor Coffij, "hoping to remain in peace," agreed to a truce. He understood that he had to be patient "till letters arrived from Holland." He swore "on God Almighty" that if the Dutch refrained from attack, his forces would do likewise. He hoped that the Dutch, too, would swear to peace. Coffij suggested a Dutch delegation visit the rebel camp to pick up the two young women in exchange for twenty barrels of gunpowder, thirty guns, and a barrel of tobacco. Perhaps as a further sign of his goodwill, he specified that the exchange could wait until word "about the four plantations" arrived from Holland, at which time he would trade the two hostages for the desired supplies.[27]

A few years earlier, Tempati rebels in Suriname had offered a similar truce to encourage their European opponents to meet their demands. Coffij may also have decided a delay would allow him to retain his hostages until a formal peace agreement was made, at which time the Dutch might be more inclined to supply him with weapons. It is unclear whether he actually expected the Dutch to hand over weapons or merely wanted to test them. When Ndyuka Maroons in Suriname in the late 1750s did not receive powder and shot as part of the goodwill gifts at peace negotiations, they reproached the colonial negotiators visiting their camp, saying that even if they had brought but a bit of ammunition, "we would have seen [your] good intentions, but now, no!" Post-treaty Maroons in Suriname, too, regularly requested ammunition and weapons, but rarely received them in the quantities they wanted, since colonists were leery of arming potential enemies.[28]

Governor Coffij's tone was one of good-natured levity between peers. He closed with affable greetings to Governor van Hoogenheim, his councilmen, and "all good Christians" along with a "very friendly greeting from my Abina George, and from [her] sister to Mr. Schermeister and all our good friends." Georgina herself, or someone writing for her, added, "I hope that you will do your utmost to buy my freedom."[29]

It turned out that the Dutch were not keen to do their "utmost." In his reply on August 9, Van Hoogenheim agreed to a truce, but he "could not swear to it without an order from Holland," as the land was not his. He was eager to ransom the two women and children. If Coffij would send them over right now, Van Hoogenheim would hand over textiles, tobacco, salted meat, bacon, and "any other supplies we have that you desire." The rebels should also return the corporal as a further sign of their sincerity. It was impossible to supply the rebels with weapons at the moment, Van Hoogenheim explained, because doing so went against his oath of office. Once the Dutch received word and permission from Holland, the rebels upriver could have what they wanted: gunpowder and weapons, "all you need." Until then, they had to wait and, Van Hoogenheim insisted, "first send us the young women and children and the corporal." [30]

The Dutch received no answer to their procrastinating offer.

Coup d'État

Why did Governor Coffij end the negotiations? Clearly, Van Hoogenheim's unwillingness to swear an oath cementing the truce made Coffij deeply suspicious. In West Africa, oaths were sacred and necessary to seal any agreement. [31] Van Hoogenheim's refusal to hand over weapons might also have been interpreted as a sign of ill will. [32] Or perhaps Captain Accara and his soldiers, returning from their expedition to fight the Indians, reduced Coffij's freedom to negotiate. When the Dutch questioned recaptured slaves in the spring of 1764, they asked few questions about Coffij or about the internal workings of the rebellion. Consequently, references to Coffij are surprisingly scant. But clues suggest that his diplomacy led to a major political crisis in rebel ranks and to his own demise. [33]

Coffij's attempts at dialogue deeply disturbed many of his fellow leaders, who rejected what looked at best like a willingness to compromise and accommodate the Europeans or, at worst, capitulation. Accabiré van Stevensburg, a leader from the Canje River and a major player in the rebellion, claimed during his interrogation that many of the rebels "turned against Governor Coffij, because he wrote to the Christians." It is possible that Coffij had reopened the negotiations without the approval of his fellow leaders, who may not have been keen on diplomacy at all. In neighboring Suriname, Tempati rebel spokesman Boston had allegedly expressed his reluctance to negotiate with the colonial authorities in 1757 without the full support of his followers, "because otherwise the other *neegers* would be suspicious that he was scheming with the whites to betray them, and they might shoot him dead."[34] Perhaps Coffij was up against similar pressures and had been willing to take this risk.

Leading the opposition was a recently arrived African named Atta. Also an Amina, Atta came from Altenklingen, one of the first plantations involved in the rebellion. Atta had been a leader from the start of the insurgency; he rose quickly through the ranks to a captaincy and a seat on Coffij's council. He participated in the Peereboom massacre and was deeply suspicious of Coffij's renewed efforts at diplomacy.[35] An angry Atta had "called his officers together and asked them whether Coffij, did right or not and they decried it," Accabiré alleged in his interrogation, "and then Coffij called his officers together, too, and asked them to support him which they promised." Abbreviating what was no doubt a painful and lengthy process of debate and deliberation, Accabiré recounted that after leaders had lined up supporters, "conflict ensued between them."[36] Accabiré, born in West Africa and head of the "Gangoe," or Ganga, faction, appears to have been on Atta's side in the coup against Coffij, though subsequently they became enemies.[37] In his interrogation, Atta denied having called the rebel council in order to remove Coffij and Accara from office "and chase them out." He did concede that he and Coffij had a falling-out, but, he claimed, it was not related to the negotiations. Rather, Atta claimed, he and Coffij disagreed about the Ganga, "whom Coffij wanted to kill and he [Atta] wanted to retain."[38]

As a result of this conflict, which signaled a profound lack of confidence in his leadership, Coffij shot himself, though the date remains unclear. The coup likely happened in September, after Coffij reopened, and then ended, the second round of negotiations in August. The Dutch learned in mid-October that Governor Coffij had killed himself, that Captain Accara had been enslaved, and that Atta was the new "chieftain."[39] Coffij, the leader of the largest slave rebellion in the Caribbean to date, a man who had dared to dream of a new colonial order, who, had he succeeded, might well have governed the first black republic, slipped out of history with barely a notice.

In trying to understand Governor Coffij's suicide, we gain insight into how he perceived his position at that moment. Among the Yoruba people in precolonial Oyo, for instance, which covered parts of what are now Nigeria and Benin in West Africa, kings who lost the support of the council of chiefs were expected to kill themselves to avoid public shame, earn respect, and prevent further violence. Governor Coffij's suicide should be seen in a similar vein. Allegedly he committed this ritual suicide in front of some of his closest supporters, ensuring his followers would know he had not been murdered. Amelia van Hollandia & Zeelandia, Coffij's counselor who had been either his cook or his wife, or both, claimed that she had seen him shoot himself. While in Oyo society, suicide by ordinary people was condemned, chiefs who committed ritual suicide for political reasons were given honorable public internments.[40]

Coffij's funeral was a momentous occasion. Everyone at the fort, except for Captain Quassie, who remained with a skeleton crew of six armed men, went upriver to attend.[41] In keeping with West African beliefs that death was a portal into a new life where the deceased political leader would need an entourage, at least five people were killed to accompany Coffij in the afterlife.[42] These included several European children and a female *wisiman*, or witch. The Dutch later accused (and executed) Amelia van Hollandia for having killed two children "to run their blood over Coffij's grave." Understandably, Amelia denied this charge, but the accusation was in keeping with cultural practice.[43] Enslaved informants on the Caribbean island of St. John spoke about blood sprinkled on graves among the Amina in West Africa.[44]

While the political upset appears to have been fought out among men, it also affected women who had been members of Coffij's inner circle. An enslaved "mulatto" woman named Cariba, who reportedly had served as Coffij's cook (or wife) at Fort Nassau, now became a wife to Atta.[45] Several other "wives" took advantage of the crisis to run away. They may have feared being sacrificed at Coffij's funeral or been apprehensive about having to marry the new leaders. One was a free native woman named Maria or Marie, "one of Coffij's wives," who according to surgeon Mangmeister fled to the Corentyne River.[46] The other was Georgina, the young Dutch woman who had been made Coffij's wife. She had seen her parents murdered in the first days of the uprising and she may also have been present at the sacrifice of her younger sister at Coffij's funeral, along with another young Dutch girl who had been her companion. The traumatized woman, a real survivor, chanced an escape, hoping to make her way to the Dutch with the help of two Amerindians. She did not get far before she was recaptured.[47]

Coffij's wives may have worried that they, too, would be killed at his funeral. Among many West African peoples, along with an entourage, a leader's closest servants and family members, those with the most access to the leader and his body, were expected to die with him. This practice ensured their loyalty to, and protection of, their leader, as his demise also spelled their own death. Enslaved Africans interviewed on the Danish Caribbean island of St. John in the 1760s confirmed such practices among the Amina. One of them told the minister who questioned him that the Amina "killed the most important wife" as soon as the king or governor died. Others suggested that the first wife was allowed to live, but all the wives he had obtained in war were buried with him, along with his cook, his servants, his slaves, and others.[48]

Reports indicate that before he killed himself, Coffij buried his remaining gunpowder to keep it out of the hands of his opponents. He shot dead the man or men who had helped him so they could not divulge the location. One European commander claimed Coffij had buried twenty-five barrels.[49] That number seems too high, but he may have buried the powder he had recently received from the mutineers. If these reports about buried gunpowder are true, it is hard to know the motive. Was it done out of spitefulness, or was it a further indication of Coffij's intent to have the rebellion end in a peace treaty with the Europeans rather than in deadly warfare?

After Coffij's sudden death, as rebel leaders vied for power, Atta seized the number one spot. There is some indication that after Coffij's fall, several men became governors, but that either Atta, a major leader in the coup, muscled them out or they died. However it happened exactly—the records are inconclusive—Atta became the new governor.[50]

His ascent spelled change not just for women close to Coffij, but for everyone else as well. Those who had been part of Coffij's cabinet, such as Captain Accara, were demoted or killed or had their European clothes and valuables taken.[51] Atta elevated others as a reward for their support or to ensure their continued loyalty. Quassie van Hardenbroek, for instance, claimed that "while Coffij was alive," he was a mere soldier, tasked with the mundane job of guarding supplies. When Atta became governor, Quassie was promoted to captain and put in command of twenty-four men. Some of the mutineers who had grown close to Governor Coffij were moved from rebel headquarters at Fort Nassau to lesser posts. Mutineer and surgeon Mangmeister was sent to Company plantation Hooftplantage to "distill liquor for Atta."[52]

The situation for Creoles deteriorated further. Shortly before Coffij's downfall, twenty-two men, women, and children, Company people from Fort Nassau, had escaped from the rebels. Taking advantage of a moonless night, they had slipped away in five canoes. Their leader was Van Hoogenheim's former messenger to the rebels the carpenter Christiaan, who had been kept hostage among the rebels since May. The escapees had related to the Dutch that the insurgents closely watched the Creoles, especially Company Creoles.[53] After the coup, militant Africans belonging to private plantations reportedly gained the upper hand among the rebels, mistreating Creoles, in part because they had resisted a military solution.[54]

Indian informants claimed that the rebels were newly determined to attack the Dutch as soon as they finished making bows and arrows to arm "all blacks who don't have a gun."[55] They fortified their rebel camps, especially plantation Vigilantie.[56] Clearly, all possibilities for diplomacy had passed. If Governor Coffij had hoped to increase political cohesion by making an agreement with the Dutch, the attempt at diplomacy created the opposite effect. The defeat of Coffij and his supporters and the demotion of Creoles meant that the rebellion now increasingly became an African affair. Coffij's death did little to unite the rebels. The lack of supplies and internal strife, which Coffij had hoped to solve with diplomacy, grew only more urgent. Cornered and divided, rebel leaders would increasingly turn toward desperate measures.

Coffij's lack of a global trade network was his undoing. His strategy was solid. Taking advantage of the rebels' position of strength, he worked to convince the Dutch to end all hostilities. A treaty would have allowed him to redeploy his resources from military to peaceful ends, cultivate gardens, and rebuild his political coalition. Possession of the upper end of the colony provided access to a vast hinterland and opened prospects for increasing trade with Amerindians. Living side by side with the Dutch as neighbors and running four sugar plantations would potentially have enabled him to engage in international trade. But to get the Dutch to the table in a meaningful way he needed allies. Thirty years later, the slave revolt in St. Domingue succeeded and became the Haitian Revolution in part because its leaders received weapons from the Spanish, who sought to hurt the French. Without allies, Governor Coffij could neither put enough pressure on the Europeans nor quell dissent in his own ranks.[57]

10

The Turning of the Tide

By fall, as the rainy season abated, death and disease continued to bring out the worst in the surviving Europeans. Burghers, officials, and officers quarreled, profiteered, and generally acted poorly. Planters and ships' captains sold supplies intended for general distribution, and did so at inflated prices. The death toll for seamen from disease was so high that one ship had only one sailor well enough to take charge; he could neither read nor write. The two leading commanders of the Suriname forces returned home to recuperate, leaving a young and inexperienced lieutenant in charge of restive troops. The slim civil bureaucracy was increasingly crippled. Van Hoogenheim no longer had a healthy clerk left to help with correspondence and record keeping, nor a steward to inventory and distribute dwindling victuals. Exhausted and defeated, the Dutch governor begged to be replaced, once the colony was "cleansed," by a man "of greater ability and capacity."[1]

Further denting morale, Van Hoogenheim had not received any word from home about military assistance. Everyone knew that news of their plight would take time to reach Europe. Still, it was crushing to have no communication at all about what the directors had decided to do to save their colony, and when, or even whether, they were sending aid. Since the uprising, only one ship had reached Berbice from Holland, in June, but it had set off on its voyage before news of the rebellion had reached the directors. "We are becoming hopeless about the arriving of our national secours," Van Hoogenheim lamented in his journal. "We hear or learn nothing. . . . Will Christendom here be entirely forgotten, and sacrificed to a barbarian enemy?" he cried. "I see nothing but a sad ending for us."[2]

His officers once again urged Van Hoogenheim to abandon Dageraad; the Dutch governor again refused, determined to hang on. "If I could bring the gardens for the whites and the slaves with me downriver," he responded, "I would not hesitate a moment," but, "the distress and misery that would result without them would be indescribable." He wrote letter after letter to the directors (sent to Holland via Suriname and Essequibo, a multistage and lengthy journey), asking why there had been "neither word nor sign" from them. "Have your honors entirely forgotten us?" he despaired, echoing Jesus on the cross. "We are here at the brink," he wrote, invoking a quintessential Dutch metaphor about drowning, "the water has been brought to our lips."[3]

Amsterdam

Word of the rebellion had in fact arrived in the Dutch Republic. In late May, ships from St. Eustatius and Barbados brought the news, which was immediately reported in local and national newspapers. Sipping their tea and coffee sweetened with sugar in the country's numerous coffeehouses, Dutch citizens shuddered as they read the accounts of murdered planters and determined insurgents. Almost every inhabitant of the republic at this time consumed the luxury goods brought from overseas colonies. Few made the effort to connect their addictive and well-sweetened drinks with the bloodshed abroad.[4]

Ship captains arriving in Amsterdam traveled to the Society of Berbice to deliver letters from Berbice refugees in Essequibo. Amsterdam was no longer the entrepreneurial powerhouse and trading hub it had been in the fabled "Golden Age." The city's port had been surpassed by those of Hamburg and London by the middle of the eighteenth century. Manufacturing stagnated although industries associated with colonial production like shipbuilding, sugar processing, and calico printing remained robust. Rather than producers, Amsterdammers became consumers, especially of colonial products like coffee and sugar, while the city's wealthy merchants and regents turned into international financiers, lending enormous sums abroad. Amsterdam bankers helped Britain and Prussia finance the Seven Years' War, which had ended the very month the Berbice Rebellion broke out. Yet colonial Atlantic trade was opening up new markets for Amsterdam traders in the German hinterlands, blunting economic decline.[5]

In the absence of official word from the governors of Essequibo and Berbice—their letters were still en route—the directors were skeptical that the situation was as bad as refugee planters' letters suggested. After all, they surmised, the planters had "to justify their retreat." Nevertheless, the sober Dutchmen concluded, "at best, the situation does not look favorable," and they rented two merchant ships to dispatch fifty soldiers to Berbice, and perhaps a third ship with a few more. The directors realized that so few men would not suffice, but they were short on funds. They turned to the government for help, since the 1732 charter of the Berbice Company stipulated that the Company's directors operated "under the sovereignty and protection" of the States General. The directors mobilized plantation owners, merchants, and financiers living in Amsterdam with commercial interests in Berbice. Together, these stakeholders lobbied the States General for soldiers to reconquer the colony. They requested an expeditionary force of several warships and at least six hundred men.[6]

To justify the cost in men and money, the directors made their case that Berbice was simply, in modern parlance, too big to fail. They conceded that Berbice was still in its infancy and not nearly as large as Suriname, "about whose importance all are convinced." Nevertheless, they claimed, the colony's coffee, cacao, cotton, and sugar were sold in the Dutch Republic for 1.5 million guilders a year. While a spokesman privately conceded that this estimate was inflated by a third (and even in reduced form it is likely too high), it was no doubt a considerable traffic. Moreover, the directors stressed, the colony imported just about everything from the republic, providing work and income for Dutch "merchants, artisans, shopkeepers and laborers." The directors were correct about the importance of the Atlantic colonies for the economy of the Dutch Republic, and even more so for the province of Holland

and the city of Amsterdam. Given the economic contributions of Berbice, the directors urged, surely it deserved public aid. And there was the domino effect to consider. If the uprising went unchecked, the enslaved in neighboring colonies might follow the example of the Berbice rebels, causing "irreparable loss" to individual Dutch citizens, not to mention to the Dutch Republic as a whole.[7] Without government intervention, the entire Dutch Wild Coast could collapse.

Berbice stakeholders were well connected at the highest levels of Dutch politics, especially in the chamber of Holland, which had much weight in the States General. Recent calculations suggest that the economy of the province of Holland depended to a considerable extent on Atlantic slavery. Holland's deputies persuaded the representatives of sister provinces that were less involved in the colonies to agree to pay their part of the cost of a military intervention. By the time the States General deliberated in July, letters from Governor van Hoogenheim had finally arrived, detailing the extent of the uprising and the scope of the rescue mission required. Officials in neighboring Suriname and Essequibo, along with the directors of the Society of Suriname, urged the deployment of state troops in Berbice. So, too, did the powerful Louis Ernest Brunswick-Wolfenbüttel. The corpulent forty-four-year-old Prussian duke commanded the Dutch army as regent for the teenage Prince of Orange, Willem V. All concurred that without "the strong hand of the state," Berbice was doomed.[8]

In July, the States General agreed to rescue the colony. They requested that the Duke of Brunswick organize the logistics for an eighteen-month deployment of troops. They demanded that the directors of the Company of Berbice draft a plan to reimburse the state for its expenditures. They also ordered them to report on their management of the colony. It was widely suspected that the directors had not fulfilled the terms of their charter regarding defense or the stipulation that one European be settled for every fifteen enslaved people, a measure thought to reduce despotic behavior among slave owners and the chance of slave revolt. In their defense, the Berbice directors, disingenuously, if tellingly, replied that more European men only led to more debauchery with enslaved women.[9]

Robert Douglas and Louis Ernst van Brunswick-Wolfenbüttel, 1786, painted by Jacobus Vrijmoet, photograph by Peter Cox. The Duke of Brunswick was famously corpulent. (Collectie Het Noordbrabants Museum-'s-Hertogenbosch, The Netherlands.)

While Brunswick organized the expeditionary force, the States General provided emergency relief. They redirected to Berbice the frigate *St. Maartensdijk*, about to set sail from Zeeland for the Mediterranean against Barbary pirates, and ordered the preparation of two more ships. These three vessels, carrying an additional four hundred soldiers, disembarked from Holland, one in late July and the other two in August. The eleven hundred soldiers sent by the Dutch Republic, in addition to the fifty fighting men dispatched by the Company directors and the Suriname and St. Eustatius forces already in Berbice, were about to confront an enemy that at most numbered fifteen hundred rebel combatants.[10]

Brunswick decided against sending an entire regiment of two battalions. Instead, he required each garrison throughout the country to send a quota of healthy volunteers. Enticed by the prospect of bounty pay and adventure, just shy of seven hundred officers, soldiers, and support personnel stepped forward. It was an international mercenary army. Likely close to half the soldiers, and perhaps a quarter of the officers, were English, French, German, Austrian, and Swiss. Brunswick appointed as commander Colonel Jan Marius de Salve, a career soldier from Zeeland in his midfifties. While De Salve had extensive military experience, none of it had been overseas. As second-in-command, Brunswick chose thirty-six-year-old Lieutenant Colonel Robert Douglas, a Scottish officer and personal friend. Douglas owned a plantation in Demerara gifted to him by his older brother James, who served in the Caribbean as a rear admiral in the British navy.[11]

Given the susceptibility to disease of Europeans in the tropics, Brunswick reached out to military and medical experts for advice about how to preserve the soldiers' health. The recommendations reflected the three pillars of eighteenth-century maritime and military medicine: ventilation, diet, and hygiene. The prescription was followed to the letter.[12]

Since the Berbice River was too shallow to accommodate warships, the duke rented for the mission seven smaller armed ships. The space between their decks was increased and air holes were added high above the waterline to allow for a refreshing breeze in the sleeping quarters even "with stiff wind and a hollow sea." Additional sails were stretched over the decks to shield the men from the tropical sun. As "good health depends on good nourishment," the holds were packed with provisions from the Dutch Republic. Dried fruits, meats, hams, eggs, cheese, nuts, tea, coffee, wines, and liqueurs along with live pigs, sheep, ducks, and chickens were brought aboard for the officers. For the ordinary soldiers crewmen stored away peas, groats and oats, cabbages, dried fish, bacon, cheese, "Irish meat," and 202,743 pounds of "bread," likely hardtack, along with tobacco and beer. To take care of the sick and wounded, the fleet carried chests full of medicines along with enough supplies to outfit a hospital.[13]

The men were dressed in linen, rather than the customary wool, to keep them more comfortable in the tropics. Each man received a blue coat "with flat tin buttons," along with shirts, long and short pants,

and a sleeping cap, daintily "hemmed with blue ribbon." Their luggage also included a leather cap, a duffel coat, a soldier's hat, short
boots, and shoes. The boots proved mostly unwearable, because they
were "too short, too narrow," and, the men later complained, "the
leather tears like paper." [14] Military suppliers were notorious for skimp-
ing on quality to increase their profits.

Since the state of the colony remained unknown (there was specu-
lation Berbice "might have to be reconquered as an abandoned land"),
the ships were loaded with arms, lots of them—more than 4,000 weapons. The loading list of "ordinary weapons" included 1,893 "ordinary
guns with bayonets and steel ramrod," another 120 guns of superior
quality for officers and sergeants, and 180 pistols. The list of artillery,
ammunition, and guns included another 1,600 "snaphaunces," or muskets with bayonets, along with another 120 for officers, and 120 pistols.
Supplies also included spare parts, and materials to repair weapons
were also provided. And they supplemented this considerable arsenal
with 12 hand mortars and 1,200 hand mortar grenades; 1,000 hand grenades; 2,000 pounds of wick; 20,000 flints; almost 60,000 live rounds
of various sizes; 2,000 pounds of cast lead in a variety of weights; and
2,000 pounds of "uncast lead" to make more bullets.[15]

For building warehouses and shelters, officials placed on board
9,300 nails of varying sizes, 1,200 spades, 800 axes, 500 pickaxes,
400 machetes, 36 saws, and endless lengths of oilcloth and rope. Finally, they added a chest filled with "presents" for the crucial allied
Indians—"differente Neurenberger waaren," specialty homewares
manufactured in Nuremberg, Germany, including knives, scissors,
buttons, fishhooks, mirrors, painted metal boxes, combs, toys, and
other curiosities. Surprisingly lacking was "salempoeris," a plain blue
calico cloth from the Coromandel coast of India that Amerindians preferred as compensation for their services. It would prove to be a costly
oversight.[16]

The extensive global trading networks of the Dutch made possible
this impressive cargo. The republic still controlled prodigious wealth
even as its economy was stagnating. The Berbice rebels facing the
Dutch possessed mostly battered shovels and machetes, with little

remaining in the way of guns and powder, and whatever food they could scavenge or grow themselves. Wars, while costly, were a boon to business for an imperial nation. Dutch merchants supplying equipment for the military suppression of a colonial slave revolt cashed in. The Dutch were fighting to preserve their investment portfolios. The rebels were fighting for their lives.

The ships were loaded at a string of islands that separated the inland Zuider Zee from the North Sea. Texel, the largest of these islands, was the staging ground for Dutch oceanic voyages from Holland. Merchant and warships alike anchored in the shallow waterway east of the island to be loaded with crew and cargo, bound for destinations in Europe, Africa, the East Indies, and the Americas. Against a backdrop of gray dunes and red-roofed villages, pilot boats, admiralty yachts, and supply barges maneuvered Texel waters, sails full and flags flapping. The prevailing winds in the republic blew across the North Sea from the west, and ship crews regularly had to wait weeks before finally unfurling their sails. The little fleet bound for Berbice was ready on October 21, yet the wind continued to blow from the wrong direction. It was an expensive delay, Brunswick explained to the States General, because "the troops were provided with fresh bread and meat" while waiting at Texel. Finally, on Sunday November 6, a stiff easterly whipped up whitecaps on the sea. A nearby man-of-war heralded the departing fleet with an eight-cannon salute, answered by De Salve's artillery.[17]

Canje Expedition

In mid-October, the governor of Essequibo relayed the welcome news to Berbice officials that the States General was outfitting four warships and two battalions of soldiers, to arrive soon. In actuality, these ships did not depart the Dutch Republic until November. But in late October, the first of the ships sent earlier with emergency relief appeared at the mouth of the Berbice River. *St. Maartensdijk* carried 150 soldiers. The ship had made a quick stop for intelligence in Paramaribo, where the captain received an earful about the deadly epidemics in Berbice and the need to fight a quick war before his soldiers were felled by disease.[18]

Armed with this information, that the infectious illnesses were rampant at Dageraad, Captain Maarten Haringman refused to sail up the Berbice River. So Van Hoogenheim hurried by tent boat to meet him at the coast. Haringman's commission from the States General called for him to make decisions jointly with the Dutch governor, but on first meeting the two men disagreed over the best course of action. Van Hoogenheim pushed his plan to wait until Indians closed off the colony's borders and there was a force large enough to attack all rebels quickly and at once. Haringman wanted to fight before disease struck down his soldiers, believing that as long as they "remained on the move," they were less likely to fall ill.[19]

Against his better judgment, Van Hoogenheim compromised. Agreeing they did not have the forces to undertake an expedition on the Berbice, the two men decided they could, as Van Hoogenheim wrote, "provisionally retake the Canje River without overly alarming our rebels on the Berbice." Since the rebels manned only a few posts, there was a good chance of a favorable outcome. Retaking the Canje would secure the border with Suriname, restore overland communication with that colony, and allow the Dutch to control the paths between the Canje and Fort Nassau on the Berbice. Haringman and Van Hoogenheim would jointly command the expedition. Although the governor believed that the captain "pretends to higher command than he is legally entitled to," Van Hoogenheim was willing to share power if that was what it took. In his journal, he expressed his fears that the expedition would only induce the Canje rebels to flee to the rebel stronghold Fort Nassau on the Berbice, meaning that "none will fall into our hands."[20]

Preparations were made quickly to preserve the element of surprise. A detachment of 45 soldiers, a few burghers, and an officer were left to protect Dageraad. Everyone else, some 180 soldiers and officers, embarked on two merchant ships fortified with cannons. The Canje River, even more so than the Berbice, was too narrow for tacking, so the two ships made their way upriver slowly, relying on the tide and wind when possible. Whenever the tide ebbed, they struck their sails and anchored. The warship was too deep to enter the Canje River and remained anchored in the mouth of the Berbice.[21]

If the slow-moving Europeans thought they could sneak up on the rebels, they were gravely mistaken. Their opponents had men stationed in the woods on the lower Canje River both to keep an eye on the Dutch at Fort St. Andries and to monitor who entered the colony. Leapfrogging from station to station, the lookouts alerted rebel leaders to the arrival of the Dutch warship, the preparations for an expedition, and the lumbering progress of the two boats up the Canje River. The Dutch did surprise a few lookouts, who departed from their posts so hastily they left behind their canoes as well as their supplies of dried and barbecued fish, salt, and cooking pots.[22]

Runners alerted Governor Atta at Fort Nassau as the ships came up the Canje River. The Canje rebels requested powder because they had none left. Atta refused to share his dwindling supplies. Instead, he ordered them to retreat to the Berbice to combine forces in anticipation of a Dutch attack on that river. One man later testified that Atta had directed Captain Fortuin van Helvetia, the commander of the Canje River, "to come to Berbice with all the negroes, and to behead those that refused."[23]

The Europeans advanced unimpeded up the lower Canje, a section with few plantations. Some fifty miles up the river, they reached plantation Don Carlos, the start of the most densely inhabited stretch of the river. Here, 120 men went ashore. Officers ordered them to march to plantation Stevensburg, so the Dutch could attack the Canje's main rebel post simultaneously from land and water.[24]

As the Canje rebels could not mount a military defense for lack of powder and shot, they prepared a hasty retreat. Everyone was ordered upriver toward plantation Horstenburg, the start of the path through the forest and savanna to Fort Nassau. From there large numbers of Canje people made their way to the fort. Before they left, the rebels placed tar and kindling in plantation buildings and lit fire after fire as the Dutch approached. By waiting until the last moment to burn buildings, the rebels achieved the maximum psychological effect on the Dutch. Passengers onboard the advancing ships observed the "sad spectacle" of plantations in full flame. The Europeans could do little about the infernos, which they watched all night with "great sorrow." By the time the expedition reached Stevensburg, some seventy miles upriver, rebel commanders Fortuin van Helvetia and Accara van de Brandwacht torched and abandoned that plantation too. Troops sent overland set to work extinguishing the flames. One of the Dutch ships continued up the river a few more miles to Horstenburg but encountered no one to apprehend. Van Hoogenheim's prediction played out: taking the Canje River with no captives was an empty military gesture.[25]

With no enemies to fight or to capture, there was little for the Dutch to do but turn back. The objective now became holding on to the river. The Dutch governor ordered one hundred soldiers and five burghers posted at Stevensburg to prevent a rebel return. For further protection, one ship remained at Stevensburg as well. On Tuesday, November 15, Van Hoogenheim and Haringman boarded the *Hoop*. As they descended the river past the charred remains of once thriving plantations, they noticed campfires here and there onshore and heard occasional shouting in the bush, indications, the governor penned, that while the river was nominally back in Dutch hands, it was not entirely "cleansed and safe."[26]

Three days later, in the middle of the night, the Dutch arrived back at St. Andries. They had lost only one soldier on their expedition—not to their opponents, but to nature. The man had died "of a swoon," or heatstroke, on the overland march. They had been gone only a week, but on Dageraad several sailors and soldiers who had stayed behind had succumbed to disease. The men Captain Haringman had dispatched to the plantation to operate the cannon in case of a rebel attack were also in the hospital.[27] Clearly, staying behind had been more dangerous than going shadowboxing with elusive rebels on the Canje River.

The Canje expedition had not exactly been a success, but the day after his return Van Hoogenheim received good news. He welcomed to Fort St. Andries a ship sent by the Society of Berbice. The *Jonge*

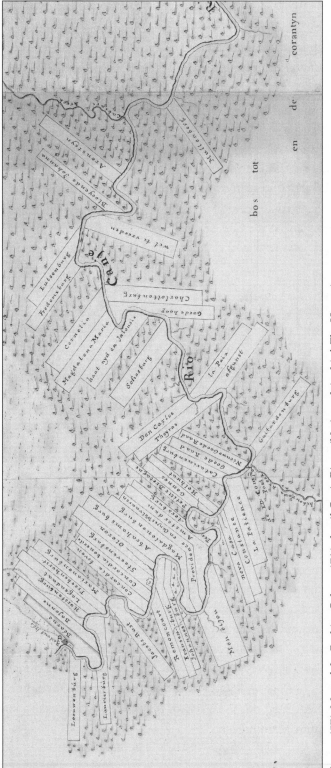

Leupe 1571, Map of the Berbice Colony, 1764, detail Canje River. (Nationaal Archief, The Hague.)

Thomas brought an additional thirty-six soldiers, a few new Company employees, and, finally, letters from the directors detailing the long-awaited military help being prepared in Holland. What's more, the ship's captain relayed that two warships sent by the States General in August along with two additional merchant marine ships sent by the Company had reached the Atlantic "wine" island of Madeira off the North African coast, a customary stop on the voyage from Holland to the Wild Coast, and would soon continue on to Berbice.[28]

In another stroke of good fortune, the Dutch captured one of the Suriname mutineers as the Canje expedition wrapped up. He related "many particulars" about what the Dutch called "rebel housekeeping."[29]

Rebel Housekeeping

Before Governor van Hoogenheim set off on the Canje expedition, he had ordered the ship *Zeven Provintien* on a reconnaissance mission to Company plantation Hooftplantage to ascertain whether the *bomba* and his people remained loyal to the Dutch. As the ship passed rebel camp Vigilantie, insurgents fired on it. The captain returned their volley with his "big guns," scattering the attackers. Armed soldiers sent ashore found only "a lot of blood," numerous warm cooking fires, and machetes. As *Zeven Provintien* approached Hooftplantage that night under a quarter moon, those on board saw the house, the mill, and other buildings in flames, stenciled against the black night sky.

The next morning, Hooftplantage appeared deserted, except for two men who dared the Dutch to come ashore. One of them rang the plantation bell (perhaps in mockery of this call to work or as a signal to his friends). Then he patted his buttocks and yelled, "Lick my ass." That seemed a clear answer regarding loyalty, so the captain turned his ship around. By the time the boat passed Vigilantie again, that plantation, too, had collapsed in a mound of ashes. Shortly after, the ship's lookout spotted a European in a canoe. The man claimed to be on his way to Dageraad and refused to come aboard. Brought on ship by force, he turned out to be one of the Suriname mutineers, surgeon Johan Carolus Mangmeister.[30]

The surgeon had been a favorite of Governor Coffij's, but after Coffij's death, Mangmeister's fortunes shifted radically. Governor Atta, unimpressed by European healing skills or eager to rid himself of Coffij's allies, sent the medic from Fort Nassau to Hooftplantage to "distill liquor." When *Zeven Provintien* exchanged fire with rebels on plantation Vigilantie—the river carried the sound of the booming shots far and wide—the startled insurgents retreated to Fort Nassau, taking Mangmeister along. Before they reached the fort they met up with more rebels. While the men debated what to do, Mangmeister escaped. It is unclear whether, as he claimed, he intended to rejoin the Dutch or, more likely, aimed for Spanish territory on the Orinoco. By his own account, the surgeon had spent five days in the woods with no food before he found the canoe.

As soon as he was spotted by sailors on *Zeven Provintien*, Mangmeister pushed overboard an iron pot and a bag, the incriminating evidence of his collaboration with the rebels. Despite repeated attempts, the loot was not retrieved. But the surviving luggage contained silver and clothes given to the surgeon by Governor Coffij in reward for his medical services. The stash would have made good barter on an escape to Venezuela. The sailors found in his canoe a silver knife, fork, and spoon engraved with "George," tableware obviously belonging to the father of Coffij's "wife" and hostage Georgina. Mangmeister would later declare that another of Coffij's wives, whom he did not name, had given him these pieces after he cured her. Perhaps he just took them.[31]

Mangmeister told the Dutch that when the Berbice rebels heard about the Canje expedition, they beat a retreat to Company plantation Peereboom to make their stand. Peereboom's advantageous situation, on a hill overlooking the Berbice River, made it easier to defend than other plantations. At the beginning of the rebellion, Dutch burghers had taken refuge there for the same reason. The surgeon added that as rebels went upriver, they left behind a deliberate trail of destruction, as the sailors on *Zeven Provintien* had already witnessed. Governor van Hoogenheim's fears—that the Canje expedition would push the insurgents upriver, along with any lukewarm supporters and noncombatants, and that many plantations would be incinerated—had been realized, not only on the Canje, but also on the Berbice.

Mangmeister divulged many particulars of the rebels' *huishouding*, or management, much of it showing signs of internal conflict. He asserted that the Amina slaves were in full control, suggesting that the succession crisis after Coffij's death had been settled, at least for the time being. Mangmeister also related that the "Crioles had to serve [the Aminas] as slaves." The fact that rebel generals re-enslaved others did not surprise the Dutch. Coercion and forced labor were the law of the land.[32]

More puzzling, Mangmeister asserted that the Aminas had "destroyed or chased into the bush most of the Angolans." Two other mutineers, caught in Demerara after escaping the rebels in late November, claimed that "Angola" people, "100 strong with guns though no powder" had installed themselves in the Wiruni Creek. It is not clear who these "Angolans" were. No enslaved people questioned by the Dutch after the rebellion identified themselves as such. Perhaps the three mutineers, like many Europeans, referred to all West Central Africans (including Loango, Congos, and Angolans) as "Angolans." Perhaps Mangmeister's story referred to the conflict between Accabiré and Atta. Accabiré was the leader of the "Gangoe," which sounds a lot like "Congo."[33] At the time of the coup, Accabiré supported Atta against Coffij, but afterward the two men became bitter enemies.[34]

Mangmeister described what turned out to be a splintering of the rebel forces into several factions and the emergence of a low-level civil war. Under later questioning, Accabiré explained to the Dutch that the falling-out was due to his refusal to "be a slave of Atta." Others who identified as Ganga also testified that Atta tried to force them to do the backbreaking work of creating new food gardens. By their own admission, Accabiré and his men plundered Atta's camp before settling down on or near plantation Essendam, near the Wiruni Creek.[35] The Amina retaliated by defeating the Ganga in a battle on Essendam. Captain Accara, formerly Governor Coffij's second-in-command, was reportedly killed during the fight, along with many others on both sides. Accabiré himself was wounded. As Accabiré later asserted repeatedly, and in self-defense, he had become a leader, or *"Heer,"* to "fight the Amina, not the Christians." The timing of this schism was particularly unfortunate, likely coinciding with the Dutch expedition up the Canje.[36]

The falling-out among various factions of rebels involved diasporic ethnic divisions but, even more so, conflicting political visions. With Coffij's death, the notion of a nation-state or an independent colony died. But questions remained over social hierarchy, military strategy, and, most important, the shape of the post-slavery future. Coffij had sought to reproduce a Dutch-style colony. Atta had his own designs for a centralized chain of command. For both leaders, the promise of liberty included the practice of forced labor. Mangmeister's intelligence suggests that while the Creole Coffij had envisioned the creation of an independent black state that would coexist with a Dutch colony, his successor Atta, an African, imagined a more conventional Maroon polity, removed from the institutions of European colonization, chattel slavery, and merchant capitalism. Officers such as Accabiré had wearied of Atta's authoritarian ways and became his adversaries. Perhaps Atta's rivals had come around to a non-state solution: decentralized communities with subsistence gardens requiring less coercion and granting more autonomy. This solution probably appealed to many rank-and-file rebels as well as dodgers, who had resisted participation in the rebellion.[37]

So there it was: if they had a choice, this was what ranged before them. Self-emancipated people faced the prospect of a liberty that embraced forced labor, like later rebellions in the American colonies and Haiti, or an autonomy that involved a retreat to self-subsisting Maroon communities. For low-level rebels and dodgers the choice was easy. Rather than being forced to grow sugar and coffee, their actions before and testimony after capture suggest they preferred being left alone on their plantations or in the savanna to get by as best they could. Such preferences were likely also fueled by people's experiences back home. As the Atlantic slave trade fomented powerful, hierarchical, and militarized states in the eighteenth century, West African commoners had grown weary of rulers who appropriated their labor through taxes, turned too many young men into soldiers, and fed growing numbers of captives to Europeans on the coast.[38]

Mangmeister had little concrete information about the rebels' future plans. He reported that he had been told the rebels still had thirty-two barrels of powder. Van Hoogenheim deemed this large quantity "an untruth."[39] The surgeon also informed the Dutch that the rebels had toyed with the idea of leaving Berbice to make their way to the "Cupanama or Saramaka" with "intention to settle there and make a treaty with the runaways from Suriname and keep the peace," but "misunderstandings and discord among their headmen" had always prevented the execution of such plans.[40]

Fourteen Company slaves, all Creoles, who escaped the rebels in early December after the Canje expedition reported that the insurgents did not let anyone stay behind as they moved up the Berbice River. Atta's enforcers were most "insistent," to put it mildly, which had led to "much murder and killing." Van Hoogenheim reported, on the basis of this information, that the rebels "are acting in a desperate manner with any slaves who won't follow them voluntarily, murdering and killing many of them." The escapees confirmed that rebels had congregated in an area near the Wiruni Creek, including at plantation Beerensteijn, a bit higher up the river. They predicted that by the time the Dutch sailed up the Berbice, all estates along the river would be "sacrificed to fire." The two mutineers questioned in Demerara similarly claimed that Atta, after the Essendam battle, had made his headquarters on Beerensteijn, captive Georgina's home.[41]

The Dutch were not the only threat the revolutionaries faced. As they were distracted by defections and political conflict, groups of Indian combatants were forming a noose around them. Essequibo's governor Storm van 's Gravesande had been working for months to induce his native allies to help. Some of these men had finally arrived in the upper Berbice. In late November, a coalition of seventy Caribs, Akawaios, and Arawaks attacked plantation Boschlust, where, as described earlier, formerly enslaved people had been enjoying their autonomy after their owners fled to Demerara at the start of the rebellion. The Indians killed at least five Boschlust people. Survivors fled to plantation Debora, where Captain Bobé was in charge. They were joined by people from nearby estates who came to help or were on the run from the Indians themselves. They fortified the plantation house with a palisade of wood planks, leaving holes through which to shoot at their attackers. From behind this barricade, the besieged Africans took aim at the Indians, using their guns and bows and arrows. They wounded and killed several natives, forcing a retreat.[42]

That night, the Indians changed tactics. They crept up to the palisade and set fire to the house, burning alive many of the people inside. Months later, a witness to the fire carefully listed by name fifteen people from her plantation, including at least three boys, several girls, and a baby, who had perished in the fire, along with "many people she knows from other plantations." Those trapped in the flames included two Akawaios who saved themselves by jumping out of the windows, only to be killed by their native adversaries. The attackers figured the pair must be spies for the rebels and, "despite them being of their own nation, beat them to death."[43] The Indians later handed over four captives, all children, to Governor van 's Gravesande in Essequibo.[44]

Pressed on multiple fronts, the rebels appeared to be in a rapid free fall. Only three months earlier, they had pressed down on the Dutch, threatening the colony's existence. Although differences over strategy divided them then, they had remained united as a movement. Now that was changing. Despite these setbacks and being outgunned by Dutch forces, revolutionaries had the advantage of mobility, local knowledge, finely tuned guerrilla tactics, and, for many, a desperate willingness to fight to the death. The revolution was by no means defeated; in fact, splintered, the rebel forces became yet more difficult to vanquish.

11

The Battle for the Berbice

To Van Hoogenheim's great relief, at long last two merchant ships, promised by the Company of Berbice six months before, arrived in late November with fifty new fighters. They were soon followed by the two naval ships authorized for emergency relief by the States General, adding 260 more soldiers. The two warships—*Dolphijn*, a three-masted frigate, and *Zephyr*, a two-masted snow—were small enough to navigate the Berbice. Still, the overloaded vessels needed a "spring tide," the higher tide that followed a full moon, to clear sandbars in the river's delta. Further delays were the result of a shortage of enslaved workers usually employed to unload incoming ships. In the absence of slaves, soldiers unaccustomed to the tropical heat struggled to unload the vessels and build their own shelters. Meanwhile, the men on Haringman's ship, which had been in the colony for a month, were falling sick in ever greater numbers. As the hospital filled with feverish bodies and medicine ran low, Van Hoogenheim, regularly confined himself to his hammock with fevers and headaches, supplied the next best thing—red wine. Funerals once again became a daily occurrence.[1]

It took several weeks for the Europeans to prepare for their expedition up the Berbice River. One armed merchant ship remained anchored at Dageraad to provide protection; the second one anchored to the south near plantation Vigilantie to block rebels from fleeing downstream. Van Hoogenheim sent sixty soldiers to rendezvous with thirty mercenaries from British Barbados stationed in Demerara. The combined forces had orders to march from Demerara to the upper Berbice

Woman with child and tree trunk, anonymous, c. 1675–1725. (Rijksmuseum, Amsterdam.)

to form a wall to prevent rebels from disappearing into the hinterlands. Colonial soldiers posted on the Canje and the Corentyne Rivers were commanded to stop rebels from crossing into Suriname to join the Samaaka, or any other Maroon groups. Allied natives being armed in Essequibo and Suriname formed a second line of defense.[2] With help from their neighbors and allies and with reinforcements from abroad, the Dutch set up a dragnet around the colony. Moreover, the rainy season was about to begin. It should have been an easy victory.

Just after midnight on December 19, five ships, armed with cannons and swivel guns, left Dageraad, floating upriver on the rising tide. They transported some four hundred European soldiers and sailors along with unknown numbers of enslaved and Amerindian men to serve as scouts and patrols. Governor van Hoogenheim and Captain Haringman shared command. The ships—floating forts—projected more power than they possessed. The range of their artillery stopped just beyond the plantation buildings at the river's edge. A unit of one hundred men, taken from the ships near Fort Nassau and sent overland, offered little help because they were short on guides and enslaved laborers to carry their luggage and equipment. Slow, unsure, and ill provisioned, they were unable to stay out long.[3]

The main expedition's goal was not just to reestablish colonial control over the river but also to conduct a massive slave hunt in an attempt to recapture Dutch lost property. The protection of private property, after all, was at the heart of the Dutch Republic's motive to finance the rebellion's suppression. Fancying himself a liberator of the people he intended to re-enslave, Van Hoogenheim sought to "deliver all loyal slaves who remain quietly on their plantations or are in hiding" from "the fury and coercion of the rebels." The governor ordered his men to reassure noncombatants that they would not be harmed if they turned themselves in. At the same time, he instructed troops to do as much damage as possible to enemies who attacked either the soldiers or the ships. To encourage their fighters, the authorities offered the usual bounty monies for captured or killed rebels. A premium for bodies, dead or alive, intensified the violence in a war where it was already difficult to distinguish rebels from noncombatants. All valuables, clothes, household goods, or weapons soldiers recovered had to be turned in; after appraisal, half would be restored to the men as prize money. These measures, the Dutch trusted, would increase "courage and loyalty." Privately, the governor did not expect that many former slaves would fall into his hands, due to the "obstinacy" of the rebels. Instead, he believed, they would melt away as they had done on the Canje River. Now, as then, he surmised, rebel leaders would force everyone to retreat with them, egged on by the "treacherous white mutineers."[4] Van Hoogenheim was wrong on that last score. The archival record does not support his persistent, chauvinistic fantasy that African rebels allowed the European mutineers to direct them.

Retreat

The insurgents, understanding that they were no match for the Dutch on their heavily armed ships, retreated upriver even before the Dutch expedition moved up the Berbice. Rebel leaders urged, and forced, people to withdraw south with them. They wanted to resettle as many people upriver as possible, both to protect them and for strategic reasons. It was imperative that the rebels prevent noncombatants from either capture or turning themselves in. Defectors could provide not only valuable intelligence to the Europeans but work for the less-than-capable European soldiers. The tactic was targeted at the Europeans' greatest weakness: their difficulty functioning in the colony without coerced labor. Like burning down plantations, relocating people denied the Dutch crucial resources. The success of the rebellion depended on the support and control of formerly enslaved people. The capture of bodies more than territory became the goal of the battle.[5]

What were the rebels' plans after their retreat? Their grand strategy is harder to gauge than that of the Dutch, recorded so exhaustively in the archives. Did the rebels intend to fight the Dutch at some point, hoping to draw their adversaries onto the shore away from the ships' cannons? Was the plan to live in the bush away from the plantations, so they could regroup and attack the Dutch at a later date, as some suggested? Or were the rebels mostly focused on trying to get out of the colony, preparing food and collecting supplies in order to establish Maroon villages? Did the political and leadership crises following Coffij's death, and the subsequent conflict between Accabiré and Atta, preoccupy and fracture the rebels so extensively that there was little opportunity to do more than organize flight in advance of the ships?[6] None of the rebel officers discussed strategy in their post-rebellion interrogations, and the judges did not ask. So to discern their intentions one must rely on reading their actions as told to Dutch interrogators by recaptured people. That exercise is like watching a film in a hall of mirrors.

The assets of this war, the noncombatants, faced tough decisions. People were terrified about what might happen to them if they fell into Dutch hands. Rumors swirled about. Rebels warned that "the Christians would kill everyone, including the smallest of children." Foot soldiers and leaders alike knew the Dutch judicial punishments in store for them would be grisly and deadly. But the people who had lived quietly on their plantations or had supported the rebellion only minimally, halfheartedly, or intermittently also had reason to feel dread. Everyone was familiar with the savage and arbitrary nature of planter "justice."[7]

Even so, some people were not keen or able to march upriver with the rebels. They had already moved around a lot, either voluntarily or at gunpoint, and they did not want to relocate again. Others figured their best bet was once again to hide in the bush behind their plantations, remaining close to gardens and in familiar surroundings. It was a strategy that had kept them alive so far. And so, once more, individuals made their own decisions on the best course of action.

As had happened on the Canje, the rebels reduced plantations to ashes as they moved up the Berbice. From the safety of their ships, the Europeans saw for themselves the extent of the colony's destruction. The insurgents had leveled the seat of colonial government. Former Fort Nassau and the hamlet of New Amsterdam surrounding it presented a "spectacle of horrific destruction," the disheartened Dutch governor noted. Whatever the fires had spared, former slaves had chopped up with axes or torn down with their bare hands. The houses of the fort slaves along with their gardens had also been ruined. The extent of the devastation was disorienting—nothing, Van Hoogenheim lamented, looked "familiar" anymore. No structures were left standing except for the church and the minister's house. The insurgents had not torn these down, a Dutch official surmised, "out of some sort of superstition."[8] Was this an ill-stated insight, or simply another typical piece of colonial condescension?

Over and over, plantations went up in smoke as soon as the ships approached. The rebels made sure to set fires when the Dutch were close enough to see but too far away to douse the flames. With their well-timed blazes, arsonists made a mockery of the tall ships with their powerful cannons, turning their opponents into impotent spectators of destructive infernos.

Before they left, rebels scattered foot traps in the woods to protect their camps and make it harder for the Dutch to advance on land. These cruel devices, known in military circles as caltrops, were commonly fashioned of two or more nails or spikes twisted together so that no matter how they were thrown down, a sharp point always stuck up, much like barbed wire. Soldiers in cheap footwear stepped right through the spikes. The foot traps hobbled soldiers, causing painful injury and the risk of fatal infection. Van Hoogenheim was impressed. He had fifty traps, made "in the manner of the negroes," brought to him so he could study "the rarity of the invention."[9] His curiosity suggests that the rebels had found a clever way of fabricating or improving the Roman traps familiar to Europeans.

With the rebels in retreat as the Dutch ascended the river, there was little fighting. The rebels simply dissolved on contact. When lookouts at the top of the ships' masts sighted what appeared to be armed men close to the river's edge, the captains gave orders to fire the cannons. The speeding iron projectiles usually landed with a useless thud on the shore, the enemies having scattered. Soldiers and sailors rushed ashore but rarely caught a soul. On a few occasions, the Dutch and rebels exchanged fire. More often, rebels and noncombatants melted into the woods behind their plantations at the approach of their enemies. Still-warm cooking fires suggested that people had decamped only minutes before. Occasionally, European soldiers or, more often, African and Indian patrols sent to inspect estates stumbled upon people left behind, either too old or too sick to move. Some were brought on the ships; others were not. The patrols left a child whose caretakers were hiding in the woods "because it had the Indian pox, which is very contagious." Several older men suffering from "dropsy," or edema—an accumulation of fluid under the skin caused by infection, injury, or starvation—were also deemed "untransportable." This was no humanitarian operation. Only people the Dutch deemed valuable property were worth rounding up.[10]

Surgeon Mangmeister and fleeing Company slaves had told the Dutch that rebels intended to congregate at the Wiruni Creek near Company plantation Peereboom. Either they were wrong or rebel plans had changed, because when the ships approached the area, the black scouts found no one. A few hours later, lookouts on the ships noticed smoke from Peereboom. Amerindian patrols hastily sent out to reconnoiter reported that rebels, somehow unnoticed, had brazenly come back downriver to set ablaze the plantation's valuable sugar mill. Two large canoes could be seen openly moored at the pier.[11]

Two sick women belonging to private plantations paddled up to the Dutch in a canoe to give themselves up. They affirmed that the rebels had left Peereboom three days earlier; then some had returned the previous day to set the fires. They claimed that "the people of Peereboom were well intentioned, but compelled to flee." Fleeing colony slaves asserted that Atta had coerced many Company people and so-called fort's *volk* into the woods or into his band. One woman from Company plantation Hardenbroek related that her son Doeffi, or Jacob as the Dutch knew him, had recently killed himself "because Governor Atta forced him to stay with his gang." Hostage Georgina George would later confirm this story.[12]

Yet despite ambivalence or even outright opposition to the rebellion, few people willingly turned themselves in to the advancing Dutch. For some, rebel vigilance stood in their way or they feared unpredictable European soldiers and vindictive Dutch officials. Others likely did not want to give up what measure of self-determination they had gained, nor were they willing to be re-enslaved, at least not yet. Those who surrendered first were those with the fewest choices and mobility, typically the elderly, women with children, or those who were desperately hungry, sick, or wounded.[13]

As the rebels feared, those who did make their way back to the Dutch talked. Despite the fact that people were no doubt strategic about what they divulged, their claims for the most part appeared correct and matched Dutch intelligence. Take, for instance, Titus, who, along with a man named Joris and native Elizabeth and her child (all from Company plantation Goede Hoop), fled to the Dutch in a canoe on December 20. Titus, who was reportedly ancient, was a font of information. He related that the insurgents on his plantation had bolted at the approach of the Dutch, as fellow Goede Hoop captives later confirmed. He accurately identified another enslaved man from his plantation, Mars, as "one of the biggest rebels." He suggested that the insurgents planned to congregate just south of Savonette at the Accoway Indian Post "with intention of settling there," a claim that also turned out to be on target. Titus revealed that most of the European mutineers were dead by now and that many rebels "had killed each other." He added that "they had been eating dogs, cats and horses for a long time." He also shared the news, already confirmed, that when Coffij was buried, several white men had been killed as "offerings."[14]

Others told similar stories. Two "old people," Gratie and Maria, both from Company plantation West Souburg, arriving a day apart, claimed that there was now "great misery" among the rebels, who had little left in the way of food or gunpowder. Maria also shared that many Company slaves were held against their will and would defect to the Dutch when they had a chance.[15] A Dutch patrol found six decapitated people in the gardens of plantation Debora, a major rebel camp, a discovery that seemed to confirm accounts of internal strife.[16] Other refugees bore signs of conflict on their own bodies. One woman had "a big cut" on her head and her arm was partially severed. The rebels had attacked her, Van Hoogenheim reported, "because she wanted to come to us."[17] The surgeon amputated her arm. A young woman named Dina from private plantation Antonia was found in the woods "half dead, with more than 20 wounds in her head." Despite her serious injuries, she tried to get away from the Dutch soldiers, whom she feared would kill her. Brought before Van Hoogenheim, she related that she had been wounded the previous day by "the Delmina" (Amina), who had murdered her husband along with several others. She described the location of four fresh graves containing their bodies. Dutch patrols indeed found the graves. She also claimed that "many well-disposed people from her plantation remained hidden in the forest."[18] Others echoed claims of "good people" in hiding.

One might think that captured people made up such stories to ingratiate themselves with the Dutch. Perhaps their injuries were not inflicted by insurgents but by European soldiers paid bonuses for bringing in live captives. Yet their claims, volunteered to the Dutch, are likely true, as many people told stories that matched these. A major rebel strategy was to prevent people from going to the Dutch, and they used coercion to make that happen.

Two "Victories"

Three days before Christmas, on December 22, the special detachment from Demerara approached plantation Savonette, the place Titus had identified as the new rebel camp. English captain Smith commanded thirty mercenaries from Barbados, the sixty Berbician soldiers dispatched by Van Hoogenheim in mid-December, and untold numbers of native troops. Guided by native scouts, they had set out from Demerara for the upper Berbice five days earlier. The men had worn themselves out on a "fatigueing" march, slogging through "immense forest" and sleeping out in the open at night with "trees only for their covering."[19]

Between one hundred and two hundred people were congregated on Savonette. Twenty armed rebels patrolled or stood watch. The rest were unarmed. Savonette's African-descended residents were there, along with rebels and refugees from other plantations, many of whom had left Fort Nassau when it was set on fire. They were preparing for

Maroon life. As the last estate on the river, Savonette was a logical staging ground. For months, rebels had put people to work making gardens near the plantation, where they had also stored food, salt, iron, and other supplies. Women must have been busy drying fish and extracting the poison from cassava roots before processing them into meal and bread. Men fished and made forays into the rain forest to cut paths, scout for suitable settlement locations, and begin the hard work of carving out new provisioning grounds. No doubt they made spiritual preparations as well.[20]

The rebels on Savonette failed to notice the detachment's approach until they were within firing range. Rebel soldiers rushed for their weapons. Sources conflict on what happened next. A report from Demerara claimed some 150 Africans "made bold resistance" before running for their canoes. Van Hoogenheim related that the rebels "had no time to fight back." Given that the Dutch sustained only one wounded, he may have been closer to the mark. Many people from the rebel camp dove into the water, desperately trying to save themselves.[21]

Taking careful aim at their opponents from the shore, the Europeans and native guides picked off the swimmers and runners, one by one. The Amerindians let loose poisonous arrows.[22] Soldiers eager for bounty followed people into the water. One Englishman dove in when he spotted two Africans paddling away with a chest in their canoe. He caught up with them and, Van Hoogenheim admiringly reported, "pierced them through one by one with his bayonet." The two dead rebels would secure a bounty for the English mercenary, but it is unclear whether he recovered the chest.[23]

Despite reports that Atta had ordered gold, silver, and other valuables brought upriver, little made its way back to the Dutch. Van Hoogenheim reported that "the daily loot mostly consists of trivia of little value—little cash, or silver has emerged." Possibly the soldiers failed to turn in what they recovered, distrustful that the authorities would distribute the prize money equitably and in a timely manner. As the Dutch governor noted, "it is impossible to check exactly what the troops actually find." Meanwhile, the authorities of Essequibo and

Demerara, convinced that Captain Smith had single-handedly prevented the Berbice rebels from spreading into their colonies, rewarded
him a bonus of 1,000 guilders, a colossal sum.[24]

Dutch and Indian soldiers killed some fifty to sixty people, including a French soldier who had deserted from Dageraad in September.
Only twenty-seven were captured, mostly women and children.[25] Two
of the women were wives of Fortuin van Helvetia, the governor of
the Canje River. The Dutch considered the one-sided slaughter of ill-
armed opponents a victory.[26]

The day after the massacre, the European soldiers decapitated the
corpses at Savonette, burned the bodies, and staked the heads. Amid
the grizzly evidence of their savagery, they dug an entrenchment to
protect the plantation house from future attack. In the following days,
several dozen corpses floated downstream amid the flotsam. The bodies, along with accounts of the massacre, would have given pause to
anyone contemplating surrender. Once again, the Berbice had become
a river of blood.[27]

The survivors of the massacre made their way to nearby plantations
Debora and Goed Land en Goed Fortuin, where Governor Atta and
his first lieutenant Captain Bobé had reportedly assembled several
hundred fighters and supporters. Bobé had turned plantation Debora,
where he came from, into a fortified camp surrounded by wooden
fences with holes for firing. The intelligence about the casualties, the
loss of crucial supplies, and the impossibility of escape into the hinterlands discombobulated the rebels. With the Dutch ships closing in,
they had little time to make new plans. Some immediately took off for
the woods, leaving behind on the river's bank their possessions and
canoes.[28]

Governor Atta and Captain Bobé and the rest of their followers hur-
riedly paddled down the river to Wikki Creek, hoping to follow the
stream to the Canje and on to the Corentyne River on Suriname's western border. On Monday, December 26, the rebels reached the creek just
ahead of the Dutch on their ships. Atta ordered several of his trusted
lieutenants, including Gousarie van Oosterleek and Amina Quakoe (or
Quaco) van Nieuw Caraques, to hold off the Dutch, while he and Bobé

hurried up the Wikki Creek with a large contingent, including women and children and those brought along by force.[29] Quakoe and his men hid in the woods near the creek's entrance. The first Dutch vessel to approach the landing at Hardenbroek carried, against regulations, all of Van Hoogenheim's remaining officers. Without waiting for their Indian scouts to pronounce the area safe, the tent boat, rowed by Amerindians, entered the creek. A terrifying noise broke out as Quakoe's men, yelling, summoned by drums and horns, advanced. The Indians at the oars dove into the river, leaving the boat dead in the water. The rebels killed three of the Dutch officers and wounded two others, including a councilman, along with two scouts.[30] After a firefight with losses on both sides, the insurgents set fire to Hardenbroek's buildings and retreated up the Wikki, leaving the Dutch to bury their dead in a fierce rain.[31]

The next day, Dutch soldiers rowed their armed sloop up the Wikki. Within fifteen minutes, they encountered people who hurried upstream when the soldiers fired their cannons at them. A small detachment sent to give chase found only two children, one of them a newborn boy. The men carried the children to the ships, where Van Hoogenheim placed the baby with an enslaved woman to nurse.[32] The Dutch governor wanted to send a detachment of fifty men overland to Wikki Creek to "harass" the rebels, but he had only ten soldiers and twenty-nine sailors on hand; all the others were either sick or employed at the military posts set up along the way.[33]

After Van Hoogenheim arranged for a military post at Hardenbroek, the ships continued up the Berbice to Savonette, the site of the massacre, where Van Hoogenheim was briefed by the officers responsible. The governor set up a hospital for his sick soldiers and sailors. Short on workers, he left the captives on the plantation to bake bread and distill rum for the sick and the sailors and soldiers who would remain at the post.[34] He took with him in chains on the ship only the rebel captain Vogel, who had commanded on Savonette. Having organized everything to his satisfaction, Van Hoogenheim directed the ships back toward Dageraad on the last day of 1763.

Eyewitnesses

If the Dutch expedition up the Berbice River yielded few captives, it did provide news about a number of Europeans whose whereabout had been unknown: deserters, mutineers, and hostage Georgina George.

The body of one Berbice soldier who had deserted in September was seen floating down the Berbice River after the massacre on Savonette. Two Suriname mutineers had been spotted among the rebel leaders during the fight on Hardenbroek. They were dressed with distinction, sporting gold and silver piping on their shirts. Perhaps, as one Company plantation returnee claimed, they served as Atta's councilmen. If Atta indeed retained these men, whether as advisers or for some other purpose, their usefulness ran out soon after the Wikki fight. Commander Quassie van Hardenbroek later confessed that he and Captain Bobé had murdered the two, fearing that they were planning to desert. "They wanted to walk [off] and kill us," he explained, "they already had their knives ready to do us in." Other rebel leaders confirmed parts of his account.[35]

Several mutineers, besides surgeon Mangmeister, who had been captured in November, ended up back in Dutch hands alive. In mid-December, three mutineers were arrested in Demerara after fleeing the rebels. Another, Jean Renaud, the Frenchman from Languedoc who had been a leader in the mutiny, was captured at gunpoint near Savonette. He had brandished a sword, in a bid either to fight alongside his rebel comrades or to resist capture. Mutineer Jacques Montagnon turned himself in to the Dutch on Christmas Eve, claiming to have escaped from the rebels.[36]

Montagnon had news about Georgina, the young woman who had been a hostage for almost ten months. In October, the Dutch had learned that she had been caught, and punished, trying to escape. She was still alive, the Frenchman reported. He had seen her a few days earlier on her father's plantation Beerensteijn, a rebel stronghold near Peereboom. The intrepid Georgina had recently tried to flee once more, he related, again unsuccessfully. "Punished with slaps to the head and face," she was now carefully guarded. When Atta and his people retreated upriver to the Wikki Creek, Georgina was brought along.[37]

But Georgina did not remain among the rebels much longer. Right around the same time that Montagnon was discussing her plight with Van Hoogenheim, she was released. Georgina's legs had swelled so badly that she had trouble walking. Unable to move swiftly as Atta led his troops in retreat, she became a liability and was abandoned. She spent five days and nights alone, starving and ill, until she met a man named Chocolat who agreed to help her in exchange for a pardon. Chocolat managed to find a canoe and paddled the young woman to the warship *Zephyr*. They arrived in a steady downpour on the eve of the New Year.[38]

Georgina came on board "in a deplorable condition" and "unrecognizable," Van Hoogenheim recorded. Sickness had disfigured her, but even more appalling to the governor was her state of undress, "for the most part naked, wearing nothing but an old linen skirt, like the female slaves wear when they work in the fields." The Dutch equated nudity with slavery. The governor probably also found Georgina "unrecognizable" because of the way her captive existence had altered her. Along with her clothes, she must have shed her previous confidence about her European superiority, her right to food, leisure, and luxuries, her capacity to command work from others, and her expectations of safety, security, and physical sanctity. Though not subjected to the horrific Middle Passage, Georgina had experienced kidnapping, forced separation from her family, the torture and murder of loved ones, violence, forced marriage, and, perhaps, rape. Perhaps she recognized the parallels between her recent experiences and the lives of those her family had held in bondage, though it is equally possible that racism prevented her from recognizing similarities. She may have formed emotional bonds with some of her captors, as is common among hostages. But if she did, she likely did not confide those feelings to Van Hoogenheim, and he disclosed little of what she did share.[39]

The governor wrote about Georgina's ordeal with great delicacy, perhaps to protect the reputation of a yet-to-be-married Dutch woman of means. He merely mentioned that "the misery and inconveniences she has suffered . . . are indescribable." Alluding to her position as Coffij's wife and the possibility of sexual violence, he continued that even more "inexpressible" were "the shame and disgrace, and what all else has happened to her." These events, he concluded obliquely, leaving us in the dark as to her actual experiences, "make her the un-happiest creature in the world." Months later, Van Hoogenheim would insist that Georgina be questioned by the court about her time among the rebels, but the resulting "declaration" seems not to have been pre-served. In late spring, she took passage on a ship to the Dutch Repub-lic, and as she sailed off, she disappeared from the archival record.[40]

In her meeting with Van Hoogenheim, Georgina provided much in-formation, though fewer details than one would wish made it into the governor's notes. She divulged that "the rebels had carried out atroc-ities and unbelievable things." There is no way to know whether she was referring to the murder of her family members and other Europe-ans, or incidents involving African-descended people or Amerindians, or both. She asserted there were still a great number of insurgents, but they had little gunpowder left, a point that was made repeatedly by Amerindians as well. She stressed that "all the colony slaves were good people." They had been forced to participate in the rebellion and were badly mistreated and closely guarded to prevent escape. She recounted the story of Doeffi, or Jacob, from Company plantation Hardenbroek, who had killed himself along with two women "out of desperation" because the rebels would not let him go, a story the Dutch had already heard from the bereft young man's mother.[41]

With respect to the rebels' future plans, Georgina affirmed that Governor Atta was high up Wikki Creek in a boat with a small group of followers, intending to make his way overland to the Canje River. Several other "governors" were also on the run in Wikki Creek, but with much larger numbers of people, she noted, and less certain of where to go. They fought, and even killed, one another, as groups sub-divided and leaders peeled off. She claimed that many people were hiding in the woods, suffering from acute hunger, prepared to return to the Dutch if they could be assured they would not be punished. Captives and refugees corroborated Georgina's claims. Amerindians living on the Wikki confirmed that people were "everywhere dispersed through the woods," mostly on the west side of the Berbice.[42] A few traveled far. Two Loango women and a child wandered west for weeks in a desperate search for sustenance and shelter before Indians caught them and delivered them to the Suriname postholder on the Corentyne River. After eighty-three days, Masoeta and Lukemi were taken back to Berbice, along with a bill for 140 guilders for their "capture" and "board."[43]

Much as Van Hoogenheim had feared, rebels and noncombatants had scattered, hiding individually near plantations or in camps deeper in the bush, or moving from place to place. No more than a few hundred people in total, children included, had so far been recovered. Of these, about a hundred had been taken by force and held in chains.[44] The expedition had put the Dutch in nominal control of the Berbice River. They could send boats up and down without hindrance or danger. Plantations were back in Dutch hands. Soldiers at newly established posts on Company plantations Savonette and Johanna, at Wikki and Wiruni Creeks, at Fort Nassau and on the Canje River guarded escape routes from the colony.

But the most important objective, to catch rebels and to recover the workers without whom the colony yielded no profits, had yet to be accomplished. While the only "victory" of the Berbice campaign, the massacre at Savonette, had denied the rebels a way out of the colony, it had simultaneously forced people to flee the river region for the deep forest and savanna. Locating rebel leaders and rounding up the others would be more difficult now, complicated further by the fact that illness continued to take out more and more European soldiers. As the ships began their descent down the river from Savonette back to Dageraad, Van Hoogenheim received word that Dutch sails had been spotted in the mouth of the Berbice River. It seemed at long last his deliverance, seven hundred fresh fighters sent by the States General, had arrived. Van Hoogenheim must have thought his long ordeal was about to end. If so, he was mistaken.

12

Wild Sang and Little Glory

The seven hundred state troops commanded by Colonel de Salve—the officer who shipped out from Texel with his fleet in early November for his first command abroad—passed the equator on December 2, 1763. After a quick voyage, on which five soldiers died, they spotted the coast of Suriname on December 18. Maneuvering into the river, they passed two Dutch slave ships on their way home. Colonel de Salve asked their captains, both of whom had in the past sold slaves in Berbice, to convey several letters to the Duke of Brunswick. But both men, evidently in a hurry, refused to wait and sailed off. After a short stop for intelligence, De Salve's convoy set course for Berbice on Christmas day. Two days later, by nightfall, it seemed the ships had missed the mouth of the Berbice River, as the "dark and heavy air" obscured the coast. The next day, to everyone's relief, the lookouts spotted the river's entrance.[1]

Arriving at Fort St. Andries, De Salve was briefed about the Canje and Berbice expeditions. The commander concluded that the just-completed campaign up the Berbice River was a mistake. "It would have been better," he reported home, "if they had not pressed the pursuit of the blacks, but had let them stay where they were." He was confident his troops would have been able to "exterminate" the rebels all at once. Now he feared they would "maintain themselves high in the bush." After an earful about the struggles with Maroons during his stop in the neighboring colony, he worried that in Berbice, "the situation will become as it is in Suriname." De Salve's concerns were not entirely strategic. He had sailed across the Atlantic in search of fame. The scattering of the rebels dashed his hopes for a decisive victory and professional acclaim. He fretted that "others have picked the laurels" and predicted that "our expedition will be crowned with little glory." "I hope," he closed his letter wistfully, "that there will be a little left for me."[2] His officers, whom he put in charge of military posts throughout the colony and tasked with defeating rebels, would indeed soon find out that military honor was elusive in Berbice.

For Want of Negroes

The new force made its headquarters in the ruins of Fort Nassau and the hamlet of New Amsterdam. Although it placed him in a central location, this decision put De Salve thirty miles by river from Van Hoogenheim on Dageraad. In order to share intelligence and coordinate their efforts, the two men wrote each other daily. In addition, the post commanders sent regular reports about rebel location and movement along with lists of captives and returnees. Officers leading commandoes submitted details of their expeditions in writing. Colonel de Salve kept a log, or *verbael*, which included daily events and copies or excerpts of letters and reports. Trusted native and enslaved men made the flow of information possible, paddling or guiding European soldiers who carried the documents on their bodies for safekeeping. This one-sided military archive details Dutch attempts to win back their colony.[3] For an understanding of what the rebels were up to, one must read between the lines.

At Fort Nassau, the Lutheran Church was repurposed as a hospital while the minister's house served as De Salve's lodgings. Since all other buildings had been destroyed, the soldiers were housed in the savanna behind the fort in huts with palm roofs built in the manner of the Indians.[4] To preserve his men's strength in the tropical heat, De Salve demanded of Governor van Hoogenheim slaves to cut down trees, to construct shelters and warehouses, and to assemble shallops, shallow boats equipped with oars and a mast intended to ferry men and supplies along the Berbice River, brought from Holland in pieces.

Van Hoogenheim sent the military commander three women to laun-
der, sew, and cook, along with two enslaved masons, a carpenter, and
a cooper.[5] But the governor had trouble providing additional workers,
porters, and rowers. Re-enslaved Company people, especially the artisans, were already employed. The returned people who belonged to
private planters, most of them first-generation Africans, were, in Van
Hoogenheim's estimation, of limited utility, as it was difficult to communicate with them.[6] As a result of this shortage of enslaved workers, setting up camp proceeded slowly, as second-in-command Robert
Douglas explained, "for want of Negroes, not chusing to Let our Men
work."[7]

Native laborers were in short supply, too. When Van Hoogenheim
sent Hein, a member of the Broer family, with several indigenous
men to Fort Nassau with palmetto leaves to roof the soldiers' huts,
De Salve ordered Hein Broer to stay and find him additional Indians.
"I can't possibly spare the young man," Van Hoogenheim explained
as he quickly disallowed the plan, "and the few Indians I have I need
to carry messages." Initially, the colonel took such refusals as a lack
of cooperation from the young governor, making for frosty interac-
tions. But he quickly came to appreciate Van Hoogenheim's challenges
in managing a colony that had, until recently, been utterly dependent
upon enslaved laborers. From that moment on, the two men cooperated "with mutual pleasure."[8]

The lack of enslaved and native laboreres hindered swift settlement
of the troops, and, more crucially, it impeded their military deployment. De Salve and Van Hoogenheim reluctantly decided that a large
expedition up Wikki Creek, where most rebels were thought to be hiding, was impossible because there were insufficient slaves to serve as
porters. In Europe, wagons transported military matériel. In Berbice,
enslaved men carried and paddled supplies through the rain forest. In
neighboring Suriname, at least twenty enslaved carriers accompanied
a detachment of sixty men, transporting the ammunition, food, medicine, axes and spades, the sick and wounded, and "the officers' boxes."
In addition, they needed so-called pioneers to cut paths through the
jungle. Matching this kind of support structure would have required

Leupe 1634, Sketch of De Salve's camp at the former Fort Nassau and New Amsterdam. The artist carefully labeled the ships in the river, the location of officers' huts, the hospital, newly created gardens, cooking huts, and Indian dwellings, but not where enslaved people or refugees were housed. (Nationaal Archief, The Hague.)

at least 200 carriers alone for De Salve's entire force. With few healthy and trustworthy enslaved men and only a handful of boats that could travel up the shallow creeks, the two commanders settled on the short-term strategy of ordering small commando units to search for the rebels, and where possible to drive them into the arms of the Amerindians. The first order of business was to ship De Salve's soldiers to the various posts along the Berbice and Canje Rivers to relieve the increasingly ill and incapacitated troops stationed there. Post commanders were instructed to use "due diligence" to locate rebels "by spies or otherwise." They were instructed to bring back the right hand of any rebels who were killed and to welcome people who returned of their own accord.[9]

Officers newly stationed at the military posts were eager to prove themselves; they responded to their orders with enthusiasm. They quickly realized, much like British troops had during the recently concluded Seven Years' War, that fighting in the Americas was a world away from fighting in Europe. It was easy to get lost without reliable maps and knowledgeable guides, much of their "intelligence" was untrustworthy, and their men, primarily used to garrison duty, lacked necessary jungle conditioning for a tropical rain forest. To add to their woes, rebel forces disappeared before they could be attacked, or carried out quick strikes, dissolving into the tangled green forest mass before the Europeans regained their bearings. Orders from headquarters were outdated by the time they were received, as rebels changed positions frequently, leaving post commanders to act on their own rather than on orders. A series of expeditions from post Hardenbroek serves as illustration.[10]

Futile Expeditions

In mid-January an African man, unnamed in the reports, hailed the guards at the Dutch post on Company plantation Hardenbroek at the mouth of Wikki Creek. Speaking through an interpreter, he said that Atta and other leaders had gathered on the west bank of the Berbice, near plantation Goed Land en Goed Fortuin, the scene of the 1762 breakout. This was surprising news. The Dutch had assumed that Atta was still high up the Wikki Creek, as Georgina, Mangmeister, and most recently the enslaved scout and translator Frederik had claimed. In fact, the Dutch had heard that Atta and his men had attacked an Amerindian village in order to raid its cassava gardens. Yet the new intelligence seemed to fit with more recent information brought by returnees that Governor Atta's lieutenants and their followers were abandoning him. There had also been recent sightings of people near plantation Goed Land en Goed Fortuin.[11]

Hardenbroek's commander, Major de Brauw, immediately acted on the intelligence, though he was not quite sure of Goed Land en Goed Fortuin's exact location. Burned-down plantations looked alike, none had signs, and there was no reliable map. In fact, two hand-drawn military maps made for the use of the troops place Goed Land en Goed Fortuin in two different spots. As luck would have it, the informer offered to show the way. Two hours later, at dusk, Captain Perrin set off with fifty volunteers in an armed boat rowed by six sailors. By ten that evening, the commando unit arrived at what their guide claimed was Goed Land en Goed Fortuin. He was wrong. It was not until the next morning at sunrise that the soldiers arrived at the correct location.[12]

Behind Goed Land en Goed Fortuin lay "dense forest" that eventually gave way to savanna. All morning, the men struggled through the soggy bush, crawling over and under fallen trees and cutting their way through tangled thorny undergrowth along a "narrow footpath," their water bottles and hammocks corded over their shoulders, muskets in hand. Hemmed in by the jungle, the troops could not march several abreast in common military fashion. Instead, they cautiously snaked along "bad paths" in a long single "Indian file," at times wading knee- or waist-deep through flooded woods and grasslands. Perhaps they put the few unarmed "negro carriers" in the middle of the human train, just as European soldiers did while hunting Suriname Maroons, to better guard them. Even with a guide, it was easy to get lost. Navigating by the sun or stars was difficult, as bushes obscured the horizon and the leafy crowns of tall trees concealed the sky. The lush jungle closed in after the nervous soldiers as they looked back over their shoulders.[13]

After several hours of trudging through marshy woods, up an "incline" and across several "plains" (the vague geographic markers in the expedition reports testify to the Europeans' meager knowledge of the terrain), the sweating soldiers arrived at a large grassy plain dotted with "very many" huts and people. None of the reports describe the dwellings, but they were likely made with walls of woven reeds or boughs roofed by palmetto leaves.[14] The soldiers took aim and fired at the rebel encampment. They missed their targets as most of the inhabitants fled, abandoning their possessions and food supplies, yielding the Dutch "big spoils." It appears they killed no one; thirty-two people, mostly women and children, were taken captive.

Instead of returning to his post to report on what he had found, a brazen Captain Perrin pressed on, leaving the loot in the care of several of his men. Five other soldiers led the captives all the way back to post Hardenbroek. Reinforced with a lieutenant and six privates who brought fresh supplies, Perrin ordered his remaining men to march in the direction people had fled. At Perrin's orders, the soldiers fired at

March thro' a swamp or Marsh in Terra-firma.

March Through a Swamp, 1793, after a drawing by John Gabriel Stedman. Soldiers hold their muskets and bundles over their heads. The African-descended man in the foreground may have been a guide, while the black figure with the basket on his head would have been a carrier. Soldiers in Berbice traveled through the jungle in the same manner. (John Carter Brown Library, Providence.)

random as "the best way to deal with blacks." When the men began to exhaust their shot, the rebels seized the opportunity. They lured the intruders into an open field, while they hid behind trees on three sides. As customary, they descended on their adversaries while "yelling in a terrifying manner." They used drums and horns to command their soldiers to advance or retreat, just as European armies used trumpets in the field. The fearsome noise of the shouting combined with the deafening drums and horns made the rebel forces appear more numerous than they actually were and flustered their opponents. One gunless rebel soldier armed himself by boldly snatching the musket right out of his stunned opponent's hands.[15]

Feeling overwhelmed, the Dutch panicked. Perrin, a Frenchman, yelled out, "*Sauve qui peut!*" The commander's orders, "Save yourselves!" echoed up and down the line, and the men fled "in great confusion." The rebels wounded Perrin with an arrow. No doubt others would have been shot, but at that moment thirty additional soldiers appeared, stopping the rebels' advance. One of the Dutch officers claimed they were fired on for some fifteen minutes before the enemy slipped away into the woods, but other reports, probably more accurately, suggest that the rebels fired little because they had few guns. The Dutch made their retreat back to the river over the course of that day and night. Perrin, along with several other injured soldiers, was taken captive. One rebel later claimed that Atta participated in this fight. Atta denied this, stating that the action had been commanded by Gousarie van Oosterleek "with ten men who had muskets."[16]

Badly shaken by their defeat, Dutch officers were quick to scapegoat Perrin. They decided that he had acted irresponsibly and was the cause of his own demise. "If he had had as much sense as bravura," his superior reported to Colonel de Salve, "and he had executed my orders, he would have lost no men, brought back large spoils, inspired our men, the negroes would have been robbed of a large part of their victuals, which I had directed him to destroy and which he controlled for three hours." Perrin's order had been to discover the rebels' location, not to attack them with an insufficient force. "It is possible," the officer continued, "that we will never have such a perfect opportunity to exterminate that riffraff, since we now again have to guess where they are hiding." Van Hoogenheim and De Salve concurred with his assessment of the captured fighter. They ordered the post commanders to do all they could to "find out from the Negroes who are daily captured or who return to us of their own accord, where the major force of the rebels may be found."[17]

Over the next week, the Dutch dispatched additional soldiers to the area to search for the rebels who had taken Perrin. The first patrol found the camp empty, the inhabitants gone without a trace. A second scouting party caught a man who told them that "the rebels had rejoined each other, and retired deep into the woods." He refused to lead the Dutch there, claiming not to know the location. He did divulge that the rebels were short of food and their plan was to leave the women and children in the camp while the men traveled to nearby plantation Debora close to Wikki Creek to raid the gardens. Another escapee confirmed this intelligence.[18]

The soldiers exhausted themselves clambering through the hot and swampy forest and savannas without locating rebels or noncombatants. They did find, as their adversaries no doubt intended them to, the remains of Captain Perrin and three more soldiers. Perrin's body, half-buried, leaned against a tree. All four corpses were badly maimed and had their right arms cut off, no doubt in retaliation for the dismembered right hands of dead rebels, which Dutch soldiers exchanged for bonuses. Blind to the symbolism, the European soldiers at seeing the mangled bodies felt only "great bitterness."[19]

At last, enslaved scouts reported having seen many Africans "in the third savanna" behind plantation Hardenbroek, some armed and others carrying palmetto baskets with provisions on their heads, likely procured at plantation Debora. If the soldiers followed the trail, scouts proposed, they might find Atta's camp. After feverish preparations, some seventy soldiers and eighty sailors took off the next day before dawn. Since there were no healthy officers to command the sailors, Captain L. H. van Oijen of the man-of-war *Zephyr* eagerly came along, leaving his ship in the hands of several sick lieutenants. As usual, several officers, including Captain Anthonij Hamel, who commanded the soldiers, and Van Oijen, in charge of the sailors, filed lengthy reports on the expedition.[20]

Just two hours into their march, the troops ran into one of Atta's lookouts. The man disappeared before the Dutch could catch him. For the next five hours, "through six woods and four savannas," the Dutch saw no further signs of rebels, though they were likely being observed by them. Around noon, the men found huts—one report speaks of "several" and the other of "a great quantity"—nestled at the edge of the woods. The inhabitants fled as soon as the soldiers approached, leaving behind precious food supplies. The soldiers captured two boys, and after marching a few more hours, they overtook several women and children, who directed them deeper into the woods toward Atta's camp. Van Oijen and Hamel divided their troops and sent them in different directions.

Van Oijen was ahead of his main force with five men when, he later reported, he first encountered ten to twelve rebels with guns who shot at him and fled when he returned fire. A bit later, he confronted "more than a hundred rebels all armed." Careful to stay out of range, the rebels yelled "Atta, Atta." They taunted their opponents, evidently in Berbice Creole, to "bring it on, if you dare, bring it on, we are brave men." The few shots they aimed at Van Oijen whizzed over his head. When the rest of Van Oijen's men came running, alerted by the commotion, the African soldiers faded away inexplicably. Shortly afterward, another commando unit encountered a "large number of armed blacks," perhaps the same men, who advanced with their usual "dreadful screaming and the loud noise of drums and horns." They, too, largely remained out of reach, likely low on shot or powder. A third group of Europeans, however, were fired at so heavily they were forced to retreat—or so they claimed. That night, the detachments reunited and the entire force camped out in the open, exhausted.[21]

The next day, the soldiers at last located Atta's settlement. It was a "large camp" nestled between the branches of a creek. Several people taken captive related that Lieutenant Quakoe and his people had arrived only the previous day. Tipped off by spies, Quakoe and Atta had left just that morning with the majority of their followers. With the two leaders and their warriors gone, resistance was minimal. The Europeans killed five people while the rest fled, leaving behind food, tools, a few guns, clothes (including many women's petticoats), and some silver. The Dutch burned the huts. Since they lacked enslaved carriers, they took only the silver and the petticoats, torching "more loot than twenty men could carry," including many tools and "considerable food supplies." Soldiers sent after the fleeing people returned before long, unsure of where to go when the trail split. After another night in the bush, on January 31, the spent troops returned to their post. They had in tow just "fourteen captives," both "great and small." The Dutch had suffered several wounded and one dead. We do not know the total numbers of rebels and refugees killed and wounded. One Dutch soldier mysteriously disappeared after handing his gun to a comrade—perhaps he deserted to the rebels, fed up with the hardship of his service.[22]

War of Attrition

The expeditions clarified a number of things.

African-descended people, both insurgents and those who stayed aloof from the revolutionary upheaval, had moved inland from the river to the savannas that stretched beyond the plantations, with most concentrated upriver from Company plantation West Souburg. Some lived in large villages, others in small camps. Dutch sources offer little description of the settlements. Some people may have planted small patches of cassava, yams, and plantains. Frogs, lizards, snakes, monkeys, birds, and fish were plentiful, if a person could catch them. Wild cacao trees may have provided berries and leaves for chewing. Those who knew about it may have made use of "famine foods," eaten by Maroons and fugitives in Suriname, like the spicy and bitter fruits of *Montrichardia arborescens*, prevalent in swamps, or the flowerhead of the costus shrubs, which contained water, a godsend for those living apart from creeks. The rain forest also contained poisonous plants, some of which looked deceptively like harmless ones, such as the red berries of *Doliocarpus* major, which resembled coffee berries, or the fleshy poisonous flowers of *Annona muricata,* which some mistook for its edible fruits. Many people returned to the Dutch hungry, so perhaps the unusually heavy rains of the early months of 1764 had made gardening and foraging difficult. Or wartime disruptions forced most to move around too much to cultivate crops. The food supplies found in the various rebel encampments were likely only for committed rebels, leaving people disconnected from the camps hungry.[23]

Rain hampered the Dutch as well since it made finding and capturing fugitives almost impossible. Large expeditions could go out for only a few days, since they lacked sufficient numbers of enslaved porters to bring supplies for a longer trip. This meant that even when they located rebels, they could not pursue them very far. Yet even on short expeditions, the Europeans were not up to the task of hunting rebels. One officer complained "how difficult it is to chase them out of the forest." The enemy was better equipped to deal with the terrain and the climate than European soldiers. Having fished and hunted in the area while enslaved, African men were more familiar with their surroundings, and they made their way through the woods more capably than colonial soldiers. In Suriname as in Berbice, European soldiers were rarely able to follow or find their opponents in the rain forest. One Suriname planter involved in Maroon fighting likened them to "hares": "you barely got to see them but they saw you." He characterized his experience as "marching blind."[24] The most the Dutch could do was chase their opponents from place to place, making it harder for many rebels and their followers to settle and feed themselves.

Like Jamaica and Suriname Maroons, rebel soldiers fought guerrilla style, maximizing their small numbers and limited weapons and ammunition, and drawing on their African military training. While West African armies certainly fought large battles in highly disciplined fashion, they also favored smaller units who made "harrassing attacks . . . followed by rapid retreats." Such units, like the Berbice rebels, used spies and lookouts posted among the hanging vines in the towering greenheart and bullet trees to stay ahead of their opponents. They rarely showed themselves, using the large buttress roots of trees, bushes, and tall grass as cover. They did not fire their weapons simultaneously, as in volley fire. Each man took aim and fired as necessary. They used drums and horns for coordination and gave out sharp cries during an attack to scare their opponents. They made swift raids or lured their pursuers into ambushes, avoiding long battles and rapidly dispersing into the jungle to avoid sustaining too many casualties.[25] In terms of adaptation to the conditions of fighting in the Berbice rain forest, the rebel forces excelled.

The creeks, the quagmires, and the heat greatly challenged the Europeans. Blood-sucking bats left bleeding sores on soldiers' toes. The Europeans were fearful of snakes, which came in many sizes and colors—the brightly colored and venomous coral snake, the tiny green and yellow parrot snake, the nervous green labaria, which bit four or five times in lightning strikes, large constrictor snakes such as the anaconda, or the man-sized, slow-moving venomous pit viper morabana, which signaled its passage through camp at night with a rustling of dry leaves. Then there were the insects: mosquitoes, inch-long wasps, and bullet ants with their excruciating stings. Scratching turned bites into running sores covering a man's body.

The Europeans could not deal with the "swaare fatiques," the physical and mental exertions the environment dished up. In short, Dutch brass concluded, "a small number of Negroes can wear out a large detachment, and massacre many in the forest." Governor van Hoogenheim agreed that Dutch military actions did little but "chase them from one place to another," and might push "the enemy" beyond plantation Savonette, where, in fact, Amerindians had recently spotted, and killed, rebels. The governor judged that the expeditions "exhausted the troops, used up a lot of provisions, and led to nothing." The missions carried out so far were, he concluded, "nothing but wild Sang," an archaic Dutch expression denoting wasteful recklessness, "without consultation and not based on a shred of intelligence."[26]

Colonel de Salve agreed with Van Hoogenheim's assessment. "These detachments do little else," he echoed, "than dislodge the rebels." De Salve soon forbade his post commanders from undertaking any and all expeditions, since they served only to "ruin the troops and render them unfit for duty."[27] Amazingly, he directed that the European soldiers who had shipped thousands of miles across the Atlantic stay in camp. Commanders should only send out small scouting parties, mostly consisting of loyal slaves and Indians, to try to locate rebels. Instead of directly engaging the enemy, the Dutch turned to environmental warfare. The soldiers were ordered to destroy the food gardens at abandoned plantations to deny sustenance to rebels and refugees alike. Unable to defeat people in the bush, the Dutch decided instead to starve them out.[28]

Even such orders were easier given than carried out. One naval officer sent his marines to dig up the provision grounds at plantation Debora. But he hastily ordered his men back onto the ship, noting, "it was impossible for our people to do this heavy work in the heat of the sun." The job "would take more than eight days," he explained, suggesting the size of the provision grounds. The commander of post Stevensburg on the Canje River cagily suggested that destroying gardens would make it difficult for plantation owners and managers to reoccupy their estates. He was ordered to proceed anyway, as the Dutch repeatedly heard from captives and returnees that rebels and refugees alike were suffering much from starvation and gravitated to the plantations in hopes of finding food. In early February, several men and a woman were picked up in the fields of plantation Vigilantie. They had recently left Atta, among whose followers, they claimed, "hunger and misery" reigned. Their bodies supported such assertions, as they looked, Van Hoogenheim remarked, "skinny like sticks, though young people."[29] People who lose so much body weight become depressed, listless, and prone to disease.

Despite Dutch bungling, the situation for the rebels was increasingly dire. The destruction of camps, especially Atta's, once more dislodged people, who fled with little food and weapons and faced shrinking options for refuge. The rebels had few remaining canoes and boats, and their mobility was further diminished by increasing numbers of Indians patrolling the colony's hinterlands.[30] Heavy rains in the first months of the New Year flooded the savannas and made trying to subsist in the woods difficult.[31] Some captives alleged that the rebels intended "to retire to the woods till the Christians shall have thought all is quiet." Once the Europeans settled back on their plantations, they would "then sally forth, put all to the sword & so get new powder to fight the Christian soldiers."[32] Whatever the rebels' ultimate plans, hunger and Indian patrols drew people back toward the plantations and their gardens. Many wandered the hilly savanna between the Wikki and Cimbia Creeks, while others settled on the other side of the Berbice, hiding in the Wironi Creek. Growing numbers reluctantly decided that the only way to stay alive was to turn themselves in to the Dutch.

13

Outsourcing the War

The scene of shifting alliances on the Berbice is almost cinematic. In mid-February, Governor van Hoogenheim traveled to Fort Nassau to confer in person with Colonel de Salve about "the further extermination of the rebels" and the challenges of catching Governor Atta, whose whereabouts were unknown after the destruction of his camp. Arawaks and Caribs claimed he had escaped from the colony and he had people cultivating food gardens beyond plantation Savonette. The two Dutchmen feared a long struggle ahead.

In the midst of their meeting, two native couriers arrived at De Salve's lodgings with better news. They handed over a letter detailing the claim by native spies that Atta was still in the colony, still near Wikki Creek. Eager to confirm this promising news but unable to speak the men's native tongue, Van Hoogenheim called for "one of my faithful blacks who well understands Indian languages."

Who was the facile linguist? Van Hoogenheim did not name the man, but it was probably Frederik, who was of mixed African and native descent and on whom the governor relied frequently for all manner of service. Regardless of his identity, the interpreter proceeded to question the two indigenous men in the presence of the uncomprehending Dutch officials. To Van Hoogenheim's relief it became clear "from all that they tell" that the story was "real and based in truth," as, he noted with early modern faith in eyewitnessing, "they have seen and spied it themselves."[1]

As Van Hoogenheim and De Salve began planning an expedition to capture Atta, an officer arrived with fifty refugees. In the midst of his report that there were many more people willing to come back, Accara van de Brandwacht materialized. Acarra had been a commander on the Canje River with Fortuin van Helvetia. Van Hoogenheim knew of Accara's exploits as a rebel leader, and he considered him a "grote Quaedoener," a scoundrel of the first order. He had surrendered a few days earlier at the fort along with Gousarie van Oosterleek. The latter was a former lieutenant of Atta's who had led the negotiations with the European refugees at Peereboom and then had double-crossed them by ordering the massacre. Instead of facing trial, the two men had convinced De Salve of their usefulness and made a deal: in exchange for rounding up rebels and refugees, their lives would be spared.[2]

Now, freshly returned from a scouting trip, Accara stood before the two Dutch commanders. He confirmed that "everywhere in the woods there are people very eager to return to the Dutch but afraid to do so." In the short time he had been working for the Dutch, Accara had provided living proof of his claims. On this day, he had brought with him fourteen people. The day before he rounded up thirty-nine, and the day before that he had returned with eighteen. In light of these developments, the two Dutch leaders called off their plans for an attack because they did not want to scare away potential returnees since "so many accrue to us daily from all sides." They decided to hold off sending a large expedition as long as Accara and Gousarie and other allies yielded results.[3]

Indigenous soldiers, rebel slave catchers, mixed-race interpreters—just as the Dutch outsourced the labor of making cacao, coffee, and sugar, so they outsourced the war itself.

Amerindians

As rebels and refugees moved away from the plantations up the creeks and into the savannas, indigenous people living in these expanded conflict zones were drawn into the fight either because they felt threatened or because rebels attacked them. Others used the war to revenge previous injuries, to prove themselves in battle, or to supply themselves with European goods.[4]

Knowing how much the Dutch needed them, Indians capitalized on colonial dependency. Like everyone else, they harnessed the revolution to their own goals. When De Salve urged one native leader and his men to join the Caribs and Arawaks in the upper Berbice, promising to "richly reward" them for every black person "killed or caught south of Savonette," the indigenous men stalled. Colonists had treated them poorly in the past, they explained. They might be willing to support the colony now, De Salve recorded their words, "as long as they are well treated, and rewarded," but the decision would require a village-wide discussion. Their point made, the Indians left with ample trade goods and textiles from India, and armed with a pass ordering all planters to assist them as needed with food and weapons. The Dutch paid dearly for this mission to the upper Berbice. It cost him, De Salve noted, "just about all the cloth I own in this world."[5]

In the first months of 1764, local Amerindians along with Arawak and Carib allies pursued rebels and refugees. They searched them out from narrow creeks, patrolled the plantations, and crisscrossed the savannas. Native captains turned in chopped-off hands, as well as sticks with *krapjes* (marks) indicating the additional number of people they had killed. Occasionally they brought along live captives, whom the Dutch interrogated. A live captive was rare. Corentyne River indigenes did not often bring prisoners, one officer explained, "because their embitterment towards them is too great." In May, the postholder sent Van Hoogenheim bills for 108 hands of murdered people and just twenty-two live captives. The Dutch preferred having their workers brought back alive (they paid five times more for a person than for a hand), yet they were desperate for native men to patrol the colony's borders. If native leaders refused to deal with live captives, the Dutch went along to appease their allies.[6]

It did not take long for newcomer Colonel de Salve to acknowledge that Indian warriors were vastly superior to European ones. "They are better," he judged, "than the soldiers the Directors have sent from time to time, who consist of vagabonds, deserters, the lame and the crippled." Governor van Hoogenheim too appeared to have lost faith in European soldiers' superiority: "as long as the Indians stand firm," he declared, the rebels could not escape, "caught as in a fish-trap."[7] Of course, how to ensure Indian resolve was the big issue. Indians were not like hired mercenaries under strict military discipline. As in North America, when natives sustained too many casualties, they went home. When they tired of working for the Dutch or had more pressing concerns, they absconded. Fewer resident indigenes had returned to the colony than the governor had hoped, despite his best efforts to lure them back.

Without more native help, the Dutch were in a bind. "No matter how successful our expeditions may be, this land will never be cleansed or made safe," Van Hoogenheim explained to his superiors, "unless the Indians join hands to help and take matters to heart." So far, he judged, the Indians were only half in the war. Their actions, he wrote, did not represent "what they are capable of if they were truly serious." He fretted over "how much patience and time is required, before one can make those people act." He did all he could to "encourage them, because without them, I repeat again," he stressed, "the work will be difficult and lengthy."[8] The challenge to win over the hearts and minds of indispensable native allies added to the governor's mounting list of concerns.

Aid, again, came from neighbors. Over the course of the spring, Essequibo's Governor van 's Gravesande organized large numbers of Caribs. He hired a mixed-descent trader named Veth who went up a tributary of the Essequibo, the Mazaruni River, to enlist fighters. Veth turned out to be a miraculous recruiter, returning with "such a band," the Essequibo governor enthused, "that I must declare that I have never seen so many Indians together before." His house was overflowing. Van 's Gravesande had been unaware, he confessed, that "such a number of Caribs lived in that river alone." They had only asked "for twelve rifles, powder and shot for the Chiefs." Several hundred Mazaruni Caribs arrived in Berbice in March and April. They were unwilling, for reasons not explained, to be guided by men of African descent, so Van Hoogenheim hired some of the male members of the Broer family, who knew the hinterlands well and were of partial Amerindian descent, along with translator Frederik, whose background was similar, to be their guides. When De Salve expressed apprehensions about provisioning so many natives, Van Hoogenheim told him, "I would rather feed a 1,000 Indians, than a 100 whites." Besides cheap rum, he explained, all native soldiers required were cassava and fish.[9]

Van Hoogenheim contrasted Van 's Gravesande's efforts to arm Amerindians with the laxity of the Suriname authorities. He repeatedly requested that the Suriname officers stationed on the Corentyne River, the border with Berbice, send natives to his aid. But the officers lacked trade goods and liquor to compensate the Indians, who would not fight without payment. The "Suriname gentlemen economize mightily," Van Hoogenheim complained, a trait he found admirable in theory, but certainly not when it hurt "an unhappy neighbor." Nevertheless, some sixty to seventy Caribs from the Corentyne River demanded payment later that summer for patrolling and killing rebels in the upper Berbice. They brought along sticks with marks as proof.[10]

Despite the importance of Amerindians in closing off the borders of the colony and pursuing rebels in the rain forest, these crucial allies remain shadowy and faceless in the records. Berbice officials rarely called anyone by name, identifying local native leaders merely with the generic and derogatory term "bok captain." "Foreign" Indian fighters were usually designated only by their ethnic affiliation, for instance, Carib or Arawak, catchall terms given to natives by colonial authorities whose knowledge and understanding of the intricacies of Amerindian societies were limited. Likely the refusal to name and identify their allies was also a subconscious way for the Europeans to downplay native importance and disguise their own dependence on the martial skills of people they were supposed to dominate. Naming their allies would have drawn attention to the tenuous nature of Dutch colonialism.

Returnees

Harassed by European and turncoat African rangers and with Amerindian bounty hunters crisscrossing the hinterlands, self-emancipated people returned to the Dutch in ever greater numbers. The destruction of Atta's camp and torrential rains that made the woods all but unlivable for rebels and refugees accelerated the flow of returnees. Even the Dutch governor recognized that many refugees returned only because they suffered "unbelievable misery." By mid-January, some 230 adults and children, from Company and private plantations, had turned themselves in to the Dutch, including 64 people from West Souburg alone. But only a month later that number had multiplied to 1,200, almost a fifth of the total pre-rebellion enslaved population of 5,000 to 6,000 people. Among them were 250 suspected rebels. By the end of March, 2,600 people, of whom a third were Company people, had returned to the Dutch. By early April, one European officer (over)estimated the total at 4,000.[11]

Some returned in sizable groups, often representing most of the slave community of one or two plantations. Others arrived with just a few friends or family members. Large numbers of Company folks let it be known that they were ready to abandon their hiding places in the forest behind their estates. People turned themselves in at the posts or hailed Dutch warships on the river. Sometimes individuals came to ask for an escort of soldiers to bring out others. A few returnees were kept at the posts to serve as guides, porters, rowers, or general workers, but most were brought to Dageraad or Fort Nassau. Rapidly, both posts became massive refugee camps and prisons.[12]

It is hard to imagine the anguished decisions that drove people to return to their Dutch enslavers and to chattel slavery. Even for those who had been swept up in the rebellion against their will, the reestablishment of Dutch rule must have been a demoralizing and terrifying prospect. Starvation, rain, and illness forced the hands of many. Others, especially Creoles and Company slaves, saw no viable future among the rebels. Or they were not keen to live as Maroons. Some came back in hopes of being reunited with loved ones. People whose main "crime" during the rebellion had been to claim a measure of self-determination may have calculated that those who turned themselves in voluntarily were less likely to be punished than those captured by force.

Some people volunteered the reasons for their return. Not surprisingly, most claimed the rebels had forced them to join and they had never done any *quaad*, or evil. These claims were true in some cases, but not in every case. People had lived through a year's worth of revolution. The returnees had grievances against one another, and some used their interrogation to air these complaints before the Dutch. Captives were not altogether free to make up whatever story they thought would save them, as others stood ready to accuse those falsely claiming innocence, just as others were falsely accused. Unfortunately, the detailed lists made by European officers of returnees' names and plantations are missing from the archives. The absence of those documents makes it difficult to know exactly who returned and when. Van Hoogenheim reported at the end of February that most Company slaves were back in Dutch hands.[13] From which private plantations did people come? How were groups composed? Were more of the returnees women and children? Only anecdotal evidence remains.

To encourage more people to return, and to hunt down those wanting to remain free and at large, the colonial authorities increasingly relied on volunteers of African descent, in particular the two former rebel commanders turned slave catchers, Accara and Gousarie. These two men were astonishingly effective hunters. Many captives pointed to the pair as the reason for their return or capture. The two went out in the bush for days on end, sometimes together, sometimes separately. They became so trusted that when they requested armed enslaved men from the Dutch posts to assist them, their request was immediately fulfilled.[14]

Neither Accara, an Amina, nor Gousarie, who may have identified as Ganga, explained why they turned on their former enslaved comrades. Neither man was formally questioned by the Dutch, and so no documents shed light on the motives each might have had for recalibrating their moral compass. Perhaps they decided that working for the Dutch was the surest way to stay alive and one day become legally free. Perhaps they acted out of animosity toward Atta, with whom they were at odds. Was their choice to switch sides an agonizing one? Perhaps their collaboration should not be surprising. Joining the enemy is an old survival tactic and many others did the same, though few with greater impact on the conflict. As a Suriname Maroon proverb puts it, *mati koli mati*—betrayal among friends always lurks.[15]

Accara and Gousarie were not the only Africans to assist the Dutch in tracking rebels and refugees. Free and enslaved men served as pathfinders, slave catchers, and soldiers. Some, like Frederik (scout, Indian interpreter, and intermediary), did so from the start of the uprising. Others, like Accara and Gousarie, joined the Dutch when the time seemed opportune or service became unavoidable. Every Dutch post employed enslaved African or Creole men as scouts and patrollers. No European soldiers went on any mission without at least one such guide. Some enslaved men were promoted to serve as soldiers. On the post plantation Johanna, the commander employed "ten loyal *negers*" who could be "used on an expedition with guns."[16]

Others aided the Dutch, willingly or not, as circumstances dictated. Captive aides sought protection or favors for themselves and their families; they hoped to avoid punishment, or they opposed the rebellion. One captive offered to get his wife "and others" out of the woods. Accompanied by a soldier and an enslaved man, he paddled down the Wironi Creek while an officer and several soldiers followed overland so as not to alarm the refugees. They captured twenty-five people, including a native woman. A few days later, two other captives directed the Dutch to an encampment of thirty-four men, women, and children, including three native men. Three "honest blacks" betrayed their former comrades after their return by leading a commando unit back to a small settlement of some twenty huts. This foray failed. All but two men and two children managed to flee as the soldiers' guns malfunctioned in the heavy rain.[17] As the fortunes of the revolutionaries dimmed, choices for former enslaved people narrowed, and survival hung in the balance.

When people were captured, or returned of their own accord, they were sorted. Those who had resisted capture or were suspected of serious misdeeds and rebel leadership were arrested and restrained. Yet their sheer numbers exceeded the available supply of manacles and chains, leaving some free to move about despite "standing accused of many ill deeds." The lack of shackles demonstrates how Dutch material resources had been stretched thin by the long-lasting conflict. Instead of hardware, they deployed humans. Black guards and European soldiers patrolled at night, both around the quarters and where captives were lodged. Not surprisingly, some men managed to escape. Both Dageraad and Fort Nassau overflowed with people in and out of chains. "Good God," Van Hoogenheim lamented not long after he opined the loss of enslaved people, "what am I to do with all those captives. I have neither food nor room for them, nor enough healthy men to guard them."[18]

The records provide scattered information about what happened to the great majority of returnees who were not locked up. Some lived in the quarters, while others built huts in designated areas near Dageraad and the fort. Not surprisingly, many were put to work, maintaining the many people, black and white, living at the two camps. The most trusted men served as valets and house servants to European officials and officers. Others worked on military construction projects, rowed canoes and tent boats, drew water, chopped wood, or herded cattle in the savana. De Salve's troops had come without the usual female camp followers. Consequently, the soldiers were in need of women to cook, bake, clean, wash, sew, nurse, and serve at the officers' tables. Still other women worked in the fields or tended the food gardens. In short, those who returned were quickly redeployed as slaves, keeping the Dutch going. De Salve and Van Hoogenheim also decided to provisionally hand over people to managers and owners who had reoccupied their plantations. As none of these people had yet been cleared in the judicial procedures that began in early March, the plan was that they could be called back if evidence turned up that implicated them in the rebellion.[19]

Not all returnees were well enough to work. Refugees and captives arrived "lean as rakes" and "crazed with hunger." They looked "as

gaunt," Van Hoogenheim reported in a revealing comment on colonial medical care, "as if they came out of a hospital." De Salve noted
that among the six hundred captives at Fort Nassau, more than a third
could not labor due to "illness, injuries, and other inconveniences." Yet,
he added, piqued, "they get their rations just like the healthy ones." Returning to the Dutch did not spell the end of hunger. They had several
thousand people to feed who had previously fed themselves largely
from their own gardens. Most plantation provision grounds had been
destroyed, either by the rebels or by the European soldiers. At the fort,
"all subsistence gardens had been ruined," creating shortages, Van
Hoogenheim worried, for the "good and loyal slaves" belonging to
the Company. The governor set enslaved people to work expanding
the gardens at Dageraad, but this took time.[20] People were given small
weekly rations, which they were expected to supplement with gardening, fishing, and foraging. Some resorted to eating rats. One refugee
at the fort was whipped and shackled for sharing meat he had stolen
from soldiers.[21]

The records are for the most part mute on how slaves and soldiers,
packed together at Fort Nassau and at Dageraad, coexisted. But it is
clear that the colonial authorities were keen to prevent cross-racial
socializing, as it might lead to trouble. De Salve banned his men
from visiting the "negro huts," while those caught in the presence of
"groups of blacks" were punished by regulation with the gauntlet. Officials realized that soldiers and enslaved had a lot in common. Both
groups were poorly fed, poorly clothed, and overworked. Soldiers
would have been eager to trade pilfered military supplies for the produce of slave gardens, creating a lively underground economy. Sexual
relations between soldiers and enslaved women, whether coerced or
consensual, might lead to sexual jealousy, competition, and fighting.
De Salve forbade his officers from "swapping" the enslaved men and
women assigned them as servants, without his express permission.[22]
This regulation was likely intended to prevent officers from replacing
older "housekeepers" with younger women. The records are silent,
too, about sexual violence endured by enslaved women, and likely

some men.[23] Others may have benefited for a bit from a liaison with a European soldier with regular rations.

With large numbers of people crammed together under poor sanitary conditions, *roode loop*, or amoebic dysentery, began to spread in January, among both the soldiers and the enslaved. By the end of April, when conditions had become much more crowded, there was "seldom a day without three or four people being put in the ground." Some captives ended up in the hospital. The archives hold a list with the names, plantations, and dates of stay for 173 enslaved people hospitalized for the first five months of 1764. Unfortunately, the list only notes whether each person's illness was "internal" or "external," which probably corresponds to disease and visible injuries, respectively. Of the 173 people, 57 suffered from illness, 106 from injuries, and 10 from both. Most people stayed in the hospital for weeks. Just over a third of them belonged to the Company, a slightly higher proportion than their proportion of the overall slave population of Berbice.[24]

The records do not comment on psychological injuries. Yet most returnees had suffered serious trauma. They had seen family members and friends killed in battle, or murdered on the run by European soldiers, Amerindians, or rebels. Others had watched loved ones die of hunger, exposure, or illness, and they felt the guilt of survivors who had been unable to provide lifesaving help. Families and communities had been ripped apart. Lutijn van Helvetia, a Creole, claimed that a rebel leader "took him with his mother and little brother" from their plantation. The rebel had "killed his mother and kept them [himself and his brother] as slaves and later on the Gangoe murdered his brother." Parents had been separated from their children. Then there were the ordeals people did not discuss with the Dutch and thus remain obscure to us: the violence perpetrated by European soldiers, the agony of returning to Dutch enslavement, and fear of gruesome punishment or death. The records also do not indicate how people helped themselves and one another to cope and, to the extent possible, to heal.[25]

Despair about the rebellion's unraveling, terror of Dutch reenslavement and punishment, African notions of honor, or the belief that after death one's spirit could continue fighting injustice led some captives to attempt suicide. As soon as a boat that transported prisoners arrived at the landing at Dageraad, one shackled man deliberately jumped into the river and drowned. At other times, several men unsuccessfully tried to cut their throats, prompting one officer to inquire pragmatically about how he would have to display the corpse afterward. Should the captive be "hung from a tree by his legs?" Colonel de Salve answered that the man should be buried "at the edge of the forest." (The poor man survived, only to have his neck snapped on the gallows once he recovered enough to be questioned and convicted.) One determined, or desperate, captive, held at a post before transportation to Dageraad, was "found with a firelock plac'd under his Chin where the Ball had gone through his head, he having drawn the Trigger with his great Toe, to which it was fastn'd with a string." [26]

Ganga

Coralling several thousand returned captives did not net the most important hostages—the armed combatants who could do damage to colonial forces. The Dutch commanders, confronted with competing rumors, remained in the dark as to the actual whereabouts of Atta and his comrades. Officials had been informed by Amerindian spies, the mutineers, and returnees that internal discord was forcing the rebels apart. "Their Chiefs have separated, each is with his own Corps, or Country Negroes," one officer, an Englishman, reported. Quakoe remained with Atta until Quakoe's death in early March, but other leaders, such as Fortuin, Accabiré, and Bobé, had gone their separate ways. The Dutch could only guess at the size and whereabouts of each group. Intelligence was contradictory and frequently wrong. Information obtained from captives quickly grew outdated as rebels moved constantly. Returnees from Atta's band claimed that he did his best to prevent people from leaving, threatening to "cut off the head" of anyone who tried to flee to the Dutch.[27]

A major Dutch attack generated several military reports that shed light on the trajectory of one such band, the "Guango," or Ganga. Ac-cabiré, initially an ally of Atta and then his nemesis, commanded the targeted group. After their defeat on plantation Essendam at the hands of Atta, Accabiré's band made a break for Demerara but Amerindians stopped them. Several of Accabiré's men later related that after they fought with Indians on the way to Demerara, they turned back toward the Berbice River. In the early months of 1764, the Ganga built a vil-lage on an island in the middle of a swamp a walk of several hours behind plantation Landskroon. They placed short, poisonous wooden spikes in the underbrush on the paths leading up to their camp, an-gled upward to wound any approaching stranger.[28] Armed rebels who had deserted Atta, fed up with being mistreated, joined them. Some of these men identified as Ganga; others did not. Regardless of affiliation, they were all integrated into Accabiré's forces.[29]

Accabiré also enlarged his band with refugees who later claimed they had been forced to join him after they fled the massacre at Savonette.[30] Newly arrived African Job and his unnamed sister were among this number. After the Ganga killed his sibling, Job managed to flee their camp. Lena survived the Savonette massacre along with her husband, only to have him fall into the hands of the Ganga and be killed. Marietje described to her Dutch interrogators how the Ganga held her to prevent her "from returning to the Christians and divulg-ing where they were." Piramus claimed that he and his wife and chil-dren had been captured by Accabiré and sixty Ganga with guns. They told him they would eventually let him go back to his plantation but for now they would kill him if he tried to escape. The Ganga had put him to work procuring heart of palm and cutting wood.[31]

Like Maroons, the Ganga regularly raided plantations. One man di-vulged in his interrogation that the Ganga intended to start a "planta-tion," likely a village, on the Abary River on the border with Essequibo. In mid-March, perhaps to supply themselves for such a venture, Ac-cabiré's men attacked Landskroon, one of a growing number of es-tates newly reoccupied by the Dutch. The warriors carried away food, powder, and lead, and they wounded the plantation manager, Daniel

Bachelin. Reportedly, the raiders also took along five women, whether voluntarily or not is unclear. The rest of the slaves on Landskroon escaped the attackers "by swimming."[32]

When his men returned to camp and made their report, Accabiré was angry. He reportedly told them that they should have caught Bachelin, "so he could write to their masters." Apparently the irate leader was eager to return to the Dutch, because, as he would explain after being captured, he and his men "had done *geen quaad*," no evil. They had fought against the Amina, not the Dutch.[33] Accabiré must have found someone who was literate, because just days later he sent two emissaries with a letter negotiating a return to the Dutch. Unfortunately, the letter has not survived, but the contents were reported by Colonel de Salve. Accabiré emphasized that he did not want to fight "the Christians." He offered to turn in the men who had wounded Bachelin as a show of good faith. He proposed two Europeans (one of them was Georgina George's only surviving brother) to negotiate the conditions of surrender with his two ambassadors.[34]

A year earlier, when Coffij negotiated for half the Dutch colony, he wrote from a position of strength. Accabiré, down on his luck, faced very different conditions. The Dutch had been eager to negotiate with Coffij because at the time they were desperate, but now the situation had reversed. Word of Accabiré's note arrived in the midst of preparations for a large-scale expedition against him. The mid-March raid on Landskroon had only strengthened De Salve's determination to wipe out the remaining revolutionaries. He emphatically forbade his officers from "agreeing to any peace treaties or anything else with that *canaille* [scum]." He issued savage instructions to his men to "mow down all that oppose you with weapons" or "cut the [achilles] tendon in the back of their legs, like one does with horses, to prevent them from running off."[35]

As the conflict wore on, De Salve became increasingly brutal and convinced of the rebels' racial inferiority. Based on intelligence, he surmised that Accabiré's troop consisted of four hundred well-armed combatants (a figure Van Hoogenheim thought exaggerated). Defeating a force this size required an elaborate plan. The Dutch archives

G. H. Luck, Military bush camp commanded by Colonel Fourgeoud in Suriname, fighting the Boni Maroons, 1770s. Expeditions against the Berbice rebels may have yielded similar scenes of African-descended carriers and slaves making camp for European soldiers. (Nationaal Militair Museum [NMM], Soesterberg.)

hold a "figurative sketch," drawn for the occasion, indicating both Accabiré's camp and the projected locations of the European and African soldiers. De Salve took the risk of arming enslaved men. He doubted Europeans could get the job done: "no Christian is able to traverse the woods to which the Guangoo have repaired." After several days of feverish preparations, an expedition of some two hundred men set off on March 22. Closely guarded enslaved bearers carried the ammunition, grenades, and small portable cannons called coehoorn mortars.[36]

Before sunset the next day, the forces deployed their mortars against Accabiré's camp. It was still dark, they could not see much, but they could hear the cries of women and children and the sound of people "running about in the woods." The mortars did not hit anyone, but they scared people badly. It quickly became clear that the Europeans had been misinformed about the strength of their opponents. Rather than 400 rebels, the camp held fewer than 160 people, including women and children, living in fifty huts. Over the course of the day, the Dutch killed 20 and took 50 captives, including Accabiré "and his entire court." Some 80 people escaped. Given that Accabiré's men had few guns, it is not surprising the Dutch suffered no casualties. The defensive spikes surrounding the village wounded several European soldiers as they stumbled on them in the thick undergrowth. The expedition's commander, Major de Brauw, had to be carried back to his post by four enslaved men, unable to walk after he punctured his thigh. To the soldiers' disappointment, they found no gold or silver in the camp. De Brauw concluded that all reports of "the courage, riches and state" of these rebels had been vastly exaggerated.[37]

De Salve and Van Hoogenheim were impressed with the charismatic Accabiré when he was brought before them a few days later. Perhaps Accabiré was of exalted birth in West Africa. He clearly cultivated the image of an honorable noble. The man had "the presence of a prince," De Salve marveled. He recommended that Accabiré be kept alive, at least for now, rather than speedily executed, as he thought the captive leader could provide information. Van Hoogenheim was similarly impressed, calling him *"een schoon Kerel,"* a valiant man. When

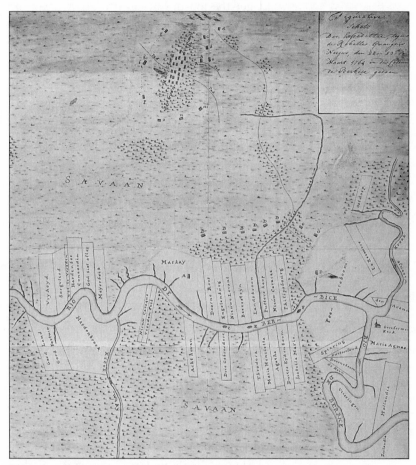

Leupe 1655, figurative sketch of the expedition against the "Rebelle Guangous,"
or Ganga, March 1764, detail. At the top are the huts of the Ganga surrounded by
European and African soldiers. (Nationaal Archief, The Hague.)

asked "whether he had not been a commander en *Groot Heer* among the rebels," Accabiré answered, Van Hoogenheim recorded, that "Yes, he had commanded and he had been a *Heer* among his people, but he was my slave." Stressing his supposed loyalty to the Dutch, Accabiré again asserted that he had fought "against the Amina, but not against the Christians" and boasted that he had beaten Atta several times.[38]

Strange accusations swirled around the Ganga. The Dutch received reports that they ate their opponents, a claim De Salve at first thought absurd. Yet after talking to captives, the colonel reported that "they admit they have eaten Negroes but they do not want to hear about having eaten Christians."[39] When the Dutch questioned the captives taken in Accabiré's camp, further details emerged. All were emphatic that the Ganga never ate Europeans. All but one denied having consumed humans themselves, though many claimed they had heard, or in some cases seen, men who did. Accabiré maintained that while some of his men had eaten their enemies, he had not. Several men testified they had not eaten human flesh because they were "Gangoe of a different nation." Only one man, La Rose van La Providence, admitted to consuming his enemies, yet he did not identify as Ganga. Faced with a witness who claimed he saw him "cook human flesh in iron pots," La Rose responded that "Amina, who were bad people, killed several of his nation and out of revenge, he and others killed several Amina and ate them." Asked how many he had consumed, La Rose answered that he "helped kill and eat eleven." The Dutch evidently believed him, as they condemned him to die for having been "a man eater" (the only person so convicted) as well as "a soldier and drummer." Another witness, Frits van de Heer Abbensets, explained how cannibals' victims were supposedly killed. "They sent them to the water or out to get wood and then others met them and said to them you are no *neger*, you don't have marks such as we, you are just meat, and they killed them."[40]

What should we make of these charges and claims? Cannibalism was a common accusation for Europeans eager to assert their superiority over the supposed barbarians in the rest of the world. People may have responded to Dutch questions with fabrications, hoping to satisfy their inquisitors' appetites for fables. Yet in that case, one would expect these stories to be somewhat indiscriminate and more frequent. But the subject is raised only with respect to the Ganga. Ritual cannibalism, the ceremonial eating of the human flesh of one's enemies, was not widespread in West Africa. But there is evidence that members of secret societies in Upper Guinea, where the Ganga came from, ritually ate their enemies.[41] Ganga interviewed by a Moravian missionary in the 1760s on the Caribbean island of St. John spoke of people in their country consuming war captives. One man explained that his people cooked and ate enemies killed in battle out of anger that they "had done them so much harm." It is also possible that the Ganga threatened people held among them against their will with cannibalism and such threats became reality in people's minds. Ten years later, Gabriel Stedman, the Maroon fighter in Suriname, mentioned that the "Gango Negroes are Reckon'd Anthropophagi or Cannibals" and that pots with flesh had been found in the village of Boni, an important Suriname Maroon leader.[42]

These grim matters appear to have been of little concern to Dutch leaders, who remained preoccupied with their own business of warfare. Defeating the Ganga was the first major victory for the Dutch since the destruction of Atta's camp at the end of January. Yet Atta continued to elude them.

The Rebellion Broken

Governor Atta no doubt heard about the capture of Accabiré, and that must have magnified his anxieties for his own safety. The leader's following rapidly dissolved. His band kept subdividing, partly as the result of Atta's reportedly harsh conduct toward his lieutenants and perhaps also because small groups could move faster in attempting to avoid detection. One unit, commanded by Adou van de Prosperiteit and Hendrik van de Hooftplantage, was overcome at the end of February, despite fierce resistance. Accompanying them was one of Atta's wives and her little son. The woman was dressed poorly, not as one would expect to see a governor's wife. Weeping, she tried to convince the Dutch that she was merely the maid of Atta's wife. When a female returnee unmasked her, she admitted Atta had confiscated her clothes.[43] She shared that he "no longer had many people with him" and that he was trying to cross the Berbice River in order to make his way to the upper Demerara and beyond.

If escaping the colony was Atta's aim, he did not succeed. He eluded his native and African-descended captors for weeks, but Gousarie and Accara, his former comrades, caught him in mid-April. Contrary to expectations, he had only a few gold coins on him. De Salve asked him where his forces were. Atta answered that a few men were still scattered in the woods, but their number was small and they were starving. De Salve reported that "very quietly" Atta added "that he knew he deserved to die, and that he did not want to live." He asked for some food and drink after which he "would welcome death." He advised that "if they would cut off his head, and put it on a pole, the rebellion would be over." Perhaps Atta alluded to an understanding in some parts of West Africa that a ruler's severed head signaled to his followers that they should no longer count on his supernatural protection. It is also possible that Atta's suggestion was inspired by preferring death to re-enslavement, a punishment particularly humiliating for a ruler.[44] The next day, Atta was brought before Van Hoogenheim in public. He threw himself on the ground and tried to kiss the Dutch governor's feet. The Dutchman interpreted this performance as submissive behavior and it surprised him. Van Hoogenheim noted in his daily record that Accabiré, who evidently watched the incident, had a loud, long laugh at his opponent and made fun of him.[45]

Now the most important leaders remaining at large were Bobé van Debora and Fortuin van Helvetia. Gousarie and Accara captured Bobé two weeks after Atta, along with his wife and child and thirty others. The group was evidently the remnant of Accabiré's followers. Whether reporting facts or catering to prejudices, Accara and Gousarie claimed to have found in the camp huge quantities of human bones "and several cooking pots with Negro flesh."[46] Several enslaved men nabbed the last major rebel leader, Fortuin van Helvetia, on the Canje River in early June. They shackled Fortuin on plantation Stevensburg, but when his guard fell asleep, Fortuin escaped with the help of two of his wives. Van Hoogenheim feared that the "sophisticated villain" would try to make his way by sea to the Suriname Maroons. But instead Fortuin turned back to the Berbice River. Two weeks later, Accara and Gousarie, who had previously served under him, caught Fortuin near his former plantation Helvetia. He was delivered to Dageraad on June 14. Questioned the next day, Van Hoogenheim noted, he "candidly confessed to all his atrocities." With the capture of Fortuin, the Dutch were sure the revolution was over.[47]

Sensing that there was little left for them to do, the Mazaruni River Caribs decided to return home. They had patrolled the colony's borders and prevented rebels from making their way beyond the Berbice and Canje Rivers. Governor van 's Gravesande judged that they had been "bold and enterprising beyond habit and expectation, yea, even reckless." Their slave hunting, he noted, relishing his divide-and-conquer strategy, "caused a great embitterment between the blacks and them, which, if well and reasonably stimulated, cannot fail to be of much use and service in the future to the Colonies." The Dutch West India Company later handed out medallions to three indigenous leaders for their role in suppressing the rebellion.[48]

The Caribs had been effective at keeping people from becoming Maroons, but Gousarie and Accara rounded up many more people than the Indians did. Dutch officials estimated that together the two men were responsible for the return of some six hundred rebels and refugees. De Salve later argued, sharing in the victory, that without "their assistance, and their demonstrated loyalty to me," it would have taken a lot longer to "quell the rebellion so thoroughly.[49]

14

Justice Sideways

Hercules sat in lockup, his legs and wrists shackled, staring at the river as he awaited his interrogation. One can only imagine his fatigue, hopelessness, and terror. The sun beat down fiercely, intensifying his misery and thirst. Hercules was from Juliana, one of the first plantations to combust in rebellion the previous year. He had been taken captive in late February 1764 and returned to his plantation. The manager at Juliana, Johannes Dell, suspected it was Hercules who had murdered his wife in the first hours of the uprising. After killing her, the rebels had staked the woman's head at the river's edge. Dell delivered Hercules in shackles to Dageraad in early April for interrogation. Van Hoogenheim ordered Hercules sequestered with prisoners accused of the most serious crimes, including "Christian murder," arson, or leadership in the rebellion. Those crimes carried the death sentence.[1]

Hercules's fellow captives likely filled him in on what was to come. He would be brought before the three remaining members of the governor's council. The three were all slaveholders, and by then they had interrogated several hundred people. The councilors, acting as judges, sought confessions or relied on credible witnesses to reach their verdicts. Some suspects confessed; others did not. Cracking under the pressure, many prisoners leveled accusations against others. The number of captives swelled as the scribe took down the names of the newly accused. The councilors ruled on guilt and handed out grisly sentences.

A few weeks before Hercules was detained, the governor and the three councilors had ordered the enslaved executioner to kill the first fifty-one people, including three women, condemned to death. The court specified in its verdicts how each prisoner would die. Some of the condemned were to have every bone broken on the rack with an iron bar, before dying from either a "mercy blow" to the heart or a merciless blow to the skull. Others were to be burned at the stake with a regular fire, which took an hour, or with "small fire," where the victim smoldered alive for four hours. Some faced the additional torture of having their flesh ripped with hot pincers. The "lucky" ones were hanged, their heads staked. As in Suriname, French Louisiana, and St. Domingue, the public executioners in Berbice were enslaved men.[2]

Hercules knew that more rounds of executions would follow, as the number of shackled captives grew. Waiting days or weeks in the stockade, the prisoners had time to make alliances and to discuss the best strategies for evading the councilors' questions. But all understood the difficulty of maintaining loyalty to friends when faced with capital punishment. No stranger in the colony, Hercules was familiar with the cruel reality of Dutch "justice."[3]

Good Law

"I am in a delicate situation with respect to the captured negroes," Governor van Hoogenheim wrote early in 1764. For him the situation was without precedent. The colony had never had a large uprising before; never had so many enslaved required a trial. He fretted to his superiors, "It is true that most came to us voluntarily, but they should be examined carefully to determine whether they are not guilty in some way."[4] The question was how.

Berbice, like other colonies steeped in Roman law, did not have a separate slave court. The same councilmen who presided over the trials of free individuals also tried enslaved people.[5] The colony's prosecutor had died and Van Hoogenheim was too overextended to do that job himself. The entire operation would have to be carried out by a trio of hardly impartial council members. Van Hoogenheim understood that their "private concerns and self interests" as slaveholders could both draw out the process and lead to the dismissals of guilty rebels who were valuable laborers. The governor suspected that the councilmen wanted their own enslaved back to work wholly abled, justice or not. He suggested a fix. He proposed that "all who engaged in murder or arson, or those who took up weapons against Christians," or "all those seen with weapons in their hands or caught armed," could receive the death penalty solely on the testimony "of their own comrades, or other blacks." As long as such testimony had "a semblance of truth," no other witnesses or proof would be required. With this shortcut, he assured the directors in Amsterdam, the commissioners could conclude the business expeditiously and "execute good law."[6]

How did the Dutch define "good law"? The *Ordre van Regieringe*, issued by the States General in 1629 to create uniformity in government and law in the Dutch West Indies, and still in force in 1763, provided only the most general guidelines. It stipulated that criminal cases be heard by three councilors. These men, chosen from the local planters, were rarely schooled in law. They were supposed to apply Dutch laws and procedures, preferably in an expedited process. Where Dutch laws were lacking, as in the case of people ensnared in slavery, which did not exist in the United Provinces, the order mandated Roman law. Given the fragmented legal landscape of the Dutch Republic, colonists most often turned to the laws and practices of the seaboard province of Holland and the city of Amsterdam, which was so deeply involved in the colonial enterprise. That sounds easy—follow the law—yet it was anything but.[7]

Early modern law and its application in the Dutch Republic had no uniformity or regularity. Not only did suspects face opaque legal processes and judges with little formal training, but the principle of equality before the law did not exist. Defendants were tried and punished in accordance with their social status. Throughout early modern Europe, the law was shaped to reinforce class hierarchies. The Dutch drew a clear line between respectable settled citizens and vagrants. This second class of citizens was an expansive category of poor that included day laborers, seasonal workers, peddlers, street vendors, beggars, migrants, prostitutes, unemployed soldiers and sailors—in short, anyone without steady work, a permanent abode, or respectable community ties. Such people had few rights, received summary justice, and were treated to painful physical punishments.[8]

Poor suspects had no right to counsel and were kept in custody during the proceedings. The public prosecutor brought an accusation on behalf of the government and had to prove its validity, ideally in the form of a confession, with torture if necessary. A confession opened the door to capital punishment and revoked the right to appeal. The prosecutor collected the facts, deposed witnesses, and examined the suspect using predetermined questions—all behind closed doors. Suspects could be confronted with witnesses to induce confession. If the suspect did not admit guilt, a judge might order torture, if there was evidence, or even just a strong suspicion, that the suspect might be guilty. After confession, the judges followed with a sentence. Juries, so important in British practice, were not used in the Netherlands. Courts disagreed about how to punish a suspect who did not confess. In Amsterdam, both the death penalty and corporal punishment were rare without a confession. In other cities, withstanding torture saved one from death, but not from the rack or whipping post. Only those who did not confess had the right to appeal.[9]

In suggesting a shortened process, Van Hoogenheim was on solid ground. He was less so when he proposed lowering the bar for execution by foregoing confessions and accepting the testimony of accomplices, moves that were problematic under Dutch law. Indeed, when the directors of Berbice received his suggestion, they swiftly rejected it, in part, as they pointed out, because Dutch law already mandated capital punishment for murder and arson. But they were also thinking about their bottom line. Combining ethics with capitalist logic, they deemed it "both extremely dangerous and unjust" (given such "loose evidence") and "of the most detrimental consequence to extend the death penalty" to those who had merely engaged in combat or were caught with weapons. While they wanted to make examples of the ringleaders, all others should be treated less "rigorously," so as not to damage further slave owners who had already "suffered so much in the present fatal circumstances." They did not need to spell out that dead slaves produced no coffee and no sugar.[10]

The directors' rejection of Van Hoogenheim's proposal and their plea for leniency did not reach the colony until much of the judicial process had been completed. No evidence survives of any explicit discussion among the three councilmen as to how they intended to proceed. Unaware of the directors' disapproval and unfamiliar with a process usually carried out by a prosecutor, it appears they followed Van Hoogenheim's suggestions. Like colonial elites elsewhere, they bent existing legal procedures for controlling the poor at home to facilitate dominion over those they so grossly exploited abroad. The fabric connecting class control in the metropole to racialized coercion abroad was tightly woven. The need to control slaves, made alien by their legal status and manufactured racial differences, justified the hollowing out of an already weak and arbitrary judicial system.[11]

Court

Once the councilors had decided on procedure, the "examinations" began in early March 1764 and continued intermittently until the end of the year. Re-enslaved people held on Dageraad were first, followed by those at Fort Nassau. The captives faced the councilors in two overlapping groups. One included those, like Hercules, kept in chains, who were suspected of arson, murder, and armed resistance. The other group involved bystanders, who might be guilty of participation in the rebellion, but only "sideways," as the directors phrased it. Between March and mid-June, the councilors heard 230 suspects and 650 detained bystanders. Another twenty captives were questioned five months later in December. Since the process took a long time, many enslaved people were sent to their plantations to work before being interrogated. They lived in a state of constant fear. Should someone point a finger at them, they could still be called before the court and be killed. Almost half of the recaptured enslaved adults were interrogated, a fact that points to the scale of the Dutch enterprise of judicial revenge. Nothing this extensive had ever occurred on the Berbice or elsewhere before.[12]

In mid-April, after several weeks in chains, Hercules was escorted into Dageraad's plantation house, the governor's temporary residence, to face the three officials in frock coats and wigs, flanked by soldiers. The barefoot captives were almost naked, clad in rags. Earlier that day, the commissioners questioned fourteen bystanders. Then, after lunch, they turned to suspected rebels. Two women preceded Hercules. The clerk wrote down the councilmen's questions and the prisoners' answers, translating Creole into standard Dutch, summarizing answers, and writing in the third person. Unfortunately, he did not summarize everything, occasionally noting that someone "said much more, none of it relevant" to the concerns of the Dutch. Hercules did not require a translator, as did recently arrived Africans. Some people could not be questioned at all because there was no translator or because the court deemed them "simpleminded." [13]

Hercules steeled himself for the specific and leading questions favored by the commissioners. Their queries aimed at eliciting a confession rather than getting at any larger truth. Hercules knew that as he stood accused of murder, his life hung in the balance. But he may also have known that several prisoners in their interrogations had pointed to another man as Dell's wife's killer. With careful answers, maybe he could elude the death penalty.[14]

The commissioners wasted no time getting to the case against Hercules. Their very first question asked: "Who killed your mistress last year, when the war began?" Hercules named two men, Mars van Elisabeth & Alexandria (already fingered by two others) and Attabane van Hollandia. Evidently familiar with how much stock the Dutch set by eyewitnesses, Hercules added that he had seen the murder himself, as, he added, had everyone else on his plantation. "What about your wife," the commissioners followed up, "did she see it?" Hercules answered in the negative, either truthfully or trying to shield his wife from interrogation, explaining that "she was in the gardens." To the next question, "Did Mistress Dell not beg you to let her go and aid her," Hercules countered, "Master Dell claims that, but it is not true." "When Mistress Dell was dead, did your wife not come in and set the table and you ate like lords?" the councilors pressed. "No," Hercules answered, "those are all lies," but, he added, perhaps proudly and somewhat foolishly, "later, after his master had left for the seaside, he ate with his wife and children at his master's table." Admitting to what must have been a deeply satisfying inversion of social practice suggested to the councilors that Hercules had indeed been a leader in the rebellion, someone with enough command to dine at Dell's table.

The councilors then took a different tack. "Who," they wanted to know, "had plundered his master's possessions?" Hercules implicated Attabane again, and added that there had been "sharing" and he had "received a dress."

Asked, "Did you not help kill many Christians?" Hercules answered that was not true; "Coffij wanted to make him a lieutenant but he had not accepted." Instead, he claimed, a fellow rebel from his plantation had taken the role: "then August became captain." "Had he gone along to fight on plantation Peereboom?" Hercules reportedly answered "yes," but he claimed he did not have a firearm. By denying he had a gun, Hercules tried to establish that he could not have participated in the killing of Europeans during the Peereboom massacre. Then he added that he had gotten hold of two of Mr. George's guns (he did not say how he obtained the guns of Georgina's father, killed at Peereboom) but that he "gave them to his commander Captain Pokko."

Next the councilors inquired whether Hercules "had not served at the fort under Lt. Quassie van Hardenbroek, and was sent on patrols to Hooftplantage" likely to pick up rum, produced under duress by Company people on that plantation. According to the clerk, Hercules replied, "That is not true and he had no soldier's gun but he had a gun of his own and came with it to plantation Dageraad but had stayed on the boat as a guard." Again, his answer was meant to prove that he had not participated in any battles on Dageraad, where, importantly, Europeans, or "Christians," had been killed.

It is hard to tell from the clerk's transcription whether Hercules was volunteering too much self-incriminating information, as anxious people under pressure tend to do, or whether the clerk had collapsed several questions and answers in a convoluted way. In either case, Hercules admitted to having been at Dageraad and Peereboom, where Europeans had been killed, two potentially incriminating events in the eyes of the councilors. To the last question, whether he bought his gun or it had been gifted to him, Hercules answered that "Amina Quakoe van de Cornelia Jacoba" had "honored him with it, with powder and shot." This damning admission, that a rebel leader had given him a gun, ended the first round of his interrogation.[15]

The records of the post-rebellion examinations are not conclusive about whether torture was used to elicit confessions, as was routine in the Dutch Republic for low-class suspects. It is unlikely that those considered mere bystanders were tortured. Their examinations were brief and the commissioners rarely challenged their careful, evasive answers. With respect to more central suspects, it is less certain whether they were tortured. If confessions were not necessary, torture, which could be time-consuming, was superfluous. Councilor Lodewijk Abbensets had in the past not been keen to use it. Even without the use of torture, suffering interrogation by a commission of three slaveholders who may have threatened violence, not to mention the possibility of horrific punishment, was terrifying in a process intended less to execute justice than to reinforce slaveholders' restored control and power.[16]

After his first interrogation, Hercules may have felt he had slipped the noose. He had denied killing Dell's wife. Yet a week later, Hercules was called in again for questioning, like many who denied wrongdoing. In their second, and final, examination, they were usually questioned further or confronted with their accusers. Hercules had admitted to having a gun and being present at the Peereboom massacre and the Dageraad battles. He was already in deep trouble. He may not have known that the day after he was questioned the first time, a fellow rebel had accused him of murdering Europeans.[17]

Hercules was "confronted" with his accuser, a returned slave named Cornelis van Petite Bayonne, who was asked whether it was Hercules who "had murdered a Christian and is guilty of much evil?" Cornelis answered, "Yes, the very same who has killed his master's wife." He stated this to Hercules *in facie*, that is, face-to-face, as Dutch law required of a credible witness.

Asked what he had to say for himself, Hercules sensibly answered that Cornelis could not have possibly known what had happened on other people's plantations. He reiterated that the culprits were Mars van Elisabeth & Alexandria and Fossoe, or Attabane, van Hollandia. He conceded that he had been present at the murder. "General rumor" claimed he was guilty, Hercules explained, but it "was not true." The councilors asked Cornelis whether Hercules had been a *heer*, a man in charge. Cornelis answered affirmatively and added that Hercules had been called *erfprins*, or crown prince. He likely spoke the truth, as this alternative name for Hercules surfaced in the records several times. Eating at his master's table, calling himself the heir apparent; Hercules's case looked grimmer and grimmer. Finally, unable to deny his leadership, Hercules granted he had been a *heer*, or lord, yet added dubiously, "He had stayed home." The councilors had what they needed and they dismissed both men. They did not call in Johannes Dell to testify. (No Europeans served as witnesses in the examinations.)[18]

For their information, the councilmen relied on people implicating each other, as Van Hoogenheim had suggested. People who made accusations, like Cornelis, were required to do so face-to-face. Naming names, accusing others, or serving as a witness did not get a defendant a more lenient sentence. The commissioners gave great weight to the testimony of Christiaan and Pieter, the two enslaved Company artisans who the previous May had served as Van Hoogenheim's messengers to rekindle diplomacy with the insurgents. The pair were detained at Fort Nassau before Governor Coffij released Pieter. Christiaan remained with the rebels for months before he escaped with twenty-one fellow Company people. The councilors relied on their accounts of what they had seen at the fort. Their statements that they had spotted someone with a gun were decisive. Hercules's accuser Cornelis, for instance, claimed that his participation in the rebellion had been entirely forced. Pieter and Christiaan testified that they had seen him with the *bomba* of his plantation at the fort, armed. Cornelis countered that he had merely carried his *bomba*'s gun. But Pieter and Christiaan retorted that they had "seen him everywhere with a gun." Despite the fact that Cornelis had served as a key witness against Hercules, Pieter and Christiaan's charges ended in Cornelis being hanged.[19] Cornelis's case is representative.

Like Hercules, suspects deployed the little bit of power they had to try to escape the death sentence. Some confessed their involvement right away. Most did not, claiming instead that they acted on orders or were forced, or that they had merely been unarmed foot soldiers. Others, like Hercules, copped to minor offenses as a way to avoid admitting to bigger ones. Most prisoners implicated others. Confronted with witnesses, or questioned a second time, many suspects ended up admitting greater involvement, even as they continued to deny the most serious charges. Given that people had every reason to distort, omit, or lie, it is hard to separate truth from fiction in an individual's careful and strategic answers.

Bystanders were more reticent to talk than suspects. While suspects sought to evade specific charges, bystanders were best served by silence to avoid inadvertently incriminating themselves or others. Asked what they knew about particular events or the rebellion as a whole, most simply answered that they had been in hiding and had seen nothing. Some divulged more detail. Most depositions of women are shorter than those of men. This reflected in part women's reluctance to condemn members of their communities to Dutch justice. It also reflected the councilors' gender norms; they assumed that women in general were less likely to be involved in insurgency, so they rarely pressed them. At other times, the clerk may have summarized women's stories. Four women were executed for their role in the rebellion. The Dutch may well have missed out on pertinent information because they failed to consider the possibility of militarized, politicized women. Yet on the whole, women were excluded from rebel leadership's military and governing structures.[20]

The proceedings were neither uniform nor consistent. People examined early on were more likely to be found guilty than those questioned later in the process. Councilmen favored their own slaves for verdicts of innocence. Several of the enslaved people accused councilor Abbensets's people of serious involvement in the rebellion. Ignoring their testimony, Abbensets declared his slaves innocent. He clearly wanted working slaves, not strung-up corpses. Over a cup of tea, Van Hoogenheim rebuked Abbensets, saying, "If the examinations will not be carried out more sharply than thus far, few rebels will be discovered." He added that he hoped "justice won't be short-changed and evil won't remain unpunished." Rather than arguing with the governor about it, or waiting for the entire court to decide on guilt and innocence, Abbensets quietly loaded his slaves onto his boat to return them to his forced labor camps. Abbensets on several more occasions acquitted his own workers and those of plantations he managed, to the chagrin of the governor and his fellow councilors. He also regularly stopped the proceedings to go attend to affairs on his plantations. No amount of cajoling could get him to resume his position on the bench until he felt like it.[21]

For his part, the governor was also eager to get the Company plantations back in production, and he pushed for those slaves to be examined quickly. Most Company captives, Van Hoogenheim noted with relief, "convincingly showed their innocence, and that they had never taken part in the rebellion." While this statement may have been in part inspired by his wish to consider Company slaves blameless, most enslaved in this category were indeed less involved than their counterparts on private plantations. Rebel masters in charge of Company plantations ruled with a familiar violence as they forced workers during the rebellion back into the sugar fields. Blind to the parallels with the colonial regime he oversaw, Van Hoogenheim wrote that Company slaves "have suffered much and they have been badly mistreated by the rebels." In the end, only one-sixth of those condemned to death were Company people. The majority of them, Van Hoogenheim noted, were of the "Amina nation."[22]

Sometimes the quarry in the court was big. In April, the councilors interrogated Atta, the former rebel governor. Like many re-enslaved people, Atta used the process as much as possible for his own ends. He acknowledged his leadership to De Salve and Van Hoogenheim upon capture. Yet under his first, brief questioning he minimized his role, claiming he had merely been a captain in the revolutionary army. He maintained that he was wrongly accused: "The people of Berbice always yelled, *Atta Atta Atta* did it, to exculpate themselves." He had only carried out orders and "never hurt any Christians." Asked whether he agreed that in addition to the harm he had done to Europeans, he had brought great misery to his own people, he countered sadly and warily to the Dutch scribe who rendered his words in the third person that "All he might say against that, we would not believe anyway." In response to the councilors' assertion that he was ultimately responsible for all the "evil" carried out by his people, "being as much as their king," Atta contradicted his earlier statements. "I know that," he confessed.[23]

Two days later Atta was brought shackled before the councilors a second time. While he offered that he knew "he had to answer for what happened during his reign," he remained defiant, using the interrogation to avenge himself against those who had betrayed him. He readily named names, yet he consistently denied involvement in the incidents of murder and arson the councilors raised. When asked "who began the war with you," he listed twenty-two prominent men, starting with Accara and Gousarie, the two traitors who had captured him, and then adding many others. He named the remaining nine men of his band still in the woods. He tried to clarify his role in Governor Coffij's demise. As he answered question after question, his fortunes fell. The councilmen's forty-fourth and final question included a moral rebuke: "What reasons did you have to destroy so many Negroes?" Atta answered simply, "Those are all just lies."[24]

The councilors could have brought in any number of witnesses to testify against Atta, but they only called in Accabiré, Atta's former comrade turned enemy who had so impressed Dutch officials with his regal bearing. Accabiré reiterated that Atta had been the top governor, who had "burned and fought everywhere," and whose frightened followers had come over to Accabiré because Atta killed so many of his own people. At the next sentencing, the court decided that Atta was "guilty of all the evil of murder, theft, arson, etc., carried out by himself and by his subordinates."[25] They sentenced him to the stake.

In June, the councilors examined Captain Fortuin van Helvetia, who had been in charge of the Canje campaign. He frankly admitted his part in the rebellion. The few men he named had all, except for Accabiré, already been executed. Fortuin related that he and Accabiré had cooperated in killing two Europeans. Brought face-to-face with Fortuin, Accabiré denied the charge, but the court deemed the claim true. On June 16, both leaders were condemned to death. For being "an important *Heer*, Governor on the Canje, murdered, robber, and arsonist, guilty of much evil, both by him and those he commanded," Fortuin was to be burned with "slow fire" while tortured with hot pincers. The princely Accabiré, "a fellow rebel and not innocent of Christian murder," was prescribed a faster end on the gallows.[26]

Executions

The court met after each round of examinations to determine guilt and punishment, but the minutes do not explain the judges' reasoning. In all, they condemned to death 120 men and 4 women. Twenty of the executed men came from Company plantations; the others, including the women, belonged to private planters. In keeping with Dutch practice, a few teenagers, due to "paucity of years," had their sentences commuted to flogging and sale out of the colony. Adults were condemned to gruesome deaths at the stake, the rack, and the gallows. Fully half of those questioned as suspects were sentenced to die. Such high rates of retribution carried out in assembly-line fashion were common in the colonial world. When some fifteen hundred enslaved people rose up in Jamaica in 1760–61, the British executed one hundred rebels by gibbeting, slow fire, and hanging. Another five hundred were sold to Honduras. After a brief revolt in Demerara, west of Berbice, in 1823, seventy-two slaves were tried. Of the fifty-one who were condemned to death, thirty-three were executed. The others, still viewed as valuable property, had their sentences commuted to whippings.[27]

As in early modern Europe, including the Dutch Republic, the executions were carried out in public to serve as an example and deterrent. De Salve's second-in-command, Robert Douglas, traveled downriver from his post to watch the executions that occurred on April 28. The judicial murders took place in a clearing behind the burned ruin of Dageraad's sugar mill. In addition to Atta, seventeen men were hanged that day, nine (including one woman, Barbara van Lelienburg, councilor to Captain Accara) were broken alive on the wheel, and five burned with slow fire. Most victims underwent their torments stoically, defiant to the end. Europeans attending public executions throughout the Caribbean commented on African-descended people's self-possession and dignity as they were tortured to death. For some victims this fortitude may have been the result of their training as soldiers in West Africa and a crucial component of masculine performance. Others may have been inspired by beliefs in transmigration, the idea that after death they would travel home, as well as faith in the endurance of the soul, which would allow them to continue their resistance as revenging spirits.[28]

Among those executed on April 28 was Hercules, sentenced to the rack. He had, Douglas noted, "not uttered a groan" while his bones were broken. In the crowd of enslaved forced to watch were friends and acquaintances, and perhaps his wife and children. While he suffered, Hercules lifted his head and spied his plantation manager and chief accuser, Johannes Dell. Upending the typical practice of spectators taunting the convicted, Hercules called out Dell. He charged that Dell was the guilty party because his abuse had turned slaves into rebels. Dell yelled back, justifying his conduct before the assembled crowd. There, behind the burned sugar mill, in the torpor of a late tropical morning, the two men, one dying, the other powerfully alive, traded insults like equals. Finally, Van Hoogenheim stepped in to silence Dell.[29]

With his dying breath, Hercules spoke truth. Dell had been named in Coffij and Accara's early letters as one of the slaveholders whose cruel treatment was responsible for the rebellion. The plantation manager had not changed his ways. A month before, colony officials had

The Execution of Breaking on the Rack, 1793, engraving after John Gabriel Stedman. (John Carter Brown Library, Providence.)

been nervously critical of Dell's propensity to drive his enslaved workers hard, too hard. He bragged that he extracted more labor from the remaining third of his slaves than from the entire pre-revolutionary workforce. He did so by punishing them with masterful ferocity. Two weeks before Hercules's execution, Dell and three other managers were accused of treating slaves with "hair-raising" cruelty. In a form of double jeopardy, they had taken justice into their own hands by "inhumanly" punishing men cleared as innocent by the court. Evidently, managers and slaveholders took vengeance for the rebellion as they saw fit, a form of vigilante justice that was a regular feature of Atlantic slavery.[30]

Colonel de Salve reported their transgression, warning that such behavior might foment yet another rebellion. Called before the council, the four planters accused of mistreating laborers denied any wrongdoing. They admitted they had flogged the slaves, but claimed it had been for good reason and not excessively. Without a prosecutor or power to punish colonists, an impotent governor could do little but berate them verbally, lamenting privately that men like Dell had not learned anything from the rebellion.[31]

After a final round of grim punishments on December 15, Van Hoogenheim, on orders from the Company, declared a general amnesty.[32]

Epilogue

In 1770, a man was baptized in a small village in the northern Dutch province of Friesland. He had been carefully educated into the Dutch Reformed faith after renouncing "the errors of paganism." He was "a black man, born in Berbice," who "during the late rebellion," a newspaper noted, had "acted with such loyalty and bravery that the Company released him from slavery." He chose the confirmation name Matthys Carel Willems.[1]

Willems was one of just eleven men, all highly valued artisans, freed by the Company of Berbice for their part in the defeat of the rebellion. All belonged to the Company; they included Christiaan and Pieter, the star witnesses in the post-rebellion trials, and Frederik, the frequent translator and scout. No thought was given to emancipating any women. But the freedom of the eleven men was a chimera. It came with the stipulation that they could never "quit the service" of the Company—in other words, their enslavement was replaced with life-long indenture.[2] Yet somehow Matthijs van de Goede Hoop, who was baptized Matthys Carel Willems, escaped bondage. No documents explain how he ended up in windy, watery Friesland or how his life after his baptism unfolded. All we know is that he served as a domestic in The Hague, in the household of Carel George, Count of Wassenaar and Lord of Twickel.[3]

In time, Accara and Gousarie, the Benedict Arnolds of the Berbice Revolution, gained their freedom. In the aftermath of the rebellion, the governor and council had wanted to try the pair as murderers, arsonists, and rebel leaders. But the commander Colonel de Salve shielded them from trial. In November 1764, De Salve and his surviving soldiers sailed home, where he was promoted to major general for his service in Berbice. The colonel left behind one hundred soldiers under Swiss émigré Major Louis Henri Fourgeoud to protect the colony for another year. When those troops repatriated in April 1765, Fourgeoud brought Accara and Gousarie to Holland "as the only way to keep them safe." As drummers, the two freed men joined a newly created permanent naval expeditionary force for service in the Dutch colonies, made up of Berbice veterans. In 1773, this force, commanded by Fourgeoud, set sail for Suriname to fight Maroons. Accara and Gousarie would be in charge of the enslaved porters. The business of suppressing resistance in the world of colonial slavery was never done.[4]

But for the great majority of enslaved Berbicians, the revolution was anything but liberating. A detailed audit of Company people reveals that one in four slaves were dead by mid-1764. It seems likely that losses on private plantations were higher, but there are no precise figures.[5] Death rates overall, combining people on Company and private plantations, can only be estimated in the absence of firm population numbers at the start of the rebellion, but it appears that between a third and a fifth of the enslaved population of Berbice did not survive the uprising and its aftermath. (These figures include people who died of disease after they had returned to the Dutch, when dysentery and other illnesses ravaged the refugee camps on Dageraad and at Fort Nassau, as well as small numbers taken from the colony by their fleeing owners.)[6]

The Company audit suggests who was most vulnerable in rebellion. Women and children fared poorly; one in four perished. Women may have been more susceptible to disease as a result of pregnancy and childbirth, miscarriages, and sharing meager food supplies with children and others under their care. The largest losses were sustained by men, of whom one-third died. Given men's roles as soldiers on both sides and their predominance among those executed by the Dutch, this is not surprising. Teenagers fared best. They were more resilient than small children and less likely to have been involved in the rebellion than adults. Saving them from execution also represented a valuable long-term investment among owners. Deaths were not distributed evenly across plantations. Some communities were hit especially hard.

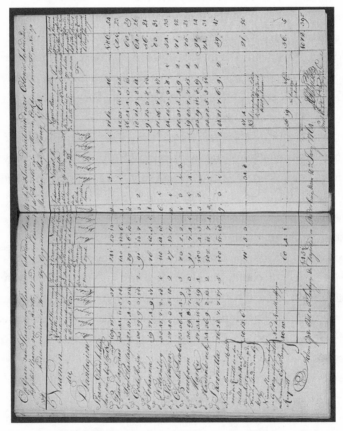

Declaration of enslaved Africans and native slaves who died, are missing, or are back in Company service, June 1764, SvB 135. (Nationaal Archief, The Hague.)

Of the eighteen enslaved people on plantation Boschlust, who had re-fused to join the rebellion in order to work their own gardens in peace, reportedly only seven survived. The others were killed by Amer-indians or perished as refugees. Half the people on Company planta-tion Savonette, site of the massacre in December 1763, lost their lives.[7]

Numbers, no matter how grim, provide no hint about how survivors absorbed the sorrows of the long rebellion's crushing final defeat, the bitter cup of re-enslavement, and the loss of spouses, parents, children, and friends. Enslaved people already suffered high death rates during the normal course of bondage. The rebellion tripled or quadrupled the customary yearly death rate of 5 percent. There was little time to mourn the dead as people worked to repair their huts, replant their gardens, and rebuild their fractured lives. They also toiled long hours to restore their enslavers' agricultural fields. As owners and investors abandoned or sold ruined estates in the years that followed, some en-slaved communities were further broken apart. Deeply indebted plant-ers spent as little as possible on their enslaved workers in the years of uncertain profit that followed.

Berbice served also as a death trap for European soldiers and sail-ors. More died of contagion than of combat. No careful accounting of their losses has been found, but it seems unlikely that more than a third survived. The departure of the state troops from Berbice was much delayed in fall 1764 because the remaining men were too ill to be transported and new crew (out of sixty seamen, only eleven re-mained somewhat healthy) had to be hired in St. Eustatius to sail them home.[8] Of the Suriname mutineers, six survived the rebellion. They were court-martialed in Suriname in the summer of 1764. Convicted of "lese majesty, high treason, mutiny, and desertion," three were con-demned to death. Surgeon Mangmeister was slapped in the face with his severed right hand before his bones were broken on the wheel, his head severed, and his decapitated body buried under the gallows. Jean Renaud, spared the dishonor of the facial slap, was similarly broken on the wheel. One more soldier was hanged. The others were whipped and had their military service extended.[9]

In 1765, when his successor finally reached Berbice, a worn-out and exhausted Governor van Hoogenheim was at last allowed to go home. Instead of a triumphant return, honor, and a promotion, as De Salve had enjoyed, to his amazement Van Hoogenheim encountered disapproval. The directors faulted him for his candor about the directors' tightfistedness with regard to the colony's defense and the vast sums required to rebuild the colony. Disillusioned with politics, Van Hoogenheim rejoined the army. His remaining connection to Berbice was an enslaved youth named Frederik, who had served him in the colony and to whom he was "much attached." He brought Frederik home with him. The records do not reveal the feelings of Jacomientje van de Dageraad, the boy's mother, or of his father (never mentioned) about their son's removal. In late 1768, sixteen-year-old Frederik confessed his faith "to great acclaim" in the Dutch Reformed Church in Arnhem in the eastern Netherlands. He received the baptismal name Frederik Wolphert Simons, after his childless patron, Wolphert Simon van Hoogenheim. Frederik's subsequent whereabouts, presumably as a free man, are not known.[10] Perhaps, like the young Amerindian Colonel de Salve reportedly took home as a souvenir, Frederik returned to Berbice, disenchanted with life in Holland and eager to reunite with family and friends.[11]

The Berbice colony never recovered economically under the Dutch. Fully one-third of the plantations were destroyed. Owners tried to sell out but had trouble as the colony became a financial risk. The Company survived thanks only to huge loans (never repaid) from the States General. Company shareholders and planters alike balked at a new tax levied to repay the cost of suppressing the rebellion. Wealthy investors like Jean Etienne Fizeaux, Amsterdam financier and collector of Vermeer paintings, spearheaded a tax protest. His banker sons later helped Ben Franklin and John Adams obtain funding for the new government of the United States.[12] But the Fizeaux family's revolutionary sympathies did not extend to their own plantations in Berbice, where abusive conditions continued. Not until 1784 did the Company of Berbice, with the approval of the States General, adopt new legal codes to improve slave treatment. The modifications were minor, and enforcement a challenge.[13] The most major consequence of the rebellion for the

Portrait study of an anonymous black servant or military musician, 1747, pastel by
Cornelis Troost. (Rijksmuseum, Amsterdam.)

Johannes Vermeer (1632–75), *The Geographer*, 1669. (Photo: Städel Museum—
ARTOTHEK, Städel Museum, Frankfurt am Main.)

Dutch was that they realized that combating rebellions and Maroons cost too much. Tired of bailing out private companies, the government took over direct management of the Wild Coast colonies in 1795.[14]

Yet Dutch influence in the Western Hemisphere was waning. Well before the Berbice Rebellion, the British had become the undisputed power in the Atlantic world. During the Napoleonic Wars at the end of the eighteenth century, Britain occupied Berbice, Essequibo, and Demerara. In the early nineteenth century, these colonies were incorporated into the expanding British Empire, briefly becoming one of Britain's most lucrative Caribbean possessions. The takeover ended Dutch rule, this time for good.[15]

The long-lasting and highly successful Berbice Rebellion foreshadowed dynamics shared by later insurgencies: rebellion morphing into revolution, political strife dissolving into civil war, total war triggering refugee crises, and victory proving elusive to those without access to the additional matériel, men, and money that global capitalism could supply. Each political rotation scaled back democratic promises and the dream of self-mastery for the enslaved. As empires shape-shifted, revolutions loosened the bonds of slavery and even dissolved them in a few places. Yet in the Atlantic world as a whole, slavery became only more deeply entrenched as the Age of Revolutions drew to a close. After the revolutions for liberty, more people than ever before lived in chains. In this respect, too, tiny Berbice was a portent.

The colony's new British masters imported slaves on a mass scale. They financed new plantations on the coast, forcing enslaved people to dig canals and trenches in soggy clay for flood control. Despite growing abolitionist agitation for better treatment of enslaved people, planters doubled down on their shrinking slave force after the British in 1807 outlawed the trade in humans. Dropping prices for coffee, cotton, and sugar deepened the exploitation of enslaved workers. In 1823, slaves on the Demerara River rose up, but their rebellion was brutally suppressed in just two days. Amelioration laws passed in the 1820s could not appease the forces of abolition, and in 1834, the British ended slavery in the West Indies. After a four-year compulsory apprentice period, many newly freed people finally had a chance to escape plantation work. They pooled resources, bought abandoned estates, and started their own farming communities, eager to achieve the self-governance their predecessors had fought for in the 1763 Berbice Rebellion.

Autonomy held for only a historical breath. European landowners used their power and wealth to chip away at the villagers' subsistence economy, eager to turn free peasants into poorly paid plantation hands laboring alongside indentured workers shanghaied from British India and Africans "rescued" by the British navy from illegal slave ships. Elites encouraged ethnic divisions to thwart collective political action, much as planters had done in the Dutch period.[16] Social justice would be equally elusive in the United States after emancipation, as freed people, seeking forty acres and a mule, found it difficult to acquire land and even harder to hold on to it when they did.[17]

At the start of the Age of Revolutions, the Berbice Rebellion tantalized African-descended people with the prospect of liberation and autonomy. As in the revolutions that followed, it brought bitter disappointments on both scores. Coffij and his fellow leaders courageously set in motion the process of self-emancipation, only to see that hope defeated by better-supplied Europeans with international allies. Yet Coffij's demand for half the colony to continue growing sugar, along with a desire for status, came at the high price of forced labor for others. Those others were dodgers of the Berbice Rebellion. Their desire for autonomy—to tend their own gardens—was not compatible with an early modern global capitalist market fueled by bonded labor. Neither rebel leaders nor the mass of self-emancipated Berbicians escaped the central dilemma of the Age of Revolutions and beyond.

Berbicians did not give up in their struggle for dignity and self-determination. Just eight years after the defeat of the Berbice Rebellion, in the fall of 1772, the authorities were deeply worried about the possibility of "conspiracies and uprisings" in the colony, especially in the upper Berbice.[18]

The human will for even a margin of freedom, it seems, does not die easily.

Acknowledgments

I want to start by thanking the kind people in Guyana who made my visit to the Berbice River so fruitful: Margaret Chan-a-Sue, Alex Mendes and his family, Dubulay manager Tedroy, Bob Sampson, Mrs. Georgiana Grimmond, Terry Fletcher, and Ben J. H. ter Welle. These modern-day Berbicians took me under their wing and helped me a great deal.

I also owe much to the librarians, archivists, and staff at Nationaal Archief (especially René Janssen, Jacqueline Reeuwijk, and Annet Waalkens), the UK National Archives, the National Archives in Guyana, het Koninklijk Huisarchief, Zeeuws Archief, Stadsarchief Amsterdam, as well as the museums and libraries that provided images to illustrate the book.

Several people kindly provided access to unpublished manuscripts. I thank Corrie en Wouter van den Hoek uit Ede with whom I spent a delightful afternoon as they shared family stories and papers related to Steven Hendrik de la Sablonière, governor of Berbice from 1768 to 1773. Unfortunately, none of the letters made it into the book, but they informed my understanding. Iris van Dalen van Antiquariaat Acanthus in Utrecht provided scans of a journal written by a Dutch officer posted to the Canje River in 1764.

Generous scholars have helped me during the many years I worked on this book. For answers, citations, conversations, documents, images, invitations, recommendations, or transcriptions, I thank Kate Adams, Tinde van Andel, Ana Lucia Araujo, Aviva Ben-Ur, Jessica Berman, Alex Bick, Kristen Block, Gijs Boink, Pepijn Brandon, Holly Brewer, Vincent Brown, Randy Browne, Natalie Zemon Davis, Victor Enthoven, Nicole Eustace, Alison Games, Ed Gould, Regina Grafe,

Quita Hendrison, Han Jordaan, Arjo Klamer, Wim Klooster, Johan de Lange, Wayne Lee, Fred Luciani, Nicole Maskiell, Michael McDonnell, Carla Pestana, Richard Price, Jenny Pulsipher, James Robertson, Esther Schreuder, Jon Sensbach, James Sidbury, Simon Smith, Barbara Sommer, Terri Snyder, Angela Sutton, Theo Thomassen, John Thornton, Joris van den Tol, Makhroufi Ousmane Traoré, Maarten van Voorst, Jeffrey Wasserstrom, Marni Weissman, Danielle Terrazas Williams, Kathleen Wilson, and Suze Zijlstra. I want to single out Paul Koulen for his generous, erudite, and enthusiastic emails. I look forward to his forthcoming work on Guyana.

Audience members at the European University Institute, Florida International University, Gettysburg College, Georgetown University, Howard University, the Johns Hopkins University, Leiden University, New York University, NiNsee (Nationaal instituut Nederlands slavernijverleden en erfenis), Omohundro Institute of Early American History and Culture, Pomona College, the University of California at Irvine, UCLA, UMBC, the University of Richmond, the University of Texas at Austin, as well as at professional conferences, made helpful suggestions.

Pieces of this story have appeared in *Geschiedenis Magazine*, *Uncommon Sense*, *The New West Indian Guide*, and the *American Historical Review* as well as in two edited collections, as indicated in the notes. I thank the editors and reviewers who helped me develop my arguments.

Much appreciated financial aid from various institutions facilitated the research and writing of this book. A Franklin Research grant from the American Philosophical Society along with funds from UMBC made possible archival trips to Guyana, the UK, and the Netherlands. Fellowships from the John Carter Brown Library, the National Endowment for the Humanities, the Dresher Center for the Humanities at UMBC, the European University Institute, the Huntington Library, and the College of Arts, Humanities and Social Sciences at UMBC freed up writing time. I want to thank my fellow colleagues for their friendship as well as each institution's employees for making my time productive. Thanks also to the staff of the American Academy of Berlin where I spent a pampered semester as a "spouse."

UMBC has been a rewarding place to work. Deans John Jeffries and Scott Casper along with Provost Philip Rouse provided financial support. Rachel Brubaker eased the fellowship application process. Joe School drew the maps in the book. Kuhn Library's interlibrary loan staff are simply the best. My chairs, Kriste Lindenmeyer and Amy Froide, were always supportive. My own six years as department chair slowed down the book's completion but my wonderful colleagues made the job a pleasure. The department's writing group (especially stalwarts Kate Brown, Christy Chapin, Amy Froide, Susan McDonough, Andrew Nolan, Meredith Oyen, and Daniel Ritschel) improved several chapters.

Many years ago, Lil Fenn turned me on to the database FileMaker and subsequently patiently answered all my software-related questions. I neglected to thank her for this in the acknowledgments of my first book and I am delighted to make up for it here. I want to also commend her for unwavering support during our many years of friendship and for pointing the way in life by being two weeks older. Woody Holton and I became friends as graduate students and over the years he has never failed to encourage me while generously sharing his prodigious knowledge of the field. I followed closely the advice of my longtime friend Rachel Toor about how to write a book proposal (see her articles in the *Chronicle of Higher Education*) and then pestered her with questions about the publishing process.

Leila Corcoran, friend and editor extraordinaire, helped me pitch the book to a wider audience—her collaboration and enthusiasm provided a wonderful boost. Several generous friends read the near final manuscript: Kate Brown, Woody Holton, Michael McDonnell, Derek Musgrove, Sharon Salinger, and Peter H. Wood. Their interventions made for a much better book, and read, even as I ignored some of their suggestions.

My wonderful agent Lisa Adams of the Garamond Agency found a great home for the manuscript. At The New Press, Marc Favreau modeled supportive editing; Eileen Chetti saved me from sloppy errors; Maury Botton patiently shepherded the manuscript through production; and Sharon Swados made my biggest book dream come true by finding it a Dutch publisher.

My parents, Geert and Tom Theunissen and George and Tineke Kars, have been supportive all the way. I am sorry my dad died before he could show off the Dutch edition. My siblings Annemarie, Erik, and Jeroen, and in-laws Holm, Mariëlle, and Marion have hosted me during research visits and their children, Marcus, Lucas, Lisan, Helena, Anne-Sophie, Emma, Sjors, and Koen, have given up their bedrooms. I am also grateful to Inge Jager for being friends since we were toddlers.

I am immensely pleased to count Tim Ahmann, Ava Ahmann, Dave Bamford, Rebecca Boehling, Warren Cohen, Leila Corcoran, Mike Fay, Michelle Feige, Lil Fenn, Kama Garrison, Lee Gould, Kevin Gould, Sally Hunsberger, Sara Hunsberger, Jupiter, Sharon Salinger (along with Aaron, Maria, Isael, and Eliana), Rachel Toor, Marianne Szegedy-Maszak, Jenny Wears, and Peter Wood as members of my American family.

Kate and Sasha came into my life near the start of this project. As I send this book into the world, Sasha Bamford-Brown has gone off to college. I could not be prouder of the wonderful man he has become. I especially admire his kindness, his level-headedness, and his wit. This book is dedicated to his mother, Kate Brown, who endures my never-ending anxieties, self-doubts, and foot-dragging with equanimity, encourages me further out on the limb, inspires me with her brilliant work, and generally makes life so very much richer.

List of Abbreviations

All references to the judicial examinations the Dutch carried out between March and December 1764 are indicated in the notes with a number, the name of the person questioned, his or her plantation, and the date. For instance, No. 215 Hercules of [or] Erfprins van Juliana, 4/12/1764, means that on April 12, 1764, Hercules, also known as Erfprins, from plantation Juliana, was "examined." In the case of a second interrogation, there is frequently no number available, just a date. Neither the names of people nor those of plantations were spelled consistently. I have standardized spelling in the text and the notes, except within quotations. The examinations may be found in SvB 135, starting with folio 152.

All translations from Dutch, German, or French are mine, unless otherwise noted.

AC	Admiraliteitscolleges, 1586–1795, 1.01.46 and inv. no., Nationaal Archief, The Hague
CB	Collectie Willem graaf Bentinck, heer van Rhoon en Pendrecht (1704-1774) G002, Koninklijk Huis Archief, The Hague
CO 116	Colonial Office and predecessors: British Guiana, formerly Berbice, Demerara and Essiquibo [sic], Miscellanea, National Archives, Kew, United Kingdom (with collection number)
DH	Dagregister van Gouverneur-Generaal W. S. van Hoogenheim, SvB 226, Nationaal Archief, The Hague
Fagel	Collectie Fagel, 1.10.29 and inv. no., Nationaal Archief, The Hague

Hartsinck   Jan Jacob Hartsinck, *Beschryving van Guiana, of de Wilde Kust in Zuid-America*, 2 vols. (Amsterdam: G. Tielenburg, 1770)

KHA   Koninklijk Huis Archief, The Hague

Leupe   Verzameling Buitenlandse Kaarten Leupe, 4.VEL and inv. no., Nationaal Archief, The Hague

Lichtveld   Ursy M. Lichtveld and Jan Voorhoeve, *Suriname: Spiegel der vaderlandse kooplieden*, rev. ed. (The Hague: Martinus Nijhoff, 1980), online at www.dbnl.org

MCC   Archief Middelburgsche Commercie Compagnie and inv. no., Archief Zeeland, Middelburg

Netscher   P. M. Netscher, *Geschiedenis van de koloniën Essequibo, Demerara en Berbice, van de vestiging der Nederlanders aldaar tot op onzen tijd* (The Hague: Martinus Nijhoff, 1888)

NHP   Notulen Hof van Politie, SvB, inv. no., folio no., Nationaal Archief, The Hague

Oldendorp   Christian Georg Andreas Oldendorp, *Historie der caribischen Inseln Sanct Thomas, Sanct Crux und Sanct Jan, insbesondere der dasigen Neger und der Mission der evangelischen Brüder unter denselben: Kommentierte Ausgabe des vollständigen Manuskriptes aus dem Archiv der Evangelischen Brüder-Unität Herrnhut*, part 1, ed. Gudrun Meier, Stephan Palmié, Peter Stein, and Horst Ulbricht (Berlin: Verlag für Wissenschaft und Bildung, 2000)

Plakaatboek Plakaatboek Guyana 1670–1816, colony, and date, online at www.huygens.knaw.nl/plakaatboek-guyana-1670-1816 -online/

SGD   C. A. Harris and J. A. J. Villiers, eds., *Storm van 's Gravesande: The Rise of British Guiana Compiled from His Dispatches* (London: Printed for the Hakluyt Society, 1911), 2 vols.

Stähelin   Fritz Stähelin, *Die Mission der Brüdergemeine in Suriname und Berbice im achtzehnten Jahrhundert: Eine Missionsgeschichte hauptsächlich in Briefen und Originalberichten*. 3 vols.

	(Hildesheim: Georg Ulms Verlag, 1997; orig. pub. 1913–ca. 1916)
Stedman	*Narrative of a Five Years Expedition Against the Revolted Negroes of Surinam, by John Gabriel Stedman*, ed. Richard Price and Sally Price (Baltimore: Johns Hopkins University Press, 1992)
SvB	Archief van de Sociëteit van Berbice, 1.05.05, inv. no. and (when available) folio no., Nationaal Archief, The Hague.
SvS	Sociëteit van Suriname, 1.05.03, inv. no. and (when available) folio no., Nationaal Archief, The Hague
TSTDB	Trans-Atlantic Slave Trade Data Base, www.slavevoyages.org
Verbael	Verbaelen gehouden bij den Collonel J. M. Desalve betreffende zijn expeditie naar de kolonie Berbice . . . , November 6, 1763–June 1764, numbered I–VII; Archief Staten Generaal, 1.01.05, inv. no. 9219, Nationaal Archief, The Hague
WIC	Dutch West India Company

Notes

Prologue

1. Part of this introduction was previously published, in slightly different form, as Marjoleine Kars, "Adventures in Research: Chasing the Past in Guyana," *Uncommon Sense* 124 (Fall 2007): 17–20.

2. The Berbice Rebellion was first narrated in two histories of the Dutch colonies on the Wild Coast, published in 1770 and 1888, respectively. See Hartsinck, 371–517, and Netscher, 195–250. Hartsinck was the son of a plantation owner and director of the Company of Berbice. Neither man used the slave examinations. Netscher quite explicitly noted (242), that the "hundreds of examinations do not contain anything new, which is the reason we did not use them." Moreover, he added, "the declarations of blacks can be but little trusted." Relying heavily on the daybook of the Dutch governor instead, these two treatments have formed the basis for all subsequent accounts: James Rodway, *History of British Guiana, from 1668 to the Present Time* (Georgetown/Demerara: J. Thompson, 1891), 171–214; Cornelis Ch. Goslinga, *The Dutch in the Caribbean and in the Guianas, 1680–1791* (Assen/Maastricht: Van Gorcum, 1985), 461–94; Alvin O. Thompson, *Colonialism and Underdevelopment in Guyana, 1580–1803* (Bridgetown, Barbados: Carib Research and Publications, 1987), 153–74. Only Ineke Velzing, "De Berbice Slavenopstand, 1763" (MA thesis, University of Utrecht, 1979), made use of the examinations.

3. For letters from Maroons in Suriname, see, for instance, Harry van den Boouwhuijsen et al., eds., *Opstand in Tempati, 1757–1760*, Bronnen voor de studie van Afro-Surinaamse samenlevingen, pt. 12 (Utrecht: Instituut voor Culturele Antropologie, 1988); and Frank Dragtenstein, *Alles voor de vrede: De brieven van Boston Band tussen 1757 en 1763* (Amsterdam/ The Hague: Ninsee/Amrit, 2009). For Brazil, see Stuart B. Schwartz, "Resistance and Accommodation in Eighteenth-Century Brazil: The Slaves' View of Slavery," *Hispanic American Historical Review* 5, 1 (February 1977): 69–81. For court testimony of some 150 enslaved men and women in

eighteenth-century Louisiana, see Sophie White, *Voices of the Enslaved: Love, Labor and Longing in French Louisiana* (Chapel Hill: University of North Carolina Press, 2019).

4. Cf. Michael A. McDonnell, "The Struggle Within: Colonial Politics on the Eve of Revolution," in *The Oxford Handbook of the American Revolution*, ed. Edward G. Gray and Jane Kamensky, 103–20, esp. 113–14 (Oxford: Oxford University Press, 2013); and *American History: Oxford Research Encyclopedias*, s.v. "The American War for Independence as a Revolutionary War," by Michael A. McDonnell, 2016. For the historiography of Atlantic slave rebellions, see Marjoleine Kars, "Dodging Rebellion: Politics and Gender in the Berbice Slave Uprising of 1763," *American Historical Review* 121, 1 (2016): 39–44.

5. According to the latest CIA figures at www.cia.gov/library/publica tions/the-world-factbook/geos/gy.htmlfield-anchor-people-and-society-de mographic-profile.

6. For recent explorations of black politics in various locales and periods in the Atlantic world, see James H. Sweet, *Domingo Alvares, African Healing, and the Intellectual History of the Atlantic World* (Chapel Hill: University of North Carolina Press, 2011); Jessica A. Krug, *Fugitive Modernities: Kisama and the Politics of Freedom* (Durham, NC: Duke University Press, 2018); Julius C. Scott, *The Common Wind: Afro-American Currents in the Age of the Haitian Revolution* (London: Verso, 2018).

7. For an in-depth assessment of enslaved testimony, see Kars, "Dodging Rebellion," 50–52.

8. James Sidbury, "Plausible Stories and Varnished Truths," *William and Mary Quarterly* 59, 1 (2002): 179–84; T. H. Been, *American Insurgents, American Patriots: The Revolution of the People* (New York: Hill and Wang, 2011); Marjoleine Kars, *Breaking Loose Together: The Regulator Rebellion in Pre-Revolutionary North Carolina* (Chapel Hill: University of North Carolina Press, 2002).

9. No. 188 Nero van Petersburg, 4/11/1763; Jan Menkenveld to the MCC, 1/25/1757 and 8/2/1757, MCC 910; Voyage 10938, TSTDB.

10. For recent incisive discussions of such archives, and ways to center the experiences of the enslaved, see Stephanie E. Smallwood, "The Politics of the Archive and History's Accountability to the Enslaved,"*History of the Present* 6, 2 (Fall 2016), 117–32; Aisha K. Finch, *Rethinking Slave Rebellion in Cuba: La Escalera and the Insurgencies of 1841–1844* (Chapel Hill: University of North Carolina Press, 2015); and Marisa J. Fuentes, *Dispossessed Lives: Enslaved Women, Violence and the Archive* (Philadelphia: University of Pennsylvania Press, 2016).

11. David Geggus, "Slave Rebellion During the Age of Revolution," in *Caraçao in the Age of Revolutions, 1795–1800*, ed. Wim Klooster and Gert Oostindie, 23–56 (Leiden: Brill, 2011). Only one other, Tacky's revolt in Jamaica in 1760, was as lengthy as the Berbice one, but the Jamaican rebels were never in charge the way the insurgents were in Berbice. Vincent Brown, *Tacky's Revolt: The Story of an Atlantic Slave War* (Cambridge, MA: Harvard University Press, 2020). Unfortunately, this book was published after my book went to press. The Haitian Revolution, which began in Saint Domingue in 1791, was the only successful slave revolt in the Atlantic world, leading to the establishment of the first black republic, Haiti, in 1804.

1: Rehearsal, 1762

1. J. P. Wyland, *Journaal of dags-aantekening van het voorgevallene in de colonie van Rio Berbiecie. Beginnende met de Revolte der Negers van den 6 July 1762 en Eyndende met des Schrijvers Arriviment in Texel op den 11 July 1763* (Amsterdam: Gedrukt voor rekening van de auteur, 1763), 4; Voyage 10806, TSTDB; NHP 1/25/1762, SvB 132/20; Hoogenheim to Directors, 1/20/1762, SvB 131/127; Ruud Paesie, "De zeven slavenreizen van het Vlissingse fregat Magdalena Maria, 1761–1771," *Den Spiegel* 32, 3 (July 2014): 7–14; Wim Klooster and Gert Oostindie, *Realm Between Empires: The Second Dutch Atlantic* (Ithaca, NY: Cornell University Press, 2018), 80.

2. TSTDB, "Trans-Atlantic Slave Trade—Estimates," www.slavevoyages.org/assessment/estimates, 1501–1760. Over the course of the Atlantic slave trade, some 12.5 million people were forced across the Atlantic.

3. Population figures for African-descended people in Berbice are inexact. Tax lists underestimate the number of enslaved people, as children under the age of three were not counted, those between three and ten counted for half a person (or "head"), and new plantations did not pay head taxes. Moreover, planters tended to evade taxes through underreporting. On the eve of the rebellion, there were 1,450 Company slaves, and private planters paid taxes on 2,260 ½ "heads." The directors of Berbice complained about the inaccuracy of the 1762 list, pointing out people and plantations not listed; see SvB 4, 12/20/1762. The directors estimated the enslaved population between 4,000 and 5,000; "Missive van Directeuren der Colonie de Berbice," 8/17/1763, SvB 49, also available on Google Books. One historian calculates a total of about 4,400 enslaved people; see Netscher, 191. For Suriname, Alex van Stipriaan calculated that eighteenth-century head-tax numbers should be multiplied on average by a factor of 1.4 to get accurate population numbers, which would bring Berbice totals to about

4,600 people. Alex van Stipriaan, *Surinaams Contrast: Roofbouw and overleven in een Caraïbische plantagekolonie 1750–1863* (Leiden: Brill, 1993), 311.

4. New Amsterdam is about seventy kilometers from the coast as the crow flies, and about fifty miles, or eighty-three kilometers, along the river. The exact timing of the rainy and dry seasons varied from year to year. See Stedman, 54. Van Hoogenheim's first name Wolphert is also spelled Wolfert. I have adhered to the spelling he used himself.

5. Robert H. Schomburgk, "Diary of an Ascent of the River Berbice, in British Guayana, in 1836–7," *Journal of the Royal Geographical Society of London* 7 (1837): 302–50.

6. Cf. the description in *The Guiana Travels of Robert Schomburgk, 1835–1844*, vol. 1, *Explorations on Behalf of the Royal Geographical Society 1835–1839*, edited by Peter Rivière, Hakluyt Society Series 3, vol. 16 (London: The Hakluyt Society, 2006), 38, 178–80. For Suriname ethnobotany, see Tinde R. van Andel et al., "Local Plant Names Reveal That Enslaved Africans Recognized Substantial Parts of the New World Flora," *PNAS*, 2014, https://www.pnas.org/content/111/50/E5346.

7. I have estimated distances on Google Earth. Contemporary sources mostly discuss distance in terms of travel time.

8. Kunkler paid poll taxes for one white, four "red" slaves, and twenty-eight "black" slaves, suggesting that there were more than thirty people of African descent on Goed Land en Goed Fortuin. "Lijst van Omschrijving van het Hoofdgeld, voor den jaare 1762," Bijlage C, Directors to States General, 7/7/1763, SvB 227.

9. Hoogenheim to Directors, 8/8/1761, SvB 131/1; SGD, 361, 362, 380.

10. Hoogenheim to Directors, 7/3/1762, SvB 132/122. See also 9/25/1762, SvB 133/3.

11. In the Dutch Republic, too, there was little separation between government and law, as the same men often functioned simultaenously as magistrates and aldermen. F. Egmond, "Recht en Krom: Corruptie, ongelijkheid en rechtsbescherming in de vroegmoderne Nederlanden," *BMGN—Low Countries Historical Review* 116, 1 (2001): 22. The account of the breakout on Goed Land en Goed Fortuin is based on the following sources: Examination Coffij, 8/17/1762 and 10/7/1762; Examination Antoinette, 10/6/1762; Hoogenheim to Directors, 9/18/1762, 11/25/1762, and 12/22/1762; Hoerle to Directors, 9/9/1762; Sentence demanded by prosecutor, Antoinette, 11/16/1762; Sentence demanded by prosecutor, Coffij, 11/26/1762; NHP 11/26/1762, 11/27/1762, all in SvB 133. "Uitgaaf der Cargazoen Goederen Anno 1762," SvB 134/158; Wyland, *Journaal*; Hoerle to Directors, 9/9/1762, SvB 133/191.

12. On drivers, see Natalie Zemon Davis, "Judges, Masters, Diviners: Slaves' Experience of Criminal Justice in Colonial Suriname," *Law and History Review* 20, 4 (2011): 947–49; and Randy M. Browne, *Surviving Slavery in the British Caribbean* (Philadelphia: University of Pennsylvania Press, 2017), chap. 3. In the Danish Caribbean, drivers were called *bombas* as well. In Suriname they were known as *negerofficier* among the Dutch and *bassia* among the enslaved, and occasionally as *bomba*. For a recent discussion of polygamy in West Africa and North America in the early modern period, see Sarah M. Pearsall, *Polygamy: An Early American History* (New Haven and London: Yale University Press, 2019), chap. 4.

13. For conjure, see Andrew Zimmerman, "Guinea Sam Nightingale and Magic Marx in Civil War Missouri: Provincializing Global History and Decolonizing Theory," *History of the Present* 8, 2 (Fall 2018): 140–41; Diana Paton, "Witchcraft, Poison, Law, and Atlantic Slavery," *William and Mary Quarterly* 69, 2 (April 2012): 249–50; Kenneth Bilby, "Swearing by the Past, Swearing by the Future; Sacred Oaths, Alliances, and Treaties Among the Guianese and Jamaican Maroons," *Ethnohistory* 44, 4 (1979): 655–89; Walter C. Rucker, *Gold Coast Diasporas: Identity, Culture, and Power* (Bloomington: Indiana University Press, 2015), 90–92; and Stedman, 72–73.

14. Hoogenheim to Directors, 9/18/1762, SvB 133/1. Wim Hoogbergen, "Binnenlandse oorlogen in Suriname in de achttiende eeuw," in *Geweld in de West: Een Militaire Geschiedenis van de Nederlands Atlantische Wereld, 1600–1800*, ed. Victor Enthoven et al., 161 (Leiden: Brill, 2013).

15. Alex van Stipriaan, "Het Dilemma van Plantageslaven: Weglopen of Blijven?" *OSO: Tijdschrift voor Surinaamse Taalkunde, Letterkunde, Cultuur en Geschiedenis* 11, 2 (1992): 122–41.

16. For the claim that Adam's murderers were vengeful fathers, see Hoogenheim to Directors, 9/25/1762, SvB 133/3. NHP 10/6/1762, SvB 133/137; "Uitgaaf der Cargazoen Goederen Anno 1762"; Antoinette claimed five people remained in the woods. One, Pieter, quietly returned to his plantation, where Kunkler failed to turn him over to the court. Pieter may have been a rebel officer during the 1763 rebellion. He was questioned but not executed. DH 8/27/1764; No. 3 Pieter van Goed Land en Good Fortuin, 12/4/1764.

17. Margaret Haig Roosevelt Sewall Ball, "Grim Commerce: Scalps, Bounties, and the Transformation of Trophy-Taking in the Early American Northeast, 1450–1780" (PhD diss., University of Colorado at Boulder, 2013), 26–27, 59–62.

18. Peter H. Wood, *Black Majority: Negroes in Colonial South Carolina from 1650 Through the Stono Rebellion* (New York: Alfred A. Knopf, 1974), 317

(quote), see also 283, 284, 311; Gwendolyn Midlo Hall, *Africans in Colonial Louisiana: The Development of Afro-Creole Culture in the Eighteenth Century* (Baton Rouge: Louisiana State University Press, 1992), 343–80.

19. Closer ("nader") information Coffij, 10/7/1762, SvB 133/133; NHP 11/27/1762, SvB 133/137. Antoinette claimed the arrows came from a captive Indian. Kunkler to Hoogenheim, no date but presened to the court on 11/20/1762, SvB 133/128. For Blake's images, see Stedman. NHP 11/27/1762. One Dutch official who lived at the fort where Coffij was imprisoned wrote that at first Coffij called out Adam's name over and over, sometimes for a half hour on end, expecting that Adam, as promised, would free him. Wyland, *Journaal*, 3–4.

20. Wyland, *Journaal*, 4–5.

21. For useful overviews of Maroons, see Alvin O. Thompson, *Flight to Freedom: African Runaways and Maroons in the Americas* (Mona, Jamaica: University of the West Indies Press, 2006); Manolo Florentino and Márcia Amantino, "Runaways and Quilombolas in the Americas," in *The Cambridge World History of Slavery*, ed. David Eltis and Stanley Engerman, 708–40 (Cambridge: Cambridge University Press, 2011); and Sylviana A. Diouf, *Slavery's Exiles: The Story of the American Maroons* (New York: New York University Press, 2014). On Spanish encouragement, see Linda M. Rupert, " 'Seeking the Water of Baptism': Fugitive Slaves and Imperial Jurisdiction in the Early Modern Caribbean," in *Legal Pluralism and Empires, 1500–1850*, ed. Lauren Benton and Richard J. Ross (New York: New York University Press, 2013), 199–232; Jane Landers, "Gracia Real de Santa Teresa de Mose: A Free Black Town in Spanish Colonial Florida," *American Historical Review* 95, 1 (1990): 9–30; and Bram Hoonhout and Thomas Mereite, "Freedom at the Fringes: Slave Flight and Empire Building in the Early Modern Spanish Borderlands of Essequibo-Venezuela and Louisiana-Texas," *Slavery and Abolition* 40, 1 (2019): 61–86.

22. Jane Landers, "Maroon Women in Colonial Spanish America: Case Studies in the Circum-Caribbean from the Sixteenth through the Eighteenth Centuries," in *Beyond Bondage: Free Women of Color in the Americas*, ed. David Barry Gaspar and Darlene Clark Hines, 3–18 (Urbana: University of Illinois Press, 2010); Van Stipriaan, "Het Dilemma."

23. For present-day Suriname Maroons, see Alex van Stipriaan and Thomas Polimé, eds., *Kunst van Overleven: Marroncultuur uit Suriname* (Amsterdam: KIT Publishers, 2009); and Marcel van der Linden, "The Okanisi: A Surinamese Maroon Community, c. 1712–2019," *International Review of Social History* 60 (2015): 463–90.

24. H. U. E. Thoden van Velzen and Wim Hoogbergen, *Een Zwarte*

Vrijstaat in Suriname: De Okaanse samenleving in de achttiende eeuw (Leiden, KITLV Uitgeverij, 2011), 46–47, 51–52, 60, 124–25 (quote).

25. Kathleen Wilson, "The Performance of Freedom: Maroons and the Colonial Order in Eighteenth-Century Jamaica and the Atlantic Sound," *William and Mary Quarterly* 66, 1 (January 2009): 45–86; on treaties, Florentino and Amantino, "Runaways and Quilombolas in the Americas," 721–25; Kathryn Joy McKnight, "Confronted Rituals: Spanish Colonial and Angolan 'Maroon' Executions in Cartagena de Indians (1634)," *Journal of Colonialism and Colonial History* 5, 3 (2004): n.p., n. 32; Charles Beatty Medina, "Caught Between Rivals: The Spanish-African Maroon Competition for Captive Indian Labor in the Region of Esmeraldas During the Late Sixteenth and Early Seventeenth Centuries," *The Americas* 63, 1 (2006): 113–36; Jessica A. Krug, *Fugitive Modernities: Kisama and the Politics of Freedom* (Durham, NC: Duke University Press, 2018), 122–24.

26. Cf. Stedman, 145–50, 450.

27. Velzen and Hoogbergen, *Zwarte Vrijstaat*, 192–93.

28. Hartsinck, 364–68. For the 1734 uprising, see also Surinaamse Gouverneurs journalen, Oud Archief Suriname: Gouvernementssecretarie, 1.05.10.01, inv. no. 1, folio 318.

29. Hoogenheim to Directors, 9/18/1762, SvB 133/1.

30. *Kortbondige Beschryvinge van de Colonie de Berbice...* (Amsterdam: J. S. Baalde Boekverkoper op den Dam, 1763), 23.

31. Hoerle to Directors, 9/9/1762, SvB 133/191. "Extrait d'une letter ecrite de Berbice le 8 Fbre 1763, par Mr. Joh. Chr. George," CB 54-I.

32. Declaration of Hoerle et al., n.d. but likely October 1762, SvB 363. About the whippings and threats, see Hoogenheim to Directors, 11/25/1762, SvB 133/67.

33. Examination Pans, 11/5/1762, SvB 363.

34. Examination Alasso, 11/5/176; Closer ["nader"] examination Panso, 1/11/1763; Examination Akkarra, 11/5/1762, all in SvB 363.

35. Examination Bomba Adam,11/10/1762, SvB 363.

36. Hoogenheim to Directors, 12/22/1762, SvB 133/69.

37. Hoogenheim to Directors, 12/22/1762, SvB 133/69; Hoogenheim to Directors, 11/25/1762, SvB 133/67; Schook to Directors, 11/25/1762, SvB 133/159.

38. "Memorie en Eijsch... Januarij 1763," SvB 363. He later claimed his conflict with Hoerle concerned his wife. No. 424 Accara van de Savonette, 6/7/1764. Accara was executed for his role in the 1763 rebellion.

2: Labor Camps in the Making

1. For Flushing's role in the slave trade, see G. K. de Kok, "Walcherse ketens: De trans-Atlantische slavenhandel en de economie van Walcheren, 1755–1780" (PhD thesis, University of Leiden, 2019).

2. On the history of the term *wilden* among the Dutch, see Susanah Shaw Romney, "Savage Comparisons: Dutch Cultural Distinctions in Seventeenth-Century Southern Africa and North America," *Genre* 48, 2 (July 2015): 315–40.

3. Wim Klooster and Gert Oostindie, *Realm Between Empires: The Second Dutch Atlantic* (Ithaca, NY: Cornell University Press, 2018), 20–24.

4. Martin van Wallenburg et al., "The Voyage of Gelein van Stapels to the Amazon River, the Guianas and the Caribbean, 1629–1630," *Journal of the Hakluyt Society* (January 2015): 1–81, www.hakluyt.com. The original journal (MS 182), in Dutch, may be found in Zeeuws Archief, Verzameling Handschriften Rijksarchief in Zeeland, inv. no. 182, Middelburg, Netherlands.

5. Netscher, 57–60, 354–55; Victor Enthoven, "Early Dutch Expansion in the Atlantic Region, 1585–1621," in *Riches from Atlantic Comerce: Dutch Transatlantic Trade and Shipping, 1585–1817*, ed. Johannes Postman and Victor Enthoven, 35n58 (Leiden: Brill, 2003); Netscher, 353–54; Van Pere had permission from the Dutch West India Company to send along six "blacks (brought from Africa)." It is not clear he actually did so. Suggestively, in 1639, the commissary at the Dutch Fort in Hartford, Connecticut, one Gysbert Opdyk, killed a "neger boy, Louis Berbice, from Dutch Guiana, belonging to him." William C. Fowler, *The Historical Status of the Negro in Connecticut* (Charleston: Walker, Evans & Cogswell Co., 1901), 4. The earliest record of the slave trade to Berbice dates from 1657.

6. Cf. Pepijn Brandon and Karwan Fatah-Black, " 'For the Reputation and Respectability of the State': Trade, the Imperial State, Unfree Labor, and Empire in the Dutch Atlantic," in *Building the Atlantic Empires: Unfree Labor and Imperial States in the Political Economy of Capitalism, ca. 1500–1914*, ed. John Donoghue and Evelyn Jennings, 84–108 (Leiden: Brill, 2015); and Klooster and Oostindie, *Realm Between Empires*, 8–11.

7. Neil L. Whitehead, "Materializing the Past Among the Lokono (Arawak) of the Berbice River, Guyana," *Anthopológica* 54, 114 (2010): 87–127.

8. Netscher, 57; Lodewijk A. H. C. Hulsman, "Nederlands Amazonia: Handel met Indianen tussen 1580 en 1680" (PhD diss., University of Amsterdam, 2009), 89, 132–33, 225–26; Hartsinck, 85.

9. Van Wallenburg, "The Voyage of Gelein van Stapels," 29–30.

10. Arie Boomert, "The Arawak Indians of Trinidad and Coastal

Guiana, ca 1500–1650," *Journal of Caribbean History* 19 (1984): 127–29, 154; H. Dieter Heinen and Alvaro García-Castro, "The Multiethnic Network of the Lower Orinoco in Early Colonial Times," *Ethnohistory* 47, 3–4 (2000): 561–79; Hulsman, "Nederlands Amazonia," 57.

11. Neil L. Whitehead, "Indigenous Slavery in South America, 1492–1820," in *The Cambridge World History of Slavery*, ed. David Eltis and Stanley L. Engerman, 248–72 (Cambridge: Cambridge University Press, 2011); Marcy Norton, "The Chicken or the Iegue: Human-Animal Relationships and the Columbian Exchange," *American Historical Review* 120, 1 (2015): 30; Boomert, "Arawak Indians," 137, 150–54.

12. Boomert, "Arawak Indians," 142–43, 146. Neal L. Whitehead, "Ethnogenesis and Ethnocide in the European Occupation of Native Surinam, 1499–1681," in *History, Power, and Identity: Ethnogenesis in the Americas, 1492–1992*, ed. Jonathan D. Hill, 24–25 (Iowa City: University of Iowa Press, 1996).

13. Report to the States General of a Dutch voyage to the coast of Guiana (December 3, 1597–Ocotober 28, 1598), submitted February 3, 1599, quoted in Cornelis Ch. Goslinga, *The Dutch in the Caribbean and on the Wild Coast 1580–1680* (Gainesville: University of Florida Press, 1971), 487; Boomert, "Arawak Indians," 160.

14. George Edmundson, "The Dutch on the Amazon and Negro in the Seventeenth Century. Part I: Dutch Trade on the Amazon," *English Historical Review* 18 (October 1903): 642–63, and "Part II: Dutch Trade in the Basin of the Rio Negro," *English Historical Review* 19 (January 1904): 1–25; Hulsman, "Nederlands Amazonia," 142–44.

15. Hulsman, "Nederlands Amazonia," 119, 189, 213. For the first documented slave voyage to Berbice, see Voyage 44117, TSTDB. Fires caused by bombardments destroyed archives in Vlissingen in 1809 and in Middelburg in 1940.

16. Klooster and Oostindie, *Realm Between Empires*, 20–22; Alan Taylor, *American Colonies* (New York: Viking, 2001), 204–21.

17. Doeke Roos, *De Zeeuwen en de Westindische Compagnie, 1621–1674* (Hulst: Van Geijt Productions, 1992), 23–24, 34; Brandon and Fatah-Black, "For the Reputation and Respectability of the State," 96.

18. Van Berkel published a book about his adventures in Berbice in 1695. For a modern annotated edition in Dutch and English, see Martijn van den Bel et al., eds., *The Voyages of Adriaan van Berkel to Guiana: Amerindian-Dutch Relationships in 17th-Century Guyana* (Leiden: Sidestone Press, 2014); for discussion of Van Berkel's origins, 46–47.

19. Over 5 percent of the 12.5 million Africans were brought across the

ocean on legally registered Dutch ships. Klooster and Oostindie, *Realm Between Empires*, 80. If we also count the numbers of captives transported by Dutch smugglers, the total is closer to 600,000. See Karwan Fatah-Black and Matthias van Rossum, "Beyond Profitability: The Dutch Atlantic Slave Trade and its Economic Impact," *Slavery and Abolition* 36, 1 (2015): 72.

20. Alison Games, "Cohabitation, Suriname-Style: English Inhabitants in Dutch Suriname after 1667," *William and Mary Quarterly* 72, 2 (2015): 200–8; Gijs Rommelse, *The Second Anglo-Dutch War (1665–1667): International Raison D'État, Mercantilism, and Maritime Strife* (Hilversum: Verloren, 2006), 188.

21. Van den Bel et al., *Voyages*, 64.

22. Van den Bel et al., *Voyages*, 81–82; Everard F. Im Thurn, *Among the Indians of Guiana Being Sketches Chiefly Anthropologic from the Interior of British Guiana* (London: Kegan Paul, Trench, & Co., 1883), 263–64.

23. Van den Bel et al., *Voyages*, 86; Hulsman, "Nederlands Amazonia," 180–81.

24. Hulsman, "Nederlands Amazonia," 139–42; Van den Bel et al., *Voyages*, 86–88.

25. Van den Bel et al., *Voyages*, 95.

26. For slaves joining the Amerindians, see R. Buve, "Gouverneur Johannes Heinsius: De rol van Aerssen's Voorganger in de Surinaamse Indianenoorlog," *New West Indian Guide* 45, 1 (1966): 14–26; Justus B. Ch. Wekker, "Indianen en Pacificatie," *OSO: Een halfjaarlijkse uitgave van de Stichting Instituut ter Bevordering van de Surinamistiek te Nijmegen* 12, 2 (1993): 174–87. See also the following, all in E. F. Molendijk-Dijk et al., eds., *Indianen in Zeeuwse bronnen: Brieven over Indianen in Suriname tijdens het Zeeuwse bewind gedurende de periode 1667–1682* (Paramaribo: Stichting, 1992): Heinsius to Chamber Zeeland, 8/21/1679, 15–17; Samuel Nassi to Heinsius, 1/30/1680, 17–18; Heinsius contra Pieter Roijs, 12/2/1680, 18–19; Governor Verboom to Zeeland Chamber, 1/23/1681, 21–22. For anger over enslavement of Indian women, see also Abram Beekman to Zeeland Chamber, 11/4/1687, quoted in Netscher, 375–77; Ben Scholtens, "Indianen en Bosnegers, een historisch wisselvallige verhouding," *SWI Forum voor Kunst, Cultuur en Wetenschap* 9, 1–2 (1992): 73.

27. For skepticism about the coalition, see Frank Dragtenstein, "Indiaanse opperhoofden rond 1700," *OSO: Tijdschrift voor Surinaamse Taalkunde, Letterkunde en Geschiedenis* 12, 2 (1993): 188; and Dragtenstein, *Stoutheid der Weglopers: Marronage en koloniaal beleid in Suriname, 1667–1768* (Utrecht: CLACS, 2002). Studies of Suriname Maroons do not mention the Indian War of 1678–86, which is surprising given how many Africans

participated. Cf. Wim Hoogbergen, "The History of the Suriname Maroons," in *Resistance and Rebellion in Suriname: Old and New*, ed. Gary Brana-Shute, 65–102, Studies in Third World Series (Williamsburg, VA: College of William and Mary, 1990). Historians have generally pointed to a revolt in 1690 on a plantation on the Cassewinica Creek as the site of the first "true slave revolt" in Suriname. See Hoogbergen, "History of Suriname Maroons," 73; and Richard Price, *Alabi's World* (Baltimore: Johns Hopkins University Press, 1990), 9. Over the course of the eighteenth century, the Caribs suffered significant population losses, making it more difficult for them to effectively police the rapidly growing slave population in Suriname, which contributed to the prevalence of marronage.

28. "Door haere vuijligheden Tiraniequen, en onrecht vaerdigen Handel," Cornelis Aarsen van Sommelsdijck to Cornelis van Pere, 5/28/1688, in Archief Staten Generaal, 1.01.02, box 5771, Nationaal Archief. I thank Angela Sutton for bringing this letter to my attention.

29. Noeleen McIlvenna, *A Very Mutinous People: The Struggle for North Carolina, 1660–1713* (Chapel Hill: University of North Carolina Press, 2009), 148–58.

30. See, for instance, "Ordonnantie of placaet nopende den handel ent coopen van roô Indiaense slave gedaen den 23 Augustij 1686 [Essequibo]," in Netscher, 367–69, and Abram Beekman to Zeeland Chamber 11/4/1687, Netscher, 375–77.

31. Cf. Proclamation Essequibo, 7/4/1729, in *British Guiana Boundary: Arbitration with the United States of Venezuela. Appendix to the Case on Behalf of the Government of Her Brittanic Majesty*, vol. 2, *1724–1763* (London: Foreign Office, 1898), 9; SGD I:250-251, 270.

32. Plakaatboek (Berbice), 5/20/1681, 9/4/1700; R. A. J. van Lier, *Frontier Society: A Social Analysis of the History of Surinam* (The Hague: Martinus Nijhoff, 1971), 76.

33. These paragraphs draw on Marjoleine Kars, " 'Cleansing the Land': Dutch-Amerindian Cooperation in the Suppression of the 1763 Slave Rebellion in Dutch Guiana," in *Empires and Indigenes: Intercultural Expansion and Warfare in the Early Modern World*, ed. Wayne E. Lee, 264–65 (New York: New York University Press, 2011).

34. Colier to Directors, 8/14 1754, SvB 120; J. Colier, "Korte Memorie wegens de tegenwoordige toestand der Colonie de Berbice . . . ," 1/8/1757, SvB 223.

35. Berbice officials paid part of the ransom in goods and sugar and 259 enslaved people: 153 "able-bodied" men, 91 women (some with nursing babies), and 15 boys, devastating families and communities. In addition,

they signed a promissory note drawn on the Van Peres. Governor and council to Johan and Cornelis van Pere, 1/2/1713, in Hartsinck, 300–5. By 1720, 895 slaves ("little and grown") lived on six Company sugar plantations and two Company cacao plantations, as well as at the fort, the company store, the smithy, the brickyard and in the households of officials. The number of enslaved people on private plantations at that time is supposed to have been considerably larger, but no figures are available. Netscher, 161–63; Hartsinck, 327–30.

36. Klooster and Oostindie, *Realm Between Empires*, 70–71; Alex van Stipriaan, *Surinaams Contrast: Roofbouw and overleven in een Caraïbische plantagekolonie 1750–1863* (Leiden: Brill, 1993), 146–47.

37. Tenhoute to Tierens, 7/27/1727; Tenhoute to Directors, 4/2/1728; Heesel to Directors, 3/12/1727 and 9/12/1727, all in SvB 61; "Inventaris van alle de slaven, Beestialen, &c. bevonden in Rio Berbice in de Maand Aug. A'o 1727," SvB 61. Many of the enslaved on Hooglande had been brought by the infamous slave ship *Leusden*. Leo Balai, *Het Slavenschip Leusden: Slavenschepen en de West-Indische Compagnie, 1720–1738* (Zutphen: Walburg Pers, 2011), 48–51. On a subsequent voyage the slaver shipwrecked in the mouth of the Suriname River on January 1, 1738. The crew sealed the ship's hold, drowning all but 16 of the 680 captives on board.

38. Tenhoute to Tierens, 7/27/1727; "Informatien genoomen over verschijdenen zaaken voorgevallen op de plantage Hoogelande," n.d.; Inventory Company plantations, 1727; Dagregister Hooglande, 1 March 1726–1 March 1727; Report Heesel to Directors, 3/18/1727, all in SvB 61. For local abortifacients, see Tinde R. van Andel et al., "Ethnobotanical Notes from Daniel Rolander's *Diarium Scurinamicum* (1754–1756): Are These Plants Still Used in Suriname Today?" *Taxon* 61, 4 (2012): 859.

39. NHP 3/23/1728, SvB 62; Commander and council to Directors, 3/25/1728, SvB 62.

40. "Caarte van de Respective Colonie en Vry-plantagen, leggende an 't Riviere de Berbice op de Custe Gujanna," Leupe 1565.

41. Cf. Trevor Burnard, *Mastery, Tyranny, and Desire: Thomas Thistlewood and His Slaves in the Anglo-Jamaican World* (Chapel Hill: University of North Carolina Press, 2004), 146–52; Nell Irvin Painter, "Soul Murder and Slavery: Towards a Fully Loaded Cost Accounting," in *Southern History Across the Color Line* (Chapel Hill: University of North Carolina Press, 2002), 15–39.

42. Netscher, 163–67, 173; Henk den Heijer, *Goud, Ivoor en Slaven: Scheepvaart en handel van de Tweede Westindische Compagnie op Afrika, 1674–1740* (Zutphen: Walburg Pers, 1999), 156–58; J. Colier, "Korte Memorie

wegens de tegenwoordige toestand der Colonie de Berbice . . . ," 1/8/1757, SvB 223; Rijswijk to MCC, 7/8/1759, MCC 59; Inventories Company plantations, October 1762, SvB 133/160–68.

43. Netscher, 173–74; Jan Daniël Knapp, "Naauekeurige Plattegrond van den Staat en den Loop van Rio de Berbice. Met dezelver Plontagian van de Geoctroyeerde colonie de Berbice gelegen. 1742, NG-477, Rijksmuseum, Amsterdam.

44. Klaas Kramer, "Plantation Development in Berbice from 1753 to 1779: The Shift from the Interior to the Coast," *New West Indian Guide* 65, 1–2 (1991): 61–62.

45. Klaas Kramer, "Hoe Berbice Niet 'Naar de Berbiesjes Ging': Economische Ontwikkeling van Particuliere Plantages in Berbice, 1753–1779, Export and Slavenopstand" (MA thesis, Universiteit van Nijmegen, 1986), 74–76.

46. Rijswijk to MCC, 7/9/1759, MCC 59, Zeeuws Archief, Middelburg. See also J. Colier, "Korte Memorie."

47. Netscher, 182.

48. Alex van Stipriaan, "Het Dilemma van Plantageslaven: Weglopen of Blijven?" *OSO: Tijdschrift voor Surinaamse Taalkunde, Letterkunde, Cultuur en Geschiedenis* 11, 2 (1992): 130; Hoogbergen, "History of the Suriname Maroons," 69.

49. According to my records, at least forty-six slave ships docked in Berbice between 1661 and 1764, bringing 6,388 people, a number that is very much an undercount, as I do not know how many people arrived on a third of these ships, nor do I know how many people may have been sold illegally, leaving no trace. Marjoleine Kars, unpublished database, based on TSTDB and archival sources such as correspondence, plantation inventories, and ships' logs. For the same period, the TSTDB shows thirty-five ships bringing 11,096 slaves to Berbice, also an undercount, as not all voyages to Berbice are in the database. TSTDB accessed 6/18/2019, with thanks to Professor Randy Browne.

50. H. U. E. Thoden van Velzen and Wim Hoogbergen, *Een Zwarte Vrijstaat in Suriname: De Okaanse samenleving in the achttiende eeuw* (Leiden: KITLV Uitgeverij, 2011), 33; Rik van Welie, "Slave Trading and Slavery in the Dutch Colonial Empire: A Global Comparison," *New West Indian Guide* 82, 1–2 (2008): 47–96; and Jelmer Vos, "The Slave Trade from the Windward Coast: The Case of the Dutch, 1740–1805," *African Economic History* 38 (2010), 29–51. Vos argues that great numbers of Windward Coast slaves were Kru speakers, of whom a majority were women and children (and more boys than girls). Silvia Kouwenberg, "The Invisible Hand of Creole

Genesis: Reanalysis in the Formation of Berbice Dutch," in *Complex Processes in New Languages*, ed. Enoch O. Aboh and Norval Smith, 115–58 (Amsterdam/Philadelphia: John Benjamins Publishing Company, 2009).

51. Gert van Oostindie, *Roosenburg en Mon Bijou: Twee Surinaamse Plantages, 1720–1870* (Dordrecht-Holland: Foris Publications, 1989), chap. 3; Van Stipriaan, *Surinaams Contrast*, chap. 3; William C. Van Norman Jr., *Shade-Grown Slavery: The Lives of Slaves on Coffee Plantations in Cuba* (Nashville, TN: Vanderbilt University Press, 2013), 44–54 (with thanks to Professor Van Norman for sending me a PDF of his book).

52. Oostindie, *Roosenburg*, 112.

53. For labor on a sugar and a coffee plantation, see Oostindie, *Roosenburg*, chaps. 3 and 6. For gardens, 12/17/1740, Plakaatboek (Berbice); Van Andel et al., "Ethnobotanical Notes," provides information on slave gardens in neighboring Suriname in the 1750s. See also Tinde R. van Andel, Amber van der Velden, and Minke Reijers, "The 'Botanical Gardens of the Dispossessed' Revisited: Richness and Significance of Old World Crops Grown by Suriname Maroons," *Genetic Resources and Crop Evolution* 63, 4 (2016): 695–710; Richard Price, "Subsistence on the Plantation Periphery: Crops, Cooking, and Labour among Eighteenth-Century Suriname Maroons," *Slavery and Abolition* 12, 1 (1991): 107–27; and Anthony Blom, *Verhandeling over den landbouw, in de colonie Suriname* (Amsterdam: J. W. Smit, 1787), 381.

54. Unlike in Jamaica, there were no specific markets in Berbice where enslaved people sold their surplus. Rather, barter was informal, and it is poorly documented, but see Governor Lösner to Directors, 1/2/1749, SvB 99/12; Schumann to Hermann, 1748, Stähelin II.2:15; Hoogenheim to Directors, 7/3/1762, SvB 132/122; "Uijtgaaf der Cargazoen Goederen Anno 1762," SvS 134/158; Blom, *Verhandeling*, 382–83; Regulation for artisans and plantation servants, 5/12/1741, Plakaatboek (Berbice), explicitly forbade colonists from trading with slaves. The classic essay on slave gardens is Sidney Mintz and Douglas Hall, "The Origins of the Jamaican Internal Marketing System," first published in 1960 and widely reprinted.

3: Overthrow

1. Barbara Blair, "Wolfert Simon van Hoogenheim in the Berbice Slave Revolt of 1763–1764," *Bijdragen tot Taal-, Land- en Volkenkunde* 140, 1 (1984): 56–76; Diarium von Pilgerhut, 12/29/1760, Stähelin II.3:188.

2. Wim Klooster and Get Oostindie, *Realm Between Empires: The Second Dutch Atlantic, 1680–1815* (Ithaca, NY: Cornell University Press, 2018), 47–48, 75.

3. Hoogenheim to Directors, 2/25/1763, SvB 133/245; Hoogenheim to Directors, 12/22/1762, SvB 133/69.

4. Hoogenheim to Directors, 2/25/1763, SvB 133/245.

5. "Journael gevoerd bij afloopinge van de Edele Societijts Post van Surinaame in Rio Correntin de dato 25e February tot dato den 5 Maart," Albert Heuer, SvS 318; Heuer to Crommelin, 3/5/1763, SvS 134/11.

6. Testimony of Heer Abbensets during examination of Cupido van Hollandia en Zeelandia, 3/12/1764. No. 77 Cupido van Hollandia, 3/8/1764 and 3/12/1764; Jacob Pool to [?], 3/26/1763, CB 54-I. *Nederlandsche Jaerboeken* 17, part 2 (Amsterdam: F. Houttuyn, 1763), 583, notes that Coffij and Accara smeared their faces with clay. About the use of white clay for ritual cleansing, see Cheryl N. Ngwenyama, "Material Beginnings of the Saramaka Maroons: An Archaeological Investigation" (PhD diss., University of Florida, 2007), 136, and for protection, see Heather Miyano Kopelson, " 'One Indian and a Negro, the First Thes Ilands Ever Had': Imagining the Archive in Early Bermuda," *Early American Studies* 11, 2 (2013): 285. Hollandia and Zeelandia were two plantations, on opposite sides of the river, with the same owner. They were often, but not always, treated as one plantation, indicated by an ampersand. So Cupido, mentioned above, could be designated in different records as being "van Hollandia" or "van Hollandia & Zeelandia." The same construction was used for a few other plantations.

7. Pieter Gillissen, *Kort Dog Waarachtig Verhaal van de Rebellie en Opstand der Negers in de Colonie de Berbice . . . By Wyze van een Brief geschreven door de Heer . . . aan zyne Vrienden in het vaderland . . .* (Amsterdam: S. J. Baalde, 1763), 6; DH 4/7/1764; No. 337 Isaac van Essendam, 5/19/1764; No. 2 Dimba van de Prosperiteit, 8/3/1764; No. 148 Jantje van Lelienburg, 3/24/1764; NHP 3/2/1763–3/8/1763, SvB 128/34; Letter from Curaçao, 5/12/1763, in *De Maandelijkse Nederlandsche Mercurius*, Amsterdam, July 1763, 14–15. On the selectivity of revenge, see, for instance, No. 173 Cesar van Castres, 4/10/1764.

8. DH 2/28/1763.

9. DH 3/1/1764; NHP 3/11/1763, SvB 134/32; Hoogenheim to Directors, 2/25/1763, SvB 133/245; Hoogenheim to States General, 3/26/1763, SvB 227. Captain Kok's name was also spelled Kock.

10. No. 21 Claas van Switserland, 3/5/1764; No. 66 Hendrik van Lagendael, 3/7/1764; No. 34 David van Helvetia, 3/12/1764; No. 8 Piramus van Engelenburg, 12/7/1764; for similar actions in Jamaica, see Trevor Burnard, *Mastery, Tyranny, and Desire: Thomas Thistlewood and His Slaves in the Anglo-Jamaican World* (Chapel Hill: University of North Carolina Press, 2004), 173.

11. Perrotet to Daniel Loofs, 5/2/1763, Fagel 1824; Jacob Pool to [?], 3/26/1763, CB 54-I; DH 3/3/1763.

12. NHP 3/2/1764 to 3/6/1764, SvB 134/28; DH 2/29/1763–3/6/1763; Hoogenheim to Directors, 4/6/1763, SvB 134/24; Gillissen, *Kort Dog Waarachtig Verhaal*, was written to defend the author, a council member, against charges of disloyalty and cowardice.

13. J. P. Wyland, *Journaal of dags-aantekening van het voorgevallene in de colonie van Rio Berbiecie* . . . (Amsterdam: Gedrukt voor rekening van de auteur; 1763), 12–14. Men are listed by name, women only with their family affiliation.

14. No. 76 Jan Banne van Saintlust, 3/8/1764; No. 222 Nero van de Prosperiteit 4/12/1764; No. 354 Coffij van Saint Lust, 5/19/1764; No. 2 Dimba van de Prosperitijt 8/3/1764. "Nota van dieGeene door de Rebellen zijn gemassacreert," n.d., SvS 319.

15. *Kortbondige Beschryvinge van de Colonie de Berbice. Behelzende de Legging, Bevolking, Uitgestrektheid, Kreeken, Forten, Plantagien, enz. dezer Colonie* . . . (Amsterdam, S. K. Baalde, 1763), 41.

16. No. 456 Lucia van de Kerk, 6/9/1764.

17. No. 458 Pansoe van d'Cornelia Jacoba, 6/14/1764. Members of the Broer family were almost always designated as "mulat" or "Christian mulat." While the word "mulat" usually indicated someone of African and European descent, I think it more likely the Broers were of European and native descent, though it is possible they were of African descent as well. Their father, Philip Broer Sr., had served as postholder, a job that required close contact with Amerindians. See "Leijste der Officiers, Coloniers, AmbagsLieden, Soldaeten, en Matroosen, soo als deselve op den 20 Sept.'r 1727 verdeelt zijn, en dienste doen in Rio Berbice," SvB 61. Broer men, especially Jan, regularly served as translators for Amerindians in court. For Hoerle, see Hoogenheim to Directors, 2/25/1763, SvB 133/245.

18. Wyland, *Journaal*, 15; Netscher, 199, claims well over sixty, including twenty-one women and children; Hooogenheim to Directors, 4/6/1763, SvB 134/24, claims forty men, women, and children.

19. Wyland, *Journaal*, 12–16; DH 3/3/1763.

20. NHP 3/6/1763, SvB 124/28.

21. NHP 3/6/1763, SvB 134/28 (quotes); see also Nader geExamineert den Neger Mars off Atta van Altenklingen, 4/18/1764, and Jacob Pool to [?], 3/26/1763, CB 54-I. In the documents, Gousarie (or Goussarie) is often referred to as Cossaal. See Governor and council to Salve, 8/25/1764, SvB 135/79. A Dutch publication noted without any irony that the Europeans on Peereboom now got to know how little one could trust those [Africans]

"who sell each other into the meanest slavery, who are cruel, and think nothing of murder, adultery, and thievery." *Nederlandsche Jaerboeken* 17 (1765), part 2, 593.

22. Wyland, *Journaal*, 16; No. 222 Nero van de Prosperiteit, 4/12/1764; No. 3 Paul van Essendam, 3/3/1764; "Confrontatie van de neger Harlecijn van de Prosperitijt, onder no. 3 in de Examinatie van den 3. Augustus met Majalla, Bedje, Dongo & Sibi van de Peereboom," 12/8/1764; No. 7 Andries van de Prosperitijt, 12/7/1764.

23. No. 86 Cupido van de Prosperiteit, 3/13/1764; Hoogenheim to Directors, 12/22/1762, SvB 133/69; Jacob Pool to [?], 3/26/1763, CB 54-I; No. 117 Daniel van Lelienburg, 5/9/1764, and Confrontation Hans van Elisabeth & Alexandria with Daniel van Lelienburg, 6/9/1764. The Dutch word *tronk* may be related to the Portuguese *tronco*, and designates a primitive kind of jail: a heavy block of wood with holes through which a person's legs were locked with iron bands, immobilizing the person.

24. About Hoerle's abusive management style, see DH 6/10/1764; No. 458 Pansoe van d'Cornelia Jacoba, 6/14/1764. About Hoerle's escape after the massacre, NHP 4/13/1763, SvB 134/32; for Schröder (or Schreuder) see Wyland, *Journaal*, 19.

25. Jacob Pool to [?], 3/26/1763, CB 54-I; Wyland, *Journaal*, 14, 17; "Nota van dieGeene door de Rebellen zijn gemassacreert," SvS 319, n.d.

26. Schook to Directors, 3/20/1762, SvB 132; Hoogenheim to Directors, 12/22/1762, SvB 133/69.

27. See also Chirurg Majoor Gerard Toussijn to [?], 9/24/1750, SvB 107/15; Londa Schiebinger, "Scientific Exchange in the Eighteenth-Century Atlantic World," in *Soundings in Atlantic History: Latent Structures and Intellectual Currents, 1500–1830*, ed. Bernard Bailyn and Patricia L. Denault, 307–16 (Cambridge, MA: Harvard University Press, 2009), shows how physicians routinely experimented on Caribbean slaves. Even a relatively compassionate doctor who practiced in Essequibo in the late eighteenth century experimented on healthy slaves to learn more about the effects of various remedies. Ernst Karl Rodschied, *Medizinische und Chirurgische Bemerkungen über das Klima, die Lebensweise und Krankheiten der Einwohner der Hollaendischen Kolonie Rio Essequebo* (Frankfurt: In der Jaegerschen Buchhandlung, 1796), 33–34.

28. Hoogenheim to Directors, 7/3/1762, SvB 132/122; Netscher, 396n79.

29. No. 128 Claas (bomba) van de Prosperiteit, 5/10/1764; No. 80 Fortuin behoorende aan de Kerk, 5/8/1764; No. 83 Elsje behoorende aan de Kerk, 5/8/1764; No. 468 Lamoura van Altenklingen, 6/15/1764.

30. See, for instance, No. 8 and 9 Lomingo en La Fleur van den Arend,

3/3/1764; No. 190 kleijn Fortuin van Lindeboom, 5/11/1764; No. 157 Dongo van de Peereboom, 5/11/1764; No. 148 Capita van de Peereboom, 5/11/1764.

31. DH 3/4/1763; Codicil, dated 12/1/1761, of Jan en Jeremias Broer about the illegitimate sons (Klaas and Hendrik) of their brother Philip with a native woman. The sons would inherit Philip's share in plantation Philipsburg, jointly owned by the three brothers, CO 116/99, p. 393, National Archives, Kew, UK. Jan Broer also owned plantation Eenzaamheid; Jeremias owned Duytse Eikenboom and Philip owned De Drie Gebroeders; see *Naam-Lyst der Bestierders . . . Op de Colonie de Berbice. . . .* (Amsterdam: Petrus Schouten, Drucker in de Kalverstraat, 1763).

32. DH 3/5/1763; No. 456 Lucia van de Kerk, 6/9/1764. DH 3/5/1764; Hartsinck, 376; Netscher, 200; Hoogenheim to Directors, 4/7/1763, SvB 134/35. The Barkeys were a powerful family in Berbice. Anthony Barkey hailed from a prominent merchant family in Hamburg, Germany. He had arrived in Berbice in 1735 as a plantation manager. He married Elisabeth van Weeningen, granddaughter of Matthijs de Feer, a former governor of Berbice. When Barkey died in a 1759 fever epidemic at age forty-eight he owned a plantation with more than forty slaves and he was a member of the governor's council. His son, Anthony Jr., took over the management of Lelienburg. The young Barkey and his mother, the widow Barkey, frequently tangled with the governor; in fact, they were at the heart of an anti-Company "cabal" in the colony. Other members included slave auctioneer and tax collector Abraham Wijs (also mentioned by the rebels), who was Barkey Jr.'s uncle; secretary and prosecutor Eilardus Harkenroth, who was married to one of Wijs's daughters; and Pastor Jonas van Petersom Ramring, married to a sister of Barkey Jr. See www.brouwertree.com /waangene5.html. It is an indication of the rebels' discernment that while they hated Barkey Jr. and tried to kill him, they spared his sisters. In 1766, Barkey Jr. left for Batavia, in modern-day Indonesia, where he became a merchant and government official.

33. NHP 3/6/1763, SvB 134/28; DH 3/3/1763–3/7/1763. "Verzoekschrift aan Gouverneur en Raaden," reproduced in Hartsinck, 384. NHP 3/7/1763, SvB 134/28; DH 3/7/1764.

34. Schrijven to Brunswick, Amsterdam, 7/19/1763, CB 54-I; "Copie missive van de negers Coffij en Akkarra, ontvangen den 8ste Maart. Letter D" and "Waarschouwing aan de Heer Gouverneur van de Captijn koffie van D h'r Barkeij, akkarra ook van Barkeij," SvB 227. Mistress Schröder wrote the letter herself; see NHP 3/8/1763, SvB 134/28; Wyland, *Journaal*, 19.

35. DH 3/5/1763–3/9/1763; NHP 3/8/1763, SvB 134/28.

36. NHP 3/11/1763, SvB 134/32; DH 3/9/1763, 3/10/1763. Closer (nader) examination Apollo van de Vigilantie, 3/14/1764.

37. DH 3/9/1763; see No. 89 Hendrik alias Blankenburg en Coudio van de Hooftplantage, 3/13/1764; DH 3/12/1764 and NHP 3/23/1763, SvB 134/33. Mara slaves eventually divided about evenly: half went with the rebels and half ran into the woods; see DH 3/31/1763.

38. DH 3/11/1763-3/12/1763; NHP 3/11/1763–3/12/1653, SvB 134/32.

39. DH 3/13/1663 (quote). It is possible that the two men in the canoe joined the rebels voluntarily, though the Dutch later exonerated them. See No. 1 Mulat Dirk van de Colonie, 12/4/1764; No. 2 Mulat Cobus van de Colony, 12/4/1764; No. 214 Claertje vrij Mulattin, 4/12/1764. Piramus would die of pleurisy early in 1764; see report J. H. Buse, 3/21/1764, SvB 135/64.

40. VH 3/15/1763 (quote) and 3/30/1763; No. 91 Coffij van de Herstelling, 3/13/1764.

41. De Vrije report about Post Andries, CB 54-IB; Salve to Brunswick, 12/31/1763, Fagel 1824.

42. DH 3/17/1763.

43. DH 3/17/1763 to 3/31/1763, quote on 3/25/1763; Abbensets et al. to the Lutherse Gemeente in Amsterdam, 4/21/1763, in 213, Archief van de Evangelisch-Lutherse Gemeente te Amsterdam, Resoluties van de gewone kerkenraad betreffende de gemeente te Berbice, Stadsarchief Amsterdam; NHP 3/23/1763, SvB 134/33; Rijssel and Texier to Crommelin, 4/13/1763, SvS 318.

44. Governor and council to States General, 3/23/1763, SvB 227; Governor and council to Directors, 3/23/1763, SvB 227; Hoogenheim to States General, 3/26/1763, SvB 227. NHP 3/21/1763, SvB 134/15; Crommelin to Hoogenheim, 3/26/1763, SvB 135/4 (quote). Crommelin also sent cloth from India, as well as knives, combs, scissors, shaving knives, beads, and mirrors to pay the Amerindians on the Corentyne River; Crommelin to Heuer, 3/22/1763, SvS 318. For the ship captain, see founders.archives.gov /documents/Franklin/01-08-02-0017.

45. Hoogenheim to States General, 3/26/1763, SvB 227; DH 3/28/1764 and 3/29/1763. Hoogenheim to Directors, 4/6/1763, SvB 134/24. Bernard Texier would serve as governor of Suriname from 1779 until his death in 1783. J. van Rijssel had served in the same regiment as Van Hoogenheim.

46. NHP 4/2/1763, SvB 134/37 (quote); DH 3/29/1763, 3/28/1763; "Generaale Detaille en Repartitie der Troupes," 3/28/1763, SvB 135/; Rijssel and Texier to Crommelin, 4/5/1763, SvB 134/62. The ships were three merchant ships: *Berbice Welvaren* (Captain Ramelo); *Standvastigheid* (Captain

Laurensen); *Hendrik* (Captain Pijnappel), and the slaver *Adriana Pietronella* (Captain Kok). The *Betsy* left Berbice on 4/3/1763; on 4/8/1763, Pijnappel and Kok left for the Dutch Republic.

4: Governing

1. On Amina scarification, see Oldendorp, 383; and Paul Lovejoy, "Scarification and the Loss of History in the African Diaspora," in *Activating the Past: History and Memory in the Black Atlantic World*, ed. Andrew H. Apter and Lauren H. Derby, 99–138 (Newcastle upon Tyne: Cambridge Scholars, 2010).

2. Hartsinck, 382 (quote). About women who came on the ship with Coffij, see No. 80 Amelia van Hollandia, 3/10/1764; Veronica and Claartje van Hollandia, in confrontation with Favoriet van de Wed'w Jansen, 6/15/1764. Lieutenant Texier called Coffij a Creole in a letter to the directors of Suriname, 11/14/1763, SvS 320. One enslaved woman mentioned that Coffij had a wife at the start of the rebellion but did not name her; see No. 70 Pallas van Antonia, 3/8/1764. About Coffij being wise, see No. 116 Adam van Hollandia & Zeelandia, 5/9/1764. About Accara, see No. 213 Barbara van Lelienburg, 4/12/1764; No. 449 Ariaantje van Lelienburg, 6/8/1764; and No. 281 Jan Broek van 't Fort, 5/12/1764. For Akan leadership, see Emmanuel Akyeampong and Pashington Obeng, "Spirituality, Gender, and Power in Asante History," *International Journal of African Historical Studies* 28, 3 (1995): 481–508.

3. Some people were identified by the name of their owner, "Simon van Abbensets," or a nation label, "Amina Quakoe." For the Coromantee, see John K. Thornton, "War, the State, and Religious Norms in 'Coromantee' Thought: The Ideology of an African American Nation," in *Possible Pasts: Becoming Colonial in Early America*, ed. Robert Blair St. George, 180–200 (Ithaca, NY: Cornell University Press, 2000); Robin Law, "Ethnicities of Enslaved Africans in the Diaspora: On the Meaning of Mina (Again)," *History in Africa* 32 (2005): 247–67; and John Thornton, "The Coromantees: An African Cultural Group in Colonial North America and the Caribbean," *Journal of Caribbean History* 39 (1998): 161–78. For a thorough discussion of the historiography about the "Akan," see Rebecca Shumway, *The Fante and the Transatlantic Slave Trade* (Rochester, NY: University of Rochester Press, 2011), 17–21; and Walter C. Rucker, *Gold Coast Diaspora: Identity, Culture and Power* (Bloomington: Indiana University Press, 2015).

4. For debates about "nation," see Alexander X. Byrd, "Eboe, Country, Nation, and Gustavus Vassa's Interesting Narrative," *William and Mary Quarterly* 63, 1 (January 2006): 123–48; and James Sweet, "Defying Social

Death: The Multiple Configurations of African Slave Family in the Atlantic World," *William and Mary Quarterly* 70, 2 (April 2013): 258–59. For a view that "nation" was primarily a political tool, see Jessica A. Krug, "Social Dismemberment, Social (Re)membering: Obeah Idioms, Kormanti Identities and the TransAtlantic Politics of Memory, c. 1675–Present," *Slavery and Abolition* 35, 4 (2014): 537–58; and Jessica A. Krug, *Fugitive Modernities: Kisama and the Politics of Freedom* (Durham, NC: Duke University Press, 2018), esp. 14–18.

5. Rucker, *Gold Coast Diaspora*, 5, 119, 158; Thornton, "War, the State, and Religious Norms," 186; J. K. Fynn, *Asante and Its Neighbours, 1700–1807* (Evanston, IL: Northwestern University Press, 1971), 32–34. When the Dutch questioned close to 900 people in 1764, the scribe noted the "nation" for 540, presumably on the basis of self-identification, though there is no way to know how people defined "nation." Of the 540, 34 were Creoles, 6 "small on arrival in the country," 6 "mulat," 28 "new," and 3 Amerindian. The others ranged across some fifty "nations," including Amina, Bambarra, Dagarij, Fonsa, Louango, Gangoe, Mamine/Mamina/Mamini, Socco, and Tjamba, among many more obscure designations.

6. Cf. No. 21 Claas van Switserland, 3/5/1764, and the story about Boschlust, later in this chapter. For the terms "junior managers" and "shop stewards," see J. H. Lean, "The Secret Lives of Slaves: Berbice, 1819 to 1827" (PhD thesis, University of Canterbury, 2002), 233. For similar dynamics in St. Domingue, see Carolyn E. Fick, *The Making of Haiti: The Saint Domingue Revolution from Below* (Knoxville: University of Tennessee Press, 1990), 132.

7. See, for instance, No. 34 David van Helvetia, 3/5/1764, and confrontation on 3/12/1764; No. 21 Claas van Switserland, 3/5/1764; No. 66 Hendrik van Legendael, 3/7/1764; No. 67 Prins van Frederiksburg, 3/7/1764; No. 31 Wellekom van Helvetia, 3/5/1764; No. 98 Lucretia van Hardenbroek, 3/21/1764; No. 354 Coffij van Saintslust, 5/19/1764. For Louis, see No. 48 Antoni van Hoogstraten, 5/7/1764; No. 254 Claartje van Lelienburg, 4/16/1764; and No. 1 Mulat Dirk van de Colonie 12/4/1764. For Fortuin, see No. 145 Jantje van Lelienburg, 3/24/1764; and No. 254 Claartje van Lelienburg, 4/16/1764. For the *bomba* of La Providence, see No. 62 Carel van La Providence, 3/7/1764. Fick, *The Making of Haiti*, 86, 97, 100; John Thornton, *Africa and Africans in the Making of the Atlantic World, 1400–1800* (Cambridge: Cambridge University Press, 1998), 332.

8. Examinations passim, but see No. 34 David van Helvetia, 3/5/1764; No. 215 Hercules of Erfprins van Juliana, 4/12/1764; No. 73 Alexander van Maria Agnes, 3/8/1764; No. 138 August van de Juliana, 3/23/1764; No. 46 Jannetje van de Heer Schirmeister, 3/20/1764.

9. "Copie missive van de negers Coffij en Akkarra, ontvangen den 8ste Maart. Letter D" and "Waarschouwing aan de Heer Gouverneur van de Captijn koffie van D h'r Barkeij, akkarra ook van Barkeij" in SvB 227 (quote). For similar complaints among Maroons in Suriname, see Frank Dragtenstein, *Alles voor de Vrede: De brieven van Boston Brand tussen 1757 en 1763* (Amsterdam/The Hague: Ninsee/Amrit, 2009), 32; and Hartsinck, 793–94.

10. See, for instance, Stuart B. Schwartz, "Resistance and Accommodation in Eighteenth-Century Brazil: The Slaves' View of Slavery," *Hispanic American Historical Review* 51 (February 1977): 69–81; Michael Craton, *Testing the Chains: Resistance to Slavery in the British West Indies* (Ithaca, NY: Cornell University Press, 1982), 16; Emilia Viotti da Costa, *Crowns of Glory, Tears of Blood: The Demerara Slave Rebellion of 1823* (New York: Oxford University Press, 1994), 71–74; Thorton, *Africa and Africans*, 302–3; Trevor Burnard, *Hearing Slaves Speak* (The Caribbean Press, Guyanan Classics Library online, 2010), introduction; Wim Klooster, "Slave Revolts, Royal Justice, and a Ubiquitous Rumor in the Age of Revolutions," *William and Mary Quarterly* 71, 3 (July 2014): 403; Randy M. Browne, *Surviving Slavery in the British Caribbean* (Philadelphia: University of Pennsylvania Press, 2017).

11. Several historians have argued that under Dutch rule, enslaved people had the right to complain to the fiscal. I have seen no such complaints in the eighteenth century, nor does it appear that the office of the fiscal was used for this purpose in the period up to the Berbice Rebellion. When enslaved people wanted to complain, they approached the governor. For the most recent exploration of these records, see Browne, *Surviving Slavery*. For an insightful discussion of such tugs-of-war in the United States, see Anthony E. Kaye, *Joining Places: Slave Neighborhoods in the Old South* (Chapel Hill: University of North Carolina Press, 2007).

12. James C. Scott, *Weapons of the Weak: Everyday Forms of Peasant Resistance* (New Haven, CT: Yale University Press, 1987), and *Domination and the Arts of Resistance: Hidden Transcripts* (New Haven, CT: Yale University Press, 1992). Rutger Tenhoute to [?], 2/14/1727, SvB 61 (quote). For an account of the many people who had escaped from various plantations at the end of the year 1750, see Governor C. F. Collier to Directors, 12/23/1750, SvB 107.

13. For a useful theoretical treatment of internal social movement conflict, by participants and later scholars, see Sherry B. Ortner, "Resistance and the Problem of Ethnographic Refusal," *Comparative Studies in Society and History* 37, 1 (1995): 173–93.

14. For names of the councilors, No. 38 Apria van de Colonie, 3/6/1764;

for the executioner, or beul, see No. 185 Frans van Antonia, 4/11/1764; No. 229 Piekenieni van Hollandia & Zeelandia, 4/14/1764; DH 2/12/1764.

15. For clothing, see, for instance, No. 79 Pokko van Hollandia, 3/10/1764; Groot Coffij van de Vigilantie 3/12/1764; No. 420 Hans van Elisabeth & Alexandria, 6/6/1764. For salutes and tent boats, see No. 265 Paul of Gaudia van Stevensburg, 4/19/1764; No. 37 Claas van Sublieslust, 3/20/1764 (quote); No. 216 Cornelis van Petite Bayonne, 4/18/1764. For the "ennobling ceremony," see Thornton, "War, the State, and Religious Norms," 186, 194–200. For similar ceremonies among Suriname Maroons, see Richard Price, *Alabi's World* (Baltimore: John Hopkins University Press, 1990), 314–15.

16. No. 2 mulat Cobus van de Colonie, 12/4/1764 (quote); No. 27 Jan Cat van de Colonie, 3/5/1764.

17. Jan Kat contra Pieter and Christiaan, 3/12/1763; No. 95 Provoost van de Colonie, 3/15/1764.

18. For an example of Accara picking lieutenants, see No. 13 Frans van de Elisabeth & Alexandria, 12/10/1764. See also No. 181 Brutos of Accabiré van Stevensburg, 4/11/1764, for *grote heren* calling their officers together. No. 79 Pokko van Hollandia, 3/10/1764. No. 74 Fortuin van Maria Agnes, 3/8/1764 (quote). Harlecijn van Prosperiteit claimed that Thomas van Vlissingen begged Coffij to be made a *"groot Heer"* [big lord] given that he killed an important Dutchman. Witnesses later claimed that in fact it was Harlecijn who killed the Dutchman. No. 3 Harlecijn van de Prosperiteit, 8/3/1764; Confrontatie Harlecijn with Majalla, Bedje, Dongo & Sibi van de Peereboom, 12/8/1764. For the meaning of cutting off an enemy's head, see Richard Price, "Uneasy Neighbors: Maroons and Indians in Suriname," *Tipití: Journal of the Society for the Anthropology of Lowland South America* 8, 2 (2010): 12n13; and Robin Law, " 'My Head Belongs to the King': On the Political and Ritual Significance of Decapitation in Pre-Colonial Dahomey," *Journal of African History* 30, 3 (1989): 399–415.

19. This paragraph and the next draw on Marjoleine Kars, "Dodging Rebellion: Politics and Gender in the Berbice Slave Uprising of 1763," *American Historical Review* 121, 1 (2016): 53–56. See also Rucker, *Gold Coast Diasporas*, 44–45, 207–14.

20. Pernille Ipsen, *Daughters of the Trade: Atlantic Slaves and Interracial Marriage on the Gold Coast* (Philadelphia: University of Pennsylvania Press, 2015), 31.

21. Edna G. Bay, "Belief, Legitimacy and the Kpojito: An Institutional History of the 'Queen Mother' in Precolonial Dahomey," *Journal of African History* 36, 1 (1995): 1–27. See also R. S. Rattray, *Ashanti* (London: Clarendon Press, 1923), 81–82; Susan Herlin Broadhead, "Slave Wives, Free Sisters:

Bakongo Women and Slavery c. 1700–1850," in *Women and Slavery in Africa*, ed. Claire C. Robertson and Martin A. Klein, 160–84 (Madison: University of Wisconsin Press, 1983).

22. No. 132 Quassie van de Savonette, 3/22/1764 (quote). DH 6/19/1763. No. 206 Hendrik van de Goede Hoop, 4/12/1764; No. 142 Thomas van God Ziet Alles, 3/26/1764; No. 48 Asso van de Debora, 3/20/1764. See No. 29 Matthijs van Sublieslust, 5/7/1764; and No. 32 Fortuijn (jongetje) van Sublieslust, 5/7/1764, for the claim that people hid their animals.

23. Texier and Rijssel to Crommelin, 4/5/1763, SvB 134/62, claim that when the colonists fled, many left behind their guns and ammunition.

24. Hoogenheim to States General, 3/26/1763, SvB 227; No. 40 Coffij van Vigilantie, 3/6/1764; No. 63 Mars van La Providence, 3/7/1763 (quote).

25. J. K. Fynn, *Asante and Its Neighbours, 1700–1807* (Evanston, IL: Northwestern University Press, 1971), 32–33, notes that in Asante armies, the "musketeers commanded the greatest prestige," but that as late as 1807, the Asante fought with both guns and bows and arrows.

26. No. 40 Coffij van de Vigilantie, 3/6/1764 (quotes); No. 13 Frans van de Elisabeth & Alexandria, 12/10/1764; No. 61 Cariba, Altenklingen, 3/7/1764.

27. Ineke Velzing, "De Berbice Slavenopstand, 1763" (MA thesis, Universiteit van Amsterdam, 1979), 113; NHP 3/8/1763, SvB 134/28. No. 13 Frans van Elisabeth & Alexandria, 12/10/1764 (quote); Fick, *The Making of Haiti*, 111. For similar discipline among Maroons in Jamaica, see Barbara Klamon Kopytoff, "Guerilla Warfare in Eighteenth-Century Jamaica," *Expedition Magazine* 19, 2 (1977): n.p.

28. For an examination that suggests that Coffij was reluctant to kill Europeans, see No. 13 Frans van de Elisabeth & Alexandria, 12/10/1764. For Widow Jansen, see No. 254 Claartje van Lelienburg, 4/16/1764; Confrontation Favoriet van Juff. Jansen with Laurens van Horstenburgh, 6/9/1764; and Confrontation Favoriet van de wed'w Jansen with Claartje and Veronica van Lelienburg, 6/15/1764. Jan Abraham Charbon to [?], "Kurassau," 5/12/1763, in *Kortbondige Beschryvinge van de Colonie de Berbice . . .* (Amsterdam: J. S. Baalde Boekverkoper op den Dam, 1763), 42; see also Hartsinck, 406, and NHP 3/8/1763, SvB 134/28. For an example of such twisted relationships in Suriname, see Hilde Neus-van der Putten, *Susanna du Plessis: Portret van een slavenmeesteres* (Amsterdam: KIT Publishers, 2003); and in Barbados, Marisa J. Fuentes, *Dispossessed Lives: Enslaved Women, Violence, and the Archives* (Philadelphia: University of Pennsylvania Press, 2016), chap. 3. For a recent discussion of relations between female slaveholders and enslaved women in the United States, see Stephanie E. Jones-Rogers, *They Were Her Property: White Women as Slave Owners in the American South*

(New Haven, CT: Yale University Press, 2019). For a similar dynamic in the St. Domingue slave uprising, see David P. Geggus, "Slave and Free Colored Women in Saint Domingue," in *More Than Chattel: Black Women and Slavery in the Americas*, ed. David Barry Gaspar and Darlene Clark Hine, 272 (Bloomington: Indiana University Press, 1996).

29. Hartsinck, 375–76 (quote). Hoogenheim to Directors, 4/6/1764, SvB 134/24; Rijssel en Texier to Crommelin, 4/5/1763, SvB 134/57; Coffij to Hoogenheim, 7/27/1763, SvB 135/25. The Dutch expressed few anxieties about rebels and white women.

30. Schrijven to Brunswick, 7/19/1763, 54-I (quote); DH 3/8/1763.

31. For claims that black Berbicians were killed, see, for instance, Messinga van de Dageraad, who testified that a woman from his plantation was "bound and thrown in the water alive" and another woman had her head cut off. No. 452 Messinga van de Dageraad, 6/9/1764; No. 82 Aboi van Nieuw Caraques, 3/10/1764; No. 94 Jacouma van de Colonie, 3/15/1764; No. 1 Groot Jacob van de Geertruijt, 5/5/1764; No. 80 Amelia van Hollandia, 3/10/1764.

32. No. 4 Simon van Hollandia & Zeelandia, 12/4/1764 (quote); No. 145 Jantje van Lelienburg, 3/24/1764; No. 77 Cupido van Hollandia, 3/8/1764.

33. No. 168 Jacob van Castres, 4/10/1764 (quote); Cesar reportedly used this line to withhold the spoils from younger men wanting their share. Cesar was executed for "theft" and for selling slaves. Sentences, 4/27/1763, SvB 135/154.

34. Crommelin to "Weledele Gestrenge Heeren," 4/22/1763, SvB 134; translation of Edict of 4/20/1763, in R. A. J. van Lier, *Frontier Society: A Social Analysis of the History of Surinam* (The Hague: Martinus Nijhoff, 1971), 41. Original in *West-Indisch Plakaatboek*, ed. J. A. Schiltkamp and J. Th. de Smidt, vol. 2, *Plakaten, Ordonantiën, en andere wetten, uitgevaardigd in Suriname, 1667–1816* (Amsterdam: Emmering, 1983), 2:766–67.

35. Cf. No. 32 Fortuin (jongetie) van Sublieslust, 5/7/1764. For similar ambivalence elsewhere, see Fick, *The Making of Haiti*, 147–50; Ray A. Kea, " 'When I Die, I Shall Return to My Own Land': An 'Amina' Slave Rebellion in the Danish West Indies, 1733–1734," in *The Cloth of Many Colored Silks: Papers on History and Society Ghanaian and Islamic in Honor of Ivor Wilks*, ed. John Hunwick and Nancy Lawler, 188 (Evanston, IL: Northwestern University Press, 1996); and Trevor Burnard, *Mastery, Tyranny and Desire: Thomas Thirslewood and His Slaves in the Anglo-Jamaican World* (Chapel Hill: University of North Carolina Press, 2004), 170–74.

36. Kea, " 'When I Die' "; Jon F. Sensbach, *Rebecca's Revival: Creating Black Christianity in the Atlantic World* (Cambridge, MA: Harvard University Press, 2005), chap. 1. The oft-quoted passage in Edward Long, *The*

History of Jamaica, Or, General Survey of the Antient and Modern State of That Island . . . (London: T. Lowndes, 1774), 2:447, reads that the object of the Jamaican rebels was "no other than the entire extirpation of the white inhabitants; the enslaving of all such Negroes as might refuse to join them; and the partition of the island into small principalities in the African mode; to be distributed among their leaders and head men." Oldendorp, 383.

37. The Dutch noted early on that many slaves, even "loyal" ones, joined the rebellion "provisionally, just to plunder." NHP 3/6/1763, SvB 134/28. On "neutral" people stripping their masters' houses in St. John in 1733, see Aimery P. Caron and Arnold R. Highfield, *The French Intervention in the St. John Slave Revolt of 1733–34* (Occasional Paper No. 8, Bureau of Libraries, Museums, and Archaeological Services, St. Thomas, 1981), 10. See also Thornton, *Africa and Africans*, 332–33.

38. One *bomba*, for instance, claimed his own former slaves deposed him as the new *heer* of the plantation, telling him "he had been in charge long enough under the Christians." No. 308 Hans, bomba van de Hooftplantage, 5/19/1764.

39. No. 223 Abram van Rosenburg, 4/13/1764. For an extended argument about anti-state behavior, see James C. Scott, *The Art of Not Being Governed: An Anarchist History of Upland Southeast Asia* (New Haven, CT: Yale University Press, 2010).

40. Michael A. McDonnell, "Resistance to the American Revolution," in *A Companion to the American Revolution*, ed. Jack Greene and J. R. Pole, 342 (New York: Blackwell Publishing, 2000).

41. Pierre Perrotet to Daniel Loofs, 5/2/1763, Fagel 1824 (quotes). Perrotet had bought Boschlust in 1746 from its former owner; see SvB 118/25.

42. For similar considerations in Suriname, see Alex van Stipriaan, "Het Dilemma van Plantageslaven: Weglopen of Blijven?" *OSO: Tijdschrift voor Surinaamse Taalkunde, Letterkunde, Cultuur en Geschiedenis* 11, 2 (1992): 122–41.

43. For similar desires among self-emancipated people to live as free peasants, see Alex van Stipriaan, "Tussen Slaaf en Peasant: De Rol van de Kleine Landbouw in het Surinaamse Emancipatie-Proces," in *De Erfenis van Slavernij*, ed. Lila Gobardhan-Rambocus et al., 29–55 (Paramaribo: Anton de Kom Universiteit, 1995); Michel-Rolph Trouillot, *Silencing the Past: Power and the Production of History* (Boston: Beacon, 1995), 103–4; Carolyn E. Fick, "Emancipation in Haiti: From Plantation Labour to Peasant Proprietorship," *Slavery and Abolition* 21, 2 (2000): 11; and Johnhenry

Gonzales, *Maroon Nation: A History of Revolutionary Haiti* (New Haven, CT: Yale University Press, 2019).

44. Gert Oostindie, *Roosenburg en Mon Bijou: Twee Surinaamse Plantages, 1720–1870* (Dordrecht-Holland: Foris Publications, 1989), 53.

45. According to Hartsinck (330), plantations Johanna, Savonette, Cornelia Jacoba, Hardenbroek, and Dageraad were started in 1722. Peereboom had been a farm and plantation since 1627. Hooftplantage is mentioned by Van Berkel in 1672, as is De Berg (later renamed Johanna). I have found inventories for Vlissingen and Markey dating back to the 1720s, but they likely existed earlier. At the start of the rebellion, a quarter to a third of the enslaved people in Berbice lived on Company plantations. On all but two Company plantations (Johanna and Goede Hoop), sugar was grown; see Report J. H. Buse, 3/21/1764, SvB 135/64. On St. John in 1733, Creoles refused to join the Amina in their rebellion; see Kea, " 'When I Die,' " 188.

46. Netscher, 59–60. According to the inventory of 7/31/1762, SvB 133/160, there were 28 healthy men, 7 invalids and aged men, 35 healthy women, another 12 invalids and aged women, 7 boys, 2 girls (one more had just died), 14 children under the age of 10, and 1 Indian woman, for a total of 106. Frederik, a youth of sixteen or seventeen, killed Jacob with a hatchet in the forest at the command of his father, David, whom the rebels had put in charge of West Souburg. See No. 137 Klaartje van West Souburg, 3/22/1763; "Weeder Examinatie van den Neger fredrik van WesSouburgh zijnde reets op no. 14 in deeze geExamineert," 3/23/1764 (quote); and testimony from witnesses Calvies en Piramus, 3/23/1764, and No. 332 David Metselaar van West Souburg, 5/19/1764; "Confrontatie van David van WesSouburgh met Claartje van d'o plantagie en Calvin & Pieramus van de Colonie," 6/15/1764.

47. No. 22 Animba van West Souburg, 3/19/1764 (quote); No. 18 Kikomba van West Souburg, 3/19/1764 (quote); No. 25 Lucretia van West Souburg, 3/19/1766; No. 13 Mars van West Souburg, 3/19/1764.

48. No. 137 Klaartje van Ijdem [West Souburg], 3/22/1764; No. 332 David Metselaar van West Souburg, 5/19/1764; No. 13 Mars van West Souburg, 5/19/1764; See also "Confrontatie van David van WesSouburgh met Claartje van d'o plantagie en Calvin & Pieramus van de Colonie," 6/15/1763. In his examination, rebel leader August claimed Klaartje had been sold to Solomon, an Amina and a *heer*, thereby confirming that enslaving people as punishment was common practice. See No. 138 August from Juliana, 3/23/1763, who claimed that Klaartje had been given as a wife to the man who killed her husband. Klaartje and at least two of her

children by Mathebi, Lucretia and Mars, survived the rebellion. See also DH 1/4/1764. For rebel leaders selling people in St. Domingue, see Laurent DuBois, *Avengers of the New World: The Story of the Haitian Revolution* (Cambridge, MA: Harvard University Press, 2005), 159.

49. For Coffij's words, see No. 65 Jantje van Vlissingen, 3/21/1764.

50. No. 67 Magiel van Vlissingen, 3/21/1764, and No. 68 Kinkie van Vlissingen, 3/21/1764.

51. DH 5/14/1763, 5/25/1763, 5/26/1764, 5/29/1763, 6/10/1763, 6/29/1763, 7/1/1763; witnesses in case of No. 12 Jacob alias Antonij van Landskroon, 12/8/1764 (quote); "Aboi van Nieuwe Caraques nader geexamineert en geconfronteert teegens den Bomba Jan van Markey," 3/15/1764. On June 29, an Indian who had been on a mission to contact the Company plantation slaves told Governor van Hoogenheim that "most of the Company plantations upriver such as Savonette, Markey, and Hardenbroek had always kept themselves apart from the rebels, but finally had to submit, and with violence were brought under their command."

52. For a discussion of West African slavery and notions of honor, see Toby Green, *A Fistful of Shells: West Africa from the Rise of the Slave Trade to the Age of Revolution* (Chicago: University of Chicago Press, 2019), chap. 6. There is a large literature on freed people owning slaves in Latin America, and, to a lesser extent, in North America. For a recent discussion of some of this literature, see Danielle Terrazas Williams, " 'My Conscience Is Free and Clear': African-Descended Women, Status, and Slave Owning in Mid-Colonial Mexico," *The Americas* 75, 3 (July 2018): 525–54.

5: The Long Atlantic Reach

1. DH 3/30/1763, 3/31/1763; NHP 4/2/1763 about events on 3/31/1764 (quote), SvB 134/37. Inventory Dageraad October 1762, SvB 133/161; Hoogenheim to Directors, 2/25/1763, SvB 133/197.

2. DH 3/13/1763, 3/31/1763 (quote).

3. DH 3/10/1763, 4/2/1763 (quote).

4. DH 4/2/1763; Stedman, 397–98. For African rebels' fighting tactics elsewhere in the Caribbean, see David Geggus, ed., *The Haitian Revolution: A Documentary History* (Indianapolis, IN: Hackett Publishing, 2014), 94–95; and Wim Hoogbergen, "De binnenlandse oorlogen in Suriname in de achttiende eeuw," in *Geweld in de West: Een militaire geschiedenis van de Nederlandse Atlantische wereld, 1600–1800*, ed. Victor Enthoven et al., 166 (Leiden: Brill, 2013).

5. DH 4/2/1763, 4/3/1763; NHP 4/3/1763, SvB 134/126; Hoogenheim to Crommelin, 4/5/1763, Fagel 1824. Hoogenheim to Directors, 4/8/1763,

SvB 134/34; Rijssel and Texier to Crommelin, 4/5/1763, SvB 134/62; NHP 4/2/1763, SvB 134/37.

6. DH 4/2/1763, 4/4/1763. NHP 3/25/1763–5/5/1763, SvB 134/37.

7. Bercheijck to "Groot Achtbare Heeren," 4/21/1763, CO 116-33, folio 185 (quote). Cf. Crommelin to Directors Suriname, 4/27/1763, SvS 318; Gravesande to Crommelin, 4/27/1763, SvB 134/82; Gravesande to WIC, 5/2/1763, SGD II:420 (quote).

8. Bercheijck Journaal, 3/10/1763-3/24/1673, CO 116/33; Bercheijck to WIC, 3/13/1763 and 4/21/1763, CO 116/33. Gravesande to WIC, 3/17/1763, SGD II:416-19. Bercheijck to WIC, 4/21/1763, CO 116/33, folio 374 (quote).

9. NHP 4/18/1763, SvB 134/93 (quote); Gravesande to WIC, 5/2/1763 and 2/29/1764, SGD II:421–24, 444–45.

10. Bercheijck to WIC, 4/21/1763, CO 116/33, folio 374; Jack D. Warren Jr., "Washington's Journey to Barbados," George Washington's Mount Vernon, www.mountvernon.org/george-washington/washingtons-youth/jour ney-to-barbados; Gravesande to WIC, 2/29/1764, SGD II:444; Clarke to Bentinck, 4/3/1763, SGD II:421–22n3, 483; and S. D. Smith, "Gedney Clarke of Salem and Barbados: Transatlantic Super-Merchant," *New England Quarterly* 76, 4 (December 2003): 499–549, esp. 519–21 and 536–37; WIC to States General, 7/11/1763, in Extract uit de Resolutien van de Heeren Staaten van Holland en Westvriesland . . . 20 July 1763, SvB 227.

11. Crommelin and council to Hoogenheim and council, 4/22/1763, SvB 134/66.

12. Edict 4/20/1763, in R. A. J. van Lier, *Frontier Society: A Social Analysis of the History of Surinam* (The Hague: Martinus Nijhoff, 1971), 57; Crommelin to Rijssel and Texier, 4/22/1763, SvB 134/70; Journal, 5/10/1763, Gouvernementssecretarie Suriname tot 1828, 1.05.10.01 inv. no. 8, Nationaal Archief, The Hague. The Society of Suriname estimated that the colony contained 36,000 slaves and 1,300 whites. Resolutien van de Heeren Staten van Holland en Westvriesland, 7/23/1763.

13. NHP 3/21/1763 (quote); Crommelin to Hoogenheim, 3/26/1763, SvS 318.

14. Crommelin to Heuer, 3/22/1763, SvS 318; Gravesande to Hoogenheim, 5/20/1763 and 6/6/1763, SvB 135.

15. Extract uijt de Extraordinaire Notulen van den Hove van Politie en Crimineele justitie [Suriname], 7/10/1763, SvB 227; Crommelin to Directors Berbice, 7/13/1763, SvB 134/113; Gravesande to WIC, 2/11/1765, SGD II:483; D. Luijck Massis and A. Duvelaer to Directors, 11/19/1763, SvB 134/104. Suriname alone presented a bill for more than 51,000 guilders. "Notitie van het geene de Edele Heeren Directeuren van de Colonie de Berbice

306 Notes

Debet zijn aan Directeuren der Edele Geoctroijeerde Sociëteit van Suriname," 2/20/1766, SvB 56.

16. Declaration De Windt, 3/28/1763, Extract Uyt het Register der Resolutien van de . . . Heeren Staaten Generaal der Vereenigde Nederlanden, 9/22/1772, Fagel 1825; De Windt to Directors, 7/9/1764, SvB 135/176; Gravesande to WIC, 6/20/1763, SGD II:426; Clarke to Bentinck, 12/28/1763, in "A Contribution Towards the History of Demerara—1763. From the Correspondence of Sydney Clarke," *Timehri: Journal of the Royal Agricultural and Commercial Society of British Guiana* 2 (December 1888): 258–59.

17. Clarke to Bentinck, 12/28/1763, SGD II:433.

18. NHP 4/5/1763, SvB 134/37.

19. Neil L. Whitehead, *Lords of the Tiger Spirit: A History of the Caribs in Colonial Venezuela and Guyana, 1498–1820* (Dordrecht: Foris Publications, 1988): 160–61; Netscher, 117–18.

20. See, for instance, Gravesande to WIC, 12/7/1747, 12/2/1748, in SGD I:225, 239–40; Edward Bancroft, *An Essay on the Natural History of Guiana, in South America* . . . (London: T. Becket and P. A. De Hondt in the Strand, 1769), 263–64; Stähelin II.2:59, 60; letter of the Prefect of the Missions (Frey Benito de la Garriga) to the Commandant of Guiana, Senor Don Felix Ferreras, 6/9/1758, in *British Guiana Boundary: Arbitration with the United States of Venezuela, Appendix to the Case on Behalf of the Government of Her Britannic Majesty*, vol. 2, *1724–1763* (London: Foreign Office, 1898), 145–50.

21. Neil L. Whitehead, "Native Peoples Confront Colonial Regimes in Northeastern South America (ca. 1500–1900)," in *The Cambridge History of the Native Peoples of the Americas*, vol. 3, *South America*, part 2, eds., Frank Salomon and Stuart B. Schwartz, 399 (Cambridge: Cambridge University Press, 1999). For the Dutch-Carib alliance, see also Whitehead, *Lords of the Tiger Spirit*, 162–63.

22. Gravesande to WIC, 8/27/1755, SGD I:342.

23. Marjoleine Kars, " 'Cleansing the Land': Dutch-Amerindian Cooperation in the Suppression of the 1763 Slave Rebellion in Berbice," in *Empires and Indigenes: Intercultural Alliance, Imperial Expansion, and Warfare in the Early Modern World*, ed. Wayne E. Lee, 265–66 (New York: New York University Press, 2011).

24. "Uitgaaf der Cargazoen Goederen anno 1762," SvB 134/158.

25. "Verhandlungen Schumanns mit dem Gouverneur und Herrn Boulée," November 1750, Stähelin II.2:52.

26. DH 6/19/1763.

27. Rijssel and Texier to Crommelin, 4/13/1763, SvS 318; Stähelin

II.3:316–17; DH 4/26/1763, 6/19/1763, 7/27/1763; Heuer to Crommelin, 5/13/1763, SvB 134/81.

28. Stähelin II.3:277, 278.

29. J. Colier, "Korte Memorie wegens de tegenwoordige toestand der Colonie de Berbice . . . ," 1/8/1757, SvB 223; Christlieb Quandt, *Nachricht von Suriname* . . . (Görlitz: Gedruckt bey J. G. Burghart; zu finden bey dem Verfasser, und in Kommission bey P. G. Kummer in Leipzig, [1807]), 72. For examples of alliances between Indians and Maroons, see Ben Scholtens, "Indianen en Bosnegers, een historisch wisselvallige verhouding," *SWI: Forum voor Kunst, Cultuur en Wetenschap* 9, 1–2 (1992): 70–98.

6: Expanding the Revolution

1. Charbon's story is based on DH 4/3/1763; Charbon to Directors, 5/12/1763, in *Kortbondige Beschryvinge van de Colonie de Berbice* . . . (Amsterdam: J. S. Baalde, 1763), 41–44; Lichtveld, 72–76 (quote on 75); NHP 4/3/1763, SvB 134/137.

2. In Suriname Maroons made Europeans swear African oaths, not trusting European promises much, as they were so often broken, "whereas for a Negro to break his Oath is absolutely without Example." Stedman, 71. Several enslaved men later testified that they had captured Mittelholtzer in the cornfield of plantation Prosperiteit and had taken him to Coffij's headquarters. They may have spoken the truth, or they may have sought to disclaim responsibility for his death. See No. 70 Pokko van Hollandia, 3/10/1764; Hans van van Staden, testifying in the examination of No. 467 Jupiter van Engadina, 6/9/1764.

3. NHP 4/3/1763, SvB 134/126; DH 4/3/1763.

4 Several copies of the letters, with slight variations, but not the originals (which appear to be lost), are in SvB 134/41, SvB 134/54, and SvB 227. The letters have also been published in Lichtveld, 77–97. For accessibility's sake, I have quoted from the versions in Lichtveld.

5. Lichtveld, 78–79. Insurgents in St. Domingue expressed similar sentiments, though at greater length and in loftier language (bad masters forced their hand, they would fight to the death yet they desired peace); see David Geggus, ed., *The Haitian Revolution: A Documentary History* (Indianapolis, IN: Hackett Publishing, 2014), 82–83.

6. Lichtveld, 79. See also Rebels to Hoogenheim, n.d., SvB 134/41.

7. Ineke Velzing, "De Berbice Slavenopstand, 1763" (MA thesis, Universiteit van Amsterdam, 1979), 110–12, also suggests that one of the letters was sent earlier, but she dates it to early March, which I think is too early.

8. On slave communication networks, see Julius Scott, *The Common Wind: Afro-American Currents in the Age of the Haitian Revolution* (London: Verso, 2018).

9. See chapter 1 in this volume.

10. Perrotet to Daniel Loofs, Amsterdam, 5/2/1763, Fagel 1824. On St. John in 1733, the Amina similarly intended to keep plantations in production as "the material basis of the new political order." Ray A. Kea, " 'When I Die, I Shall Return to My Own Land': An 'Amina' Slave Rebellion in the Danish West Indies, 1733–1734," in *The Cloth of Many Colored Silks: Papers on History and Society Ghanaian and Islamic in Honor of Ivor Wilks*, ed. John Hunwick and Nancy Lawler, 183 (Evanston, IL: Northwestern University Press, 1996).

11. DH 4/3/1763.

12. NHP 4/3/1763, SvB 134/126; DH 4/3/1763.

13. Lichtveld, 79–80, and copy letter Hoogenheim to rebels, 4/3/1763, in SvB 134/55.

14. Lichtveld, 81; copy letter from rebels to Hoogenheim, n.d., SvB 134/41. Frank Dragtenstein, *Alles voor de vrede: De Brieven van Boston Band tussen 1757 en 1763* (Amsterdam/The Hague: Ninsee/Amrit, 2009), 52.

15. DH 4/4/1763. For Van Hoogenheim's assessment of the correspondence, see also Hoogenheim to Gravesande, 4/18/1763, SvB 227.

16. DH 4/3/1763; Lichtveld, 82–83, and Hoogenheim to rebels, 4/5/1763, SvB 134/42 and 134/55.

17. Relaas van Coffj en Charlestown, 9/6/1759, in Harry van den Bouwhuijsen et al., *Opstand in Tempati 1757–1760*, Bronnen voor de Studie van Afro-Surinaamse Samenlevingen in de Guyana's, dl. 12 (Utrecht: Centrum voor Caraïbische Studies, 1988), 104.

18. Van den Bouwhuijsen et al., *Opstand in Tempati 1757–1760*, 102. One of their leaders related that such peace agreements had worked well in Jamaica, where he himself had lived. After much discussion, the Tempati Maroons had drawn up a list of things they required.

19. D. J. E. Maier, "Military Acquisition of Slaves in Asante," in *West African Economic and Social History: Studies in Memory of Marion Johnson*, ed. D. Henige and T. C. McCaskie, 119 (Madison: University of Wisconsin Press, 1990).

20. Clarke to Bentinck, 4/3/1763, in SGD II:421n3 (quote on 422). Bercheijck to WIC, 4/21/1763, CO 116.

21. Gravesande to Directors, 7/18/1763, CO 116.

22. DH 3/31/1763 (quote). Cf. No. 189 Daniel van Lagendaal, 4/11/1764;

Haringman to "Hoog Mogende Heeren," 11/20/1763, Fagel 1824. DH 3/6/1763, 3/17/1763, 3/18/1763.

23. No. 31 Willekom van Helvetia, 3/5/1764; No. 32 Don Quischot van Helvetia, 3/5/1764; No. 74 Fortuin van Maria Agnes, 3/8/1764; No. 75 Februarij van Maria Agnes, 3/8/1764.

24. No. 466 Fortuin van Helvetia, 6/14/1764; No. 461 Lisette van Helvetia, 6/14/1764. "Timmini" comes up in the Berbice records only once.

25. No. 88 Anna [van Helvetia], 3/13/1764; No. 74 Fortuin van Maria Agnes, 3/8/1764; No. 466 Fortuin van Helvetia, 6/14/1764. No. 39 Groot Coffij van de Vigilantie, bomba, 3/6/1764; No. 28 La Rose van La Providence, 5/5/1764. Report Knollart aan Hattinga, 4/2/1763, SvB 134 (quote); No. 461 Lisette van Helvetia, 6/14/1764, and No. 59 Lonkje van Petite Bretagne, 3/20/1764; for firing at ships, No. 52 Quamina van Vigilantie, 3/6/1764; Jeremias van de Vigilantie, 3/6/1764. For Accara van de Brandwacht, see No. 83 Marquis van Helvetia, and No. 63 Mars van La Providence, 3/7/1764. For the use of red feathers in Tacky's Revolt, see Maria Alessandra Bollettino, "Slavery, War, and Britain's Atlantic Empire: Black Soldiers, Valors, and Rebels in the Seven Years' War" (PhD diss., University of Texas at Austin, 2009), 223–24. For the color red, see Toby Green, *A Fistful of Shells: West Africa from the Rise of the Slave Trade to the Age of Revolution* (Chicago: University of Chicago Press, 2019), 370–71, 394.

26. For Accara, see, for instance, "Nader geExamineert den Neger Mars off Atta van Altenklingen," 4/18/1764; No. 33 Marquis van Helvetia, 3/5/1764; No. 32 Don Quichot van Helvetia, 3/5/1764; No. 73 Alexander van Maria Agenes, 3/8/1764; No. 265 Paul of Quadia van Steevensburg, 4/19/1764. For Adou, who was known as Claas among the Dutch, No. 33 Marquis van Helvetia, 3/5/1764; No. 41 David van de Heer Schirmeister, 3/20/1764; No. 40 Prins van de Heer Schirmeister, 3/20/1764; No. 118 Jan Broek van de Goede Hoop, 3/22/1764; No. 120 Filida van de Goede Hoop, 3/22/1764; No. 200 Adam van de Goede Hoop, 4/12/1764; No. 15 Roosje van de Geertuijd, 5/5/1764; No. 12 Alida van d'Geertruijd; No. 29 Charmoes van Roosendael, 3/5/1764; No. 39 Fortuin van de Heer Schirmeister, 3/20/1764.

27. Natalie Zemon Davis, "Judges, Masters, Diviners: Slaves' Experience of Criminal Justice in Colonial Suriname," *Law and History Review* 29, 4 (November 2011): 956–58; H. U. E. Thoden van Velzen and Wim Hoogbergen, *Een Zwarte Vrijstaat in Suriname: De Okaanse samenleving in the achttiende eeuw* (Leiden: KITLV Uitgeverij, 2011), 9. Jan Speelman to Governor van Rijswijk, n.d. (but referring to events in 1759), SvB 128; DH 4/15/1764.

28. DH 4/26/1763.

29. Report Knollart to Hattinga, 4/6/1763, SvB 134/75; Bomba Jantje van Catharinenburg was beaten to death according to his wife and others on that plantation. See No. 62 Johanna van Catharinenburg, 3/21/1764, who hid in the bush; No. 63 Dorothea van Catharinenburg, 3/21/1764, who was taken to Berbice, where "she had to work like a slave." The *bomba* of Stevensburg was tied up and, with his wife and children, taken away by the rebels; see Report Knollart to Hattinga, 4/6/1763. Bomba Coffij van Peetersburg was beaten for helping his manager; see No. 64 Africa van Peetersburg, 3/21/1764, and No. 97 Thomas van Peetersburg, 3/21/1764.

30. Cf. No. 61 Thomas van Blijendaal, 3/7/1764, and No. 431 Assalij van Stevensburg, 6/7/1764; No. 434 Henriette van Stevensburg, 6/7/1764.

31. For Alla, see No. 12 Mavo van Sophiasburg, 3/9/1763. For people ending up on plantation Agthoven, see No. 15 Ariaentje van Sophiasburg (with her small child), and her husband, No. 13 Sam van Sophiasburg and No. 9 Flip van Sophiasburg, all on 3/9/1764. For Prosperiteit, see No. 16 Simba van Sophiasburg, 3/9/1764; No. 17 Boerika van Sophiasburg, 3/9/1764, who claimed they were "kept as slaves"; No. 11 Catoen van Sophiasburg, 3/9/1764. No. 16 Simba van Sophiasburg, 3/9/1764. No. 14 La Haije van Sophiasburg, 3/9/1763. No. 96 Moses van Markeij, 3/15/1764.

32. No. 10 Cacauw van Sophiasburg, 3/9/1763. No. 9 Flip van Sophiasburg, 3/9/1763.

33. No. 63 Mars van La Providence, 3/7/1763.

34. DH 4/19/1764; No. 181 Brutos off Accabiré van Stevensburg, 4/11/1764.

35. "Nader examinatie van den Neeger Thomas van Blijendael," 3/23/1764 (quote); No. 50 Oranje van Blijendael, 3/20/1764; No. 190 Paij van Blijendaal, 4/11/1764 (quote); No. 191 Hector van Blijendaal, 4/11/1764; "Confrontatie van Paij van Blijendaal teegens de Neegers," 4/25/1764; "Confrontatie van de Neger Hector van Blijendaal tegens de Neegers Coffij & Daniel van Elisabeth Adriana en Orange van Blijendaal," 4/25/1764; No. 460 Louis van Blijendaal, 6/14/1764. Stedman, 73, describes a blood oath.

36. Report Knollart to Hattinga, 4/6/1763; Rijssel and Texier to Knollart, 4/4/1763, SvB 135/10.

37. DH 6/2/1763.

38. Hoogenheim to the States General, 3/26/1763, SvB 227; DH 4/15/1763 for pretend guns. Report Knollart to Hattinga, 4/6/1763, SvB 135/9; DH 4/8/1873; Rijssel and Texier to Crommelin, 4/13/1763, Fagel 1824. No. 189 Daniel van Lagendael, 4/11/1764; No. 466 Fortuin van Helvetia, 6/14/1764; No. 461 Lisette van Helvetia, 6/14/1764; No. 235 Petra van Horstenburg, 4/14/1764.

39. Rijssel and Texier to Crommelin, 4/13/1763, Fagel 1824; DH 4/8/1763.

NHP 6/13/1763, SvB 134/95; Meel to [?], 10/21/1763, Fagel 1824. DH 4/8/1763, 4/26/1763, 6/13/1763, 7/2/1763, November 1763.

7: Stalemate

1. Rijssel and Texier to Crommelin, 4/13/1763, SvS 319 (quote); Hoogenheim to Gravensande, 4/18/1763, SvB 227. DH 4/8/1763, 4/15/1763, 4/22/1763; NHP 5/2/1763, SvB 134/94.

2. Douglas to Bentinck, 4/25/1764, CB 54-IB; J. R. McNeill, *Mosquito Empires: Ecology and War in the Greater Caribbean, 1620–1914* (Cambridge: Cambridge University Press, 2010), 6, 196.

3. Stedman, 127, 46; McNeill, *Mosquito Empires*, 195–98.

4. DH 5/1/1763, 5/8/1763, 5/10/1763.

5. DH 5/3/1763 (quote); NHP 5/6/1763, SvB 134/94. Lichtveld, 83, or Hoogenheim to Coffij and Accara, 5/3/1763, in SvB 134/55. Van Hoogenheim's letters have no salutation or signature.

6. For what happened to the two men at the fort, see NHP 5/6/1763, SvB 134/95; No. 89 Hendrik alias Blankenburg en Coudio van de Hooftplantage, 3/13/1764; Groot Coffij van de Vigilantie contra deselve, 3/12/1764. DH 5/4/1763; NHP 5/6/1763, SvB 134/94.

7. NHP 5/6/1763, SvB 134/94.

8. DH 5/4/1763 (quote). NHP 5/6/1764, SvB134/94. According to Hartsinck, 285, there were some twenty houses in New Amsterdam.

9. DH 5/3/1763, 5/5/1763; Heuer to Crommelin, 4/24/1763, SvB 134/76, and 5/13/1763, SvB 134/81; Crommelin to Heuer, 5/12/1763, Fagel 1824.

10. DH 5/3/1763, 5/5/1763; NHP 5/4/1763, SvB 134/94. The two ships were *De Zeven Provintien* (Captain Jacob Hendriks), with ten four-pound cannon and twelve swivel guns, and *St. Eustatius* (Captain Dabbadij). NHP 5/6/1763, SvB 134/94; Advice Rijssel en Texier 5/8/1763, SvB/227 (quotes).

11. Plakaatboek (Berbice), 5/8/1763; DH 5/8/1763. Peter Way, "The Cutting Edge of Culture: British Soldiers Encounter Native Americans in the French and Indian War," in *Empire and Others: British Encounters with Indigenous Peoples, 1600–1850*, ed. Martin Daunton and Rick Halpern, 133–34 (London: University College of London Press, 1999); John Grenier, *The First Way of War: American War Making on the Frontier, 1607–1814* (Cambridge: Cambridge University Press, 2005), esp. 39, 129, 141, 144. Grenier shows how, starting in the second half of the seventeenth century, inducing colonists to enlist in the Rangers depended on providing bounties for scalp hunting. Margaret Haig Roosevelt Sewall Ball, "Grim Commerce: Scalps, Bounties, and the Transformation of Trophy-Taking in the Early American Northeast, 1450–1780" (PhD diss., University of Colorado at Boulder,

2013), 69, 140–61. Ball argues (76–78) that the Dutch were the first in North America to offer prize money to Indians and colonists, starting the practice in New Netherland, later New York, in 1641.

12. Lichtveld, 84–85; Also, Hoogenheim to rebels, 5/4/1763, SvB 134/55. DH 5/9/1763.

13. Lichtveld, 83–84. Also, rebels to Hoogenheim [n.d. but 5/9/1763], SvB 134/54. Lichtveld and Voorhoeve misdate this note. They place it before Van Hoogenheim's May 4 letter, when it was in fact a response to it, as the summary of the letter in the minutes and Van Hoogenheim's journal indicate. Christiaan was kept by the rebels until his escape in August, DH 8/12/1763.

14. DH 5/9/1763; NHP 5/9/1763, SvB 134/94.

15. Lichtveld, 86–87; Van Hoogenheim to rebels, 5/10/1763, SvS 134/55.

16. DH 5/29/1763.

17. Heuer to Crommelin, 5/13/1763, SvB 134/81; Heuer to Hoogenheim, 5/17/1763, SvB 135/15, and Heuer to Directors Suriname, 5/17/1763, SvS 319. Gravesande to Governor of St. Eustatius, 5/9/1763, CO 116/33; NHP 5/11/1763, SvB 134/94.

18. DH 5/12/1763, 5/29/1763 (quote); Reijnet to Crommelin, 6/28/1763, SvS 319. One man claimed that Coffij ordered everyone to Dageraad "on pain of death"; No. 129 Isaac Smits neger van de colonie, 5/10/1764.

19. The Dutch had three ships, the two barks from St. Eustatius (see note 283) and *Standvastigheid*. Hartsinck, 416; DH 5/13/1763. No. 227 Quassie van Hardenbroek and No. 74 Fortuin van Maria Agnes, 3/8/1764.

20. Hoogenheim to Directors, 5/29/1653, SvB 134/50; DH 5/13/1763 (quote).

21. DH 5/13/1763; NHP 5/14/1763, SvB 135/95; Hoogenheim to Directors, 5/29/1763, SvB 134/50; Hartsinck, 417; Netscher, 215.

22. DH 5/13/1763 (quotes); Hoogenheim and council to States General, 5/20/1764, SvB 227; Gravesande to Directors WIC, 6/20/1763, CO 116/33; Bercheijck to Directors WIC, 6/20/1763, CO 116/33.

23. DH 5/13/1763 (quote); Plakaatboek (Berbice), "Vergoeding by verminking in de strijd," 5/14/1763 (quotes); Hartsinck, 413–14; NHP 5/14/1763, SvB 134/94. Netscher, 214, notes that these premiums caused great anger among the directors and shareholders, who claimed that premiums were appropriate only in foreign countries, but that in Berbice any booty was merely property that should be returned to the directors, shareholders, or planters. Netscher claims, without attribution, that these premiums were later disallowed. See also Hoogenheim to Directors, 10/15/1764, SvB 136/3.

24. DH 5/24/1763 (quote), 5/25/1763, 5/26/1763, 5/27/1763, 5/28/1763, 6/2/1763, 6/21/1763, and Journal Rijssel and Texier, 5/13/1763, SvS 319.

25. Journal Rijssel and Texier, 5/13/1763, SvS 319; DH 5/11/1763, 5/24/1763, 6/1/1763, 6/10/1763, 6/6/1763, 6/21/1763, 8/22/1763, 9/28/1763, 10/15/1763, and 10/16/1763; NHP 7/8/1763, SvB 134/129. Cf. Peter Way, "Rebellion of the Regulars: Working Soldiers and the Mutiny of 1763–1764," *William and Mary Quarterly* 57, 4 (2000): 761–92.

26. NHP 6/20/1763, SvB 134/127.

27. DH 5/2/1763, 6/2/1763, 6/8/1763, 6/25/1763 (quote), 6/28/1763, 7/2/1763 (quote). Gravesande to WIC, 5/28/1763, CO 116/33, quoting Hoogenheim (quote); Hoogenheim to Directors, 6/14/1763, SvB 134/97.

28. DH 5/22/1763.

29. DH 5/25/1763 (quote), 5/26/1763, 5/29/1763, 6/17/1763, 6/29/1763, 10/31/1763; Hoogenheim to Gravesande, 7/12/1763, SvB 227. One of Broer's assailants, Fortuin van Eenzaamheid, was later executed for his murder; see No. 18 Isaac van Jan Broer, 3/5/1764; No. 84 Frans van Eenzaamheid, 3/10/1764; No. 85 Fortuin van Eenzaamheid, 3/10/1764; and Sentences, 3/16/1763, SvB 135/124.

30. DH 5/13/1763; Hoogenheim to Directors, 5/29/1763, SvB 134/50 (quote); Hartsinck, 415–17; Netscher, 214–16; if we assume a high limit of five thousand enslaved people in the colony, at most two thousand would have been men, and this number would have included the infirm and the old, several hundred men who belonged to the Company, as well as many enslaved people living on the Canje River, and all those who were hiding in the woods. See also Netscher, 215–16.

31. DH 6/11/1763, 6/19/1763, 6/29/1763.

32. John Thornton, *Africa and Africans in the Making of the Atlantic World, 1400–1800* (Cambridge: Cambridge University Press, 1998), 329–33. Cf. "Inwerken van nieuwe slaven," 12/17/1740, Plakaatboek (Berbice). In the Haitian Revolution, some thirty years after the rebellion in Berbice, Africans and Creoles similarly were at odds. John K. Thornton, " 'I Am the Subject of the King of Congo': African Political Ideology and the Haitian Revolution," *Journal of World History* 4, 3 (1993): 199–201; Michel-Rolph Trouillot, *Silencing the Past: Power and the Production of History* (Boston: Beacon, 1995), 43; David Geggus, *Haitian Revolutionary Studies* (Indianapolis: Indiana University Press, 2002), chap. 2.

33. DH 6/19/1763, 6/29/1763 (quote); Rijssel to Reijnet, 8/7/1763, Fagel 1824; Gravesande to WIC, 7/18/1763, in Bercheijck Journal, CO 116/33.

34. Wim Hoogbergen, "De binnenlandse oorlogen in Suriname in de

achttiende eeuw," in *Geweld in de West: Een militaire Geschiedenis van de Nederlandse Atlantische Wereld, 1600–1800*, ed. Victor Enthoven, Henk den Heijer, and Han Jordaan, 156–57 (Leiden: Brill, 2013). Frank Dragtenstein, *Alles voor de Vrede: De brieven van Boston Brand tussen 1757 en 1763* (Amsterdam/ The Hague: Ninsee/Amrit, 2009), 51, suggests rebels stayed in Tempati for only six weeks.

35. Crommelin to Hoogenheim, 7/23/1763, SvS 319. See also Hartsinck, 420.

8: Rebellious Soldiers

1. M. J. Lohnstein, "De Werving voor de militie in Suriname in de 18e eeuw," *OSO: Een halfjaarlijkse uitgave van de Stichting Instituut ter Bevordering van de Surinamistiek te Nijmegen* (1987): 67–84; Peter Way, "Rebellion of the Regulars: Working Soldiers and the Mutiny of 1763–1764," *William and Mary Quarterly* 57 (October 2000): 761–92. The Berbice soldiers' mutiny is briefly mentioned in Edward Bancroft, *The History of Charles Wentworth*, 3 vols. (London: T. Becket and P. A. De Hondt, 1770), 2:255–62.

2. Information from Captain Baron von Canitz, Post Ephraim, 8/12/1763, SvS 324 (quote); "Copie, De Blanke Rebellen aan Crommelin," n.d., SvS 319. A slightly edited version may be found in SvS 324; Information from . . . two deserters from the Correntine, 12/15/1763, SvB 135/42; Report Kaeks, Paramaribo, 7/28/1763, SvS 319; Information from Lieutenant Marchal, 8/13/1763, SvS 324. The court later accepted the soldiers' view of the officers' behavior; see Minutes court-martial Paramaribo, 7/19/1764, SvS 324; DH 8/21/1763.

3. Reijnet to Crommelin, 6/28/1763, SvS 319.

4. "Informatie ten Overstaen van den WelEdele Heer Majoor van Ewijk over den Heer Lieutenant Marchal," 8/13/1763, SvS 324 (quote); "Copie, De Blanke Rebellen aan Crommelin," n.d., SvS 319.

5. Reijnet to Crommelin, 6/28/1763, SvS 319; Journal Von Canitz, June 13–19, 1763, esp. entries 6/17/1763 (quote) and 6/18/1763, SvS 319.

6 "Informatie ten Overstaen van den WelEdele Heer Majoor van Ewijk over den Heer Lieutenant Marchal," 8/13/1763, SvS 324.

7. Journal Von Canitz; Report Kaeks,Paramaribo, 7/28/1763, SvS 319; Examination Mangmeister, 4/9/1764 (quote) and 4/10/1764, SvS 324; "Informatie ten Overstaen van den WelEdele Heer Majoor van Ewijk over den Heer Lieutenant Marchal," 8/13/1763, SvS 324; "Nadere Informatie Corporael Weicks," 8/20/1763, SvS 324.

8. The mutineers also rehearsed their grievances in a letter to Governor Crommelin; see note 312 above.

9. Information or "scherper Examen" Dijmens, 7/18/1764 and 7/19/1764, SvS 324.

10. "Informatie ten Overstaen van den WelEdele Heer Majoor van Ewijk over den Heer Lieutenant Marchal," 8/13/1763, SvS 324. For soldiers protesting, see Jeannette Kamp, "Between Agency and Force: The Dynamics of Desertion in a Military Labour Market, Frankfurt am Main 1650–1800," in *Desertion in the Early Modern World*, ed. Matthias van Rossum and Jeannette Kamp (London: Bloomsbury, 2016), 60. Mangmeister was born in Augsburg, in Bavaria.

11. "Informatie ten Overstaen van den WelEdele Heer Majoor van Ewijk over den Heer Lieutenant Marchal," 8/13/1763; Information Captain Baron von Canitz, Post Ephraim, 8/12/1763 (quote); Report Kaeks, "intrims militaire Fiscaal," Paramaribo, 7/28/1763; Information Steven Andries "vrije mulat," 4/5/1764; Confrontation Mangmeister with Steven Andries, 5/5/1763, all in SvB 324. Steven Andries managed to escape the mutineers and reunited with the Suriname officers.

12. In 1746, nine soldiers had deserted their post on the Berbice River and taken off for the Orinoco River, where they allegedly mustered on a ship from Trinidad engaged in disrupting Dutch trade in Essequibo. Gravesande to WIC, 12/7/1746, SGD I: 225. It seems likely that what the Dutch called *de breede water* is Ikuruwa Lake at 5°33'0" N 57°27'0" W.

13. Examination Fiderer, 7/4/1764, SvS 324.

14. Report Kaeks, Paramaribo, 7/28/1763, SvS 319. Examination Renaud, 4/25/1764. See also Examination Mangmeister, 4/9/1764, SvS 324; "Informatien gehouden 12e August 1763 over de Soldaten Pieter Bormans, van Majoor Reijnet Compagnie, Frederik Claasen van de Comp. van den Capitein Texier, Henrik Charton van de Compagnie van de Lt. Collonel Meijer, Albert Jansen, van de Comp. van de Majoor Ewijk," 8/12/1763, SvB 320. For a complete list of all the men involved in the mutiny, see "Lijste der manschappen van 't Detachement onder den Majoor Rijnet in rio Correntijn dewelke op den 3 Julij 1763 hebben gerebelleert en sijn gedeserteert," SvS 319. I have used this list to determine that the sergeant among the mutineers was called Adam Niesse, though most of his fellow mutineers refer to him as "de Niesse."

15. For the killing of natives, see Reijnet to Crommelin, 7/8/1763, SvS 319, and Crommelin to Directors Suriname, 7/27/1763, SvS 319. Curiously, neither the killing of Indians nor the abduction of the women was brought up in any of the examinations of captured mutineers. Renaud relates spending the night in the Indian village but, perhaps not surprisingly, does not mention murdering anyone or abducting any women. Examination

Renaud, 4/25/1764 and 4/26/1764, SvS 324. For the fact that some men got drunk, see "Confrontatie en Informatie Mattheus Dijmens, Jan Renaudt, Jacques Montagnon, Johan Mangmeister, en Michiel Fredrik Schott," 5/16/1764, SvS 324. Not all clerks spelled names in the same way.

16. "Informatie of Scherper Examen van Matthias Dijmens," 7/18/1764 and 7/19/1764, SvS 324; Sentence Mangmeister, 7/20/1764, SvS 324.

17. Reijnet to Crommelin, 7/8/1763, SvS 319; Journal Van Ewijk, 8/5/1767 to 8/17/1764, SvS 320.

18. Examination Fiderer, 7/4/1764; Examination Mangmeister, 4/9/1764; Information Sergeant T. Keller, 7/2/1764, all in SvS 324.

19. On the running away of one "*bok*" and the killing of the other, see Examination Mangmeister, 4/9/1764 and 4/10/1764, SvS 324.

20. The path ran from the Corentyne River to the Berbice. Gerrit Bos, "Some Recoveries in Guiana Indian Ethnohistory" (PhD diss., Free University, Amsterdam, 1998), 62–63.

21. Examination Mangmeister, 4/9/1764 and 4/10/1764, 1764, SvS 324; J. Reijnet to Crommelin, 8/2/1763, SvS 319.

22. Examination Mangmeister, 4/9/1764 and 4/10/1764, SvS 324; Examination Renaud, 4/25/1764 and 4/26/1764, SvS 324. The commander may have been Adou van Prosperiteit; see No. 466 Fortuin van Helvetia, 6/14/1764.

23. Sentence Mangmeister, 7/20/1764, SvS 324 (quote). Former slaves living on Stevensburg watched the execution; see No. 59 Lonkje van Petite Bretagne, 3/20/1764.

24. Examination Renaud, 4/25/1764 and 4/26/1764 (quotes), SvS 324; Examination Mangmeister, 4/10/1763, SvS 324; No. 6 Adou (or Boas) van Plantation Prosperiteit & Zion, 3/3/1764, SvB 135. Adoe claimed he was sent by Coffij to bring the mutineers from Stevensburg plantation to Fort Nassau.

25. "De Heeren Capiteins der Zurinaamse militie aan 't gemuitineerde detachement van de Corentijn, dat zig bij de rebelle neegers heeft toevoegt," 7/30/1763, SvB 135.

26 Rijssel to Reinet, 8/7/1763, Fagel 1824.

27. Andries ended up in Suriname, as Governor Crommelin reported that he had in his custody a "new boy Andries," who claimed "not to know his master or plantation," but who, or so Crommelin had been informed, had been given by Coffij as a *voetebooij* (servant) to Mangmeister. Crommelin to Hoogenheim, 1/14/1764, SvS 321.

28. Examination Renaud, 4/25/1764 and 4/26/1764; Examination Mangmeister, 4/10/1763; Examination Schuijlen, 7/3/1764; Examination Fiderer, 7/4/1764; Examination Montagnon, 4/5/1764, all in SvB 324.

29. Crommelin to Hoogenheim, 1/14/1764, SvS 321; Examinations Mangmeister, 4/9/1764 and and 4/10/1764, and Examination Renaud, 4/25/1764 and 4/26/1764; Examination Schuijlen, 7/3/1764; Examination Fiderer, 7/4/1764, all in SvB 324.

30. DH 7/8/1763; see also Hoogenheim to Gravesande, 7/12/1763, SvB 227.

31. St. Domingue rebels were eager to be trained in European warfare; see John K. Thornton, " 'I Am the Subject of the King of Congo': African Political Ideology and the Haitian Revolution," *Journal of World History* 4, 3 (1993): 204; Hoogenheim to Directors, 12/6/1763, SvB 134/189.

32. DH 7/14/1763 and Gravesande to Hoogenheim, 6/6/1763, SvB 135.

33. Hoogenheim to Gravesande, 7/12/1763, Bijlage in Bercheijk Journal, CO 116/33.

34. DH 7/27/1763, 8/31/1763. See also Reflections Captains Rijssel and Texier, 8/3/1763, SvB 135/29; Crommelin to directors Suriname, 7/30/1763, SvS 319, referred to French soldiers as "members of [Louis] Mandarin's smugglers band" and "Fischer's highway robbers." For more information on eighteenth-century French smugglers and their call for social change, see Michael Kwass, *Contraband: Louis Mandarin and the Making of a Global Underground* (Cambridge, MA: Harvard University Press, 2014).

35. NHP 7/8/1763, SvB 134/114.

36. DH 9/19/1763. The men were Jean Pierre, of the Berbice militia, and I. Fransisco of Suriname. Jean Pierre would be killed by Dutch forces at Savonette in late December 1763. See Neil Lancelot Whitehead, "Carib Ethnic Soldiering in Venezuela, the Guianas, and the Antilles, 1492–1820," *Ethnohistory* 37, 4 (Fall 1990): 380n10, about native reluctance to attack white men.

37. DH 9/27/1763 (quote), 9/19/1763, 10/2/1763; NHP 9/29/1763, SvB 134/126.

38. DH 6/21/1763, 8/22/1763 (quotes). Besides supplies and twelve soldiers, the Dutch ship *Hendrik* (Captain H. M. Rolwagen) brought five new employees for private planters, and for the governor two surgeons and a new fiscal, Laurens van Fick, who died a few months later, on November 28, 1763; see "Lijste van Overleedene," 12/17/1763, SvB 134/186. The *Demerarij Welvaren* (Captain Salvolani) from St. Eustatius carried forty soldiers. By mid-August, Van Hoogenheim complained that he had not yet received any of the victuals on board. DH 8/11/1763.

39. DH 9/28/1763 (quotes); NHP 9/29/1763, SvB 134/126; Reflexien Rijssel en Texier, 8/3/1763, SvB 135/124.

40. DH 10/14/1763, 10/15/1763 (quote).

41. Gouverneur en Raad to Directors, 9/29/1763, SvB 134/126 (quote); DH 9/27/1763. For other instances of conflict, see DH 7/27/1763, 9/19/1763, 9/27/1763, and 11/11/1763.

9: Palace Revolution

1. DH 7/27/1763.

2. Lichtveld, 87–90; see also Coffij to Hoogenheim, 7/27/1763, SvB 135/25.

3. Coffij may have been inspired by a provision of the 1760 Suriname treaty with the Ndyuka that specified that those Maroons were allowed to bring their products to coastal markets. Coffij inverted the power dynamic by making this concession to the Dutch. See H. U. E. Thoden van Velzen and Wim Hoogbergen, *Een Zwarte Vrijstaat in Suriname: De Okaanse samenleving in the achttiende eeuw* (Leiden: KITLV Uitgeverij, 2011),193.

4. DH 7/24/1763, 7/26/1764.

5. DH 8/9/1763, 8/12/1763 (quote); Rijssel to Reynet, 8/7/1763, Fagel 1824.

6. Heuer to Crommelin, 8/17/1763, SvS 320; DH 7/24/1763, 8/19/1763.

7. No. 132 Quassie van de Savonette, 3/22/1764; No. 232 Makongo van Lelienburg 4/14/1764; Confrontatie Damon van Lelienburg met Fredrik van West Souburg, 4/19/1764; No. 211 Andries van Perrotet [Boschlust], 4/12/1764; DH 7/27/1763, 7/29/1763, 8/12/1763, 9/25/1763. Hoogenheim to Heuer, 8/8/1763, in Extract uit de Resolutien van de Heeren Staaten van Holland en Westvriesland . . . 6 Januarij 1764, SvB 227; Bercheijck Journal, 8/9/1763, 8/17/1763, CO 116/33; Gravesande to WIC, 9/27/1763, SGD II:438.

8. Lichtveld, 87, suggests that Georgina George wrote the letters in this round of negotiations. This is wrong; see DH 7/27/1763; Examination Renaud, 4/24/1764 and 4/25/1764, SvS 324.

9. Hoogenheim to Gravesande, 7/12/1763, SvB 227; DH 7/27/1763 (quote), 7/30/1763. Hartsinck, 511, notes Cupido's capture in 1764.

10. DH 7/27/1763. Indian spies had told Van Hoogenheim on July 23 that they had seen some fifty rebels, "all armed with snaphaunces and sabels or hatchets," board canoes at plantation Vigilantie and head upriver, DH 7/23/1763.

11. Rijssel to Major Reijnet, 8/7/1763, in Extract uit de Resolutien van de Heeren Staaten van Holland en Westvriesland . . . 6 Januarij 1764, SvB 227 (quote); NHP 8/3/1763, SvB 134/129; Hartsinck, 431; DH 8/1/1763 (quote); Report Hattinga, Rijssel and Texier, 7/10/1763, SvB 134/124; DH 7/24/1763.

12. DH 7/15/1763, 7/24/1763, 7/22/1763 (quote).

13. Reflexions Rijssel en Texier, 8/3/1763, SvB 135/29; DH 7/31/1763, 8/4/1763; Rijssel to Reijnet, 8/7/1763 (quote); and Hoogenheim to Heuer, 8/8/1763 (quote), both in Extract uit de Resolutien van de Heeren Staaten van Holland en Westvriesland . . . 6 Januarij 1764, SvB 227.

14. DH 7/27/2014 (quote); "Memorie" Ewijk, Rijssel, Texier, 10/3/1763,

SvB 135/38; Notulen Hove, 7/29/1763, SvB 134/129; DH 7/29/1763 (quote), 7/30/1763.

15. Lichtveld, 91–92 (quotes); see also Hoogenheim to Coffij, 7/30/1763, SvB 135/26.

16. DH 8/2/1763, 8/3/1763; NHP 8/3/1763 (quote).

17. The note rendered these plantations as "Saffanet, Marquaij Ossaburg Barbon," which may be further proof that it was written by a Suriname mutineer, who would not have been familiar with the names of these Company plantations well known to every Berbician. See also Governor and council to Suriname, 8/24/1763, SvB 134/125. The letter may be found in Lichtveld, 92–93 and in SvB 135/28.

18. For similar accusations by Maroons in Suriname, see Frank Dragtenstein, *Alles voor de vrede: De brieven van Boston Band tussen 1757 en 1763* (Amsterdam/The Hague: Ninsee/Amrit, 2009), 33–34, and Hartsinck, 793–94.

19. Johnhenry Gonzales, *Maroon Nation: A History of Revolutionary Haiti* (New Haven, CT: Yale University Press, 2019). Edward Long, *The History of Jamaica, Or, General Survey of the Antient and Modern State of That Island . . .* (London: T. Lowndes, 1774), 2:460, suggests something similar for the Jamaica rebels.

20. The letter read: "wat ons Christen aan belangt weeten wij weel, dat God is aan allen orde en wij verblijve bij haare volk bis aan dat eend." This ambivalent phrasing may be translated as "we know that God is the source of all order and we stay with those people till the end." Or, conceivably, "we know that God rules over all and we stay with those people till the end." Or, and this reading yields a different meaning: "as far as we Christians are concerned, we know very well that God is the source of all order and we remain a part of his people [i.e., Christians] till the end."

21. Lichtveld, 93–94. See also Coffij to Hoogenheim, 8/2/1763, NHP 8/3/1763, SvB 134/129, also in SvB 135/28. DH 8/2/1763.

22. NHP 8/3/1763, SvB 134.

23. Mutineer Mangmeister suggested that Niesse had not shared the news of the letter from the Suriname officers with Governor Coffij. Frenchman Renaud reportedly told Coffij about it, and Coffij was very angry. It is possible that Coffij forced Niesse to add this note to his letter. Closer (*nader*) Information Renaud, Mangmeister and Tomas Keller, SvS 324.

24. "De Heeren Capitains der Zurinaamse militie aan 't gemutineerde detachement van de Corentijn, dat zig bij de rebelle neegers heeft toevoegt, Ind. den 30. Julij 1763," SvB 135. See also "Vertaling van den hoog duijtsche

brief aan de gerebelleerde Surinaamse Soldaten, Dageraat, den dertigsten July 1763," SvB 324. Mutineer Renaud claimed that Niesse had kept this letter a secret from the other mutineers. Examination Renaud 4/25/1764 and 4/26/1764, SvS 324. There is also some indication that one of the mutineers, perhaps Renaud, told Coffij about the letter from the Suriname officers, which may have gotten Niesse in trouble. "Nadere Informatien genomen van Renaud, Mangmeister en Keller," 7/2/1764, and Examination Fiderer, 7/4/1764, SvS 324.

25. DH 8/3/1763.

26. Lichtveld, 94; See also Hoogenheim to Coffij, 8/3/1763, SvB 134/120 and 135/30; NHP 8/8/1763, SvB 134/129.

27 Lichtveld, 95–96; see also Coffij to Hoogenheim, 8/7/1763, SvB 134/129 and 135/32.

28. For the Suriname case, see "Journaal van Abercrombie en Zobre" (1759) in *Opstand in Tempati, 1757–1760*, Bronnen voor de studie van Afro-Surinaaamse samenlevingen, pt. 12, ed. Harry van den Bouwhuijsen et al., 112 (quote), 118–19 (Utrecht: Instituut voor Culturele Antropologie, 1988); 121–22, provides a list of what the Dutch sent, including, as requested by the Maroons, "six dolls, nicely dressed in women's and men's clothing, big and strong," 11/3/1759.

29. Lichtveld, 96. For Tempati rebels, see Dragtenstein, *Alles voor de vrede*, 53.

30. Lichtveld, 96–97; see also Hoogenheim to Coffij, 8/9/1763, SvB 134/33 and 135/33.

31. Kenneth Bilby, "Swearing by the Past, Swearing to the Future: Sacred Oaths, Alliances, and Treaties Among the Guianese and Jamaican Maroons," *Ethnohistory* 44, 4 (Autumn 1997): 655–89; and Edmond Kwam Kouassi, "Negotiation, Mediation and Other Non-Juridical Ways of Managing Conflicts in Pre-Colonial West African Societies," *International Negotiation* 13 (2008): 233–46.

32. Cf. Stedman, 70–71.

33. For similar divisions about peace among Maroons, see Herbert S. Klein and Francisco Vidal Luna, *Slavery in Brazil* (Cambridge: Cambridge University Press, 2010), 196, and Richard Price, *Alabi's World* (Baltimore: Johns Hopkins University Press, 1990), 33.

34. Examination of No. 181 Brutos of Accabiré van Stevensburg, 4/11/1763. Bouwhuijsen et al., *Opstand in Tempati*, 49. For similar concerns among the Samaaka, see Richard Price, *To Slay the Hydra: Dutch Colonial Perspectives on the Saramaka Wars* (Ann Arbor, MI: Karoma, 1983), 34.

35. DH 11/15/1763; No. 12 Kinkia van Altenklingen, 3/3/1764, and for

Atta as a leader, see No. 146 Damon van Lelienburg, 3/24/1763. Cf. No. 3 Paul van de Plantagie Essendam, 3/3/1764, No. 61 Cariba Slavin Altenklingen, 3/7/1764, and No. 38 Apia van de Colonie, 3/6/1763.

36. Examination of No. 181 Brutos of Accabiré van Stevensburg, 4/11/1763. For other mentions of conflict between Atta and Coffij, see No. 145 Jantje van Lelienburg, 3/24/1764.

37. In the judicial proceedings that followed the rebellion, many people self-identified as "Gangoe," spelled various ways by the Dutch scribes. For their identification as Ganga from the Windward Coast, west of the Gold Coast, see chap. 13 in this volume.

38. Closer ("nader") Examination Mars of Atta van Altenklingen, 4/18/1764. See also No. 256 Sicilia van Landskroon, 4/17/1763, who claimed that "many Amina [on her plantation] joined Coffij to fight the Kangoes."

39. DH 10/19/1763 (quote). For Accara's death, see No. 166 Prins van Castres, 4/10/1764, and No. 76 Quassie van Lelienburg, 5/8/1764.

40. Olufunke Adeboye, " 'Iku Ya J'esin': Politically Motivated Suicide, Social Honor, and Chieftaincy Politics in Early Colonial Idaban," *Canadian Journal of African Studies/Revue Canadienne des Études Africaines* 41, 2 (2007): 189–225; John Iliffe, *Honor in African History* (New York: Cambridge University Press, 2005); and Toby Green, *A Fistful of Shells: West Africa from the Rise of the Slave Trade to the Age of Revolution* (Chicago: University of Chicago Press, 2019), 269–70. For Coffij's suicide, see DH 10/19/1763; No. 181 Brutos of Accabiré van Stevensburg, 4/11/1764; No. 2 Den mulat Cobus van de Colony, 12/4/1764. Surgeon Mangmeister also claimed Coffij had killed himself; see DH 11/28/1763. It is of course possible that Coffij's suicide was forced or that it was murder disguised as suicide, but no records even hint at these possibilities.

41. No. 227 Quassie van Hardenbroek, 4/13/1764.

42. For a lucid discussion of human sacrifice, which was widespread in West Africa, see Robin Law, "Human Sacrifice in Pre-Colonial West Africa," *African Affairs* 84 (1985): 53–88. See also Oldendorp, 389.

43. No. 80 Amelia van Hollandia, 3/10/1764 (quote); No. 82 Aboi van Nieuw Caraques, 3/10/1763, who claimed Captain Accara helped Amelia; DH 11/23/1763.

44. Oldendorp, 389, 433–36. See also Law, "Human Sacrifice," 53–87, and Vincent Brown, *The Reaper's Garden: Death and Power in the World of Atlantic Slavery* (Boston: Harvard University Press, 2008), 39–40.

45. No. 38 Apia van de Colonie, 3/6/1764. When she was captured, Cariba claimed she had been a maid to Atta's wife. In her examination a few days later, she claimed she had been merely Atta's cook, just as she

had cooked for Coffij. See No. 61 Cariba Slavin Altenklingen, 3/7/1764. Other witnesses were adamant that she had been Atta's wife, Verbael V, 3/1/1764.

46. DH 10/19/1763; Examination Mangmeister, 4/10/1764, SvS 324.

47. DH 10/19/1763; Salve to Brunswick, 12/29/1763, Fagel 1824. According to Mangmeister, Georgina spoke at least one native language.

48. Oldendorp, 388–89 (quote), 435–36. See also Adeboye, "'Iku Ya J'esin,'" 199; Brown, *Reaper*, 39–41; David Brion Davis, *Inhuman Bondage: The Rise and Fall of Slavery in the New World* (New York: Oxford University Press, 2006), 352n28.

49. Texier to Directors Suriname, 11/14/1763, SvS 320.

50. There is confusion about whether he was chosen right away or someone else took over first. Atta himself related that "when Coffij and Accara were dead, they met in council and they made Boi van Beeren-steijn the top governor, and him [Atta], with others, lesser governors, but when Boi died, he became the upper governor." Closer Examination Mars off Atta van Altenklingen, 4/18/1764. When surgeon Mangmeister, one of the leaders of the mutineers, was captured in November of 1763, he corroborated Atta's claim that someone else had preceded him as governor. Mangmeister alleged that "the man chosen as governor in Coffee's place, is an old man, belonging to plantation Altenklingen, belonging to Mrs. Boulé." This man, Mangmeister continued, much "detests" their "godless behavior and cruelties" and lives quietly on his plantation. DH 11/23/1763. If Mangmeister was correct, this would mean that two men from Altenklingen were prominent after Coffij's death, Boi and Atta. It is also possible that Mangmeister mixed up Boi van Beerensteijn with a Boi van Altenklingen, a man who otherwise remains invisible in the records. When Bobé van Debora was questioned, the interrogators asked, "Did you not become governor after the death of Coffiji and Mars van Beerensteijn?" No. 413 Bobé van Debora, 6/6/1764. Mars was also known as Aboi. Paulus, the mixed-descent son of a postholder who had escaped the rebels in early October, may have had the most accurate account. He had been a captive among the insurgents, forced to serve Governor Coffij as his "boy." He related to the Dutch that after Coffij had killed himself, Accara had been enslaved. He described the man who had become the new governor as "a young neger from the plantation of Mrs. Boulé [i.e., Altenklingen]," which would suggest Atta. See DH 10/19/1763. Paulus did not mention anyone older or anyone named Boi. By mid-November, two recently escaped slaves informed Van Hoogenheim that the new governor was indeed Atta, "a new neeger from the plantation of Mrs. Boulez." DH 11/15/1783. See also

No. 227 Quassie van Hardenbroek, who mentioned that he first worked for Coffij and "when Atta became Governor he made him lieutenant."

51. Cf. the testimony of two of Coffij's councilors, No. 229 Piekenieni van Hollandia & Zeelandia, 4/14/1764, and No. 230 Nouakou van Hollandia & Zeelandia, 4/14/1764.

52. No. 227 Quassie van Hardenbroek, 4/13/1764 (quote). Examination Mangmeister, 4/10/1764, SvS 324 (quote); Information Mangmeister, 1/31/1764, SvS 324; No. 113 David van de Hooftplantage, Criool, 3/22/1764.

53. DH 8/12/1763 and 10/19/1763. The twenty-two also brought news of people still among the rebels to their family members on Dageraad; see "Informatien slaaf mulat Adriaen in zaake van zeekere vrijmulattin Claartje," 4/25/1764, SvB 135.

54. DH 11/13/1764 and 11/22/1763. Texier to Directors of Suriname, 11/14/1763, SvS 320.

55. DH 9/20/1763.

56. DH 10/6/1763 and 10/9/1763.

57. Gonzales, *Maroon Nation*, 61; Philippe Girard, *Toussaint Louverture: A Revolutionary Life* (New York: Basic Books, 2016), 132–33; Laurent DuBois, *Avengers of the New World: The Story of the Haitian Revolution* (Cambridge, MA: Harvard University Press, 2005), 107–8, 116, 152–53, 166.

10: The Turning of the Tide

1. Hoogenheim to Directors, 10/4/1763, SvB 134/122.

2. DH 9/27/1763.

3. DH 10/4/1763; Hoogenheim to Directors, 10/4/1763, SvB 134/122.

4. *Nouvelles extraordinaires de divers endroits* (Leiden), 5/24/1763; *Opregter Groninger Courant*, 5/27/1763; *Amsterdamse Courant*, 5/31/1763; *Oprechte Haerlemsche Courant*, 5/31/1763. Anne E. C. McCants, "Poor Consumers as Global Consumers: The Diffusion of Tea and Coffee Drinking in the Eighteenth Century," *Economic History Review* 61, 1 (2008): 179, 196; Wim Klooster and Gert Oostindie, *Realm Between Empires: The Second Dutch Atlantic, 1680–1815* (Ithaca, NY: Cornell University Press, 2018), 218–23.

5. Meeting directors, 5/30/1763, SvB 4; Resolutien Staten van Holland en Westvriesland, Google Books; Geert Mak, *Een Kleine Geschiedenis van Amsterdam* (Amsterdam/Antwerp: Uitgeverij Atlas, 2005), 181–83, 199; Cle Lesger, "Stagnatie en stabiliteit: De economie tussen 1730 en 1795," in *Geschiedenis van Amsterdam. Zelfbewuste stadstaat 1650–1813*, ed. Willem Frijhoff and Maarten Prak (Amsterdam: Sun, 2005), 219–65, 506–8. Pepijn Brandon and Ulbe Bosma, "De Betekenis van de Atlantische Slavernij voor de Nederlandse Economie in de Tweede Helft van de Achttiende Eeuw,"

Tijdschrift voor Sociale en Economische Geschiedenis 16, 2 (2019): 6, argue that as much as 40 percent of the economic growth of the province of Holland in the second half of the eighteenth century rested on Atlantic slavery.

6. Graafland to Raadspensionaris, 5/31/1763, Fagel 1824 (quotes); Netscher, 221–22. The directors were correct that trade with the colonies and distribution of processed colonial goods in the Dutch market and abroad were the lifeblood of the Amsterdam economy. Lesger, "Stagnatie," 265; Brandon and Bosma, "Betekenis."

7. Graafland to Raadspensionaris, 6/28/1763, Fagel 1824 (quotes); Petition Sociëteit van Berbice, 7/18/1763, in Extract Resolutien Staaten van Holland en Westvriesland, 7/20/1763, SvB 227 (quote). Brandon and Bosma state that imports from Suriname into the Dutch Republic amounted to more than 8 million guilders a year between 1765 and 1769, but Suriname had ten times as many slaves as Berbice. They calculate that around 1770, about 10 percent of the GDP (gross domestic product) of the province of Holland depended on Atlantic slavery, while the corresponding number for the entire Dutch Republic was about 5 percent; see Brandon and Bosma, "Betekenis," 31. Their calculations are likely too low. See also Klooster and Oostindie, *Realm Between Empires*, 88–97. On the importance of colonial commerce to Amsterdam, see Lesger, "Stagnatie." For an assessment of the slave trade, see Pepijn Brandon and Karwan Fatah-Black, " 'For the Reputation and Respectability of the State': Trade, the Imperial State, Unfree Labor, and Empire in the Dutch Atlantic," in *Building the Atlantic Empires: Unfree Labor and Imperial States in the Political Economy of Capitalism, ca. 1500–1914*, ed. John Donoghue and Evelyn Jennings, 84–108 (Leiden: Brill, 2015).

8. Graafland to Raadspensionaris, 6/3/1763, Fagel 1824 (quote). The other provinces, such as Utrecht, Gelderland, and Overijssel, less involved with the colonies, grumbled that unless they were better kept informed about the state of the colonies, they would not agree to bail them out again. They also wished that the Society of Berbice would repay the States General—a wish in which they were disappointed. The province of Zeeland stipulated that the troops would go fight in Essequibo and Demerara, if necessary, and that if Berbice was lost, and Essequibo was in danger, the soldiers would rescue Essequibo before reconquering Berbice. Extract Register der Resolution van de Hoog Mogende Heeren Staten General der Vereenigde Nederlanden, 7/7/1763, 7/20/1763, SvB 227; Meel to [?], 6/25/1763, and enclosures, Fagel 1824; Graafland to Raadspensionaris, 6/28/1763, Fagel 1824. On the West Indian lobby, see Klooster and Oostindie, *Realm*

Between Empires, 65–68, and Pepijn Brandon, *War, Capital and the Dutch State (1588–1795)* (Leiden: Brill, 2015), esp. 137–38.

9. Berbice directors [to States General], 8/17/1763, in Extract Register Resolutien van de . . . Staten Generaal der Vereenigde Nederlanden, 9/9/1763, SvB 227; *Middelburgse Courant,* 7/7/1763.

10. Haringman to [?], 1/3/1764, SVB 227, estimated potential fighting men between twelve hundred and fifteen hundred.

11. Brunswick to "Hoog Mogende Heeren," 7/11/1763, SvB 227; Bijlagen (appendices) A (Lijst der Officieren) and C (Lijst Onderofficieren en Gemeenen), SvB 227. H. L. Zwitser, *De Militie van den staat: Het leger van de Republiek der Verenigde Nederlanden* (Amsterdam: Van Soeren, 1991), 50–51. On De Salve, see H. L. Zwitzer, J. Hoffenaar, and C. W. van der Spek, *Het Staatse Leger. Deel IX, De Achttiende Eeuw, 1713–1795* (Amsterdam: De Bataafsche Leeuw, 2012), 803, 826; Han de Leune, *Pieter de la Rocque (1679–1760) en de capitulatie van Hulst in 1747* (Broek op Langedijk: GigaBoek, 2014), appendix 5, www.hanleune.nl/pieter-de-la-rocque-en-de-capitulatie-van -hulst-in-1747. On Douglas, SGD II:391–92, 394, 399, and www.douglashis tory.co.uk/history/robert_douglas.htm.

12. "Memorie weegens den Toestand van de Colonie de Berbice . . . Door den Lt. Admiraal [Cornelis] Schrijver aan den Hertog overgegeven, rec. 7/3/1763," CB 54-IA. See also Salomon de Monchy, *Korte Onderrigting en Raadgeving aan de Bevelhebberen van het Krijgsvolk naar de Kolonie de Berbice geschikt . . .* (1763). De Monchy was a Rotterdam doctor and scientist.

13. Memorie Schrijver; Report Brunswick 10/24/1763, and appendices F–N; here appendix H. Lijst der Provisie voor de Officieren; Lyste der Victualie ten dienste der Troupes; L. Lyst der Medicamenten en Instrumenten, all in Extract Resolutie Holland en Westvriesland, 9/12/1764, SvB 227.

14. Report Brunswick, Appendixes M. Notitieboekje der Goederen and N. Meede gesonden om te verstellen; Report C. C. Pusch, 1/19/1764, Verbael III (quotes) and 3/12/1764, Verbael V. For the poor quality of soldiers' shoes in Suriname, see Stedman, 135.

15. Report Brunswick, Appendix I. Lijst der Ordinaris Geweeren, Pistoolen, en andere Ysergoed tot reparatie meegegeeven; Appendix K. Lyste van Artillery, Amunitie, Geweeren, en Handgereedschappen &c.

16. Report Brunswick, Appendix K. Lyste van Artilerie, Amunitie, Geweeren, en Handgereedschappen &c.; Appendix G: Lyst van Camalie-Wand en andere noodwendigheeden. On "Nuremburg wares," see *Nederlandsch handelsmagazijn, of Algemeen zamenvattend woordenboek voor*

handel en nijverheid (Amsterdam: Gebroeders Diederichs, 1843), and Lesger, "Stagnatie," 258; Salve to Gravesande, 3/27/1764, Verbael V. See also Salve to Hoogenheim, 2/10/1764 and 2/11/1764, Verbael III.

17. Report Brunswick, 10/24/1763, SvB 227; Verbael I, 11/6/1763.

18. DH 10/11/1763, 10/28/1763.

19. DH 11/4/1763; Hoogenheim to Crommelin, 11/22/1763, Fagel 1824 (quote).

20. DH 11/6/1763, 11/7/1763; Hoogenheim to Crommelin, 11/22/1763.

21. DH 11/5/1763; 11/15/1763, Netscher, 231.

22. DH 11/12/1763.

23. No. 63 Mars van La Providence, 3/7/1763 (quote); No. 190 Paij van Blijendaal, 4/11/1764.

24. DH 11/13/1763.

25. DH 11/15/1763; Hoogenheim to Crommelin, 11/22/1763, Fagel 1824. Examinations of Canje people confirm this account; DH 11/14/1763 (quote); No. 68 Debora van Frederiksburg, 3/8/1764; DH 11/14/1763; Haringman to "Hoog Mogende Heren," 11/20/1763, Fagel 1824.

26. DH 11/16/1763.

27. DH 11/14/1763 (quote), 11/20/1763.

28. DH 11/19/1763; NHP 11/21/1763, SvB 134/165; Hoogenheim to Crommelin, 11/22/1763, Fagel 1824.

29. DH 11/22/1763.

30. DH 11/22/1763; Report Abrams to Hoogenheim, 11/22/1763, SvB 135/41; NHP 11/21/1763, 11/22/1763, SvB 134/165.

31. Continuation Examination Mangmeister, 4/10/1764, SvS 324.

32. Examination Mangmeister, 4/10/1764; Information Renaud, 2/6/1764; Examination Schuijlen, 7/3/1764; "Informatien gehouden tegen Renaud, Mangmeister and Fiderer," 7/4/1764, all in SvS 324; Hoogenheim to Crommelin, 11/22/1763, SvS 320 (quote).

33. DH 11/22/1763 (quote); "Informatien gehouden op de plantagie Amsterdam in Rio Demerarij den 15e Xber 1763 over twee Deserteurs uit de Correntijn die alhier opgebragt zijn," 12/15/1763, SvB 135/42 (quote). Rather than Congo, however, I identify Accabiré's "Gango" as Ganga (or Kanga) from the upper Guinea Coast, especially Sierra Leone and Liberia; see Marjoleine Kars, "Dodging Rebellion: Politics and Gender in the Berbice Slave Uprising of 1763," *American Historical Review* 121, 1 (February 2016), 49n30. In the eighteenth century, the Dutch purchased as many as ninety thousand people on the Windward Coast—a quarter of the total Dutch trade in African slaves in that century. Jelmer Vos, "The Slave Trade from the Windward Coast: The Case of the Dutch, 1740–1805," *African*

Economic History 38 (2010): 33–34; Klooster and Oostindie, *Realm Between Empires*, 84–85.

34. Accabiré's own testimony, at least as the clerk recorded it, is ambiguous: No. 181 Brutos of Accabiré van Stevensburg, 4/11/1764. But see No. 265 Paul of Gaudia van Stevensburg, 4/19/1764. Gaudia was a "brother" of Atta and a "big man," who testified that after Coffij tried to enslave him, he fought with Atta and Accabiré, though later he supported Atta on Essendam. See also No. 256 Sicilia van Landskroon, 4/17/1764, who testified that many Amina "joined Coffij to fight against the Ganga," and No. 116 Adam van Hollandia & Zeelandia, 5/9/1764; Information from two deserters from Correntijn, 12/15/1763, SvB 135/42.

35. No. 181 Brutos of Accabire van Stevensburg, 4/11/1764. For other claims that the Amina tried to enslave the Ganga, see No. 48 Antoni van Hoogstraten, 5/7/1764; No. 116 Adam van Hollandia & Zeelandia, 5/9/1764; No. 130 Acca van de Colonie, 5/10/1764; No. 115 Quamina van Doornboom, 5/9/1764; No. 222 Nero van de Prosperiteit, 4/12/1764; No. 227 Quassie van Hardenbroek, 4/13/1764.

36. No. 221 Simon van Rosenburg, 4/13/1764; No. 181 Brutos of Accabiré van Stevensburg, 4/11/1764 (quote); No. 97 Jan Bomba van Markeij, 3/15/1764; No. 275 Baron van de Vigilante, 4/25/1764; for timing of Essendam fight, No. 13 Mars van West Souburg, 9/13/1764; No. 76 Quassie van Lelienburg, 5/8/1764; DH 12/5/1763; Hartsinck, 465; Ineke Velzing, "De Berbice Slavenopstand, 1763" (MA thesis, University of Utrecht, 1979), 131.

37. Maroon regimes ranged from more to less egalitarian. See Alvin O. Thompson, *Flight to Freedom: African Runaways and Maroons in the Americas* (Jamaica: University of the West Indies Press, 2006): 211–23; Manolo Florentino and Márcia Amantino, "Runaways and Quilombolas in the Americas," in *The Cambridge World History of Slavery*, ed. David Eltis and Stanley Engerman, 731, 735–37 (Cambridge: Cambridge University Press, 2011).

38. Toby Green, *A Fistful of Shells: West Africa from the Rise of the Slave Trade to the Age of Revolution* (Chicago: University of Chicago Press, 2019), chaps. 6 and 7.

39. Hoogenheim to Crommelin, 11/22/1763, SvS 320; for the enslavement of other Africans and Creoles, see also Hoogenheim to Directors 12/7/1763, SvB 227.

40. DH 11/23/1763. It is doubtful that the Samaaka Maroons would have welcomed large numbers of strangers who would jeopardize food supplies and treaties with the Dutch.

41. Six men, five women, and three children of twelve were from the fort and two from Company plantation Goede Hoop, DH 12/6/1763 (quote);

Hoogenheim and council to Directors, 12/7/1763, SvB 134/161 (quote); Hoogenheim and council to States General, 12/17/1763, in Extract Resolutien Staten van Holland en Westvriesland, 9/9/1764, Faber 1824 (quote); "Informatien gehouden op de plantagie Amsterdam in Rio Demerarij den 15e X'ber 1763 over Twee Deserteurs uit de Correntijn die alhier opgebragt zijn," 12/15/1763, SvB 135/42.

42. DH 12/2/1763; No. 211 Andries van Boschlust, 4/12/1764.

43. No. 48 Asso van de Debora, 3/20/1764 (quote); DH 12/2/1763; No. 229 Acceba van de Debora, 5/11/1764; Inventory plantations Debora, Catharina, Manepad, Overbeek, 10/25/1760, CO 116/99, Kew. Scheepsjournaal *Zephyr*, 1/1/1764, AC 1161a (quote).

44. Gravesande to WIC, 12/21/1763, in SGD, 442–44.

11: The Battle for the Berbice

1. DH 11/28/1763, 12/7/1763, 12/17/1763.

2. Netscher, 231; SGD II:441–43; Gravesande to WIC, 12/19/1763, SGD I:239. See also Hoogenheim to Directors, 12/17/1763, SvB 134/190.

3. DH 12/19/1763, 12/22/1763, 12/25/1763; Haringman Journal, 12/19/1763, AC 2985; Hartsinck, 462–63. Netscher, 231.

4. Plakaatboek, 5/8/1763, reissued in December 1763; Hartsinck, 464; Hoogenheim and council to States General, 12/17/1764, Fagel 1824.

5. See, for instance, No. 114 Jan van de Hooftplantage, 3/22/1764; No. 8 Jappa van Geertrui, 5/5/1764; no. 281 Jan Broek van 't Fort 5/12/1764; No. 41 David van de Heer Schirmeister 3/20/1764; No. 278 Jillis van 't Fort, 5/12/1764.

6. Douglas to Bentinck, 1/26/1764, CB 54-IB; DH 9/20/1763; Haringman to "Hoog Mogende Heeren," 12/18/1763, Fagel 1824.

7. Thomas van Oostermeer, contra deselve, 3/12/1764 (quote); No. 22 Animba van West Souburg, 3/19/1764.

8. DH 12/18/1763–12/20/1764 (quotes); Closer examination Quassie of Alexander van Hardenbroek, 4/19/1764; Verbael II, 1/7/1764; Hoogenheim to Directors, 1/16/1764, SvB 135/43; Haringman Journal, 12/19/1763, AC 2985 (quote).

9. DH 12/25/1763; Robert W. Reid, "Weaponry: The Caltrop," History-Net, www.historynet.com/weaponry-the-caltrop.htm; No. 97 Jan Bomba van Markeij, 3/15/1763.

10. DH 12/19/1763, 12/21/1763 (quote), 12/22/1763 (quote).

11. No. 66 Hendrik van Lagendael, 3/7/1764, blamed Piramus van Engelenburg for the fire, as did several others; see "Confrontatie van de neger

Piramus van Engelenbug no. 8 in de Exam. met Capitan Bedje, Dongo en Sibi van de Peereboom," 12/8/1764; DH 12/23/1763.

12. DH 12/24/1763 (quote). The testimony of Peereboom slaves in 1764 neither contradicts nor corroborates such claims. Only eighteen people from Peereboom were examined by the Dutch. Two of them, both Amina, were executed as rebels. The other sixteen, at least ten of whom were Creoles, offered little in the way of detail, claiming they had seen nothing, as they had been in the woods when the rebels showed up; No. 77 Cupido van Hollandia, 3/8/1764; Aboi van Nieuwe Caraques nader geexamineert en geconfronteerd teegens den Bomba Jan van Markey, 3/15/1764; DH 12/27/1763 (quote). See also No. 98 Lucretia van Hardenbroek, 3/21/1764; Haringman Journal, 12/25/1763, AC 2985; DH 1/2/1764.

13. DH passim; Haringman Journal AC 2985; Scheepsjournaal *Zephyr*, AC 1161a.

14. DH 12/20/1763. In a postscript, Van Hoogenheim added: "the before mentioned Titus came into the country on a ship of Mr van Goetdem for the Van Peeres. That ship sank in this river." The slave voyages website lists a Goethem who was a slave captain in the 1690s, which would have made Titus rather old. Titus's voluntary return to the Dutch set a pattern. When people turned themselves in, either they were questioned or they volunteered information. Such intelligence sometimes made its way into Van Hoogenheim's journal and officers' reports. It is not clear to what extent the words used are those of the informants, as conversations were commonly summarized, rather than noted verbatim.

15. For Maria, see DH 12/27/1763. For Gratie, DH 12/28/1763 (quote).

16. DH 12/28/1763.

17. DH 12/25/1763.

18. DH 12/25/1763.

19. Hoogenheim to Directors, 1/16/1764, SvB 135/43; SGD II:441–43 (quotes). The *Gazette van Ghent*, 4/16/1764, claimed the Indians numbered two hundred to three hundred.

20. DH 12/29/1763 claims one hundred people were on Savonette; Hoogenheim, "Corte Memorie vervattende een waaragtige en beknopte beschrijvinge van het gepasseerde in de Berbice . . . ," 6/18/1766, CB 54-IA, 40, states that the soldiers killed one hundred and captured sixty, suggesting a larger initial number given that some people managed to flee; Confrontation Quipay van de Goede Hoop with Jan Broek and Christian and Pieter van de Colonie, 6/14/1764; No. 205 Diro van de Goede Hoop, 4/12/1764; No. 241 Lena van Sublieslust, 4/16/1764; No. 2 Frans van

Abbensets, 3/3/1764; Confrontation Damon van Lelienburg with Fredrik van West Souburg, 4/19/1764; No. 135 Sander van West Souburg, 3/22/1764; No. 132 Quassie van de Savonette, 3/22/1764. For iron, see No. 94 Jacouma van de Colonie, 3/15/1764; "Rapport ... weegens de bevindinge van de Edele Comp's Plantagien &c ... Maart 1764," SvB 135/64.

21. DH 12/29/1763; SGD II:441–43 (quote); Hoogenheim to Directors, 1/161764, SvB 135/43 (quote); No. 4 Dikkie van Blijendaal "Surinaamse Criool," 8/3/1764.

22. Gravesande supplied Akawaios and Caribs on their way to Berbice with guns because the Indians noted that poisonous arrows could not penetrate the walls of the "Christian houses" in which the rebels were living. Gravesande to Hoogenheim, 6/6/1763, SvB 135/18. European travelers were fascinated by the use of native poison. On native bows and arrows, see Edward Bancroft, *An Essay on the Natural History of Guiana ...* (London: T. Becket and P. A. De Hondt in the Strand, 1769), 281–96; George Pinckard, *Notes on the West Indies ...* (London: Longman, Hurst, Rees, and Orme, Paternoster-Row, 1806), II:405–8; Ernst Karl Rodschied, *Medizinische und Chirurgische Bemerkungen über ... Kolonie Rio Esseqebo* (Frankfurt: In der Jaegreschen Buchlandlung, 1796), discusses poisonous plants in the area.

23. DH 12/29/1763.

24. Hoogenheim to Directors, 1/16/1764, SvB 135/43; DH 12/24/1763, 12/27/1764 (quotes); SGD II:441–43, 451; Verbael II, 1/3/1764.

25. DH 12/29/1763. At the time, Van Hoogenheim claimed fifty to sixty dead and twenty-seven captured. In "Corte Memorie" (40) he claims one hundred dead and sixty captured. See also No. 4 Dikkie van Blijendaal Surinaamse Criool, 8/3/1764; No. 194 Job van de Heer Schirmeister, 4/11/1764; No. 51 Julij van Vigilantie, 3/6/1764; for the captives being women, see Scheepsjournaal *Zephyr*, 12/29/1763, AC 1161a.

26. Scheepsjournaal *Zephyr*, 12/31/1763, AC 1161a; DH 12/31/1763.

27. Scheepsjournaal *Zephyr*, 12/28/1763, 12/30/1763, AC 1161a; DH 12/28/1763–12/31/1763.

28. Scheepsjournaal *Zephyr*, 12/28/1763, 11/29/1763, 1/1/1764, AC 1161a; DH 12/27/1763–12/30/1763.

29. Atta claimed he and Bobé had rushed ahead and Lieutenant Quakoe van Nieuw Caraques had commanded; see "Nader geExamineert den Neger Mars of Atta van Altenklingen," 4/18/1764, along with No. 227 Quassie van Hardenbroek, 4/13/1764, and No. 65 Abraham van La Providence, 3/7/1764. Others claimed Bobé had commanded; see No. 140 Piramus van Elisabeth & Alexandria, 3/23/1764, and Confrontation Bobé van

de Debora and Piramus van Elisabeth & Alexandria with Coffij van de Wed. Moses van Doorn, 6/15/1764.

30. Scheepsjournaal *Zephyr*, 12/26/1763, AC 1161a. Hoogenheim to Directors, 1/16/1764, SvB 135/43; one of the scouts was Amerindian, and Van Hoogenheim identified the other as an enslaved man named Quassie. For poisonous arrows, see Haringman Journal, 12/26/1763, AC 2985.

31. Hartsinck, 477; No. 201 Jacob van de Goede Hoop, 4/12/1764, claimed rebel leader Mars van de Goede Hoop was shot in the chest and died of his wounds. Haringman Journal, 12/26/1763, AC 2985, mentions that the soldiers brought four hands; Scheepsjournaal *Zephyr*, 12/26/1763, AC 1161b, notes the weather and that the Dutch found five dead rebels and caught three alive; No. 61 Ariba van Altenklingen mentions Quakoe van Rousseau [plantation Cadeques] as leading this fight. Almost a year later Van Hoogenheim mentioned that an enslaved man named Accara was also wounded in the fight. The rebels captured him but he escaped several days later, returning to the Dutch. Hoogenheim to Directors, 11/6/1764, SvB 136/44.

32. DH 12/27/1764.

33. DH 12/28/1764.

34. DH 12/31/1763.

35. DH 12/30/1763; 12/27/1763. Quassie van Hardenbroek, 4/13/1764 (quote), and Closer Examination Quassie of Alexander van Hardenbroek, 4/19/1764. No. 82 Aboi van Nieuw Caraques, 3/10/1764, accused Quassie of their murder, as did No. 199 Michel van de Goede Hoop, 4/12/1764. It seems likely that Sergeant Niesse, who wrote some of Coffij's letters to the Dutch, was one of the two men.

36. One of the three died; the remaining two were questioned and eventually sent back to Suriname to be tried. Informatien gehouden op de plantage Amsterdam in Rio Demerarij, 12/15/1763, SvB 135/42; Information Matthias Fiderer, 7/4/1764, SvS 324; DH 12/24/1763, 12/29/1763.

37. DH 12/24/1763.

38. DH 1/1/1764, 1/2/1764; Scheepsjournaal *Zephyr*, 12/31/1763, 1161b. There is no further mention of Chocolat in the records.

39. DH 1/2/1764; Hoogenheim to Directors, 1/16/1764, SvB 135/43 (quote). Georgina likely knew quite a bit about the rebels. Cf. No. 6 Adou of Boas van Prosperiteit & Zion, 3/3/1764, who had served as lieutenant among the insurgents and who told the Dutch to check with Georgina ("who knows everything") to corroborate his claims.

40. Hoogenheim to Directors 1/16/1764, SvB 135/43 (quotes); DH 5/17/1764, 5/24/1764.

41. DH 1/2/1764 (quotes), 12/27/1763; Scheepsjournaal *Zephyr*, 1/2/1764, AC 1161a;

42. Scheepsjournaal *Zephyr*, 1/1/1764, 1/5/1764, and "rapport" 12/28/1763 to 1/8/1764, filed between entries for 1/8/1764 and 1/9/1764, AC 1161a; DH 1/2/1764, 1/17/1764, 1/24/1764, 2/27/1764; Hoogenheim to Directors, 1/16/1764, SvB 135/43. Verbael III, 1/31/1764 (quote).

43. No. 437 Masoeta van Schermeister, 6/7/1764, and No. 439 Lukemi van Schermeister, 6/7/1764; "De Kolonie de Berbice, voor weggeloopene Slaven, welke in Corentijn gevangen zijn, aan Albert Heuer Debet," 5/1/1764, SvB 56, Lt. B; DH 4/5/1764.

44. Hoogenheim to Directors, 1/16/1764, SvB 135/42; Hoogenheim to Salve, 1/2/1764, in Verbael II, 1/5/1764.

12: Wild Sang and Little Glory

1. 12/21/1763, 12/27/1763, Verbael II; Douglas to Bentinck, 1/26/1764, CB 54-IB.

2. Salve to Brunswick, 12/29/1763, Fagel 1824.

3. Missing, unfortunately, are the lists of people who were captured or received at each post, noting their names and plantations, and sometimes the crimes they were accused of. Post commanders were required to send in such lists weekly. Matched with what people claimed in their examinations, this information would have been illuminating. Cf. DH 3/20/1764.

4. Hoogenheim to Salve, 1/14/1764, Verbael III; Stedman, 192.

5. DH 1/10/1764, 1/14/1764. Hoogenheim to Salve, 1/14/1764, 1/16/1764, Verbael III.

6. Hoogenheim to Salve, 1/16/1764, 1/18/1764, Verbael III.

7. Douglas to Bentinck, 1/26/1764, CB 54-IB.

8. Salve to Hoogenheim, 1/13/1764, Verbael II; DH 1/16/1764 (quote); Hoogenheim to Salve, 1/14/1764, 1/16/1764, Verbael III; Douglas to Bentinck, 1/26/1764, CB 54-IB; DH 1/25/1764 (quote); Hoogenheim to Directors, 2/26/1764, SvB 135/54.

9. Stedman, 155 (quote); Verbael II, 1/9/1764; Hoogenheim to Directors, 1/16/1764, SvB 135/43. These posts were located south of Fort Nassau, starting with plantation Johanna on the Wironi Creek; plantation Hardenbroek on the Wikki Creek; plantation Savonette; plantation Stevensburg on the Canje River; and Fort St. Andries at the coast; Verbael II, 1/10/1764 (quote), 1/11/1764.

10. Brauw to Salve, 1/22/1764, Verbael III.

11. Scheepsjournaal *Zephyr*, 1/18/1764, AC 1161a; Report Cornelis de Vree, 1/22/1764, Verbael III; DH 1/18/1764; story of the expedition is based

on reports by De Vree, Sieborgh, De Brauw, Oijen, Blanc, and others in Verbael III.

12. Scheepsjournaal *Zephyr*, 1/18/1764, AC 1161a; the map, "Caart Figuratief," based largely on oral "information," places Goed Land en Goed Fortuin right next to Hardenbroek, which is clearly wrong; see Leupe Vel 1653. The map, "Kaarte van de Ge'octroyeerde Coloie de Berbice," Leupe Vel 1571 (Map 5 above), also drawn in 1764, appears to get it right, placing Debora closer to Hardenbroek and Goed Land en Goed Fortuin farther upriver.

13. Haringman to "Hoog Mogende Heeren," 2/9/1764, Fagel 1824.

14. Stedman, 191–93.

15. Report Vree, 1/22/17864 (quotes); Report Lieutenant Pichot, Scheepsjournaal *Zephyr*, 1/19/1764, AC 1161a. For another attempt to steal a soldier's gun that worked out less well, see ibid., 1/20/1764. That gun, or another, was later recovered from one of Atta's brothers, 3/3/1764, Verbael V.

16. Report Vree, 1/22/1764, Verbael IIII (quote); Douglas to Bentinck, 1/26/1764, CB 54-IB; Haringman to "Hoog Mogende Heeren," 2/9/1764, Fagel 1824; DH 1/23/1764 (quote). For claim that Atta was at this fight, No. 427 Andries van Landskroon. "Nader geExamineert den Neger Mars off Atta van Altenklingen," 4/18/1764 (quote). Cossaal van Oosterleek and Gou(s)sarie van Oosterleek are the same man.

17. Brauw to Salve, 1/23/1764, Verbael III (quote); DH 1/23/1764 (quote).

18. Relaas Blank, 1/22/1764, Verbael III (quote); Scheepsjournaal *Zephyr*, 1/21/1764, AC 1161a.

19. Scheepsjournaal *Zephyr*, 1/25/1764, AC 1161a; "Copie-Rapport Mesteeker van den 26 en 27 Janary 1764," enclosure with Haringman letter to the States General, 2/9/1764, Fagel 1824; Oijen to Haringman, 1/21/1764, Fagel 1824; Douglas to Bentinck, 1/26/1764, CB 54-IB; Brauw to Salve, 1/23/1764, Verbael III (quote); Hartsinck, 494.

20. "Rapport van het Commando gedaan door den Capt. Comm'r Hamel den 29. Jann. 1764," 2/4/1764, Verbael III; Oijen to Haringman, Scheepsjournaal *Zephyr*, 2/2/1764, AC 1161a (quote). Stedman, 404, describes baskets woven from palm leaves.

21. Oijen to Haringman, Scheepsjournaal *Zephyr*, 2/2/1764, AC 1161a; Report Hamel, 1/29/1764, Verbael III.

22. Oijen to Haringman, 2/2/1764, Scheepsjournaal *Zephyr*, AC 1161a. By the time the news reached Van Hoogenheim via Lieutenant Colonel Douglas, who himself had it secondhand, the number of huts had grown to two thousand, which is highly unlikely. DH 2/5/1764.

23. Tinde van Andel, Paul Maas, and James Dobreff, "Ethnobotanical

Notes from Daniel Rolander's *Diarium Scurinamicum* (1754–1756): Are These Plants Still Used in Suriname Today?" *Taxon* 61, 4 (2012): 855, 857. For heavy rains, see Hoogenheim to Directors, 2/26/1764, SvB 135/54.

24. Haringman to "Hoog Mogende Heeren," 2/9/1764, in Fagel 1824 (quote); Harry van Bouwhuijsen et al., ed., *Opstand in Tempati, 1757–1760*. Bronnen voor de Studie van Afro-Surinaamse samenlevingen, pt. 12 (Utrecht: Instituut voor Culturele Anthropologie, 1988), 16.

25. Stedman, xxvi; John K. Thornton, "African Soldiers in the Haitian Revolution," *Journal of Caribbean History* 25 (1993): 68; and John K. Thornton, " 'I Am the Subject of the King of Congo': African Political Ideology and the Haitian Revolution," *Journal of World History* 4, 3 (1993): 201–2.

26. Haringman to "Hoog Mogende Heeren," 2/9/1764, in Fagel 1824 (quote); Oijen to Haringman, 1/21/1764, Fagel 1824; DH 2/5/1764 (quote); DH 2/8/1764 (quote); Hoogenheim to Salve, 2/8/1764, Verbael III (quote).

27. Salve to Bisdom, 1/31/1764, Verbael III (quote); Salve to Brauw, 1/30/1764, Verbael III (quote); Report van Brunswick to States General, 10/24/1764, SvB 227.

28. Verbael IV, 2/13/1764.

29. Scheepsjournaal *Zephyr*, 2/2/1764, AC 1161a (quote); Pusch to Salve, 1/30/1764, Verbael III; DH 2/5/1764 (quote); see also Scheepsjournaal *Zephyr*, 1/17/1764, AC 1161a.

30. See assessment in Oijen to Brauw, 1/24/1764, Verbael III.

31. DH 2/20/1764; Douglas to Salve, 2/19/1764, Verbael IV; Hoogenheim to Directors, 2/26/1764, SvB 135/54; 3/11/1764, Verbael V.

32. Douglas to Bentinck, 1/26/1764, CB 54-IB.

13: Outsourcing the War

1. DH 2/17/1764. Van Hoogenheim referred to Frederik both as *mulat neger* and *neger*. He was likely of mixed descent, probably native and African. See, for instance, DH 10/9/1763, 10/26/1763, 11/28/1763, 9/17/1764. Frederik shows up as an interpreter for Indians as early as the 1750s; see SvB 105/50. On eyewitnessing, see Julia Rudolph, *Common Law and Enlightenment in England, 1689–1750* (Woodbridge, UK: Boydell Press, 2013), chap. 3; Neil Safier, *Measuring the New World: Enlightenment Science and South America* (Chicago: University of Chicago Press, 2008).

2. Cf. Verbael IV, 2/13/1764, 2/14/1764; Salve to Brunswick, 2/26/1764, Verbael V; Report Brunswick to States General, 10/24/1764, SvB 227.

3. DH 2/16/1764 (quotes) and 2/17/1764; Verbael IV, 2/14/1764–2/16/1764

4. Verbael II, 1/10/174; Salve to Bisdom, 1/11/1764, Verbael II; DS to VH,

1/11/1764, Verbael II; Salve to Brunswick, 1/13/1764, CB 54-IB; Verbael III, 1/21/1764 and 1/30/1764.

5. Verbael III, 2/10/1764 and Verbael IV, 2/11/1764. DH 2/11/1764. The captains singled out slave auctioneer Abraham Wijs (whom the rebels had also pointed out) and mapmaker David Willem Hattinga as officials who had abused them; Salve to Hoogenheim, 2/11/1764, Verbael IV (quotes). See also Verbael IV, 2/14/1764.

6. Report Brunswick to States General, 10/24/1764, SvB 227; for turning in hands, see, for instance, Verbael III, 1/30/1764; Verbael V, 2/29/1764; DH 2/3/1764, 3/9/1764; Scheepsjournaal *Zephyr*, 1/31/1764, AC 1161a; Verbael III, 2/10/1764, 2/11/1764; Marchant to Crommelin, 3/11/1764, SvS 321 (quote). "De Colonie de Berbice, voor weggelopen Slaven . . . aen Albert Heuer debet, 5/1/1764," and "De Colonie de Berbice Voor Gedaene Attaquen op de Berbice Rebellende Neegers Aen de Indiaanen in Riv. Corentijn, Debit," 5/1/1764, in SvB 56, Lt. B en C; DH 5/4/1764; Essequibo's governor noted in early 1764 that it was "custom in his colony to pay as much for a runaway's head or hand as for a [live] slave." Neil L. Whitehead, *Lords of the Tiger Spirit: A History of the Caribs in Colonial Venezuela and Guyana, 1498–1820* (Dordrecht-Holland: Foris Publications, 1988), 164.

7. Salve to Brunswick, 1/13/1764, CB 54-IB (quote); Hoogenheim to Directors, 1/16/1764, SvB 135/43 (quote).

8. Hoogenheim to Directors 2/15/1764, SvB 135/48 (quotes). See also Hoogenheim to Salve, Verbael III, 2/8/1764; DH 2/14/1764.

9. Gravesande to WIC, 4/9/1763, SGD II:447 (quote). He estimated that close to 5,000 Carib men capable of bearing arms lived on the Mazaruni River; Verbael VI, 4/11/1764; DH 4/12/1764, 4/15/1764; Hoogenheim to Salve, 4/14/1764, Verbael VI; DH 4/12/1764 (quote), 4/15/1764.

10. DH 4/13/1764 (quote), 7/5/1764.

11. DH 2/20/1764 (quote); Hoogenheim to Directors, 1/16/1764, SvB 135/43; DH 2/15/1764; DH 1/4/1764; Scheepsjournaal *Zephyr*, 1/1/1764, AC 1161a; DH 2/23/1764; Hoogenheim to Directors, 2/15/1764, SvB 135/48; Hoogenheim to Directors, 2/26/1764, SvB 135/54. Salve to Gravesande 2/24/1764, Verbael IV; Douglas to Brunswick, 2/26/1764, CB 54-IB, mentions "above 1200 surrendered"; Verbael V, 3/1/1764; Hoogenheim to Directors, 3/29/1764, SvB 135/59; Report J. H. Buse 3/21/1764, SvB 135/64; Douglas to Brunswick, 4/4/1764, CB 54-IB.

12. DH 2/11/1764; Verbael IV, 2/16/1764; Meijbaum to Salve, 2/17/1764 and 2/20/1764, Verbael IV; Hoogenheim to Directors, 2/15/1764, SvB 135/48. It appears that on at least one occasion a woman posing as a returnee lured

European soldiers into an (unsuccessful) ambush; see Douglas to Salve, 2/19/1764, Verbael IV; DH 2/23/1764.

13. Hoogenheim to Directors, 2/26/1764, SvB 135/54.

14. Report Fourgeoud, 5/8/1764, Verbael VII.

15. "Nader geexamineert den Neger Mars off Atta van Altenklingen," 4/18/1764. Atta fingered Gousarie repeatedly in his examination, claiming, for instance, that his onetime associate had been the one to capture and kill Captain Perrin; H. U. E. Thoden van Velzen and Wim Hoogbergen, *Een Zwarte Vrijstaat in Suriname: De Okaanse samenleving in de achttiende eeuw* (Leiden: KITLV Uitgeverij, 2011), 49.

16. Meijboom to Salve, 3/25/1764, Verbael V; De Brauw employed "16 armed blacks," see Report Brauw, 3/25/1764, Verbael V. Salve to Hoogenheim, 4/3/1764, Verbael V; Hoogenheim to Salve, 4/5/1764, Verbael V; Hoogenheim to Salve, 4/14/1764, Verbael VI; DH 4/3/1764; Verbael V, 3/18/1764 (quote). For a recent discussion of enslaved people in Suriname who fought on the side of enslavers, see Jeroen Dewulf, *Grijs Slavernijverleden? Over Zwarte Milities en Redimoesgedrag* (Amsterdam: Amsterdam University Press, 2018).

17. Capt. Meijbaum to DS, 2/17/1764, 2/20/1764, Vierde Verbael; the two male captives were arrested. Despite witnesses who put them at the fort with Coffij, one of them even armed, they were found not guilty. See No. 8 and 9 Lomingo en LaFleur van den Arend, 3/3/1764; "Lomingo en Lafleur van den Arend Contra de selve," 3/9/1764.

18. Hoogenheim to Directors, 2/15/1764, SvB 135/48; Hoogenheim to Salve, 2/8/1764, Verbael III (quote).

19. DH 2/7/1764, 2/20/1764, 2/24/1764; "Lijst der Slaven, die bij Stafquartier gerequireert worden," 5/21/1764, SvB 135/160.

20. Scheepsjournaal *Zephyr*, 1/17/1764, AC 1161a ; DH 2/4/1764, 2/25/1764 (quote); Verbael V, 3/2/1764, 3/24/1764 (quote); Hoogenheim to Directors, 1/16/1764, SvB 135/43. One *bomba* complained to De Salve about the miserable rations slaves were given; see Verbael V, 3/24/1764.

21. Cf. Verbael III, 1/28/1764; Salve to Fourgeoud, 5/1/1764, Verbael VII; "Lijst der Randsoenen . . . aan de gevangene neegers . . . geleevert . . . Januarij 1764 to den 20e May," 5/20/1764, SvB 135/161; Verbael V, 3/24/1764. Cf. Examination Olé [van de Dageraad?], 4/30/1764, who spoke of eating rats.

22. Verbael III, 1/17/1764; Verbael III, 2/11/1764; Verbael IV, 2/18/1764.

23. The records divulge only one instance where women may have been targeted. In November 1764 Van Hoogenheim noted that soldiers entered his house at night and went into the kitchen, "where the [enslaved] maids" slept, who "screamed with consternation," waking two officers

who promised to punish the men but evidently did not. Van Hoogenheim noted that he hoped Colonel Fourgeoud would ensure "that I am not molested by his men in my own house"; DH 11/8/1764. It is not clear whether the soldiers came to steal food or to rape the women, or both.

24. DH 1/29/1764, 2/29/1764, 4/24/1764 (quote), and 2/29/1764; Verbael V, 3/4/1764; "De namen van de negers en negerinnen . . . in 't groot Hospitaal, als uit en inwendig zijn verbonden, en geneesen geworden. . . ." 5/14/1764, SvB 135/163.

25. No. 61 Lutijn van Helvetia, 5/7/1764; Marjoleine Kars, "Dodging Rebellion: Politics and Gender in the Berbice Slave Uprising of 1763," *American Historical Review* 121, 1 (2016): 63–65.

26. DH 2/9/1764, 2/28/1764; Inventory Vlissingen, May/June 1764, SvB 135/141; Scheepsjournaal *Zephyr*, 2/16/1764, AC 1161a; DH 2/9/1764; Verbael VI, 4/21/1764 (quote) and Verbael VII, 5/8/1764; No. 131 van den Berg van Stevensburg, 5/10/1764; Verbael VI, 4/8/1764; Douglas to Brunswick, 2/26/1764, CB 54-IB (quote).

27. Hoogenheim to Salve, 1/18/1764, Verbael III; DH 1/26/1764, 2/14/1764, 2/24/1764, 2/28/1764, 3/1/1764, 3/9/1764; Douglas to Bentinck, 2/12/1764, CB 54-IB; No. 38 Apria van de Colonie, 3/6/1764; No. 34 David van Helvetia, confrontation with Christiaan and Pieter, 3/12/1764; Douglas to Brunswick, 2/26/1764, CB 54-IB (quote); cf. Salve to Hoogenheim, 2/16 1764, Verbael IV; about Quakoe's death, see 3/9/1764, Verbael V; Salve to Brunswick, 2/26/1764, Verbael V (quote).

28. No. 225 Hollandia van Switserland, 4/13/1764; No. 274 August van de Vigilantie, 4/24/1764; No. 115 Quamina van Doornboom, 5/9/1764; No. 137 Laurens van Horstenburgh, 5/10/1764; No. 221 Simon van Rosenburg, 4/13/1764; No. 97 Jan Bomba van Markey, 3/15/1764. For such defenses among Maroons, see Manolo Florentino and Márcia Amantino, "Runaways and Quilombolas in the Americas," in *The Cambridge World History of Slavery*, ed. David Eltis and Stanley Engerman, 735 (Cambridge: Cambridge University Press, 2011). For the identification of Accabiré's "Gango" as Ganga (or Kanga) from the upper Guinea Coast, see Kars, "Dodging Rebellion," 49n30.

29. No. 181 Brutos of Accabiré van Stevensburg, 4/11/1764; No. 232 Abraham van Maria Henriettta & Theodora, 4/14/1764; No. 275 Baron van de Vigilantie, 4/24/1764. On the creativity with which African and diasporic peoples created communities and the fluidity of national affinities, see James Sweet, "Defying Social Death: The Multiple Configurations of African Slave Family in the Atlantic World," *William and Mary Quarterly* 70, 2 (April 2013): 251–72.

30. See, for instance, No. 211 Andries van Perrotet [Boschlust], 4/12/1764; No. 259 Lea van de Prosperiteit, 4/17/1764; No. 263 Margriet van Stevensburg, 4/17/1764; No. 268 Hans van de Vigilantie, 4/19/1764; No. 24 Ariaantje, meisje van de Heer Gelissen, 5/5/1764; No. 183 Stoffel van Stevensburg, 4/11/1764; No. 186 Jan van La Providence, 4/11/1764; No. 209 Hendrik van de Hooftplantage, 4/12/1764.

31. No. 194 Job van de Heer Schirmeister, 4/11/1764; No. 241 Lena van Sublieslust, 4/16/1764; No. 252 Marietje van P. Masse, van de Erven Nicolay, 4/16/1764 (quote); Catharina van Mercier, 4/16/1764; No. 210 Piramus van de Hooftplantage, 4/12/1764.

32. Verbael V, 3/17/1764; No. 82 Aboi van Nieuw Caraques, 3/10/1764; Verbael V, 3/20/1764 (quote); DH 3/22/1764; No. 181 Brutos of Accabiré van Stevensburg, 4/11/1764; No. 124 Quassie van d'Heer Schirmeister, 5/9/1764; No. 129 Isaaq Smits neeger van de Colonie, 5/10/1764. Neither Quassie nor Isaac, the two men who admitted to hurting Bachelin, identified as Ganga. Neither man claimed that he had been forced to join the Ganga. Declaration Daniel Bachelin, 9/11/1764, SvB 136/22.

33. No. 176 Fritz van de Heer Abbensets, 4/10/1764.

34. Verbael V, 3/22/1764.

35. DS to Brauw, 3/21/1764, Verbael V; 3/22/1764, Verbael V.

36. Verbael V, 3/17/1764 (quote), 3/24/1764; Report Brauw, 3/24/1764, Verbael V; DH 3/22/1764; "Figurative schets der expedittie tegen de rebelle Guangous negers, den 22 en 23e van Maart 1764, in de Colonie de Berbice gedaan." Leupe Vel 1655.

37. Report Brauw, 3/24/1764 (quotes); Salve to Gravesande 3/27/1764, Verbael V (quote). Salve to Hoogenheim, 3/25/1764, Verbael V; DH 3/26/1764 mentions slightly higher numbers.

38. Salve to Hoogenheim, 3/25/1764, Verbael V; DH 3/26/1764; No. 181 Brutos of Accabiré van Stevensurg, 4/11/1764. See also No. 177 Abel van Malpomene, 4/10/1764, and Hoogenheim to Directors, 3/29/1764, SvB 135/59.

39. Verbael V, 3/9/1764, 3/13/1764; Salve to Hoogenheim, 3/25/1764, Verbael V (quote).

40. No. 288 August van de Vigilantie, 4/24/1764 (quote); see also No. 275 Baron van de Vigilantie, 4/24/1764; No. 418 Aron van Cornelia Jacoba, 6/6/1764; No. 249 Sophia van Elisabeth & Alexandria, 4/16/1764; No. 177 Abel van Malpomene, 4/10/1764; No. 28 La Rose van La Providence, 5/5/1764; No. 176 Frits van de Heer Abbensets, 4/10/1764 (quote). About Fritz, see also No. 164 Rebecca van de Heer Abbensets, 4/9/1764, and DH 4/10/1764. Many others talked in their examinations about the supposed cannibalism of the Ganga.

41. Robin Law, "Human Sacrifice in Pre-Colonial West Africa," *African Affairs* 84 (1985): 58.

42. Oldendorp, 1:380–82 (quote on 82), and see 441, 442. For a similar trajectory, see Peter Delius, "Recapturing Captives and Conversations with 'Cannibals': In Pursuit of a Neglected Stratum in South African History," *Journal of Southern African Studies* 36, 1 (2010): 7–23; Stedman, 526. Stedman clearly thought of the "Gango" as separate from the "Congo"; see 175. Stuart B. Schwartz, "Rethinking Palmares: Slave Resistance in Colonial Brazil," in *Slaves, Peasants and Rebels: Reconsidering Brazilian Slavery* (Urbana: University of Illinois Press, 1992), 127, writes about the Imbangala in West Central Africa who made a paste of human fat, which "made their . . . warriors invisible." Monica Schuler believes the Berbice Guango to have been Imbangala; see "Akan Slave Rebellions in the British Caribbean," *Savacou* 1 (1970): 20.

43. Cf. Salve to Douglas, 2/26/1764, Verbael IV; DH 2/26/1764; Verbael V, 2/28/1764; one man killed himself, 4/8/1764, Verbael VI; for Adou's capture, see 3/1/1764, Verbael V; Verbael V, 3/1/1764 (quote).

44. Verbael VI, 4/14/1764 (quotes); Hoogenheim to Directors, 4/25/1764, SvB 135/67. Robin Law, " 'My Head Belongs to the King': On the Political and Ritual Significance of Decapitation in Pre-Colonial Dahomey," *Journal of African History* 30, 3 (1989): 406, 413; see also Jessica A. Krug, "Social Dismemberment, Social (Re)membering: Obeah Idioms, Kromanti Identities and the Trans-Atlantic Politics of Memory, c. 1675–Present," *Slavery and Abolition* 35, 4–5 (2014): 537–58.

45. DH 4/15/1764. Richard Price argues that Samaaka Maroon men "affected an ironic, Sambo-like self-deprecation" as a way to taunt Moravian missionaries. *Alabi's World* (Baltimore: Johns Hopkins University Press, 1990), 201.

46. Schwaaren to Salve, 4/26/1764, Verbael VII (quote); DH 4/29/1764. One wonders how one distinguishes "negro flesh." For similar claims of cannibalism, see Brunswick to States General, 10/24/1764, SvB 227; "Ijdem van de negers Abraham van Essendam en Holland van Switserland met voorst. Negers," 4/19/1764; DH 4/29/1764; Stedman, 526; see DH 3/9/1764 for a different story about Bobé.

47. DH 6/4/1764, 6/5/1764 (quote). One of the women was caught; see Verbael VII, 6/3/1764; DH 6/5/1764; one man claimed that Fortuin "had said he was going to the Spaniards." No. 28 La Rose van La Providence, 5/5/1764; DH 6/14/1764, 6/15/1764 (quote), 6/27/1764.

48. Gravesande to WIC, 4/9/1764, SGD II:447; Netscher, 134–35.

49. DS to Governor and council, 9/8/1764, SvB 136/13.

14: Justice Sideways

1. DH 4/7/1764; No. 1 Mars van Elisabeth en Alexandra, 8/3/1764.

2. Re-Examination of Frederik van West Souburg, testimony of Calvies and Piramus van de Colonie, 3/23/1764; Natalie Zemon Davis, "Judges, Masters, Diviners: Slaves' Experience of Criminal Justice in Colonial Suriname," *Law and History Review* 29, 4 (2011): 970; Cécile Vidal, *Caribbean New Orleans: Empire, Race, and the Making of a Slave Society* (Chapel Hill: University of North Carolina Press, 2019): 399–400, 443–44; Peter H. Wood, *Black Majority: Negroes in Colonial South Carolina* (New York: Knopf, 1974), 282.

3. I am assuming that Hercules had been in Berbice quite a while, as he had a wife and children. The fact that he ate with his wife at the same table may suggest he was a Creole, as in many West African cultures men and women ate separately. For similar practices among the Samaaka Maroons in the eighteenth century and still today, see Richard Price, "Subsistence on the Plantation Periphery: Crops, Cooking, and Labour Among Eighteenth-Century Suriname Maroons," *Slavery and Abolition* 12, 1 (1991): 118.

4. Hoogenheim to Directors, 1/16/1764, SvB 135/34.

5. In British colonies, including in North America, separate slave courts existed. Diane Paton, "Punishment, Crime, and the Bodies of Slaves in Eighteenth-Century Jamaica," *Journal of Social History* 34, 4 (2001): 927.

6. Hoogenheim to Directors 2/15/1764, SvB 135/48; see also DH 1/26/1764; Hoogenheim to Directors, 5/27/1763, SvB 135/68. Prosecutor Fick died in November 1763; see "Lijste van Overleedene, en uit den dienst van de Weledele Achtb. Heeren Directeuren gegane Persoonen," 12/17/1763, SvB 134/186.

7. Jacob A. Schiltkamp, "Legislation, Government, Jurisprudence, and Law in the Dutch West Indian Colonies: The Order of Government of 1629," *Pro Memoria* 5, 2 (2003): 320–32; Davis, "Judges, Masters, Diviners."

8. Florike Egmond, "Recht en Krom: Corruptie, Ongelijkheid en Rechtsbescherming in de Vroegmoderne Nederlanden," *BMGN—Low Countries Historical Review* 116, 1 (2001): 1–33.

9. Frans Thuijs, *De Ware Jaco. Jacob Frederik Muller, alias Jaco (1690–1718): Zijn criminele wereld, zijn berechting en zijn leven na de dood* (Hilversum: Verloren, 2008), 198–99, 226–31; Egmond, "Recht en Krom"; P. van Heijnsbergen, *De Pijnbank in de Nederlanden* (Groningen: Noordhoff, 1925), 69, claims that by the late eighteenth century, people were condemned to death without a confession.

10. Minutes Meeting Directors, 4/7/1764, 6/19/1764, 7/9/1764 (quote), SvB

4; Resolutions Directors, 4/7/1764, 7/9/1764 (quote), SvB 18; Hoogenheim and council to Directors, 10/15/1764, SvB 136/3; Hoogenheim to Directors, 11/6/1764, SvB 136/44. Thuijs, *De Ware Jaco*, 223, states that incriminating testimony by accomplices was problematic in the Dutch extraordinary process.

11. For logistics, see NHP 3/2/1764, SvB 135/114. See also Hans Jordaan, "Free Blacks and Coloreds, and the Administration of Justice in Eighteenth-Century Curaçao," *New West Indian Guide* 84, 1–2 (2010): 75–78.

12. Examinations, SvB 135; NHP 3/5/1764, SvB 135/114; SvB 18, 7/9/1764 (quote).

13 Cf. No. 41 Wellekom van Vigilantie, 3/6/1764, "seems very simple, and knows nothing," or No. 43 David van Vigilantie, 3/6/1764, "is softheaded, and knows nothing;" No 2 Filida van Aurora, 3/9/1764, was considered "unreliable" as "her answer is so confused, one can't understand a word, and she even contradicts herself."

14. No. 140 Piramus van Elisabeth & Alexandria, 3/23/1764; No. 212 Daniel van Elisabeth & Alexandria, 4/12/1764.

15. No. 215 Hercules of Erfprins van Juliana, 4/12/1764.

16. Cf. Van Hoogenheim seemed to suggest he wished torture were used, DH 4/10/1764; see also DH 8/8/1763, 9/18/1763, and NHP 8/3/1763; "Memorie En Eijsch gedaan maken aan den Edele Hove van Politie . . . Jannuarij 1763," SvB 363. In French Louisiana in the 1760s, which used a judicial process similar to that of the Dutch, torture was not used in the majority of criminal cases involving slaves; see Sophie White, " 'Wearing Three or Four Handkerchiefs Around His Collar and Elsewhere About Him': Slaves' Construction of Masculinity and Ethnicity in French Colonial New Orleans," *Gender and History* 15, 3 (2003): 530, though Vidal, *Caribbean New Orleans*, 407–8, argues that it was used more frequently in the 1760s, "though it was never employed lightly."

17. No. 216 Cornelis van Petite Bayonne, 4/13/1764.

18. Confrontation Hercules van de Juliana with Cornelis van Petite Bayonne, 4/19/1764.

19. Confrontation Cornelis van Petite Bayonne, 4/26/1764.

20. Cf. No. 33 Maria van West Souburg, 3/20/1764, "knows nothing about any of the things asked about." Yet when she was first taken captive, in December 1763, she had a great deal to say, see DH 12/27/1763. Or Grietje van Castres, who had nothing to say in her own examination, but readily spoke when called in to testify against someone else; see No. 173 Cesar van Castres, 4/10/1764, and No. 172 Caatje, Marietta & Griet van

Castres, kinderen, 4/10/174. For more on women's roles overall, see Marjoleine Kars, "Dodging Rebellion: Politics and Gender in the Berbice Slave Uprising of 1763," *American Historical Review* 121, 1 (February 2016): 39–69.

21. DH 4/4/1764, 4/9/1764, 4/10/1764 (quotes), 4/24/1764, 5/10/1764, 5/14/1764, 5/28/1764, 6/5/1764.

22. DH 3/23/1764.

23. No. 236 Mars alias Atta van Altenklingen, 4/16/1764.

24. "Nader geExamineeert den Neger Mars of Atta van Altenklingen," 4/18/1764.

25. Sentences, 4/27/1764, SvB 135/125.

26. Fortuin claimed that Accabiré had drunk a man's blood. No. 181 Brutos of Accabiré van Stevensburg, 4/11/1764; No. 466 Fortuin van Helvetia, 6/14/1764; Confrontation Accabiré and Fortuin, 6/14/1764; Sentences 6/15/1764, SvB 135/167 (quotes); DH 6/15/1764.

27. Trevor Burnard, *Mastery, Tyranny, and Desire: Thomas Thislewood and his Slaves in the Anglo-Jamaican World* (Chapel Hill: University of North Carolina Press, 2004), 151; the hundred rebels were tortured and executed both by planters on their own plantations and by the court. In the absence of court records in Jamaica, it is not known how many were condemned by the court. Maria Alessandra Bollettino, "Slavery, War, and Britain's Atlantic Empire: Black Soldiers, Valors, and Rebels in the Seven Years' War" (PhD diss., University of Texas at Austin, 2009), 256, 219–20n472. Emilia Da Costa, *Crowns of Glory, Tears of Blood: The Demerara Slave Rebellion of 1823* (New York: Oxford University Press, 1994), 243–44; Vincent Brown, *The Reaper's Garden: Death and Power in the World of Atlantic Slavery* (Cambridge, MA: Harvard University Press, 2008), 137–44; Diane Paton, "Punishment, Crime, and the Bodies of Slaves in Eighteenth-Century Jamaica," *Journal of Social History* 34, 3 (2001): 923–54.

28. Douglas to Bentinck, 5/25/1764, CB 54-IB. Douglas's numbers add up to thirty, while Van Hoogenheim noted, DH 4/27/1764, 4/28/1764, that thirty-two would be executed. The discrepancy is explained when we learn that Damon van Lelienburg died the night before the executions, while Simon van de Prosperiteit escaped. See NHP 4/27/1764 and 4/28/1764, SvB 135/114; the court minutes suggest that 275 people were examined and sentenced between the March and April executions. Of these, 201 were found innocent and returned to their owners; of the 74 left to be sentenced, 3 died and 1 escaped. Of the 70 left, 2 were held over, 9 condemned to the stake, 8 to the wheel, and 17 to the gallows. The others were provisionally released. For bravery, see Richard Price, "Violence and Hope in a Space of Death: Paramaribo," *Common Place* 3, 4 (July 2003), www.common-place

.org; Stedman, 103; Brown, *The Reaper's Garden*, 148–49. See also James Do-breff et al., trans., *Daniel Rolander's Journal: Sweden, Denmark, Germany, Holland Suriname, St. Kitts and Nevis*, Linnaeus Apostles Global Science and Adventures, vol. 2, bk. 3 (London: IK Foundation, 2008), 1275. Rolander, a botanist, visited Suriname in the mid-1750s, chronicling his stay in a fascinating journal. For bravery, see also the discussion in Walter C. Rucker, " 'Earth from a Dead Negro's Grave': Ritual Technologies and Mortuary Realms in the Eighteenth-Century Gold Coast Diaspora," in *Slavery and Its Legacy*, ed. Rebecca Shumway and Trevor R. Getz, 77–80 (London: Bloomsbury, 2017).

29. Douglas to Bentinck 5/25/1764, CB 54-IB; DH 4/28/1764; Dell claimed Hercules had murdered his wife, DH 4/7/1764. See also No. 215 Hercules of Erfprins, 4/12/1764, and Confrontatie van Hercules van de Juliana met Cornelis van Petite Bayonne, 4/19/1764. A Dutch officer noted that the noose failed twice in the case of a man condemned to be hanged. Dusting himself off after his second fall, the man reportedly walked over to a rebel on the rack, kicked him, and yelled, "You are the reason I am here." He then climbed the ladder and was hanged successfully. "Landjornaal gehouden in Rio de Berbice op de post en plantasie Steevenburgh in Rio Canje beginnende den 15 Januari 1764 door A. Boonacker," 4/28/1764, with thanks to Iris van Dalen van Antiquariaat Acanthus in Utrecht for allowing me to read this manuscript.

30. Brauw to Salve, 3/2/1764, Verbael V; Verbael V, 3/24/1764; Verbael VI, 4/12/1764 (quote), 4/14/1764; DH 4/12/1764, 4/15/1764 (quote); NHP 4/16/1764, SvB 135/114; Resolutions Directors 9/25/1764, SvB 18. After Tacky's Rebellion in Jamaica, many suspected rebels were executed by their owners on plantations, rather than by the court.

31. Verbael VI, 4/14/1764, 4/18/1764; DH 4/15/176, 6/10/1764; NHP 4/16/1764 and 4/26/1764, SvB 135/114.

32. DH 12/8/1766, 12/12/1764, 12/15/1764, 12/15/1764; "Amnestie en gratie voor alle zwarte slaven die aan de opstand hebben deelgenomen," Plakaatboek, 12/12/1764.

Epilogue

1. *Leeuwarder Courant*, 3/3/1770, 2 (quote). In May, Willems was confirmed as a member of the Reformed Church in Dongjum, and given a letter of transfer to The Hague. See Nederland, Friesland Province, Church Records, 1543–1911, Nederlands Hervormd, Dongjum, 5/6/1770, Family Search, with thanks to Esther Schreuder (quote); DH 11/14/1764.

2. DH 11/28/1763; Hoogenheim to Directors, 1/16/1764, SvB 135/43;

Directors Meeting, 7/9/1764, Resolution 16, SvB 4, lists the men by name: Frederik, Calvis, Simon, and Piramus, all from the smithy at the fort, Christiaan the carpenter at the fort, Piramus van Dageraad, Jan van de Steenbakkerij (brickyard), Emanuel van de Scheepswerf (shipyard), and Jan van de Peereboom. Van Hoogenheim later added Mathijs van de Goede Hoop and bricklayer Pieter (whom he had previously overlooked by mistake). Hoogenheim to Directors, 11/6/1764, SvB 136/44.

3. The count had recently married Jacoba Elisabeth van Strijen, the very wealthy widow of Amsterdam burgomaster Dick Trip; perhaps that is how Matthijs ended up in his household. Surprisingly, Matthijs does not show up in the records of the rebellion, so I have no idea why he was emancipated.

4. Salve to the court 9/8/1764, SvB 136/3; see also NHP 9/11/1764, SvB 136/3; Extract Register Resolutien Staaten Generaal, 10/23/1765, in Resolution Staten van Holland en Westvriesland . . . in den jaare 1765, Google Books, p. 860 (quote). The directors of the Sociëteit van Berbice had wanted to sell the two men out of the colony; see Resolutien 4/25/1765 and 5/13/1765, SvB 18. By the time those orders arrived, the pair had already left the colony. The States General approved their immunity on 10/23/1765. Gousarie and Accara's activities in Suriname are chronicled in a memoir, *Narrative of a Five Years Expedition Against the Revolted Negroes of Surinam* (1796), by one of the officers, John Gabriel Stedman. For Stedman's cynical take on the reasons for the creation of the permanent naval expeditionary force, see Stedman, 111.

5. Of the 1,367 people on Company plantations at the start of the uprising, 1,000 were back in June 1764: 316 men (65 percent of pre-rebellion numbers), 367 women (75 percent), 72 boys and 53 girls (both 87 percent), 182 children (74 percent) and 9 Amerindians (38 percent). "Opgave van Slaven en Slavinnen . . . ," Jan Buse, 6/14/1764, SvB 135/142. I have adjusted the totals to account for 60 people disembarked by a slaver in January 1764 who should be subtracted for my purposes.

6. The total enslaved population at the start of 1763 lay somewhere between 4,200 and 5,000 people. In September 1764, the court reported that 1,308 enslaved men, 1,317 women, and 745 children were back in Dutch hands, a total of 3,370 people. This number represents 80 percent of the pre-rebellion population at the lower limit of 4,200 people, or 67 percent at the higher limit of 5,000. This signifies an annual death rate in the uprising of between 12 percent and 20 percent per year (calculated from to 20 percent and 33 percent per the twenty-month period from January 1763 to September 1764), compared to a death rate of 5 percent normally.

For the 5 percent, which is an estimate for Suriname (there are no figures for Berbice), see Alex van Stipriaan, *Surinaams Contrast: Roofbouw and overleven in een Caraïbische plantagekolonie 1750–1863* (Leiden: Brill, 1993), 316; Gert Oostindie, *Roosenburg en Mon Bijou: Twee Surinaamse Plantages, 1720–1870* (Dordrecht-Holland: Foris Publications, 1989), 253. I thank Mike Fay, mathematical statistician, for helping me with these calculations. It is of course possible that the total of 3,370 was underreported by planters eager to evade taxes, though the list was not made for taxation purposes. Nor can we assume that all missing people died, as some might have succeeded in becoming Maroons, though the Dutch thought few had. But see SGD II:561–63, 583. In total 116 whites remained.

7. No. 211 Andries van Perrotet [Boschlust], 4/12/1764. According to an inventory made on Savonette early in 1765, twelve men, seventeen women, and seven children were killed by natives, likely in the fight on plantation Debora in November 1763; 1765 Savonette inventory, SvB 136/125. Other communities suffered large numbers of executions. Plantation Vigilantie lost twelve men, Prosperiteit eight, and Hollandia & Zeelandia seven.

8. Hoogenheim to Directors, 9/19/1764, SvB 135/181; DH 11/11/1764; Brunswick to States General, 10/25/1765, AC 9219. Of the 1,650 soldiers sent to fight Maroons in Suriname in the 1770s, only about 200 survived; see J. R. McNeill, *Mosquito Empires: Ecology and War in the Greater Caribbean, 1620–1914* (Cambridge: Cambridge University Press, 2010), 197–98. In general, McNeill estimates that a European army arriving in the Caribbean would lose half or more of its soldiers within eight weeks (305). As the campaign in Berbice lasted well over a year, it seems likely the death toll was higher.

9. Marjoleine Kars, "Policing and Transgressing Borders: Soldiers, Slave Rebels, and the Early Modern Atlantic," *New West Indian Guide* 83, 3–4 (2009): 187–213. Of the six tried, five had been with the rebels. The sixth man had been among those who returned to their post two days after the mutiny started.

10. Hoogenheim to Directors, 5/27/1764, SvB 135/68 (quote). Since the phrasing is ambiguous, it is possible that Van Hoogenheim wrote that the boy was much attached to him; Meeting Directors, 9/20/1764, SvB 4. For the directors' critique of Van Hoogenheim, see B. Blair, "Wolfert Simon van Hoogenheim in the Berbice Slave Revolt of 1763–1764," *Bijdragen tot de Taal-, Land- en Volkenkunde* 140 (1984): 67; Directors to Hoogenheim, 4/7/1764, SvB 4. For Van Hoogenheim's defense, see Hoogenheim, "Corte Memorie vervattende een waaragtige en beknopte beschrijvinge van het gepasseerde in de Berbice, in den Jaere 1763 met Relatie tot de Revolte van

de Negros Slaeven aldaar in het gemeen, en de Persoon van Wolphert Simon van Hoogenheim in qualiteijt als tijdelijken Gouverneur Generael van den Geoctroijeerde Colonie in het bijsonder," 6/18/1766, CB 54-IA. For Frederik, see *Maandelijks Uittreksel of Boekzaal der Geleerde Waereld* 109 (January–June 1769): 93–94; Doop-, Trouw-, en Begraafboeken, 0176–114, 106, Gelders Archief, Arnhem, the Netherlands. I thank Anthonius Livius of Gelders Archief for providing me with a scan of this record. It was common in the Dutch Republic to name the first son after his father. The choice of Frederik's baptismal name is interesting for this reason. As he would not have had a last name in Berbice, his last name in Holland appears to be Simons.

11. Stedman, 466; for the uncertainty about legal status, see Dienke Hondius, "Access to the Netherlands of Enslaved and Free Black Africans: Exploring Legal and Social Historical Practices in the Sixteenth–Nineteenth Centuries," *Slavery and Abolition* 32, 3 (2011): 377–95.

12. Elias Luzac, *Hollands Rijkdom*, pt. 2 (Leiden: Luzac en Van Damme, 1781), 242–43; Netscher, 252–57.

13. P. H. Koppiers to Directors, 7/12/1780, in *Resolutien van de Heeren Staaten van Holland en Westvriesland*, 1784, NA 3.01.04.01/248. Historians of slavery in nineteenth-century Berbice mention a slave code reportedly adopted by the States General in 1772, based on a reference in Emilia Viotti da Costa, *Crowns of Glory, Tears of Blood: The Demerara Slave Rebellion of 1823* (New York: Oxford University Press, 1994), 44–45, 314n21. I have not been able to find this code in the records. In 1780, Governor Koppiers, who was tasked with curbing abuse of slaves in Berbice, was clear that there were no comprehensive codes to guide him. See also Netscher, 260–61. See also Alvin O. Thompson, *Colonialism and Underdevelopment in Guyana, 1580–1803* (Bridgetown, Barbados: Carib Research & Publications, 1987), 114–15.

14. Pepijn Brandon, *War, Capital, and the Dutch State (1588–1795)* (Chicago: Haymarket Books, 2016; first published, Leiden: Brill, 2015), 275–83, 302–3. Brandon also points to the role played by the failure of the Dutch decentralized "federal-brokerage state" and a growing interest in free trade.

15. In the same period, the British also took over, and kept, Dutch possessions elsewhere in the world, such as the Cape Colony, Sri Lanka, and Malacca. Wim Klooster and Gert Oostindie, *Realm Between Empires: The Second Dutch Atlantic, 1680–1815* (Ithaca, NY: Cornell University Press, 2018): 227–29, 234–35, 255; Randy M. Browne, *Surviving Slavery in the British*

Caribbean (Philadelphia: University of Pennsylvania Press, 2017), chronicles the world of the enslaved in British Berbice.

16. Browne, *Surviving Slavery*, 24–25. Barbara P. Josiah, "After Emancipation: Aspects of Village Life in Guyana, 1869–1911," *Journal of Negro History* 82, 1 (1997): 105–21; Walter Rodney, "Guyana: The Making of the Labour Force," *Race and Class* 22, 4 (1981): 331–52, and *A History of the Guyanese Working People, 1881–1905* (Baltimore: Johns Hopkins University Press, 1981).

17. For a series of essays that chronicles such difficulties in the United States in the 150 years since emancipation, see Debra A. Reid and Evan P. Bennett, eds., *Beyond Forty Acres and a Mule: African American Landowning Families Since Reconstruction* (Gainesville: University Press of Florida, 2010); Russell Rickford, " 'We Can't Grow Food on All This Concrete': The Land Question, Agrarianism, and Black Nationalist Thought in the Late 1960s and 1970s," *Journal of American History* 103, 4 (2017): 956–80, shows the endurance of such elusive dreams among African Americans, including (970) the attempt of a group from Brooklyn in the 1970s who intended to farm in Guyana. For more on this group, see Russell Rickford, "African-American Expats, Guyana, and the Pan-African Ideal in the 1970s," in *New Perspectives in the Black Intellectual Tradition* ed. Keisha N. Blain et al., 233–52 (Evanston, IL: Northwestern University Press, 2018). For an empowering example of agrarian activism, see Monica M. White, *Freedom Farmers: Agricultural Resistance and the Black Freedom Movement* (Chapel Hill: University of North Carolina Press, 2019).

18. Plakaatboek Berbice, 12/14/1772; P. Dekker, "Een Zijpenaar ging naar de Barbiesjes: Waardevol 18e eeuws schilderijk in Zijper boerderij," *West-Friesland oud en nieuw* 37 (1970): 15.

Index

About the Author

Marjoleine Kars is an associate professor at the University of Maryland, Baltimore County. A noted historian of slavery, she is the author of *Breaking Loose Together*. She lives in Washington, DC.

Publishing in the Public Interest

Thank you for reading this book published by The New Press. The New Press is a nonprofit, public interest publisher. New Press books and authors play a crucial role in sparking conversations about the key political and social issues of our day.

We hope you enjoyed this book and that you will stay in touch with The New Press. Here are a few ways to stay up to date with our books, events, and the issues we cover:

- Sign up at www.thenewpress.com/subscribe to receive updates on New Press authors and issues and to be notified about local events
- Like us on Facebook: www.facebook.com/newpressbooks
- Follow us on Twitter: www.twitter.com/thenewpress

Please consider buying New Press books for yourself; for friends and family; or to donate to schools, libraries, community centers, prison libraries, and other organizations involved with the issues our authors write about.

The New Press is a 501(c)(3) nonprofit organization. You can also support our work with a tax-deductible gift by visiting www.thenewpress.com/donate.